ANNUAL EDITIONS

American History Volume 1

Eighteenth Edition

Pre-Colonial Through Reconstruction

EDITOR

Robert James Maddox (Emeritus)
Pennsylvania State University
University Park

Robert James Maddox, distinguished historian and professor emeritus of American history at Pennsylvania State University, received a B.S. from Fairleigh Dickinson University in 1957, an M.S. from the University of Wisconsin in 1958, and a Ph.D. from Rutgers in 1964. He has written, reviewed, and lectured extensively, and is widely respected for his interpretations of presidential character and policy.

McGraw-Hill/Dushkin
2460 Kerper Blvd., Dubuque, IA 52001

Visit us on the Internet
http://www.dushkin.com

Credits

1. **The New Land**
   Unit photo—© by PhotoDisc, Inc.
2. **Revolutionary America**
   Unit photo—Courtesy of the Library of Congress.
3. **National Consolidation and Expansion**
   Unit photo—National Archives.
4. **The Civil War and Reconstruction**
   Unit photo—Courtesy of the Library of Congress.

Copyright

Cataloging in Publication Data
Main entry under title: Annual Editions: American History Vol. One: Pre-Colonial Through Reconstruction. 18e.
1. United States —History—Periodicals. 2. United States—Historiography—Periodicals. 3. United States—Civilization—Periodicals. I. 1. Maddox, Robert James, comp. II Title: American History, Vol. One: Pre-Colonial Through Reconstruction.
ISBN 0–07–296885–0   973'.5   74–187540   ISSN 0733–3560

Eighteenth Edition

Cover image © C. Borland/PhotoLink/Getty Images
Printed in the United States of America   1234567890QPDQPD987654   Printed on Recycled Paper

To the Reader

In publishing ANNUAL EDITIONS we recognize the enormous role played by the magazines, newspapers, and journals of the public press in providing current, first-rate educational information in a broad spectrum of interest areas. Many of these articles are appropriate for students, researchers, and professionals seeking accurate, current material to help bridge the gap between principles and theories and the real world. These articles, however, become more useful for study when those of lasting value are carefully collected, organized, indexed, and reproduced in a low-cost format, which provides easy and permanent access when the material is needed. That is the role played by ANNUAL EDITIONS.

Someone once said that studying history is like visiting another country. One can argue endlessly over what constitutes "human nature," but the means of expressing that nature vary widely from place to place and at different times. One article in this volume, for instance, deals with the Salem "witch trials" of the 1690s. How, the modern reader, might ask, could otherwise intelligent people have believed that evil spirits possess individuals causing them to bark like dogs or to assume different shapes? Is it not obvious that the people caught up in the situation were victims of some sort of mass hysteria? It was not so at the time, and at least most of those involved sincerely believed that their actions were appropriate to meet the perceived threat. One does not have to accept any particular set of assumptions in order to try to understand why people acted as they did in given situations.

Practically all of our beliefs about what is "natural" have undergone radical changes over the course of history and will continue to do so. Consider the role of women in society. Once referred to as the "weaker sex," women were assumed (at least by men) to be suited by nature to marry, maintain households, bear children, and to defer to their husbands on matters outside the home. Owing to their delicate natures and superior morality, the conventional wisdom held, they should be kept isolated from the rough-and-tumble world of politics or the sordid dealings of the marketplace. The most obvious symbol of that mindset was the question of suffrage. Women had to fight for decades (and often were vilified for their efforts) to achieve the most elementary benefit of citizenship: the right to vote. Although there is still a long way to go, women now hold high positions in government and business, and serve as police officers, construction workers, and soldiers.

The list may be extended indefinitely to almost every group. Blacks were once considered (by whites) to be lazy, shiftless, and lacking intelligence. Those of Italian descent were seen to be emotional and prone to violence. Jews were said to be avaricious and untrustworthy in financial matters. Unfortunately many of these stereotypes still exist, but most people who lived during the time period covered in this volume would have been astounded had they been able to peer into the future and see the status members of such groups have attained.

When studying history, one should avoid the arrogance of "presentism." This is the practice, all too common, of judging the past by modern-day standards and beliefs. How easy it is to look at an earlier period and condemn or patronize people for their ignorance and prejudices. It is certain that two hundred years from now many of our own assumptions will seem equally wrong-headed or quaint. One does not have to accept such obvious evils as slavery, for instance, to seek to understand how individuals could have justified as "natural" such an abominable institution. Consider the subject of immigration, for instance. The alarms sounded, by those who opposed immigration from Europe during the 19th Century, do not differ all that much from present-day warnings about immigration from Latin America and Asia.

Annual Editions: American History, Volume I is designed for non-specialized survey courses. We have attempted to present a fair sampling of articles that incorporate newer approaches to the study of history as well as more traditional ones. The sources from which these essays have been taken, for the most part, are intended for the general reader: they require no particular expertise to understand them and they avoid the dreadful jargon that permeates so much of modern academic writing.

This volume contains a number of features designed to aid students, researchers, and professionals. These include a *topic guide* for locating articles on specific subjects; the *table of contents abstracts* that summarize each essay, with key concepts in bold italics; and a comprehensive *index*. Articles are organized into four units, each preceded by an overview that provides a background for informed reading of the articles, emphasizes critical issues, and presents *challenge questions*.

Every revision of *Annual Editions: American History, Volume I* replaces about fifty percent of the previous articles with new ones. We try to update and improve the quality of the sections, and we would like to consider alternatives that we may have missed. If you find an article that you think merits inclusion in the next edition, please send it to us (or at least send us the citation, so that the editor can track it down for consideration). We welcome your comments about the readings in this volume, and a postage-paid reader response card is included in the back of the book for your convenience. Your suggestions will be carefully considered and greatly appreciated.

Robert James Maddox

Editor

Contents

UNIT 1
The New Land

Nine selections discuss the beginnings of America—the new land from pre-Columbian times, early life of the colonists, Indian revolts, Puritan wives, and the stirrings of liberty and independence.

The concepts in bold italics are developed in the article. For further expansion, please refer to the Topic Guide and the Index.

UNIT 2
Revolutionary America

Nine articles examine the start of the American Revolution. The new land offered opportunities for new ideas that led to the creation of an independent nation.

The concepts in bold italics are developed in the article. For further expansion, please refer to the Topic Guide and the Index.

UNIT 3
National Consolidation and Expansion

Ten selections examine the developing United States, the westward movement of people seeking a new life, the realities of living in early nineteenth-century America, and the first American terrorist.

The concepts in bold italics are developed in the article. For further expansion, please refer to the Topic Guide and the Index.

The concepts in bold italics are developed in the article. For further expansion, please refer to the Topic Guide and the Index.

UNIT 4
The Civil War and Reconstruction

Nine articles discuss the tremendous effects of the Civil War on America. With the abolishment of slavery, the United States had to reconstruct society.

The concepts in bold italics are developed in the article. For further expansion, please refer to the Topic Guide and the Index.

The concepts in bold italics are developed in the article. For further expansion, please refer to the Topic Guide and the Index.

Topic Guide

This topic guide suggests how the selections in this book relate to the subjects covered in your course. You may want to use the topics listed on these pages to search the Web more easily.

On the following pages a number of Web sites have been gathered specifically for this book. They are arranged to reflect the units of this *Annual Edition.* You can link to these sites by going to the DUSHKIN ONLINE support site at *http://www.dushkin.com/online/.*

ALL THE ARTICLES THAT RELATE TO EACH TOPIC ARE LISTED BELOW THE BOLD-FACED TERM.

Adams, John

19. The First Democrats

African Americans

3. Slavery in the Lower South
22. African Americans in the Early Republic
28. A Violent Crusader in the Cause of Freedom
29. "The Doom of Slavery": Ulysses S. Grant, War Aims, and Emancipation, 1861–1863
32. A Bold Break for Freedom
33. A Gallant Rush for Glory
37. The New View of Reconstruction

American Revolution

10. The American Self
12. Flora MacDonald
14. Making Sense of the Fourth of July
15. Hamilton Takes Command
16. Winter of Discontent
17. Founders Chic: Live From Philadelphia

Brown, John

28. A Violent Crusader in the Cause of Freedom

Civil War

29. "The Doom of Slavery": Ulysses S. Grant, War Aims, and Emancipation, 1861–1863
30. Richmond's Bread Riot
31. The Civil War's Deadliest Weapons were not Rapid-Fire Guns or Giant Cannon, but the Simple Rifle-Musket and the Humble Minié Ball
32. A Bold Break for Freedom
33. A Gallant Rush for Glory
34. Between Honor and Glory
35. Absence of Malice
36. America's Birth at Appomattox

Clark, George Rogers

21. Brains and Brawn: The Lewis and Clark Expedition

Colonial America

3. Slavery in the Lower South
4. Pocahontas
5. Instruments of Seduction: A Tale of Two Women
6. The Pueblo Revolt
7. Penning a Legacy

8. Blessed and Bedeviled: Tales of Remarkable Providences in Puritan New England
9. Roots of Revolution
10. The American Self
11. Ben Franklin's 'Scientific Amusements,'

Constitution

17. Founders Chic: Live From Philadelphia
18. Your Constitution Is Killing You

Culture

1. Island Hopping to a New World
2. 1491
3. Slavery in the Lower South
4. Pocahontas
5. Instruments of Seduction: A Tale of Two Women
8. Blessed and Bedeviled: Tales of Remarkable Providences in Puritan New England
10. The American Self
11. Ben Franklin's 'Scientific Amusements,'
13. Founding Friendship: Washington, Madison and the Creation of the American Republic
22. African Americans in the Early Republic
24. New Horizons for the American West
27. Little Women? The Female Mind At Work in Antebellum America

Davis, Jefferson

30. Richmond's Bread Riot

Declaration of Independence

14. Making Sense of the Fourth of July

Environment

2. 1491
21. Brains and Brawn: The Lewis and Clark Expedition
24. New Horizons for the American West

Exploration

1. Island Hopping to a New World
2. 1491
21. Brains and Brawn: The Lewis and Clark Expedition

Franklin, Ben

11. Ben Franklin's 'Scientific Amusements,'

Washington, George

Western expansion

Women

World Wide Web Sites

The following World Wide Web sites have been carefully researched and selected to support the articles found in this reader. The easiest way to access these selected sites is to go to our DUSHKIN ONLINE support site at *http://www.dushkin.com/online/*.

AE: American History, Volume 1

The following sites were available at the time of publication. Visit our Web site—we update DUSHKIN ONLINE regularly to reflect any changes.

General Sources

American Historical Association (AHA)
http://www.theaha.org

This site is an excellent source for data on just about any topic in American history. All affiliated societies and publications are noted, and AHA and its links provide material related to myriad fields of history.

American Studies Web
http://www.georgetown.edu/crossroads/asw/

Links to a wealth of Internet resources for research in American studies, from agriculture and rural development, to government, to race and ethnicity, are provided on this eclectic site.

Harvard's John F. Kennedy School of Government
http://www.ksg.harvard.edu

Starting from this home page, click on a huge variety of links to information about American history, politics, and government, including material related to debates of enduring issues.

History Net
http://www.thehistorynet.com/

Supported by the National Historical Society, this site provides information on a wide range of topics. The articles are of excellent quality, and the site has book reviews and even special interviews. It is also frequently updated.

Library of Congress
http://www.loc.gov

Examine this Web site to learn about the extensive resource tools, library services/resources, exhibitions, and databases available through the Library of Congress in many different subfields of government studies.

Smithsonian Institution
http://www.si.edu

This site provides access to the enormous resources of the Smithsonian, which holds some 140 million artifacts and specimens for "the increase and diffusion of knowledge." Learn about American social, cultural, economic, and political history from a variety of viewpoints here.

UNIT 1: The New Land

Early America
http://earlyamerica.com/earlyamerica/index.html

Explore the "amazing world of early America" through early media data at this site. Topics include Pages of the Past, Lives of Early Americans, Notable Women of Early America, Milestone Events, and many more.

1492: An Ongoing Voyage/Library of Congress
http://lcweb.loc.gov/exhibits/1492/

Displays examining the causes and effects of Columbus's voyages to the Americas can be accessed on this Web site. "An Ongoing Voyage" explores the rich mixture of societies coexisting in five areas of this hemisphere before European arrival. It then surveys the polyglot Mediterranean world at a dynamic turning point in its development.

The Mayflower Web Page
http://www.mayflowerhistory.com

The Mayflower Web Page represents thousands of hours of research, organization, and typing; it grows daily. Visitors include everyone from kindergarten students to history professors, from beginning genealogists to some of the most noted genealogists in the nation. The site is a merger of two fields: genealogy and history.

New Mexico's Pueblo Indians
http://members.aol.com/chloe5/pueblos.html

This Web site offers an overview of the history and culture of the Pueblo Indians.

UNIT 2: Revolutionary America

The Early America Review
http://www.earlyamerica.com/review/

Explore the Web site of *The Early America Review*, an electronic journal of fact and opinion on the people, issues, and events of eighteenth-century America. The quarterly is of excellent quality.

House of Representatives
http://www.house.gov

This home page of the House of Representatives will lead to information about current and past House members and agendas, the legislative process, and so on.

National Center for Policy Analysis
http://www.public-policy.org/web.public-policy.org/index.php

Through this site, click onto links to read discussions of an array of topics that are of major interest in the study of American history, from regulatory policy and privatization to economy and income.

Supreme Court/Legal Information Institute
http://supct.law.cornell.edu/supct/index.html

Open this site for current and historical information about the Supreme Court. The archive contains a collection of nearly 600 of the most historical decisions of the Court.

U.S. Senate
http://www.senate.gov

The U.S. Senate home page will lead to information about current and past Senate members and agendas, legislative activities, committees, and so on.

The White House
http://www.whitehouse.gov/

Visit the home page of the White House for direct access to information about commonly requested federal services, the White House Briefing Room, and all of the presidents and vice presidents. The "Virtual Library" provides an opportunity to search White House documents, listen to speeches, and view photos.

The World of Benjamin Franklin
http://www.fi.edu/franklin/

Presented by the Franklin Institute Science Museum, "Benjamin Franklin: Glimpses of the Man" is an excellent multimedia site that lends insight into Revolutionary America.

UNIT 3: National Consolidation and Expansion

Consortium for Political and Social Research
http://www.icpsr.umich.edu

At this site, the inter-university Consortium for Political and Social Research offers materials in various categories of historical social, economic, and demographic data. Presented is a statistical overview of the United States beginning in the late eighteenth century.

Department of State
http://www.state.gov

View this site for an understanding into the workings of what has become a major U.S. executive branch department. Links explain what the Department does, what services it provides, what it says about U.S. interests around the world, and much more information.

Mystic Seaport
http://amistad.mysticseaport.org/

The complex Amistad case is explored in a clear and informative manner on this online educational site. It places the event in the context of the issues of the 1830s and 1840s.

Social Influence Website
http://www.workingpsychology.com/intro.html

The nature of persuasion, compliance, and propaganda is the focus of this Web site, with many practical examples and applications. Students of such topics as the roles of public opinion and media influence in policy making should find these discussions of interest.

University of Virginia Library
http://www.lib.virginia.edu/exhibits/lewis_clark/

Created by the University of Virginia Library, this site examines the famous Lewis and Clark exploration of the trans-Mississippi west.

Women in America
http://xroads.virginia.edu/~HYPER/DETOC/FEM/

Providing the views of women travelers from the British Isles, France, and Germany on the lives of American women, this valuable site covers the years between 1820 and 1842 and is informative, stimulating, and highly original.

Women of the West
http://www.wowmuseum.org/

The home page of the Women of the West Museum offers several interesting links that include stories, poems, educational resources, and exhibits.

UNIT 4: The Civil War and Reconstruction

The American Civil War
http://sunsite.utk.edu/civil-war/warweb.html

This site provides a wide-ranging list of data on the Civil War. Some examples of the data that are available are: army life, the British connection, diaries/letters/memos, maps, movies, museums, music, people, photographs, and poetry.

Anacostia Museum/Smithsonian Institution
http://www.si.edu/archives/historic/anacost.htm

This is the home page of the Center for African American History and Culture of the Smithsonian Institution, which is expected to become a major repository of information. Explore its many avenues.

Abraham Lincoln Online
http://www.netins.net/showcase/creative/lincoln.html

This is a well-organized, high-quality site that will lead to substantial material about Abraham Lincoln and his era. Discussions among Lincoln scholars can be accessed in the Mailbag section.

Gilder Lehrman Institute of American History
http://www.digitalhistory.uh.edu/index.cfm?

Click on the links to various articles presented through this Web site to read outstanding, first-hand accounts of slavery in America through the period of Reconstruction.

Secession Era Editorials Project
http://history.furman.edu/~benson/docs/dsmenu.htm

Newspaper editorials of the 1800s regarding events leading up to secession are presented on this Furman University site. When complete, this distinctive project will offer additional features that include mapping, statistical tools, and text analysis.

We highly recommend that you review our Web site for expanded information and our other product lines. We are continually updating and adding links to our Web site in order to offer you the most usable and useful information that will support and expand the value of your Annual Editions. You can reach us at: *http://www.dushkin.com/annualeditions/*.

UNIT 1
The New Land

Unit Selections

Key Points to Consider

- What new evidence is there that American Indians may have come to the New World by boat at a much earlier time than previously thought?

- Conventional wisdom has it that the Americas in 1491 were only sparsely populated by native peoples who led a simple existence. How does new research challenge this view? What implications does it have on contemporary environmental issues?

- The first enslaved African Americans arrived with the Spaniards more than a century before the founding of Jamestown in 1619. Discuss their treatment and that of enslaved Native Americans.

- Consider the trials of Ann Hibben and Anne Hutchinson in the 1630s. What were they accused of, and how does this shed light on the condition of women at the time?

- Discuss the constitution William Penn framed for the colony he wished to establish. What aspects of it were "progressive" for the time?

- What prevailing attitudes and beliefs led to the persecution of at least 150 people during the Salem Witch trials of 1692?

 **Links: www.dushkin.com/online/**
These sites are annotated in the World Wide Web pages.

Early America
http://earlyamerica.com/earlyamerica/index.html

1492: An Ongoing Voyage/Library of Congress
http://lcweb.loc.gov/exhibits/1492/

The Mayflower Web Page
http://www.mayflowerhistory.com

New Mexico's Pueblo Indians
http://members.aol.com/chloe5/pueblos.html

Europeans were fascinated with the "New World" long before they were able to mount expeditions to actually go there. Artists and writers imagined all sorts of exotic plants and animals, and depicted human inhabitants as ranging from the most brutal savages to races of highly advanced peoples. These latter were reputed to have constructed cities of great splendor, where fabulous treasures of precious metals and jewels lay for the taking. The "age of exploration" had to await the sufficient accumulations of capital to finance expeditions and the advanced technology to make them feasible. Motives were mixed in undertaking such ventures: the desire to explore the unknown, national rivalries, the quest for routes to the Far East, converting the heathens to Christianity, and pure greed. Spain and Portugal lead the way, followed by France and England.

The inhabitants had lived here for a millennia without even knowing (let alone caring) that Europe existed. Estimates are that there were between 80 to 100 million people living in the Western Hemisphere at the time the explorations began. In the region that became the United States there were no powerful empires such as those developed by the Aztecs in Mexico or the Incas in Peru. There were, however, fairly sophisticated settlements such as the small city of Cahokia, located near present-day St. Louis, Missouri. European incursions proved catastrophic for peoples at whatever stage of civilization. Not only did some of the explorers treat indigenous peoples with great brutality, but they brought with them a variety of deadly diseases against which natives had no immunity. The expansion of Europe, therefore, came at the expense of millions of unfortunates in the new world.

For years the conventional wisdom was that what we call "native Americas' emigrated here from Asia across the Bering land bridge to Alaska. The first essay in this volume, "Island Hopping to a New World," discusses more recent archeological findings that indicate people may have come much earlier by boat. "1491" discusses population estimates and what is known about their societies, and suggests that they had a far larger impact on the environment than previously suspected. "Slavery in the lower South" refutes the traditional view that black slavery was introduced in the new world by the English in 1619. Actually, enslaved Africans arrived with the Spaniards more than a century earlier. "The Pueblo Revolt" provides an account of a little-known Indian uprising against the Spanish occupiers in present-day New Mexico. The Spanish were forced to flee temporarily, and when they returned showed greater respect for Pueblo religious practices.

The English came relatively late to the new world. Many, many, like the Spanish and Portuguese who preceded them, came in search of wealth. Others came to settle permanently, either to escape religious persecution or merely to build new lives for themselves. "Pocahontas" treats one such encounter between Indians and the English. Very little is actually known about Pocahontas, but much has been written about her. The article discusses the myths that grew about her, and how they have been used to promote certain agendas over the years.

"Instruments of Seduction: A Tale of Two Women" uses the trials of Anne Hutchinson and Ann Hibben in the 1630s to pro-

vide insights into Puritan religious beliefs at the time. The author's particular emphasis is upon what was assumed to be the proper role of women within marriage and within society. "Blessed and Bedeviled: Tales of Remarkable Providences in Puritan New England" treats the Salem "witch trials" of 1692. Its author analyzes the attitudes and beliefs that led to the persecution of at least 150 people.

In contrast with New England, Pennsylvania has a more liberal tradition. "Penning a Legacy" tells a story of William Penn's acquisition of the land that would bear his name. He developed a constitution that provided for religious freedom, voting rights, and penal reform. He also hoped that the Native Americans in the area would permit the new settlers to live among them "with your love and consent."

Many of those who came to be called "Americans" regarded themselves as loyal English men and women almost until the Revolutionary War. The passage of time and the great distances involved, however, periodically caused disputes between American settlements and England. The prevailing theory of empire during the 17th and 18th centuries was that colonies should be integrated in such a way as to benefit the mother country and the empire as a whole. The ideal colony would provide England with needed raw materials—in exchange the colony would purchase English manufactured goods. In the event of friction, however the government in London understandably favored the interests of England. "Roots of Revolution" provides an early example of how colonists came to resent what they regarded as the English government's heavy-handed interference in their affairs.

ISLAND HOPPING TO A NEW WORLD

The first Americans may have arrived not on foot but by boat from Asia, even Europe

BY ALEX MARKELS

Digging in a dank limestone cave in Canada's Queen Charlotte Islands last summer, 21-year-old Christina Heaton hardly noticed the triangular piece of chipped stone she'd unearthed in a pile of muddy debris. But as her scientist father, Timothy, sifted through the muck, he realized she'd struck pay dirt. "Oh my God!" he yelled to her and the team of other researchers scouring the remote site off the coast of British Columbia. "It's a spear point!"

Bear bones found near the artifact suggested that its owner had probably speared the beast, which later retreated into the cave and eventually died with the point still lodged in its loins. Radiocarbon tests soon dated the remains at about 12,000 years old, making them among the earliest signs of human activity in the region or, for that matter, in all of the Americas.

"It's not the smoking gun, but we're getting closer and closer to finding one," says Timothy Heaton, who is the director of earth sciences at the University of South Dakota. He and his colleagues are trying to rewrite prehistory and show that the people who first explored the Americas at the waning of the last Ice Age may have come earlier than archaeologists thought and by routes they never suspected.

Walk this way. Almost from the moment the first white explorers set eyes on America's indigenous "Indians," people have wondered where the natives came from. Among the first to guess right was Fray José Acosta, a Jesuit priest who in 1590 speculated that a small group from Asia's northernmost latitudes must have walked or floated to the New World. Indeed, since the 1930s archaeologists have taught that the first Americans were big-game hunters who walked across the Bering land bridge from Siberia, chasing woolly mammoths southward through Canada down a narrow corridor between two ice sheets. By about 11,500 years ago, they'd tromped as far south as Clovis, N.M., near where archaeologists first found their distinctive fluted spear points. The Clovis hunters didn't stop there. Their descendants ultimately reached the tip of South America after a footslogging journey begun more than 20,000 miles away. Or so the story goes.

Yet the Heatons' find is the latest addition to a small but increasingly weighty pile of tools and remains suggesting that the first Americans may have come from Asia not by foot down the center of the continent but along the coast in boats, centuries or millenniums before the Clovis people. The evidence, detailed in scientific articles and a new book by journalist Tom Koppel called *Lost World*, has turned up along the Pacific coast all the way from Alaska to southern Chile. So far it does not include any human remains of pre-Clovis age. But a woman whose bones were found on Santa Rosa Island off Santa Barbara, Calif., was only 200 to 300 years more recent. And scientists excavating Chile's Monte Verde site, over 6,000 miles from the southernmost Clovis find, have discovered caches of medicinal herbs, twine, and other artifacts that date back 12,500 years—even older than those of the Clovis people. Still other, more controversial digs near the East Coast may even indicate pre-Clovis travel across the northern Atlantic from Europe.

Such finds have dovetailed with genetic, biological, and climate research to paint a far more complex—and, many scientists believe, more realistic—picture of America's first explorers. Rather than a single migration of Clovis people, "there were clearly several waves of human exploration," says Douglas Wallace, a geneticist at the University of California-Irvine. Wallace's DNA studies of American natives identify at least five genetically distinct waves, four from Asia and one possibly of European descent, the earliest of which could have arrived more than 20,000 years ago. That diversity jibes with research by linguists who argue that the Americas' 143 native languages couldn't possibly have all developed from a single 11,500-year-old tongue. And if they had, then the languages would be most diverse along the mainland route the Clovis people traveled.

In fact, the number of languages is greatest along the Pacific coast, adding to suspicions that at least some of the first immigrants came that way. Until recently, many geologists assumed that the Ice-Age shore was a glaciated wasteland. But new studies of fossil records and ancient climates imply a navigable coastline full of shellfish, seals, and other foods, with patches of grassy inland tundra capable of supporting big game—and perhaps seafaring humans wending their way south.

Unfortunately, looking for evidence that could clinch the coastal-migration scenario is akin to searching for the lost city of Atlantis. Warming temperatures since the last Ice Age have helped transform the ancient tundra into thick forests, rendering most signs of early human exploration all but invisible. And as Ice-Age glaciers melted, the world's sea level has risen hundreds of feet, submerging most of the coastal campsites where the ancient mariners may have sojourned. "Most of those places are under 300 to 400 feet of water, which makes the searching a bit difficult," explains Daryl Fedje, an archaeologist with the Canadian park service who has overseen the decade-long search in the Queen Charlotte Islands.

Beginning in the mid-1990s, he traversed the waters off the foggy archipelago on a research vessel, mapping the ocean bottom and dredging up sediments including, in 1998, a 4-inch-long basalt blade that showed telltale flaking from use by an ancient hunter. Retrieved from a site that might have made an ideal beachside camp 10,200 years ago, it was one of the oldest human artifacts yet found in the region and the first inkling of the potential treasure-trove on the sea bottom. The find made headlines and inspired some to call for a comprehensive high-tech search of the seafloor.

Cave diggers. Yet the immense costs of a seafloor survey have prevented the idea from becoming more than a pipe dream. So Fedje and other researchers have instead focused on caves on the nearby islands and in Alaska, where artifacts are protected from weather and decay. "The caves have been a real windfall," says Heaton of the animal bones he has found. He's confident that "it's really just a matter of time" before he and his colleagues find pre-Clovis human remains, "because in almost every cave we put our shovels to, we find something new."

Archaeologists working on the other side of the continent are also seeking a smoking gun, for a different migration route. Clovis-style spear points recovered from barrier islands near the Chesapeake Bay and inland in Virginia and Pennsylvania bear a striking resemblance to tools made by the ancient Solutrean people of northern Spain, leading some to speculate about a prehistoric crossing of the Atlantic.

"That could explain how DNA from ancient Europeans showed up in some of the first Americans," says Dennis Stanford, chairman of anthropology at the Smithsonian Institution. In an upcoming book, Stanford and coauthor Bruce Bradley make the seemingly far-fetched case that an adventurous lot of Iberians walked over an ice bridge or boated across open water to Newfoundland during the last Ice Age.

Whether they threaded their way through Pacific archipelagoes or negotiated the ice-choked Atlantic, "we need to open our minds and give these early explorers their due," says Stanford. The first people to explore the Americas "were modern humans very much like ourselves ... smart, adventurous, and very much capable of making their way in the world."

From *U.S. News & World Report*, February 23–March 1, 2004, pp. 54–55. © 2004 by U.S. News & World Report, L.P. Reprinted by permission.

1491

*Before it became the New World, the Western Hemisphere was vastly more populous
and sophisticated than has been thought—an altogether more salubrious
place to live at the time than, say, Europe. New evidence of both the extent
of the population and its agricultural advancement leads to a remarkable conjecture:
the Amazon rain forest may be largely a human artifact*

BY CHARLES C. MANN

The plane took off in weather that was surprisingly cool for north-central Bolivia and flew east, toward the Brazilian border. In a few minutes the roads and houses disappeared, and the only evidence of human settlement was the cattle scattered over the savannah like jimmies on ice cream. Then they, too, disappeared. By that time the archaeologists had their cameras out and were clicking away in delight.

Below us was the Beni, a Bolivian province about the size of Illinois and Indiana put together, and nearly as flat. For almost half the year rain and snowmelt from the mountains to the south and west cover the land with an irregular, slowly moving skin of water that eventually ends up in the province's northern rivers, which are sub-subtributaries of the Amazon. The rest of the year the water dries up and the bright-green vastness turns into something that resembles a desert. This peculiar, remote, watery plain was what had drawn the researchers' attention, and not just because it was one of the few places on earth inhabited by people who might never have seen Westerners with cameras.

Clark Erickson and William Balée, the archaeologists, sat up front. Erickson is based at the University of Pennsylvania; he works in concert with a Bolivian archaeologist, whose seat in the plane I

usurped that day. Balée is at Tulane University, in New Orleans. He is actually an anthropologist, but as native peoples have vanished, the distinction between anthropologists and archaeologists has blurred. The two men differ in build, temperament, and scholarly proclivity, but they pressed their faces to the windows with identical enthusiasm.

---

*Indians were here in
greater numbers than
previously thought, and
they imposed their will on
the landscape. Columbus
set foot in a hemisphere
thoroughly dominated
by humankind.*

Dappled across the grasslands below was an archipelago of forest islands, many of them startlingly round and hundreds of acres across. Each island rose ten or thirty or sixty feet above the floodplain, allowing trees to grow that would otherwise never survive the water. The forests were linked by raised berms, as straight as a rifle shot and up to three miles long. It is Erickson's belief that this entire landscape—30,000 square miles of forest mounds surrounded by

raised fields and linked by causeways—was constructed by a complex, populous society more than 2,000 years ago. Balée, newer to the Beni, leaned toward this view but was not yet ready to commit himself.

Erickson and Balée belong to a cohort of scholars that has radically challenged conventional notions of what the Western Hemisphere was like before Columbus. When I went to high school, in the 1970s, I was taught that Indians came to the Americas across the Bering Strait about 12,000 years ago, that they lived for the most part in small, isolated groups, and that they had so little impact on their environment that even after millennia of habitation it remained mostly wilderness. My son picked up the same ideas at his schools. One way to summarize the views of people like Erickson and Balée would be to say that in their opinion this picture of Indian life is wrong in almost every aspect. Indians were here far longer than previously thought, these researchers believe, and in much greater numbers. And they were so successful at imposing their will on the landscape that in 1492 Columbus set foot in a hemisphere thoroughly dominated by humankind.

Given the charged relations between white societies and native peoples, inquiry into Indian culture and history is inevitably contentious. But the recent scholarship is especially controversial. To begin with, some researchers—many but not all from an older generation—deride the new theories as fantasies arising from an almost willful misinterpretation of data and a perverse kind of political correctness. "I have seen no evidence that large numbers of people ever lived in the Beni," says Betty J. Meggers, of the Smithsonian Institution. "Claiming otherwise is just wishful thinking." Similar criticisms apply to many of the new scholarly claims about Indians, according to Dean R. Snow, an anthropologist at Pennsylvania State University. The problem is that "you can make the meager evidence from the ethnohistorical record tell you anything you want," he says. "It's really easy to kid yourself."

More important are the implications of the new theories for today's ecological battles. Much of the environmental movements is animated, consciously or not, by what William Denevan, a geographer at the University of Wisconsin, calls, polemically, "the pristine myth"—the belief that the Americas in 1491 were an almost unmarked, even Edenic land, "untrammeled by man," in the words of the Wilderness Act of 1964, one of the nation's first and most important environmental laws. As the University of Wisconsin historian William Cronon has written, restoring this long-ago, putatively natural state is, in the view of environmentalists, a task that society is morally bound to undertake. Yet if the new view is correct and the work of humankind was pervasive, where does that leave efforts to restore nature?

The Beni is a case in point. In addition to building up the Beni mounds for houses and gardens, Erickson says, the Indians trapped fish in the seasonally flooded grassland. Indeed, he says, they fashioned dense zigzagging networks of earthen fish weirs between the causeways. To keep the habitat clear of unwanted trees and undergrowth, they regularly set huge areas on fire. Over the centuries the burning created an intricate ecosystem of fire-adapted plant species dependent on native pyrophilia. The current inhabitants of the Beni still burn, although now it is to maintain the savannah for cattle. When we flew over the ar-

eas, the dry season had just begun, but mile-long lines of flame were already on the march. In the charred areas behind the fires were the blackened spikes of trees—many of them one assumes, of the varieties that activists fight to save in other parts of Amazonia.

After we landed, I asked Balée, Should we let people keep burning the Beni? Or should we let the trees invade and create a verdant tropical forest in the grasslands, even if one had not existed here for millennia?

Balée laughed. "You're trying to trap me, aren't you?" he said.

LIKE A CLUB BETWEEN THE EYES

According to family lore, my great-grandmother's great-grandmother's great-grandfather was the first white person hanged in America. His name was John Billington. He came on the *Mayflower,* which anchored off the coast of Massachusetts on November 9, 1620. Billington was not a Puritan; within six months of arrival he also became the first white person in America to be tried for complaining about the police. "He is a knave," William Bradford, the colony's governor, wrote to Billington, "and so will live and die." What one historian called Billington's "troublesome career" ended in 1630, when he was hanged for murder. My family has always said the he was framed—but we *would* say that, wouldn't we?

A few years ago it occurred to me that my ancestor and everyone else in the colony had voluntarily enlisted in a venture that brought them to New England without food or shelter six weeks before winter. Half the 102 people on the *Mayflower* made it through to spring, which to me was amazing. How, I wondered, did they survive?

In his history of Plymouth Colony, Bradford provided the answer: by robbing Indian houses and graves. The *Mayflower* first hove to at Cape Cod. An armed company staggered out. Eventually it found a recently deserted Indian settlement. The newcomers—hungry, cold, sick—dug up graves and ransacked houses, looking for underground stashes of corn. "And sure it was God's good

providence that we found this corn," Bradford wrote, "for else we know not how we should have done." (He felt uneasy about the thievery, though.) When the colonists came to Plymouth, a month later, they set up shop in another deserted Indian village. All through the coastal forest the Indians had "died on heaps, as they lay in their houses," the English trader Thomas Morton noted. "And the bones and skulls upon the several places of their habitations made such a spectacle" that to Morton the Massachusetts woods seemed to be "a new found Golgotha"—the hill of executions in Roman Jerusalem.

To the Pilgrims' astonishment, one of the corpses they exhumed on Cape Cod had blond hair. A French ship had been wrecked there several years earlier. The Patuxet Indians imprisoned a few survivors. One of them supposedly learned enough of the local language to inform his captors that God would destroy them for their misdeeds. The Patuxet scoffed at the threat. But the Europeans carried a disease, and they bequeathed it to their jailers. The epidemic (probably of viral hepatitis, according to a study by Arthur E. Spiess, an archaeologist at the Maine Historic Preservation Commission, and Bruce D. Spiess, the director of clinical research at the Medical College of Virginia) took years to exhaust itself and may have killed 90 percent of the people in coastal New England. It made huge differences to American history. "The good hand of God favored our beginnings," Bradford mused, by "sweeping away great multitudes of the natives… that he might make room for us."

By the time my ancestor set sail on the *Mayflower,* Europeans had been visiting New England for more than a hundred years. English, French, Italian, Spanish, and Portuguese mariners regularly plied the coastline, trading what they could, occasionally kidnapping the inhabitants for slaves. New England, the Europeans saw, was thickly settled and well defended. In 1605 and 1606 Samuel de Champlain visited Cape Cod, hoping to establish a French base. He abandoned the idea. Too many people already lived there. A year later Sir Ferdinando Gorges—British despite his name—tried to establish an English community in southern Maine. It had more founders than Plymouth and seems to have been better organized. Confronted by numerous well-armed local Indians, the settlers abandoned the project within months. The Indians at Plymouth would surely have been an equal obstacle to my ancestor and his ramshackle expedition had disease not intervened.

Faced with such stories, historians have long wondered how many people lived in the Americas at the time of contact. "Debated since Columbus attempted a partial census on Hispaniola in 1496," William Denevan has written, this "remains one of the great inquiries of history." (In 1976 Denevan assembled and edited an entire book on the subject, *The Native Population of the Americas in 1492*.) The first scholarly estimate of the indigenous population was made in 1910 by James Mooney, a distinguished ethnographer at the Smithsonian Institution. Combing through old documents, he concluded that in 1491 North America had 1.15 million inhabitants. Mooney's glittering reputation ensured that most subsequent researchers accepted his figure uncritically.

That changed in 1966, when Henry F. Dobyns published "Estimating Aboriginal American Population: An Appraisal of Techniques With a New Hemispheric Estimate," in the journal *Current Anthropology*. Despite the carefully neutral title, his argument was thunderous, its impact long-lasting. In the view of James Wilson, the author of *The Earth Shall Weep* (1998), a history of indigenous Americans, Dobyns's colleagues "are still struggling to get out of the crater that paper left in anthropology." Not only anthropologists were affected. Dobyns's estimate proved to be one of the opening rounds in today's culture wars.

Dobyns began his exploration of pre-Columbian Indian demography in the early 1950s, when he was a graduate student. At the invitation of a friend, he spent a few months in northern Mexico, which is full of Spanish-era missions. there he poked through the crumbling leather-bound ledgers in which Jesuits recorded local births and deaths. Right

away he noticed how many more deaths there were. The Spaniards arrived, and then Indians died—in huge numbers at incredible rates. It hit him, Dobyns told me recently, "like a club right between the eyes."

It took Dobyns eleven years to obtain his Ph.D. Along the way he joined a rural-development project in Peru, which until colonial times was the seat of the Incan empire. Remembering what he had seen at the northern fringe of the Spanish conquest, Dobyns decided to compare it with figures for the south. He burrowed into the papers of the Lima cathedral and read apologetic Spanish histories. The Indians in Peru, Dobyns concluded, had faced plagues from the day the conquistadors showed up—in fact, before then: smallpox arrived around 1525, seven years ahead of the Spanish. Brought to Mexico apparently by a single sick Spaniard, it swept south and eliminated more than half the population of the Incan empire. Smallpox claimed the Incan dictator Huayna Capac and much of his family, setting off a calamitous war of succession. So complete was the chaos that Francisco Pizarro was able to seize an empire the size of Spain and Italy combined with a force of 168 men.

Smallpox was only the first epidemic. Typhus (probably) in 1546, influenza and smallpox together in 1558, smallpox again in 1589, diphtheria in 1614, measles in 1618—all ravaged the remains of Incan culture. Dobyns was the first social scientist to piece together this awful picture, and he naturally rushed his findings into print. Hardly anyone paid attention. But Dobyns was already working on a second, related question: If all those people died, how many had been living there to begin with? Before Columbus, Dobyns calculated, the Western Hemisphere held ninety to 112 million people. Another way of saying this is that in 1491 more people lived in the Americas than in Europe.

His argument was simple but horrific. It is well known that Native Americans had no experience with many European diseases and were therefore immunologically unprepared—"virgin soil," in the metaphor of epidemiologists. What Dobyns realized was that such diseases could have swept from the coastlines initially visited by Europeans to inland areas controlled by Indians who had never seen a white person. The first whites to explore many parts of the Americas may therefore have encountered places that were already depopulated. Indeed, Dobyns argued, they must have done so.

Peru was one example, the Pacific Northwest another. In 1792 the British navigator George Vancouver led the first European expedition to survey Puget Sound. He found a vast charnel house: human remains "promiscuously scattered about the beach, in great numbers." Smallpox, Vancouver's crew discovered, had preceded them. Its few survivors, second lieutenant Peter Puget noted, were "most terribly pitted... indeed many have lost their Eyes." In *Pox Americana* (2001), Elizabeth Fenn, a historian at George Washington University, contends that the disaster on the northwest coast was but a small part of a continental pandemic that erupted near Boston in 1774 and cut down Indians from Mexico to Alaska.

Because smallpox was not endemic in the Americas, colonials, too, had not acquired any immunity. The virus, an equal-opportunity killer, swept through the Continental Army and stopped the drive into Quebec. The American Revolution would be lost, Washington and other rebel leaders feared, if the contagion did to the colonists what it had done to the Indians. "The small Pox! The small Pox!" John Adams wrote to his wife, Abigail. "What shall We do with it?" In retrospect, Fenn says, "One of George Washington's most brilliant moves was to inoculate the army against smallpox during the Valley Forge winter of '78." Without inoculation smallpox could easily have given the United States back to the British.

So many epidemics occurred in the Americas, Dobyns argued, that the old data used by Mooney and his successors represented population nadirs. From the few cases in which before-and-after totals are known with relative certainty, Dobyns estimated that in the first 130 years of contact about 95 percent of the people in the Americas died—the worst demographic calamity in recorded history.

Dobyns's ideas were quickly attacked as politically motivated, a push from the hate-America crowd to inflate the toll of imperialism. The attacks continue to this day. "No question about it, some people want those higher numbers," says Shepard Krech III, a Brown University anthropologist who is the author of *The Ecological Indian* (1999). These people, he says, were thrilled when Dobyns revisited the subject in a book, *Their Numbers Become Thinned* (1983)—and revised his own estimates upward. Perhaps Dobyns's most vehement critic is David Henige, a bibliographer of Africana at the University of Wisconsin, whose *Numbers from Nowhere* (1998) is a landmark in the literature of demographic fulmination. "Suspect in 1966, it is no less suspect nowadays," Henige wrote of Dobyns's work. "If anything, it is worse."

When Henige wrote *Numbers From Nowhere,* the fight about pre-Columbian populations had already consumed forests' worth of trees; his bibliography is ninety pages long. And the dispute shows no sign of abating. More and more people have jumped in. This is partly because the subject is inherently fascinating. But more likely the increased interest in the debate is due to the growing realization of the high political and ecological stakes.

INVENTING BY THE MILLIONS

On May 30, 1539, Hernando de Soto landed his private army near Tampa Bay, in Florida. Soto, as he was called, was a novel figure: half warrior, half venture capitalist. He had grown very rich very young by becoming a market leader in the nascent trade for Indian slaves. The profits had helped to fund Pizarro's seizure of the Incan empire, which had made Soto wealthier still. Looking quite literally for new worlds to conquer, he persuaded the Spanish Crown to let him loose in North America. He spent one fortune to make another. He came to Florida with 200 horses, 600 soldiers, and 300 pigs.

From today's perspective, it is difficult to imagine the ethical system that would justify Soto's actions. For four years his force, looking for gold, wandered through what is now Florida,

Georgia, North and South Carolina, Tennessee, Alabama, Mississippi, Arkansas, and Texas, wrecking almost everything it touched. The inhabitants often fought back vigorously, but they had never before encountered an army with horses and guns. Soto died of fever with his expedition in ruins; along the way his men had managed to rape, torture, enslave, and kill countless Indians. But the worst thing the Spaniards did, some researchers say, was entirely without malice—bring the pigs.

According to Charles Hudson, an anthropologist at the University of Georgia who spent fifteen years reconstructing the path of the expedition, Soto crossed the Mississippi a few miles downstream from the present site of Memphis. It was a nervous passage: the Spaniards were watched by several thousand Indian warriors. Utterly without fear, Soto brushed past the Indian force into what is now eastern Arkansas, through thickly settled land—"very well peopled with large towns," one of his men later recalled, "two or three of which were to be seen from one town." Eventually the Spaniards approached a cluster of small cities, each protected by earthen walls, sizeable moats, and deadeye archers. In his usual fashion, Soto brazenly marched in, stole food, and marched out.

After Soto left, no Europeans visited this part of the Mississippi Valley for more than a century. Early in 1682 whites appeared again, this time Frenchmen in canoes. One of them was Réné-Robert Cavelier, Sieur de la Salle. The French passed through the area where Soto had found cities cheek by jowl. It was deserted—La Salle didn't see an Indian village for 200 miles. About fifty settlements existed in this strip of the Mississippi when Soto showed up, according to Anne Ramenofsky, an anthropologist at the University of New Mexico. By La Salle's time the number had shrunk to perhaps ten, some probably inhabited by recent immigrants. Soto "had a privileged glimpse" of an Indian world, Hudson says. "The window opened and slammed shut. When the French came in and the record opened up again, it was a transformed reality. A civilization crumbled. The question is, how did this happen?"

> *Swine alone can disseminate anthrax, brucellosis, leptospirosis, trichinosis, and tuberculosis. Only a few of Hernando de Soto's pigs would have had to wander off to infect the forest.*

The question is even more complex than it may seem. Disaster of this magnitude suggests epidemic disease. In the view of Ramenofsky and Patricia Galloway, an anthropologist at the University of Texas, the source of the contagion was very likely not Soto's army but its ambulatory meat locker: his 300 pigs. Soto's force itself was too small to be an effective biological weapon. Sicknesses like measles and smallpox would have burned through his 600 soldiers long before they reached the Mississippi. But the same would not have held true for the pigs, which multiplied rapidly and were able to transmit their diseases to wildlife in the surrounding forest. When human beings and domesticated animals live close together, they trade microbes with abandon. Over time mutation spawns new diseases: Avian influenza becomes human influenza, bovine rinderpest becomes measles. Unlike Europeans, Indians did not live in close quarters with animals—they domesticated only the dog, the llama, the alpaca, the guinea pig, and here and there, the turkey and the Muscovy duck. In some ways this is not surprising: the New World had fewer animal candidates for taming than the Old. Moreover, few Indians carry the gene that permits adults to digest lactose, a form of sugar abundant in milk. Non-milk-drinkers, one imagines, would be less likely to work at domesticating milk-giving animals. But this is guesswork. The fact is that what scientists call zoonotic disease was little known in the Americas. Swine alone can disseminate anthrax, brucellosis, leptospirosis, taeniasis, trichinosis, and tuberculosis. Pigs breed exuberantly and can transmit diseases to deer and turkeys. Only a few of

Soto's pigs would have had to wander off to infect the forest.

Indeed, the calamity wrought by Soto apparently extended across the whole Southeast. The Coosa city-states, in western Georgia, and the Caddoan-speaking civilization, centered on the Texas-Arkansas border, disintegrated soon after Soto appeared. The Caddo had had a taste for monumental architecture: public plazas, ceremonial platforms, mausoleums. After Soto's army left, notes Timothy K. Perttula, an archaeological consultant in Austin, Texas, the Caddo stopped building community centers and began digging community cemeteries. Between Soto's and La Salle's visits, Perttula believes, the Caddoan population fell from about 200,000 to about 8,500—a drop of nearly 96 percent. In the eighteenth century the tally shrank further, to 1,400. An equivalent loss today in the population of New York City would reduce it to 56,000—not enough to fill Yankee Stadium. "That's one reason whites think of Indians as nomadic hunters," says Russell Thornton, an anthropologist at the University of California at Los Angeles. "Everything else—all the heavily populated urbanized societies—was wiped out."

Could a few pigs truly wreak this much destruction? Such apocalyptic scenarios invite skepticism. As a rule, viruses, microbes, and parasites are rarely lethal on so wide a scale—a pest that wipes out its host species does not have a bright evolutionary future. In its worst outbreak, from 1347 to 1351, the European Black Death claimed only a third of its victims. (The rest survived, though they were often disfigured or crippled by its effects.) The Indians in Soto's path, if Dobyns, Ramenofsky, and Perttula are correct, endured losses that were incomprehensibly greater.

One reason is that Indians were fresh territory for many plagues, not just one. Smallpox, typhoid, bubonic plague, influenza, mumps, measles, whooping cough—all rained down on the Americas in the century after Columbus. (Cholera, malaria, and scarlet fever came later.) Having little experience with epidemic diseases, Indians had no knowledge of how to combat them. In contrast, Europeans were well versed in the brutal logic

of quarantine. They boarded up houses in which plague appeared and fled to the countryside. In Indian New England, Neal Salisbury, a historian at Smith college, wrote in *Manitou and Providence* (1982), family and friends gathered with the shaman at the sufferer's bedside to wait out the illness—a practice that "could only have served to spread the disease more rapidly."

Indigenous biochemistry may also have played a role. The immune system constantly scans the body for molecules that it can recognize as foreign—molecules belonging to an invading virus, for instance. No one's immune system can identify all foreign presences. Roughly speaking, an individual's set of defensive tools is known as his MHC type. Because many bacteria and viruses mutate easily, they usually attack in the form of several slightly different strains. Pathogens win when MHC types miss some of the strains and the immune system is not stimulated to act. Most human groups contain many MHC types; a strain that slips by one person's defenses will be nailed by the defenses of the next. But, according to Francis L. Black, an epidemiologist at Yale University, Indians are characterized by unusually homogeneous MHC types. One out of three South American Indians have similar MHC types; among Africans the corresponding figure is one in 200. The cause is a matter for Darwinian speculation, the effects less so.

In 1966 Dobyns's insistence on the role of disease was a shock to his colleagues. Today the impact of European pathogens on the New World is almost undisputed. Nonetheless, the fight over Indian numbers continues with undiminished fervor. Estimates of the population of North America in 1491 disagree by an order of magnitude—from 18 million, Dobyns's revised figure, to 1.8 million, calculated by Douglas H. Ubelaker, an anthropologist at the Smithsonian. To some "high counters," as David Henige calls them, the low counters' refusal to relinquish the vision of an empty continent is irrational or worse. "Non-Indian 'experts' always want to minimize the size of aboriginal populations," says Lenore Stiffarm, a Native American-education specialist at the University of

Saskatchewan. The smaller the numbers of Indians, she believes, the easier it is to regard the continent as having been up for grabs. "It's perfectly acceptable to move into unoccupied land," Stiffarm says. "And land with only a few 'savages' is the next best thing."

"Most of the arguments for the very large numbers have been theoretical," Ubelaker says in defense of low counters. "When you try to marry the theoretical arguments to the data that are available on individual groups in different regions, it's hard to find support for those numbers." Archaeologists, he says, keep searching for the settlements in which those millions of people supposedly lived, with little success. "As more and more excavation is done, one would expect to see more evidence for dense populations than has thus far emerged." Dean Snow, the Pennsylvania State anthropologist, examined Colonial-era Mohawk Iroquois sites and found "no support for the notion that ubiquitous pandemics swept the region." In his view, asserting that the continent was filled with people who left no trace is like looking at an empty bank account and claiming that it must once have held millions of dollars.

The low counters are also troubled by the Dobynsian procedure for recovering original population numbers: applying an assumed death rate, usually 95 percent, to the observed population nadir. Ubelaker believes that the lowest point for Indians in North America was around 1900, when their numbers fell to about half a million. Assuming a 95 percent death rate, the pre-contact population would have been 10 million. Go up one percent, to a 96 percent death rate, and the figure jumps to 12.5 million—arithmetically creating more than two million people from a tiny increase in mortality rates. At 98 percent the number bounds to 25 million. Minute changes in baseline assumptions produce wildly different results.

"It's an absolutely unanswerable question on which tens of thousands of words have been spent to no purpose," Henige says. In 1976 he sat in on a seminar by William Denevan, the Wisconsin geographer. An "epiphanic moment" occurred when he read shortly afterward that scholars had "uncovered" the existence of eight million people in Hispaniola. *Can you just invent millions of people?* he wondered. "We can make of the historical record that there was depopulation and movement of people from internecine warfare and diseases," he says. "But as for how much, who knows? When we start putting numbers to something like that—applying large figures like ninety-five percent—we're saying things we shouldn't say. The number implies a level of knowledge that's impossible."

Nonetheless, one must try—or so Denevan believes. In his estimation the high counters (though not the highest counters) seem to be winning the argument, at least for now. No definitive data exist, he says, but the majority of the extant evidentiary scraps support their side. Even Henige is no low counter. When I asked him what he thought the population of the Americas was before Columbus, he insisted that any answer would be speculation and made me promise not to print what he was going to say next. Then he named a figure that forty years ago would have caused a commotion.

To Elizabeth Fenn, the smallpox historian, the squabble over numbers obscures a central fact. Whether one million or 10 million or 100 million died, she believes, the pall of sorrow that engulfed the hemisphere was immeasurable. Languages, prayers, hopes, habits, and dreams—entire ways of life hissed away like steam. The Spanish and the Portuguese lacked the germ theory of disease and could not explain what was happening (let alone stop it). Nor can we explain it; the ruin was too long ago and too all-encompassing. In the long run, Fenn says, the consequential finding is not that many people died but that many people once lived. The Americas were filled with a stunningly diverse assortment of peoples who had knocked about the continents for millennia. "You have to wonder," Fenn says. "What were all those people *up* to in all that time?"

BUFFALO FARM

In 1810 Henry Brackenridge came to Cahokia, in what is now southwest Illinois, just across the Mississippi from St. Louis. Born close to the frontier, Brack-

enridge was a budding adventure writer; his *Views of Louisiana,* published three years later, was a kind of nineteenth-century *Into Thin Air,* with terrific adventure but without tragedy. Brackenridge had an eye for archaeology, and he had heard that Cahokia was worth a visit. When he got there, trudging along the desolate Cahokia River, he was "struck with a degree of astonishment." Rising from the muddy bottomland was a "stupendous pile of earth," vaster than the Great Pyramid at Giza. Around it were more than a hundred smaller mounds, covering an area of five square miles. At the time, the area was almost uninhabited. One can only imagine what passed through Brackenridge's mind as he walked alone to the ruins of the biggest Indian city north of the Rio Grande.

To Brackenridge, it seemed clear that Cahokia and the many other ruins in the Midwest had been constructed by Indians. It was not so clear to everyone else. Nineteenth-century writers attributed them to, among others, the Vikings, the Chinese, the "Hindoos," the ancient Greeks, the ancient Egyptians, lost tribes of Israelites, and even straying bands of Welsh. (This last claim was surprisingly widespread; when Lewis and Clark surveyed the Missouri, Jefferson told them to keep an eye out for errant bands of Welsh-speaking white Indians.) The historian George Bancroft, dean of his profession, was a dissenter: the earthworks, he wrote in 1840, were purely natural formations.

Bancroft changed his mind about Cahokia, but not about Indians. To the end of his days he regarded them as "feeble barbarians, destitute of commerce and of political connection." His characterization lasted, largely unchanged, for more than a century. Samuel Eliot Morison, the winner of two Pulitzer Prizes, closed his monumental *European Discovery of America* (1974) with the observation that Native Americans expected only 'short and brutish lives, void of hope for any future." As late as 1987 *American History: A Survey,* a standard high school textbook by three well-known historians, described the Americas before Columbus as "empty of mankind and its works." The story of Europeans in the New World, the book explained, "is the story

of the creation of a civilization where none existed."

Alfred Crosby, a historian at the University of Texas, came to other conclusions. Crosby's *The Columbian Exchange: Biological Consequences of 1492* caused almost as much of a stir when it was published, in 1972, as Henry Dobyns's calculation of Indian numbers six years earlier, though in different circles. Crosby was a standard names-and-battles historian who became frustrated by the random contingency of political events. "Some trivial thing happens and you have this guy winning the presidency instead of that guy," he says. He decided to go deeper. After he finished his manuscript, it sat on his shelf—he couldn't find a publisher willing to be associated with his new ideas. It took him three years to persuade a small editorial house to put it out. *The Columbian Exchange* has been in print ever since; a companion, *Ecological Imperialism: The Biological Expansion of Europe, 900–1900,* appeared in 1986.

Human history, in Crosby's interpretation, is marked by two world-altering centers of invention: the Middle East and central Mexico, where Indian groups independently created nearly all of the Neolithic innovations, writing included. The Neolithic Revolution began in the Middle East about 10,000 years ago. In the next few millennia humankind invented the wheel, the metal tool, and agriculture. The Sumerians eventually put these inventions together, added writing, and became the world's first civilization. Afterward Sumeria's heirs in Europe and Asia frantically copied one another's happiest discoveries; innovations ricocheted from one corner of Eurasia to another, stimulating technological progress. Native Americans, who had crossed to Alaska before Sumeria, missed out on the bounty. "They had to do everything on their own," Crosby says. Remarkably, they succeeded.

When Columbus appeared in the Caribbean, the descendants of the world's two Neolithic civilizations collided, with overwhelming consequences for both. American Neolithic development occurred later than that of the Middle East, possibly because the Indians needed more time to build up the requisite population density. Without beasts of burden they could not capitalize on the wheel (for individual workers on uneven terrain skids are nearly as effective as carts for hauling), and they never developed steel. But in agriculture they handily outstripped the children of Sumeria. Every tomato in Italy, every potato in Ireland, and every hot pepper in Thailand came from this hemisphere. Worldwide, more than half the crops grown today were initially developed in the Americas.

Maize, as corn is called in the rest of the world, was a triumph with global implications. Indians developed an extraordinary number of maize varieties for different growing conditions, which meant that the crop could and did spread throughout the planet. Central and Southern Europeans became particularly dependent on it; maize was the staple of Serbia, Romania, and Moldavai by the nineteenth century. Indian crops dramatically reduced hunger, Crosby says, which led to an Old World population boom.

In the Aztec capital Tenochtitlán the Spaniards gawped like hayseeds at the side streets, ornately carved buildings, and markets bright with goods from hundreds of miles away.

Along with peanuts and manioc, maize came to Africa and transformed agriculture there, too. "The probability is that the population of Africa was greatly increased because of maize and other American Indian crops," Crosby says. "Those extra people helped make the slave trade possible." Maize conquered Africa at the time when introduced diseases were leveling Indian societies. The Spanish, the Portuguese, and the British were alarmed by the death rate among Indians, because they wanted to exploit them as workers. Faced with a labor shortage, the Europeans turned their eyes to Africa. The continent's quarrelsome

societies helped slave traders to siphon off millions of people. The maize-fed population boom, Crosby believes, let the awful trade continue without pumping the well dry.

Back home in the Americas, Indian agriculture long sustained some of the world's largest cities. The Aztec capital of Tenochtitlán dazzled Hernán Cortés in 1519; it was bigger than Paris, Europe's greatest metropolis. The Spaniards gawped like hayseeds at the wide streets, ornately carved buildings, and markets bright with goods from hundreds of miles away. They had never before seen a city with botanical gardens, for the excellent reason that none existed in Europe. The same novelty attended the force of a thousand men that kept the crowded streets immaculate. (Streets that weren't ankle-deep in sewage! The conquistadors had never heard of such a thing.) Central America was not the only locus of prosperity. Thousands of miles north, John Smith, of Pocahontas fame, visited Massachusetts in 1614, before it was emptied by disease, and declared that the land was "so planted with Gardens and Corne fields, and so well inhabited with a goodly, strong and well proportioned people... [that] I would rather live here than any where."

Smith was promoting colonization, and so had reason to exaggerate. But he also knew the hunger, sickness, and oppression of European life. France—"by any standards a privileged country," according to its great historian, Fernand Braudel—experienced seven nationwide famines in the fifteenth century and thirteen in the sixteenth. Disease was hunger's constant companion. During epidemics in London the dead were heaped onto carts "like common dung" (the simile is Daniel Defoe's) and trundled through the streets. The infant death rate in London orphanages, according to one contemporary source, was 88 percent. Governments were harsh, the rule of law arbitrary. The gibbets poking up in the background of so many old paintings were, Braudel observed, "merely a realistic detail."

The Earth Shall Weep, James Wilson's history of Indian America, puts the comparison bluntly: "the western hemisphere was larger, richer, and more populous than Europe." Much of it was freer, too. Europeans, accustomed to the serfdom that thrived from Naples to the Baltic Sea, were puzzled and alarmed by the democratic spirit and respect for human rights in many Indian societies, especially those in North America. In theory, the sachems of New England Indian groups were absolute monarchs. In practice, the colonial leader Roger Williams wrote, "they will not conclude of ought... unto which the people are averse."

Pre-1492 America wasn't a disease-free paradise, Dobyns says, although in his "exuberance as a writer," he told me recently, he once made that claim. Indians had ailments of their own, notably parasites, tuberculosis, and anemia. The daily grind was wearing; life-spans in America were only as long as or a little longer than those in Europe, if the evidence of indigenous graveyards is to be believed. Nor was it a political utopia—the Inca, for instance, invented refinements to totalitarian rule that would have intrigued Stalin. Inveterate practitioners of what the historian Francis Jennings described as "state terrorism practiced horrifically on a huge scale," the Inca ruled so cruelly that one can speculate that their surviving subjects might actually have been better off under Spanish rule.

I asked seven anthropologists, archaeologists, and historians if they would rather have been a typical Indian or a typical European in 1491. Every one chose to be an Indian.

I asked seven anthropologists, archaeologists, and historians if they would rather have been a typical Indian or a typical European in 1491. None was delighted by the question, because it required judging the past by the standards of today—a fallacy disparaged as "presentism" by social scientists. But every one chose to be an Indian. Some early colonists gave the same answer. Horrifying the leaders of Jamestown and Plymouth, scores of English ran off to live with the Indians. My ancestor shared their desire, which is what led to the trumped-up murder charges against him—or that's what my grandfather told me, anyway.

As for the Indians, evidence suggests that they often viewed Europeans with disdain. The Hurons, a chagrined missionary reported, thought the French possessed "little intelligence in comparison to themselves." Europeans, Indians said, were physically weak, sexually untrustworthy, atrociously ugly, and just plain dirty. (Spaniards, who seldom if ever bathed, were amazed by the Aztec desire for personal cleanliness.) A Jesuit reported that the "Savages" were disgusted by handkerchiefs: "They say, we place what is unclean in a fine white piece of linen, and put it away in our pockets as something very precious, while they throw it upon the ground." The Micmac scoffed at the notion of French superiority. If Christian civilization was so wonderful, why were its inhabitants leaving?

Like people everywhere, Indians survived by cleverly exploiting their environment. Europeans tended to manage land by breaking it into fragments for farmers and herders. Indians often worked on such a grand scale that the scope of their ambition can be hard to grasp. They created small plots, as Europeans did (about 1.5 million acres of terraces still exist in the Peruvian Andes), but they also reshaped entire landscapes to suit their purposes. A principal tool was fire, used to keep down underbrush and create the open, grassy conditions favorable for game. Rather than domesticating animals for meat, Indians retooled whole ecosystems to grow bumper crops of elk, deer, and bison. The first white settlers in Ohio found forests as open as English parks—they could drive carriages through the woods. Along the Hudson River the annual fall burning lit up the banks for miles on end; so flashy was the show that the Dutch in New Amsterdam boated upriver to goggle at the blaze like children at fireworks. In North America, Indian torches had their biggest impact on the Midwestern prairie,

much or most of which was created and maintained by fire. Millennia of exuberant burning shaped the plains into vast buffalo farms. When Indian societies disintegrated, forest invaded savannah in Wisconsin, Illinois, Kansas, Nebraska, and the Texas Hill Country. Is it possible that the Indians changed the Americas more than the invading Europeans did? "The answer is probably yes for most regions for the next 250 years or so" after Columbus. William Denevan wrote, "and for some regions right up to the present time."

Amazonia has become the emblem of vanishing wilderness—an admonitory image of untouched Nature. But the rain forest itself may be a cultural artifact—that is, an artificial object.

When scholars first began increasing their estimates of the ecological impact of Indian civilization, they met with considerable resistance from anthropologists and archaeologists. Over time the consensus in the human sciences changed. Under Denevan's direction, Oxford University Press has just issued the third volume of a huge catalogue of the "cultivated landscapes" of the Americas. This sort of phrase still provokes vehement objection—but the main dissenters are now ecologists and environmentalists. The disagreement is encapsulated by Amazonia, which has become *the* emblem of vanishing wilderness—an admonitory image of untouched Nature. Yet recently a growing number of researchers have come to believe that Indian societies had an enormous environmental impact on the jungle. Indeed, some anthropologists have called the Amazon forest itself a cultural artifact—that is, an artificial object.

GREEN PRISONS

Northern visitors' first reaction to the storied Amazon rain forest is often

disappointment. Ecotourist brochures evoke the immensity of Amazonia but rarely dwell on its extreme flatness. In the river's first 2,900 miles the vertical drop is only 500 feet. The river oozes like a huge runnel of dirty metal through a landscape utterly devoid of the romantic crags, arroyos, and heights that signify wilderness and natural spectacle to most North Americans. Even the animals are invisible, although sometimes one can hear the bellow of monkey choruses. To the untutored eye—mine, for instance—the forest seems to stretch out in a monstrous green tangle as flat and incomprehensible as a printed circuit board.

The area east of the lower-Amazon town of Santarém is an exception. A series of sandstone ridges several hundred feet high reach down from the north, halting almost at the water's edge. Their tops stand drunkenly above the jungle like old tombstones. Many of the caves in the buttes are splattered with ancient petroglyphs—renditions of hands, stars, frogs, and human figures, all reminiscent of Miró, in overlapping red and yellow and brown. In recent years one of these caves, La Caverna da Pedra Pintada (Painted Rock Cave), has drawn attention in archaeological circles.

Wide and shallow and well lit, Painted Rock Cave is less thronged with bats than some of the other caves. The arched entrance is twenty feet high and lined with rock paintings. Out front is a sunny natural patio suitable for picnicking, edged by a few big rocks. People lived in this cave more than 11,000 years ago. They had no agriculture yet, and instead ate fish and fruit and built fires. During a recent visit I ate a sandwich atop a particularly inviting rock and looked over the forest below. The first Amazonians, thought, must have done more or less the same thing.

In college I took an introductory anthropology class in which I read *Amazonia: Man and Culture in a Counterfeit Paradise* (1971), perhaps the most influential book ever written about the Amazon, and one that deeply impressed me at the time. Written by Betty J. Meggers, the Smithsonian archaeologist, *Amazonia* says that the apparent lushness of the rain forest is a sham. The soils are poor and can't hold nutrients—the jungle flora exists only because it snatches up everything worthwhile before it leaches away in the rain. Agriculture, which depends on extracting the wealth of the soil, therefore faces inherent ecological limitations in the wet desert of Amazonia.

As a result, Meggers argued, Indian villages were forced to remain small— any report of "more than a few hundred" people in permanent settlements, she told me recently, "makes my alarm bells go off." Bigger, more complex societies would inevitably overtax the forest soils, laying waste to their own foundations. Beginning in 1948 Meggers and her late husband, Clifford Evans, excavated a chiefdom on Marajó, an island twice the size of New Jersey that sits like a gigantic stopper in the mouth of the Amazon. The Marajóara, they concluded, were failed offshoots of a sophisticated culture in the Andes. Transplanted to the lush trap of the Amazon, the culture choked and died.

Green activists saw the implication: development in tropical forests destroys both the forests and their developers. Meggers's account had enormous public impact—*Amazonia* is one of the wellsprings of the campaign to save rain forests.

Then Anna C. Roosevelt, the curator of archaeology at Chicago's Field Museum of Natural History, re-excavated Marajó. Her complete report, *Moundbuilders of the Amazon* (1991), was like the anti-matter version of *Amazonia*. Marajó, she argued, was "one of the outstanding indigenous cultural achievements of the New World," a powerhouse that lasted for more than a thousand years, had "possibly well over 100,000" inhabitants, and covered thousands of square miles. Rather than damaging the forest, Marajó's "earth construction" and "large, dense populations" had *improved* it: the most luxuriant and diverse growth was on the mounds formerly occupied by the Marajóara. "If you listened to Meggers's theory, these places should have been ruined," Roosevelt says.

Meggers scoffed at Roosevelt's "extravagant claims," "polemical tone," and "defamatory remarks." Roosevelt, Meggers argued, had committed the beginner's error of mistaking a site that had been occupied many times by small, unstable groups for a single, long-lasting society. "[Archaeological remains] build up on areas of half a kilometer or so," she told me, "because [shifting Indian groups] don't land exactly on the same spot. The decorated types of pottery don't change much over time, so you can pick up a bunch of chips and say, 'Oh, look, it was all one big site!' Unless you know what you're doing, of course." Centuries after the conquistadors, "the myth of El Dorado is being revived by archaeologists," Meggers wrote last fall in the journal *Latin American Antiquity,* referring to the persistent Spanish delusion that cities of gold existed in the jungle.

The dispute grew bitter and personal; inevitable in a contemporary academic context, it has featured vituperative references to colonialism, elitism, and employment by the CIA. Meanwhile, Roosevelt's team investigated Painted Rock Cave. On the floor of the cave what looked to me like nothing in particular turned out to be an ancient midden: a refuse heap. The archaeologists slowly scraped away sediment, traveling backward in time with every inch. When the traces of human occupation vanished, they kept digging. ("You always go a meter past sterile," Roosevelt says.) A few inches below they struck the charcoal-rich dirt that signifies human habitation—a culture, Roosevelt said later, that wasn't supposed to be there.

For many millennia the cave's inhabitants hunted and gathered for food. But by about 4000 years ago they were growing crops—perhaps as many as 140 of them, according to Charles R. Clement, an anthropological botanist at the Brazilian National Institute for Amazonian Research. Unlike Europeans, who planted mainly annual crops, the Indians, he says, centered their agriculture on the Amazon's unbelievably diverse assortment of trees: fruits, nuts, and palms. "It's tremendously difficult to clear fields with stone tools," Clement says. "If you can plant trees, you get twenty years of productivity out of your work instead of two or three."

Planting their orchards, the first Amazonians transformed large swaths of the river basin into something more pleasing to human beings. In a widely cited article from 1989, William Balée, the Tulane anthropologist, cautiously estimated that about 12 percent of the nonflooded Amazon forest was of anthropogenic origin—directly or indirectly created by human beings. In some circles this is now seen as a conservative position. "I basically think it's all human-created," Clement told me in Brazil. He argues that Indians changed the assortment and density of species throughout the region. So does Clark Erickson, the University of Pennsylvania archaeologist, who told me in Bolivia that the lowland tropical forests of South America are among the finest works of art on the planet. "Some of my colleagues would say that's pretty radical," he said, smiling mischievously. According to Peter Stahl, an anthropologist at the State University of New York at Binghamton, "lots" of botanists believe that "what the eco-imagery would like to picture as a pristine, untouched Urwelt [primeval world] in fact has been managed by people for millennia." The phrase "built environment," Erickson says, "applies to most, if not all, Neotropical landscapes."

"Landscape" in this case is meant exactly—Amazonian Indians literally created the ground beneath their feet. According to William I. Woods, a soil geographer at Southern Illinois University, ecologists' claims about terrible Amazonian land were based on very little data. In the late 1990s Woods and others began careful measurements in the lower Amazon. They indeed found lots of inhospitable terrain. But they also discovered swaths of *terra preta*—rich, fertile "black earth" that anthropologists increasingly believe was created by human beings.

Terra preta, Woods guesses, covers at least 10 percent of Amazonia, an area the size of France. It has amazing properties, he says. Tropical rain doesn't leach nutrients from *terra preta* fields; instead the soil, so to speak, fights back. Not far from Painted Rock Cave is a 300-acre area with a two-foot layer of *terra preta* quarried by locals for potting soil. The bottom third of the layer is never removed, workers there explain, because over time it will re-create the original soil layer in its initial thickness. The reason, scientists suspect, is that *terra preta* is generated by a special suite of micro-organisms that resists depletion. "Apparently," Woods and the Wisconsin geographer Joseph M. McCann argued in a presentation last summer, "at some threshold level… dark earth attains the capacity to perpetuate—even *regenerate* itself—thus behaving more like a living 'super'-organism than an inert material."

In as yet unpublished research the archaeologists Eduardo Neves, of the University of São Paulo; Michael Heckenberger, of the University of Florida; and other colleagues examined *terra preta* in the upper Xingu, a huge southern tributary of the Amazon. Not all Xingu cultures left behind this living earth, they discovered. But the ones that did generated it rapidly—suggesting to Woods that *terra preta* was created deliberately. In a process reminiscent of dropping microorganism-rich starter into plain dough to create sourdough bread, Amazonian peoples, he believes, inoculated bad soil with a transforming bacterial charge. Not every group of Indians there did this, but quite a few did, and over an extended period of time.

When Woods told me this, I was so amazed that I almost dropped the phone. I ceased to be articulate for a moment and said things like "wow" and "gosh." Woods chuckled at my reaction, probably because he understood what was passing through my mind. Faced with an ecological problem, I was thinking, the Indians *fixed* it. They were in the process of terraforming the Amazon when Columbus showed up and ruined everything.

Scientists should study the microorganisms in *terra preta,* Woods told me, to find out how they work. If that could be learned, maybe some version of Amazonian dark earth could be used to improve the vast expanses of bad soil that cripple agriculture in Africa—a final gift from the people who brought us tomatoes, corn, and the immense grasslands of the Great Plains.

"Betty Meggers would just die if she heard me saying this," Woods told me. "Deep down her fear is that this data will be misused." Indeed, Meggers's recent *Latin American Antiquity* article charged that archaeologists who say the Amazon can support agriculture are effectively

telling "developers [that they] are entitled to operate without restraint." Resuscitating the myth of El Dorado, in her view, "makes us accomplices in the accelerating pace of environmental degradation." Doubtless there is something to this—although, as some of her critics responded in the same issue of the journal, it is difficult to imagine greedy plutocrats "perusing the pages of *Latin American Antiquity* before deciding to rev up the chain saws." But the new picture doesn't automatically legitimize paving the forest. Instead it suggests that for a long time big chunks of Amazonia were used nondestructively by clever people who knew tricks we have yet to learn.

Environmentalists want to preserve as much of the world's land as possible in a putatively intact state. But "intact" may turn out to mean "run by human beings for human purposes."

I visited Painted Rock Cave during the river's annual flood, when it wells up over its banks and creeps inland for miles. Farmers in the floodplain build houses and barns on stilts and watch pink dolphins sport from their doorsteps. Ecotourists take shortcuts by driving motorboats through the drowned forests. Guys in dories chase after them, trying to sell sacks of incredibly good fruit.

All of this is described as "wilderness" in the tourist brochures. It's not, if researchers like Roosevelt are correct. Indeed, they believe that fewer people may be living there now than in 1491. Yet when my boat glided into the trees, the forest shut out the sky like the closing of an umbrella. Within a few hundred years the human presence seemed to vanish. I felt alone and small, but in a way that was curiously like feeling exalted. If that place was not wilderness, how should I think of it? Since the fate of the forest is in our hands, what should be our goal for its future?

NOVEL SHORES

Hernando de Soto's expedition stomped through the Southeast for four years and apparently never saw bison. More than a century later, when French explorers came down the Mississippi, they saw "a solitude unrelieved by the faintest trace of man," the nineteenth-century historian Francis Parkman wrote. Instead the French encountered bison, "grazing in herds on the great prairies which then bordered the river."

To Charles Kay, the reason for the buffalo's sudden emergence is obvious. Kay is a wildlife ecologist in the political-science department at Utah State University. In ecological terms, he says, the Indians were the "keystone species" of American ecosystems. A keystone species, according to the Harvard biologist Edward O. Wilson, is a species "that affects the survival and abundance of many other species." Keystone species have a disproportionate impact on their ecosystems. Removing them, Wilson adds, "results in a relatively significant shift in the composition of the [ecological] community."

When disease swept Indians from the land, Kay says, what happened was exactly that. The ecological ancien régime collapsed, and strange new phenomena emerged. In a way this is unsurprising; for better or worse, humankind is a keystone species everywhere. Among these phenomena was a population explosion in the species that the Indians had kept down by hunting. After disease killed off the Indians, Kay believes, buffalo vastly extended their range. Their numbers more than sextupled. The same occurred with elk and mule deer. "If the elk were here in great numbers all this time, the archaeological sites should be chock-full of elk bones," Kay says. "But the archaeologists will tell you the elk weren't there." On the evidence of middens the number of elk jumped about 500 years ago.

Passenger pigeons may be another example. The epitome of natural American abundance, they flew in such great masses that the first colonists were stupefied by the sight. As a boy, the explorer Henry Brackenridge saw flocks "ten miles in width, by one hundred and twenty in length." For hours the birds darkened the sky from horizon to horizon. According to Thomas Neumann, a consulting archaeologist to Lilburn, Georgia, passenger pigeons "were incredibly dumb and always roosted in vast hordes, so they were very easy to harvest." Because they were readily caught and good to eat, Neumann says, archaeological digs should find many pigeon bones in the pre-Columbian strata of Indian middens. But they aren't there. The mobs of birds in the history books, he says, were "outbreak populations—always a symptom of an extraordinarily disrupted ecological system."

Throughout eastern North America the open landscape seen by the first Europeans quickly filled in with forest. According to William Cronon, of the University of Wisconsin, later colonists began complaining about how hard it was to get around. (Eventually, of course, they stripped New England almost bare of trees.) When Europeans moved west, they were preceded by two waves: one of disease, the other of ecological disturbance. The former crested with fearsome rapidity; the later sometimes took more than a century to quiet down. Far from destroying pristine wilderness, European settlers bloodily *created* it. By 1800 the hemisphere was chockablock with new wilderness. If "forest primeval" means a woodland unsullied by the human presence, William Denevan has written, there was much more of it in the late eighteenth century than in the early sixteenth.

Cronon's *Changes in the Land: Indians, Colonists, and the Ecology of New England* (1983) belongs on the same shelf as works by Crosby and Dobyns. But it was not until one of his articles was excerpted in *The New York Times* in 1995 that people outside the social sciences began to understand the implications of this view of Indian history. Environmentalists and ecologists vigorously attacked the anti-wilderness scenario, which they described as infected by postmodern philosophy. A small academic brouhaha ensued, complete with hundreds of footnotes. It precipitated *Reinventing Nature?* (1995), one of the few academic critiques of postmodernist philosophy written largely by biologists. *The Great New Wilderness Debate* (1998), another lengthy book on the subject, was edited by two philosophers who earnestly identified themselves as "Euro-American men [whose] cultural legacy is patriarchal Western civilization in its current postcolonial, globally hegemonic form."

It is easy to tweak academics for opaque, self-protective language like this. Nonetheless, their concerns were quite justified. Crediting Indians with the role of keystone species has implications for the way the current Euro-American members of that keystone species manage the forests, watersheds, and endangered species of America. Because a third of the United States is owned by the federal government, the issue inevitably has political ramifications. In Amazonia, fabled storehouse of biodiversity, the stakes are global.

Guided by the pristine myth, mainstream environmentalists want to preserve as much of the world's land as possible in a putatively intact state. But "intact," if the new research is correct, means "run by human beings for human purposes." Environmentalists dislike this, because it seems to mean that anything goes. In a sense they are correct. Native Americans managed the continent as they saw fit. Modern nations must do the same. If they want to return as much of the landscape as possible to its 1491 state, they will have to find it within themselves to create the world's largest garden.

From *The Atlantic Monthly*, March 2002, pp. 41-53. © 2002 by Charles Cameron Mann. Reprinted by permission of the Balkan Agency, Inc.

Slavery in the Lower South

If you ask Americans about the origins of slavery in this country, most would doubtlessly tell you that it all began at Jamestown in 1619. Many United States history textbooks still say so, and efforts are underway to establish a museum recognizing that supposed first in concrete and mortar. The assumption is that the first slaves were Africans—which they were not—and that United States history begins with English settlement—which it does not. Conventional wisdom holds that the first blacks to arrive were slaves and that too is incorrect; the history of Africans in colonial North America is not synonymous with slavery.

In the Lower South, indigenous slavery predated the arrival of Africans; indeed, some of the first Africans to reach the shores of what would later become the United States were free. Moreover, both free and enslaved Africans arrived more than a century before 1619. A free African named Juan Garrido accompanied Juan Ponce de Leon when he claimed La Florida for Spain in 1513. Africans, free and slave, were also present in all of the major Spanish expeditions through the Lower South. Wherever these Africans traveled, they encountered Native Americans held in slavery.

During the early years of Spanish settlement, most slaves were not Africans. At first, Spain's Queen Isabella forbade the enslavement of her Indian subjects. But the alleged ferocity of the Caribs and their reputed cannibalism led her to authorize "just war" against them and, by extension, other hostile groups. After 1511, Indians who rejected Christianity or Spanish dominion could be legally enslaved. The Indians who resisted Ponce de Leon's second landing in Florida in 1521 had probably already experienced slave raids launched from Hispaniola.

The first large contingent of African slaves brought to the present-day United States arrived from Hispaniola in 1526 with the ill-fated colonizer, Lucas Vázquez de Ayllón. Ayllón landed some six hundred Spanish men, women, and children at a site believed to be near present-day Sapelo Sound in Georgia. Disease and malnutrition undermined the settlement, which was pushed to the brink with Ayllón's death. Mutiny ensued, and disaffected elements took control of the failing colony. African slaves set fire to the compound of the mutineers and the Guale Indians attacked the colony. This episode marked the first known alliance of Indians and Africans against Europeans in what came to be the United States. The surviving Spaniards straggled back to Hispaniola,

but some of the fugitive Africans took up residence among the Guale and became the region's first maroons (from the Spanish word *cimarrón*). Other maroons, or fugitive slaves, already inhabited the remote mountains and swamps of Hispaniola, Puerto Rico, Jamaica, Cuba, and Mexico.

Despite the slave rebellion at Gualdape, all subsequent Spanish expeditions to the Lower South included black slaves. Africans continued to desert, taking their chances among the indigenous nations. During the three centuries that followed the Spanish arrival in mainland North America, the Indian nations of the vast territory of La Florida—which the Spanish understood to stretch from Key West to Newfoundland and west to "the mines of Mexico"—provided a potential refuge for enslaved Africans (1). The presence of vast unsettled hinterlands populated by still-numerous Indians shaped the development of slavery in the Lower South as did differential types and rates of immigration and of economic development. Ira Berlin has described the evolution of slavery—from "charter generations" of slaves, who worked in relatively equal conditions alongside European masters in rough frontiers—to full blown slave societies—characterized by plantations and staple crops such as rice, sugar, and cotton. Plantation slavery was slow to develop in the Lower South, because Spain was more determined to plant an effective settlement and guard the Atlantic passageways of its treasure fleets than to initiate plantation economies (2).

In 1565, Pedro Menéndez de Avilés established St. Augustine, transforming La Florida into an outpost of the Spanish empire. Menéndez probably brought fewer than fifty slaves to the new settlement. He later sent some of these to plant his second settlement of Santa Elena, in present-day South Carolina. The colonization of La Florida was not easy. Earlier Spanish expeditions into the Lower South had introduced diseases which took a devastating toll on the native populations, and the new settlements only added to the burden on Indians whom the Spaniards expected to give them food, labor, and obedience. Before long, Menéndez was also facing indigenous rebellion (3).

As disease, flight, and war made native labor more problematic, Spaniards tried to acquire more Africans, but the number of slaves in the region remained relatively small, as Peter Wood's demographic study of the South has shown (4). Spain relied on Portuguese slave traders whom they contracted to import Africans into the circum-

Caribbean, but Florida was a minor post and most of the available slaves went to areas where the investment might be recouped, such as Mexico or Peru.

During the first century of Spanish occupation, a multi-tiered system of African slavery developed in the Lower South, distinguishing between unacculturated Africans called *bozales* and Spanish-speaking Catholic slaves known as *ladinos*. The *bozales* labored on cattle ranches, government fortifications, and other public works, while the *ladinos* filled a wide range of urban domestic, artisanal, and menial jobs. In general, urban slaves received better treatment than their rural counterparts, based on older metropolitan slave relations, their access to legal and religious protection, and their integration into a cash economy. In St. Augustine, as in Havana and other circum-Caribbean cities, slaves were allowed to earn money working for themselves on Sundays and feast days. They also hired themselves for an agreed upon return to their owners. With effort, slaves could accumulate sufficient income to buy their freedom or that of their kin through a legal mechanism called *coartación*. Owners and the state also freed slaves, and African freedom and enslavement coexisted in Florida, as in most Spanish colonies. Because it was basically a military outpost, supported by annual Spanish payrolls, and only secondarily a ranching and timbering economy, Florida developed as "a society with slaves" rather than "a slave society" (5).

In 1670, the nature of black life in the Lower South changed. After more than a century of Spanish settlement in the region, English planters from the island of Barbados established an English colony at Charles Town, "but ten days journey" from St. Augustine. The newcomers were intent on establishing plantations such as they had known in Barbados. Such plantations rested upon the massive importation and exploitation of African slaves. Slavery in the Spanish empire was based on Roman law which considered slavery a mutable legal condition. Slaves, then, were entitled to not only legal protection and church membership, like all men and women, but also freedom through testament, self-purchase, and state or private manumission. English planters in the Caribbean developed slave codes that considered slaves as chattel or "moveable property," not unlike their cattle or furniture. The English slave system featured harsh regulatory codes and minimal protection; it discouraged manumission.

Slaves quickly learned the differences in these slave regimes and fled southward from English South Carolina asking for religious sanctuary in Spanish Florida. In 1693, the Spanish king issued a decree "giving liberty to all … the men as well as the women … so that by their example and by my liberality others will do the same"(6). The English in Carolina denounced Spain's provocative sanctuary policy and instituted regulatory slave codes, ticket systems, and land and water patrols. But neither diplomatic negotiations nor military action stanched the flow of runaways. Spanish governors armed the men and encouraged them to return and raid the plantations of their former owners. The freedmen made an effective guerrilla force against the English in Carolina and later Georgia. As more slaves sought sanctuary, Florida's governor followed a model that had been used to pacify maroon populations in Panama, Mexico, Hispaniola, and Colombia. In 1738, he placed the runaway slaves and other black men and women in a town of their own, Gracia Real de Santa Teresa de Mose, two miles north of St. Augustine (7).

Meanwhile, South Carolina's colonists attempted to replicate the Barbadian plantation model. In the early years of settlement in Carolina, Africans experienced slavery that was much like that in Spanish Florida. Africans chased cattle through the woods and worked alongside their owners to build the first homesteads and indigo works in the colony. But with the beginnings of rice cultivation, that changed dramatically. Rice required intensive labor under the grimmest of conditions. Before long, British traders were importing thousands of slaves, mostly from the Congo-Angola region and lesser numbers from Sierra Leone. No other mainland colony imported more slaves, and Sullivan's Island in Charleston's harbor became the Africans' Ellis Island. By the early decades of the eighteenth century, Carolina was said to be "like a Negro country," and the vastly outnumbered white colonists lived in dread of slave uprisings. Their fears were not without reason. Slaves revolted in 1711 and 1714, and in 1715, they joined with Yamasee Indians in a war that almost succeeded in destroying white settlement in Carolina (8).

As the English created a slave society in the Carolinas, the French attempted the same in the Lower Mississippi Valley. During the second decade of the eighteenth century, French planters began importing "Bambara" slaves from the Senegambia region of Africa to establish a plantation regime in Louisiana. This "chatter generation" of slaves was unlike that in Florida or Carolina. Louisiana's slaves derived almost exclusively from one African nation and they came in large numbers over a brief period of intense importation. Senegambian labor enabled Louisiana planters to move rather quickly into plantation development, first of indigo, but, later, and more importantly, of sugar cane. African slaves also labored on government fortifications and public works, and built and repaired the levees that protected New Orleans. French slave law, drawn from the *Code Noir*, was—like the Spanish—based on Roman law, but its implementation had none of the humanity of the Spanish system. Unlike planters in Spanish America, French planters had no long history of milder urban slavery on which to draw. They focused on developing profitable colonial plantations. Slaves were brutalized in the process (9).

Louisiana's African slaves faced the grueling task of creating a plantation economy. As a result, their owners confronted all of the dangers of life in a slave society. Like their counterparts in Florida and Carolina, they also faced the hazards of frontier life. Spanish, English, and French colonizers all exploited Native Americans, intruding upon their lands and appropriating their labor. They cheated them, abused their women, and interfered in their religious and social practices. Inevitably, the Indians in all these regions rose against their oppressors. The history of the Lower South was scarred by warfare. The Guale, Timucuan, and Apalachee Indian wars in Florida, the Yamasee war in Carolina, and the Natchez war in Louisiana were just the most prominent. The latter was particularly deadly, for Africans and Indians joined forces to destroy the nascent French plantation system and all but pushed the French from the lower Mississippi Valley (10).

When Spain acquired Louisiana in 1769, French planters remained. The new rulers of Louisiana needed friends and they turned to the slaves, offering them freedom in exchange for service in the Spanish militia. Gwendolyn Midlo Hall and Kimberly S. Hanger have shown that Spain introduced the multi-tiered system of race relations already operating in other Spanish colonies, thus stoking the growth of a free black population. The free persons of color concentrated in New Orleans filled artisanal and occupational roles much like those of their counterparts in St. Augustine, and like them, also formed loyal black militias for Spain (11).

Such free persons of color were not the only people of African descent to win their freedom in the Lower South. Plantation slaves took advantage of the frequent periods of chaos that wracked the region to escape into the still unsettled hinterlands. The Lower South developed a rich tradition of marroonage. The Savannah River area, the swamps and bayous surrounding New Orleans, the Apalachicola River region, and the interior of central Florida all became home to large maroon communities, which local authorities and planters usually struggled in vain to eradicate (12).

The maroons of the Savannah River were runaways from Carolina and from the new colony of Georgia established by James Oglethorpe in 1732. Oglethorpe envisioned Georgia as a buffer state between South Carolina and Florida, where the debilitating system of slavery would not enter. Despite Oglethorpe's early moralizing, however, Georgian colonists soon legalized slavery, and indigo and silk-worm farms gave way to rice and cotton. Georgian planters purchased their slaves in Charleston from the same English traders who provisioned South Carolina. So African life along the Atlantic coast of the Lower South developed from a homogenous cultural base, with most slaves drawn from the Congo-Angola region of Africa (13).

At the conclusion of the Seven Years' War in 1763, Florida became a British colony and remained so until 1784. Daniel L. Schafer and David Hancock have shown that Anglo-American planters and slave traders imported thousands of slaves directly from Africa to work the large rice and indigo plantations they established in their new colony. One early investor in British Florida, Richard Oswald, imported hundreds of Africans from his slaving factory on Bance Island in the middle of the Sierra Leone River. One of Oswald's contemporaries estimated that as many as one thousand African slaves were imported into Florida in 1771 alone, a peak year of the trade between Africa and Florida. The "new Negroes" came from the Windward, Grain, Gold, and Guinea Coasts of West Africa, from Gambia, and from Angola (14).

The outbreak of the American Revolution disrupted slavery throughout the Lower South. When the Loyalists lost first Charleston and then Savannah, they evacuated over nine thousand slaves southward to the region's last remaining British colony—Florida. However, Loyalist hopes for reestablishing their plantations in Florida were dashed a few short years later when the war ended and Spain regained Florida. Hundreds of slaves belonging to the outgoing Loyalists rushed to claim the religious sanctuary Spain had established in 1693 and reestablished in 1783. They remained in Florida as free Spanish subjects. Like their predecessors who lived at Mose, these Africans became loyal defenders of the Spanish Crown that had freed them.

By the time the British evacuated Florida, slaves had built flourishing rice plantations and cattle ranches along the St. Johns River and helped extract great profits in timber from Florida's dense forests. The incoming Spanish, thus, inherited an established plantation economy (15). All they lacked was a sufficient labor force. Like the English and the French, the Spanish Crown turned to slaves. The Spanish opened Florida to American homesteaders who, like their former Loyalist enemies, brought many new slaves into the colony. Their hopes for the future were also undone, however, by raids by French-inspired revolutionaries, Seminole attacks, American-backed invasions, and pirates disguised as Latin American revolutionaries who seized Florida's most important port, Fernandina on Amelia Island. The United States, which one Spanish official described "as industrious as it is ambitious," had already acquired Louisiana by purchase in 1803 and was determined to have Florida as well. In 1819, the Adams-Onís Treaty gave the Americans legal title to Florida. Florida, the longest-lived colony in what is today the United States, ended as it began, a Spanish settlement. Many of the former slaves whom Spain had freed evacuated to Cuba with the outgoing Spaniards and their slaves. The free black subjects who trusted treaty provisions and stayed behind hoping to preserve their homesteads, like their counterparts in Louisiana, lost most of their hard-won gains over the next years as chattel slavery and all its social implications took root in Florida (16).

Jane Landers is associate professor of history and associate dean of the College of Arts & Science at Vanderbilt University. She is the author of Black Society in Spanish Florida *(1999), editor of* Colonial Plantations and Economy of Florida *(2000) and* Against the Odds: Free Blacks in the Slave Societies of the Americas *(London, 1996), and coeditor of* The African American Heritage of Florida *(1995). She has published essays on the African history of the Hispanic Southeast and of the circum-Caribbean in* The American Historical Review, Slavery and Abolition, The New West Indian Guide, The Americas, *and* Colonial Latin American Historical Review. *Her work also appears in a variety of anthologies and edited volumes.*

Endnotes

1. Jane Landers, *Black Society in Spanish Florida* (Urbana, IL: University of Illinois Press, 1999), ch. 1.
2. Ira Berlin, *Many Thousands Gone: The First Two Centuries of Slavery in North America* (Cambridge, MA: Harvard University Press, 1998).
3. Landers, *Black Society*, 14-15; Henry Dobyns and William Swagerty, *Their Number Became Thinned: Native American Population Dynamics in Eastern North America* (Knoxville, TN: University of Tennessee Press, 1983).
4. Peter H. Wood, "The Changing Population of the Colonial South: An Overview by Race and Region, 1685–1790," in *Powhatan's Mantle: Indians in the Colonial Southeast*, ed. Peter H. Wood, Gregory A. Waselkov, and M. Thomas Hatley (Lincoln, NE: University of Nebraska Press, 1989), 35–103.
5. Landers, *Black Society*; Berlin, *Many Thousands Gone*.
6. Royal edict, 7 November 1693, Santo Domingo 58-1-26, Archivo General de Indias, cited in Landers, *Black Society*, 25.
7. Peter H. Wood, *Black Majority: Negroes in Colonial South Carolina from 1670 through the Stono Rebellion* (New York: Norton Books, 1974); Landers, *Black Society*.
8. Wood, *Black Majority*, 113, 116, 127.
9. Daniel H. Usner Jr., *Indians, Settlers, and Slaves in a Frontier Exchange Economy: The Lower Mississippi Valley before 1783* (Chapel Hill, NC: University of North Carolina Press, 1992); Gwendolyn Midlo Hall, *Africans in Colonial Louisiana: The Development of Afro-Creole Culture in the Eighteenth Century* (Baton Rouge, LA: Louisiana State University Press, 1992); Kimberly S. Hanger, *Bounded Lives, Bounded Places: Free Blacks in Colonial New Orleans, 1769–1803* (Durham, NC: Duke University Press, 1997).
10. Eugene Lyon, *Santa Elena: A Brief History of the Colony, 1566–1587* (Columbia, SC: Institute of Archeology and Anthropology, University of South Carolina, 1984); Wood, *Black Majority*, 113, 116, 127.
11. Hall, *Africans in Colonial Louisiana*, 100–105.
12. Hall, *Africans in Colonial Louisiana*; Landers, *Black Society*.
13. Julia Floyd Smith, *Slavery and Rice Culture in Low Country Georgia, 1750–1860* (Knoxville, TN: University of Tennessee Press, 1985), ch.1; Betty Wood, *Women's Work, Men's Work: The Informal Slave Economies of Lowcountry Georgia* (Athens, GA: University of Georgia Press, 1995; Landers, *Black Society*, 79–80.
14. Daniel L. Schafer, "Yellow Silk Ferret Tied Round Their Wrists": African Americans in British East Florida, 1763–1784," in *The African American Heritage of Florida*, ed. David R. Colburn and Jane L. Landers (Gainesville, FL: University Press of Florida, 1995), 71–103; David Hancock, *Citizens of the World: London Merchants and the Integration of the British Atlantic Community, 1735–1785*, (Cambridge, MA: Harvard University Press, 1995), chap. 5 and 6.
15. Daniel L. Schafer, "'A Swamp of Investment?': Richard Oswald's British East Florida Plantation Experiment," in *Colonial Plantation and Economy in Florida*, ed. Jane G. Landers (Gainesville, FL: University Press of Florida, 2001), 11–38.
16. Landers, *Black Society*.

Pocahontas

Four hundred years after her birth, this Native American girl is defined
more by myth than reality. What is the truth about Pocahontas?

By William M.S. Rasmussen and Robert S. Tilton

FEW FIGURES from America's early history are better known than the Powhatan girl who has come to us as "Pocahontas." Called America's Joan of Arc by some for her virtue and her courage to risk death for a noble cause, Pocahontas has even been revered as the "mother" of the nation, a female counterpart to George Washington. Her 1607 rescue of Captain John Smith is one of the most appealing episodes in colonial history.

A number of the original chroniclers of the Jamestown colony mention Pocahontas by name and note her interactions with the English settlers. By the early 1700s her reputation was well established, but it was during the nineteenth century, when the brief history of America was recognized as containing elements useful in the construction of romantic visual and literary narratives, that saw the greatest dissemination of the Pocahontas legend. Her story was wrested from the exclusive purview of historians by novelists, dramatists, and artists, who, noting the potential in the great events of her life for stirring fictional portrayals, re-created and glamorized her accomplishments.

During the centuries since its creation, therefore, the Pocahontas narrative has so often been retold and embellished and so frequently adapted to contemporary issues that the actual, flesh-and-blood woman has become almost totally obscured by the burgeoning mythology.

This young woman, who was known among her own people as "Matoaka" and whose nickname was "Pocahontas" ("little wanton" or "little plaything"), apparently possessed a number of extraordinary qualities, including a spirited and engaging personality, but only scattered references to her appearance and character have survived. William Strachey, in his rendition of the early days of the Virginia colony (for which he was the first secretary), provided the shocking depiction of her as a naked young girl cavorting with the boys of the settlement, as well as the report that she had been married to an Indian named Kocoum. The chief architect of the Pocahontas legend, however, is Captain John Smith, who wrote of her in his *Generall Historie* published in 1624.

The trustworthiness of all the early accounts can be called into question, but the scarcity of verifiable "facts" proved in a way to be a boon to the literary and visual artists who wished to tell her story; they were therefore free to depict its events in whatever form they wished. By the end of the nineteenth century, although their historical veracity was still at times debated, their truth as sources had grown beyond the power of those who would attempt to demythologize the heroine of Jamestown.

In his *Generall Historie,* Smith recorded that after being taken prisoner by Indians in December 1607, his life was endangered by the men of the village to which he was taken. As they prepared to "beate out [my] braines," he wrote, Pocahontas—the adolescent daughter of Chief Powhatan—"got his head in her armes, and laid her owne upon his to save him from death."

Through much of the late 1800s, New England historians, intent on discrediting the South's efforts to formulate an impressive history of its own, concluded that debunking the legend of Pocahontas would cause the "Virginia aristocracy" to be "utterly gravelled." These historians ultimately succeeded in casting serious doubt on whether a rescue had ever taken place.

Ethnologists are inclined to dismiss the rescue as highly problematical because Smith did not mention it in his earliest accounts of his capture, and the behavior described does not conform to what is known of Indians of the Powhatan Confederacy.

Sharing the ethnologists' suspicion that Smith's life was never in danger, some historians have suggested that the rescue was a ritual the Englishman simply did not understand. According to that theory, Pocahontas served as a sponsor for Smith as he was adopted into Powhatan's tribe. Smith's death was only ceremonial, a prelude to his rebirth into Indian society. Ethnologists, however, have no evidence that the Indians practiced such a ritual.

A final possibility is that the incident was a test of Smith's manliness and that the outcome was left unresolved when Pocahontas intervened. Throughout their lives, the courage of

Powhatan men was under scrutiny. Because they were repeatedly tested, they often similarly tested opponents through physical torture or the threat of it.

Smith's account of the rescue was apparently accepted by his contemporaries. In 1623, when Smith testified to a commission conducting an in-depth investigation of the Virginia Company, he credited the "King's daughter as the means to returne me safe to James towne." He would hardly have lied to an investigative committee that had access to multiple witnesses with firsthand knowledge.

Did Pocahontas really rescue Smith? The question may never be answered conclusively. Although there are disturbing anthropological questions, the historical evidence is persuasive. Until proven otherwise, Pocahontas should probably be awarded credit for saving Smith, if only from a test of his composure under duress.

In the spring of 1613, Captain Samuel Argall, a navigator and administrator who had arrived in the colony in 1612, learned that Pocahontas was visiting the Patowomeck Indians of what is now northern Virginia. He arranged for her abduction in order to exchange her for several English prisoners held by Powhatan and for arms, tools, and corn.

Powhatan was "much grieved" to learn of the capture of Pocahontas. He immediately sent instructions that the Englishman should "use his Daughter well, and bring my [Argall's] ship into his River, and there he would give mee my demands." Within a "few dayes" Powhatan returned seven English hostages and three tools. This was not enough to satisfy the English, however, and a year went by before another attempt was made to resolve the impasse.

In March 1614, colonial administrator Sir Thomas Dale set out toward Powhatan's residence with Pocahontas and 150 men, determined "either to move [the Indians] to fight for her... or to restore the residue of our demands."

When the two sides met, a battle seemed imminent until "[t]wo of Powhatans sonnes being very desirous to see their sister... came unto us, at the sight of whom, and her well fare... they much rejoyced, and promised that they would undoubtedly persuade their father to redeeme her, and to conclude a firme peace forever with us."

At this point, however, colonist John Rolfe, a twenty-eight-year-old widower, announced to Dale by letter his love for Pocahontas and his interest in marrying her. Dale readily approved the pairing and thereby ended any chance for the "redemption" of Pocahontas, who had already been baptized, or who was in the process of becoming well versed enough in the religion of her captors to contemplate conversion.

There is no written account of the details surrounding Pocahontas's baptism in 1613 or early in 1614, at which she was given the name Rebecca. John Smith recorded, however, that by

Rolfe's "diligent care" she was taught to speak English "as might well bee understood," and was "well instructed in Christianitie."

During Pocahontas's captivity, "John Rolfe had bin in love with [her] and she with him." Although is "hartie and best thoughts [had] a long time bin so intangled," Rolfe agonized over what he perceived to be a moral dilemma. He attempted to convince himself that he was not motivated by "the unbridled desire of carnall affection" but was acting "for the good of this plantation, for the honour of our countrie, for the glory of God, for my owne saluation, and for the converting to the true knowledge of God and Jesus Christ, an unbeleeving creature...." Finally, Rolfe concluded that marriage to Pocahontas would be morally correct, even a "holy... worke."

Powhatan found the proposed marriage of his daughter "acceptable" and gave his consent. He sent "an olde uncle of hirs, named Opachisco, to give her as his deputy in the Church, and two of his sonnes to see the marriage solemnized."

Two years later, Pocahontas traveled to England with her husband and young son, Thomas. Her journey was an arrangement of the Virginia Company, the organization that sponsored the Jamestown settlement. The company was continually in search of investors and colonists and eager for the potential financial reward of colonization, but its leadership also had a genuine concern that Virginia's Indians be Christianized. Pocahontas, the converted daughter of a chief, was impressive evidence of the attractiveness of Virginia as an investment and of the founding's success as a missionary endeavor.

Pocahontas, Rolfe, and Thomas left Virginia in the spring of 1616 with Dale and his party. The Virginia Company provided Pocahontas with a small living allowance while in England and saw to it that she was presented to society. The reception given "Rebecca Rolfe" was warm, and her visit generated a great deal of attention and excitement. She "did not onely accustome her selfe to civilitie, but still carried her selfe as the Daughter of a King, and was accordingly respected, not onely by the company... but of divers particular persons of Honor, in their hopefull zeale by her to advance Christianitie."

The Rolfes began the return trip to Virginia in the spring of 1617 but got no further than Gravesend. There Pocahontas died at the age of twenty-two, the victim of an illness that had "unexpectedly" developed. Her Christian faith remained constant; those who witnessed her death were "joy[ous]... to heare and see her make so religious and godly an end."

Dr. William M. S. Rasmussen is Virginius C. Hall Curator of Art at the Virginia Historical Society. Dr. Robert S. Tilton is professor of American Literature at Queens College in New York.

"Instruments of Seduction": A Tale of Two Women

Sandra F. VanBurkleo

Ann Hibbens and Anne Hutchinson had much in common. Both hailed from the Puritan hotbed of Lincolnshire, England, where they had married successful merchants before emigrating to New Boston, in 1630 and 1634 respectively. Within a few years, both women stood in the dock, charged with committing crimes against the community and entertaining diabolical religious ideas. And both women lost their contests with government. At issue were Puritan teachings about "godly relations" between husband and wife, minister and church member, and magistrate and subject. In trials of Hibbens, Hutchinson (1), and other "headstrong" women, judicial decisions about whether or not to allow important procedural and substantive freedoms partly depended upon which aspect of Calvinism's two-sided vision of woman held sway at particular moments in the proceeding. On one side, women were potential Saints equal to men in God's eyes; on the other side, they were Eve-like temptresses, peculiarly susceptible to Satanic temptation. In addition, Puritan responses to fallen or treacherous women in courtrooms lay bare the essential masculin-

ity of many freedoms—among them, the right to command one's own body, the right of locomotion, liberty of speech (especially in public), the right to bring witnesses and otherwise engage in self-defense, and the privilege against self-incrimination.

The facts in the two cases differ. The charismatic teacher and spiritist Anne Hutchinson had been admitted in 1635 to the Reverend John Wilson's First Church of Boston, over the objections of several ministers who suspected her of Antinomianism—a belief in the primacy of divine revelation and related skepticism about the authority of clergy and Biblical law. With the encouragement of Governor Harry Vane, the radical theologian John Cotton (her spiritual mentor), and the Reverend John Wheelwright (her intemperate and impolitic brother-in-law), Hutchinson began to hold women's meetings at home. Such meetings were common enough among English gentlewomen, and (contrary to myth) did *not* involve promiscuous mingling of the sexes; instead—and more damagingly—Hutchinson summarized and explicated Biblical texts and criticized sermons, notably Wil-

son's, encouraging women to subject ministers, husbands, and other lawgivers to criticism.

The heyday of Hutchinson's meetings coincided with a colony-wide revival and expansion of church rolls. When spiritual malaise replaced euphoria in 1636, Cotton (2) began castigating other ministers for their abandonment, solely to attract new members, of the "covenant of grace" in favor of a "covenant of works." Hutchinson, who agreed with Cotton and had Vane's ear, emerged as the mainspring of a faction pitted against Wilson's ministry and the political ambitions of John Winthrop. Hutchinson and her followers began walking out of church during sermons; throughout the colony, women rose in mid-service to heckle pastors or to dispute theological points.

In Anglo-America, these were shocking developments: public oratory by women violated both law and custom. Anglican lecturers regularly enjoined women to "obey husbands," to "cease from commanding," and to avoid what Amy Schrager Lang calls "female authorship." The influential English scholar Thomas Hooker permitted public speeches by women only when they supported "*subjection.*" And, while Puritans expanded women's sphere to include family governance and church membership, they had qualms about female voices in public spaces. Scholars and preachers hoped to preserve "an inequality in the degree of … Authority" so that, when push came to shove, husbands might retain "a *Superiority.*" Puritan historian Edward Johnson averred that only "silly women laden with diverse lusts and phantastical madness" pursued rhetoric and theology. After the Antinomian crisis, John Cotton similarly proscribed female oratory unless women had in mind "singing forth the praises of the Lord" or confessing crime. Speech "by way of teaching" or "propounding questions … under pretence of a desire to learn," he said, usurped male prerogatives and unsettled the polity.

On one side, women were potential Saints equal to men in God's eyes; on the other side, they were Eve-like temptresses, peculiarly susceptible to Satanic temptation.

Hutchinson's moment in the sun was fleeting: in mid-1636, the political tides began to turn against the Vane faction. Pretending friendship, Wilson and other clerics visited Hutchinson's home in December, 1636, ostensibly to discuss religion (by Puritan lights, a "private" conversation ordinarily off limits to public scrutiny). Hutchinson spoke freely; Wilson surreptitiously took notes from which record the group compiled a list of doctrinal "errors."

Some weeks later, at John Cotton's invitation, John Wheelwright (3) preached an incendiary fast-day sermon in which, to Cotton's horror, he condemned every minister except his host for practicing a covenant of works, and

called for open warfare against Satan's allies in Bay Colony meetinghouses. His jeremiad revealed, among other things, the ongoing vitality of associations between Woman and the Anti-Christ. Wheelwright said Christians welcomed battles between "Gods people and those that are not"; everyone knew "that the whore [or false church] must be burnt.… [I]t is not shaving of her head and paring her nayles and changing her rayment, that will serve … but this whore must be burnt."

Fearing rebellion, the General Court confiscated firearms from suspected Wheelwright supporters, who in turn circulated a remonstrance (signed by Wheelwright's friends) threatening an appeal to royal courts. Four months later, Winthrop won the governorship and Vane fled to London. In March, 1637, magistrates commenced proceedings against Wheelwright, Hutchinson, and other minor players in the drama. Convicted of sedition, Wheelwright was exiled, though he returned after a decent interval to preach at Harvard. Significantly, the evidence used against him was a matter of public record (i.e., the contents of a sermon and written, signed remonstrance); magistrates extended a long list of procedural rights at trial—among them, the right to offer witnesses and testimony in self-defense, and the right to be silent.

His sister-in-law fared less well. In September, at an open meeting in Newport, a church-state synod examined Hutchinson, in keeping with English procedure, for evidence of sedition, heresy, blasphemy, and other crimes against authority. Unlike her kinsman, she had never occupied a pulpit, and had neither inspired nor signed petitions. Her crimes—the sowing of rebellious seeds among women, for example—occurred entirely behind the walls of a frame house.

Pregnant and faint, Hutchinson faced three rows of hostile questioners—civil magistrates, elected deputies, and clergy. In Winthrop's words, she had "troubled the peace of the

commonwealth" and "spoken divers things … prejudicial to the honour of the churches and ministers thereof." She had "maintained a meeting and an assembly" in her home—"a thing not tolerable nor comely in the sight of God" nor "fitting" for her sex. Despite criticism, she had persisted; the court hoped to "understand how things are" and "reduce" her (i.e., force her to acknowledge error). Failing that, she would be condemned for "obstinance."

For a time, Hutchinson prevailed, ably challenging the court's questionable use of evidence taken privately, the curious absence of a criminal charge, the judges' related refusal to let her examine Wilson's notebooks in advance of trial, and their refusal to administer oaths to witnesses (which they technically did not *have* to do, so long as the proceeding still could be termed a magisterial examination and not a trial). Familiar with Biblical law and common law procedure, she saw clearly how weak the governor's case really was. Winthrop, after all, had no hard evidence of sedition—by definition a crime involving public acts—and flimsy evidence of heresy, some of which tended to implicate John Cotton. She had not signed the Wheelwright petition, had criticized ministers at *home*, and had spoken with Wilson as one speaks with "friends." As she put it, Puritans respected private exchanges and "matter(s) of conscience." Nobody came forward to secure liberties for Hutchinson; but, because she managed to assert rights claims accurately and persuasively, the magistrates acceded to her procedural demands.

Gradually, however, Hutchinson lost ground. The focus began to shift from specific theological points to "natural" relations between the sexes, and especially to Hutchinson's alleged violations of the Fifth Commandment and usurpations of male prerogatives. More than once, magistrates reminded her that men need not "discourse" with women—that men need not *hear* what women said as to "facts" or "truth" in self-defense. Winthrop also gained important leverage in the control of Hutchinson's body (e.g., ordering her to stop speaking, to sit while standing, to stand while sitting). A woman could never "call a company together" to preach, he said, nor offer testimony without judicial dispensation. Why had Hutchinson failed to teach young women to "love their husbands and not to make them clash?" Why had she not learned the lesson herself? Surely her meetings, so "prejudicial to the state," led to "families — neglected" by wives who had come to believe, with their teacher, that "the fear of man, is a snare." Domestic sabotage weakened all of political society: as one minister later explained, God chose *not* to create church and state "at one stroke," but to lay "foundations both of State and Church, in a family," the "Mother Hive" from which church and state "issued forth." To attack this "little commonwealth" was to assail political government. For this reason, the court declared Wilson's notebooks a lawful source of evidence: when women attacked the polity at its foundation, confidences "counted for nothing," and private utterances could support charges of sedition (or other "public" crimes). In addition, magistrates imposed banishment instead of censure, against the letter of Bay Colony law.

Because she had been demonized, Hutchinson's decision to tell the truth and be done with it returned to haunt her. She freely described her gift of prophecy, her doctrinal positions, and the content of divine messages; she claimed a God-given ability to distinguish between true and false voices. Sensing an opportunity to gather *public* evidence of heresy, magistrates asked her to say exactly how God communicated with her. "By an immediate voice," she replied truthfully. For good measure, she reminded her accusers that, because Jesus alone controlled her "body and soul," the court could do her no harm, and instead would bring a "curse upon … posterity, and the mouth of the Lord hath spoken it."

Magistrates no doubt breathed a sigh of relief: the "American Jezebel" (as she came to be called) had admitted antinomianism before dozens of witnesses. So long as she refused to recant errors in a separate church trial, they would be rid of her.

Jailed in a private home for the winter, Hutchinson's health steadily declined. John Wilson officiated at the proceeding in March, 1638. There, the congregation would judge whether or not she had violated the First Church covenant by which Saints agreed to "walke in all sincere Conformity" with God's law as interpreted by the clergy. If guilty and unrepentant, she would be excommunicated as well as exiled. Hutchinson was too weak to attend opening sessions, where elders presented yet more evidence "taken from her owne Mouth" over the winter by seeming friends and at least one ex-disciple. As earlier, she had no knowledge of the evidence to be used against her. Because she claimed to be ruled exclusively by God and not by her husband or the clergy, several elders accused her of several obscure heresies and—more damning—of sympathy with Familism (the notorious "family of love" sect in which members collectively married Jesus and dispensed with ordinary matrimony) (4). Hutchinson stoutly denied these charges and recanted several "errors," on the ground that human language garbled God's "true" messages (which came to her *without* language) when she tried to put them into words.

On another day, in another court, recantation might have saved her from severe punishment; but this was not such a day. At one particularly delicate moment, a critic determined to portray Hutchinson as a viper in society's bosom abruptly interjected more talk about "that foule, groce, filthye, and abominable opinion held by Familists, of the Communitie of Weomen." Would she dispense altogether with patriarchal marriages? Cotton reminded parishioners that, while Hutchinson had done "much good," she was

"but a Woman and many unsound and dayngerous principles are held by her." Did she not threaten the "very foundation of Religion" with the "filthie Sinne of the Communitie of Woemen and all promisc[uou]s and filthie cominge togeather of men and Woemen without Distinction or Relation of marriage?" He even accused her of marital infidelity on the ground that Familism always led there.

At closing sessions some days later, Wilson presented a longer list of "errors," some compiled by embittered ex-disciples over the winter. Weakened by pregnancy and long detention, Hutchinson said little; in any case, theology had ceased to be the issue. She had been reconstituted as the "whore of Babylon," charged with violations of Puritan relational ideology, and tarred with Familism, the heresy for which Quakers could be hanged in Massachusetts Bay. One of the elders summarized charges: "[Y]ou have stept out of your place," he said, "you have rather bine a Husband than a Wife and a preacher than a Hearer, and a Magistrate than a Subject." Wilson called her a "dayngerous Instrument of the Divell." Said others, the "Misgovernment of this Woman's tongue" by her husband and other natural rulers portended grave "Disorder." When members objected again to punishment for conscience, Cotton found biblical authority to exile her for perjury, blasphemy, and spiritual "seduction." The writ of excommunication ordered her to leave the parish "as a Leper"; because she "dispised and contemned the Holy Ordinances," she should not "benefit by them."

Hutchinson walked out of church, followed by family members and her friend Mary Dyer (executed in 1660 for Quakerism). In March, 1638, she joined William Hutchinson in Rhode Island, where she experienced what Winthrop soberly termed a "monstrous birth"—in his view, providential evidence of grotesque theology, a "confession" that cast additional doubt upon the woman's own words. The governor noted, too, that Dyer's "familiarity with the devill" earlier had produced a stillborn "monstrous" child, which Hutchinson and Dyer had labored to conceal; both women were unnatural, poisonous, perhaps demonic. Indeed, Winthrop wondered whether or not his old nemesis had been a witch all along. In 1639, church elders (including Ann Hibbens' husband, William) visited Rhode Island to check on the progress of censured members. Hutchinson slammed the door in their faces. She wanted no part of their church, for she was an ecstatic "spouse of Christ." Disconcerted visitors pronounced her a "Harlot," begging the church to "cut her off" once and for all. Wilson gladly obliged.

The tale's end fit neatly into the narrative Winthrop later constructed to justify Hutchinson's exile. In the early 1640's, she moved to New York to find "peace." There, Indians killed the entire Hutchinson family except one child. Surely her assailants had been godly messengers: "I never heard that the Indians … did ever before this, commit the like outrage," wrote Winthrop. God had made of "this wofull woman" a "heavie example of their cruelty," and confirmed the diabolical nature of her theology.

Meanwhile, Puritans on both sides of the Atlantic had closed ranks, ruling out female ministries and antinomian experimentation. John Brinsley's 1645 sermon in Yarmouth, England, contained a typical announcement of the Puritan decision against woman preachers: "Sure we are," he said, "that … Women may not teach in publick. And were there no other Reason for it, this alone might be sufficient to silent them. The woman by her taking upon her to teach … became the Instrument of Seduction, and Author of Transgression to her husband, and consequently of ruine to him.…Henceforth then no more Women-Preachers." For women to assume "the office of Teaching," he added, was "no less than a mingling of Heaven and earth together, an inversion of the course and order of nature" (5).

Ann Hibbens, by contrast, did not claim to be a prophet. No sooner had she sailed into Boston harbor than she developed a reputation for "natural crabbedness of … temper" and squabbling with neighbors (6). But serious trouble awaited 1640, when she locked horns with a joiner (or carpenter) who raised his price after building a fancy bedstead. Hibbens not only disputed the worker's claim and investigated prices charged by other joiners, but also interrogated laborers in neighboring towns and rejected the mediating efforts of another craftsman. Says historian Jane Kamensky, Hibbens "spoke as a woman trying to participate in a rational society with a developing economy; prices, value, and collusion, not inspiration and revelation, were her province." But, after the Hutchinson debacle, wives did business and exhibited a "restless tongue" at some peril. While Puritans despised hustling and gouging, they also hated scolds; in Hibbens' case, they punished the "medium, not the message" (7).

In the autumn of 1640, the First Church commenced a magisterial examination of Hibbens, initially to ferret out evidence of "lying" about her fellows (a felony in Massachusetts); they probably sought evidence as well of scolding (a sex-specific crime punished with a dunking). The trigger had been her seemingly arrogant rejection of a male mediator and related decision to singlehandedly undertake a market survey on horseback. Judges charged Hibbens with laying "infamy, disgrace, and reproach" on the carpenter ("our Brother"). As with Hutchinson, charges multiplied to include neglect of "natural" relations between women and their male "heads."

As in Hutchinson's case, Hibbens refused to submit to false authority; Unlike her forebear, she preferred to *withhold* speech whenever the court demanded testimony, to stand when the court bade her sit, and to smile maddeningly at her accusers. Finally driven to distraction, the magistrates condemned her arrogance and especially her "carriage … so proud and contemptuous and irreverent … when

the church is dealing with her." Through a "Brother," Hibbens sardonically told her accusers that she dared not respond to queries in church because God required silence of women.

Also as with Hutchinson, Hibbens's accusers fastened upon ungodly relations—her unwomanly violations of "the rule of the Apostle in usurping authority over him whom God hath made her head and husband," and her anti-Christian decision to take "the power and authority which God hath given to him out of his hands." William had accepted the joiner's price; Ann's insistence that she could "manage it better than her husband" constituted a "plan breach of the rule of Christ," and by implication an indictment of Hibbens' husband for failing to govern his wife. Judges toyed with the possibility that her ability to rile up the neighborhood evidenced witchcraft; but, in 1640, they settled for admonition and (when she refuse to disavow "lusts and covetous distempers") excommunication. The pastor stated that Hibbens merited damnation for "slandering and raising up an evil report of … Brethren," for the "sowing of discord," and for refusing to remain at home. She had, after all, dashed "with a restless and discontented spirit … from person to person from house to house, and from place to place." She had rejected governance by the "wise … head" of her husband, usurped his prerogatives, and "grieved his spirit." Has she not behaved "as if he was a nobody," rejected "the way of obedience," and encouraged "unquietness of the family"? With Hutchinson, Hibbens had little time for "due submission." Unlike her predecessor, she celebrated the commercial spirit and ignored theology—impulse which profoundly troubled her interrogators.

Hibbens vanished from public view until 1654 when her well-respected husband died. One historian thinks that, without his protection, she no longer could fend off the "full weight of her neighbors' hatred" (8). In 1655, the General Court convicted her of witchcraft, but magistrates refused the verdict and ordered a new trial, where jurors again condemned her. In mid-1656, Massachusetts executed

Hibbens as a witch, for being "turbulent in her passion, and discontented," and possessed of a "strange carriage." Years later, a witness to the spectacle told Puritan minister Increase Mather that she had been hanged "for having more wit than her neighbors." She had "guessed that two of her persecutors, whom she saw talking in the street, were talking of her; which, proving true, cost her life."

The trials of Hutchinson and Hibbens—and analogous ordeals to which colonial magistrates subjected other female spiritist and malcontents—lay bare the extent to which gender shaped access to important freedoms, particularly when women threatened to destabilize the "Yoke-fellowship" that governed Puritan families. A reputation for self-sovereignty clearly diminished a woman's liberty prospects. The die was cast when Hutchinson rose to defend herself as God's instrument, immune to the slings and arrows of mere men. Hibbens similarly tossed freedom to the wind when she refused to let magistrates control her body, mind, and tongue. Submissiveness guaranteed nothing, but unruly or aggressive women triggered fears of the Anti-Christ. Puritan divine William Perkins suggested that, in certain cases, and never in cases of witchcraft, women's "weakness" might "lessen both the crime and the punishment"; unruliness or aggression ensured the opposite result. Mercy Brown of Wallingford Massachusetts, escaped the gallows in 1691 after killing her son; however, judges delayed passing sentence because she was "distracted," and finally jailed her. By contrast, Dorothy Talbye of Salem (hanged for child murder) resisted authority, refused to confess until threatened with torture, sat when ordered to stand, and rejected a face-cloth at the gallows. Defiance increased the odds of unmitigated punishment, and often lent credence to suspicions of witchcraft (9).

Comparisons with state trials of men are telling. Magistrates, to give one example, did not interpret Wheelwright's

silence as guilt, because regular male ministers (unlike lay female ministers) could be counted on to tell the truth in public and elsewhere, and also because his crime, while heinous, did not weaken political society at its foundation. Anne Hutchinson's brother-in-law brought witnesses on his own behalf, offered testimony for jurors' consideration, and retained sovereign command of his own body. Both Hutchinson and Hibbens confronted judges determined to police their movements and utterances better than husbands had done, and to extract confessions or damning testimony, because they acted from and upon the domestic "Hive." Ann Hibbens's mocking silence bought her a one-way ticket to the gallows; Hutchinson's eleventh-hour recantations at the church trial (which might have saved her, had critics not identified her with Satan) ultimately were used against her, as evidence of bizarre theology and *lying* at the civil trial. For women accused of treachery, public displays of courage, honesty, erudition, and physical autonomy were altogether foolhardy.

Sandra F. VanBurkleo, Associate Professor of History at Wayne State University in Detroit, is completing a book, "Belonging to the World": Women's Rights and American Constitutional Culture. *She teaches and writes in the field of American legal and constitutional history.*

Endnotes

1. For a fuller version of the Hutchinson tale, additional bibliography, and citations to material quoted here, see Sandra F. VanBurkleo, "'To Bee Rooted Out of Her Station': The Ordeal of Anne Hutchinson," in *American Political Trials*, ed. Michal Belknap, rev. ed. (Westport, Conn: Greenwood Press, 1993), 1–24, which in turn relies upon David Hall, ed., *The Antinomian Controversy, 1636–1638: A Documentary History*, 2d ed. (Durham, N.C.: Duke University Press, 1990).
2. Reverend Richard Allestree, quoted in Alice E. Natahews, "Religious Experience of Southern Women," and John Cotton, "Singing of Psalms a Gospel-Ordinance, 1650," in *Women and Religion in America*,

ed. Rosemary Radford Ruether and Rosemary Skinner Keller, vol. 2 (New York, 1983), 191–192, 206; Amy Schrager Lang, *Prophetic Woman: Anne Hutchinson and the Problem of Dissent in the Literature of New England* (Berkeley: University of California Press, 1987), 3; Hooker and Cotton quoted in David Leverenz, *Language of Puritan Feeling: An Exploration in Literature, Psychology, and Social History* (New Brunswick, N.J.: Rutgers University Press, 1980), 82; and Edward Johnson quoted in Edgar McManus, *Law and Liberty in Early New England* (Amherst: University of Massachusetts Press, 1993), 199–220.
3. John Wheelwright, "Fast-Day Sermon," in Hall, 158–170.
4. See Christopher W. Marsh, *The Family of Love in English Society, 1550–1630* (New York: Cambridge University Press, 1994).
5. Sermon of Reverend John Brinsely, quoted in Rosemary Skinner Keller, "New England Women: Ideology and Experience in First-Generation Puritanism (1630–1650)," in Ruether and Keller, 189.
6. "[Governor] Thomas Hutchinson on Ann Hibbins [sic]", *Witchhunting in Seventeenth-Century New England*, ed. David Hall (Boston: Northeastern University Press, 1991), 91.
7. [Robert Keayne], "Proceedings of Excommunication against Mistress Ann Hibbens of Boston (1640)," in *Remarkable Providences*, ed. John Demos, rev. ed. (Boston 1991), 262; Jane Kamensky, "Governing the Tongue: Speech and Society in Early New England," (Ph.D. diss., Yale University, 1993), 220. The account of Hibbens's ordeal derives from Demos's transcription supplemented by Hall, *Witchhunting*, 91.
8. Hall, *Witchhunting*, 91.
9. William Perkins, "Discourse on the Damned Art of Witchcraft," (1592) in Ruether and Keller, 154; McManus, 105; Peter Hoffer and N. E. H. Hull, *Murdering Mothers: Infanticide in England and New England, 1558–1803* (New York, 1984), 40–1.

Bibliography

Battis, Emery. *Saints and Sectaries: Anne Hutchinson and the Antinomian Controversy in the Massachusetts Bay Colony*. Chapel Hill: University of North Carolina Press, 1962.

Demos, John. *Remarkable Providences: Readings on Early American History*. Rev. ed. Boston, Mass: 1991.

Hall, David D., ed. *The Antinomian Controversy, 1636–1638: A Documentary History.* 2d ed. Durham, N.C.: Duke University Press, 1990.

————*Witchhunting in Seventeenth-Century New England.* Boston, Mass.: Northeastern University Press, 1991.

Karlsen, Carol F. *The Devil in the Shape of a Woman: Witchcraft in Colonial New England.* New York: W.W. Norton, 1989.

Schrager Lang, Amy. *Prophetic Woman: Anne Hutchinson and the Problem of Dissent in the Literature of New England.* Berkeley: University of California Press, 1987.

Morris, Richard B. "Jezebel Before the Judges." In *Fair Trial.* New York: Macdonald, 1967.

Stoever, William. *"A Faire and Easie Way to Heaven": Covenant Theology and Antinomianism in Early Massachusetts.* Middletown, Conn: Wesleyan University Press, 1978.

VanBurkleo, Sandra F. "'To Bee Rooted Out of Her Station': The Ordeal of Anne Hutchinson." In *American Political Trials*, edited by Michal Belknap. Rev. ed. Westport, Conn: Greenwood Press, 1994.

From *OAH Magazine of History,* Winter 1995, pages 8-13. Copyright © 1995 by Organization of American Historians. Reprinted with permission.

The Pueblo Revolt

The Pueblo Indians in the province of New Mexico had long chafed
under Spanish rule. In 1680 all their grievances flared into a violent rebellion
that surprised the Europeans with its ferocity.

by Jake Page

THERE WAS A CHILL in the air in the pre-dawn hours of August 10, 1680, as Brother Juan Batista Pío settled himself on his horse. The Franciscan priest had heard rumors that the Pueblo Indians were planning to revolt against the Spanish who lived in New Mexico, the most remote and least productive colony in all of New Spain. Indians had murdered a Spanish settler the night before at the pueblo of Tesuque, situated among the low hills some 10 miles from Santa Fe, and Brother Pío set off for the village in the belief that he could calm its people and turn them from rebellion to join in the fellowship of Holy Mass.

Pedro Hidalgo made a mad dash for his life after he realized that Pueblo Indians had murdered Brother Juan Batista Pío. The Franciscan's death marked the beginning of a resistance movement that drove the Spanish from New Mexico.

Brother Pío and his soldier escort, Pedro Hidalgo, proceeded through the dark green piñon pines and desert junipers that dotted the rolling, reddish-brown landscape. Finding Tesuque deserted, they continued on into the sur-rounding countryside in search of the Indians. As they descended into a shallow ravine the two men saw the villagers, carrying weapons and with their faces painted red, headed for the mountains. "What is this, children?" the Franciscan cried out. "Are you mad? Do not disturb yourselves. I will die a thousand deaths for you."

As Hidalgo rode along, he watched Brother Pío move deeper into the ravine and disappear around a corner. A short time later one of the Indians suddenly burst from the ravine, carrying the friar's shield. Close behind him came another Indian, spattered with blood. More Indians swarmed out of the ravine to attack Hidalgo, but the soldier spurred his horse into a gallop and escaped. He saw no sign of the priest. Hidalgo rode back to Santa Fe to alert the Spanish governor of New Mexico, Antonio de Otermín, that the uprising was no longer a rumor.

BROTHER PÍO'S MURDER that morning was among the first actions of the Pueblo Indian revolt, an uprising that profoundly and permanently altered the history of the American Southwest. The violence had been a long time coming. The Indian's resentment against the Spanish had begun to smolder with Francisco Vásquez de Coronado's trek through their country in 1540–42. The Spaniard had demanded food and supplies from the Indians and had attacked any pueblos that refused him. The resentment intensified with the arrival of set-tlers, soldiers, and friars in 1598. The colonists found communities of trim multi-storied houses built of dried mud and surrounded by green fields all along the river the Europeans called the Rio Del Norte. They called the Indian towns *pueblos,* after the Spanish word for village. The settlers moved in between the pueblos, the friars moved into the villages, and the secular authorities established a capital in one of the northern pueblos, which they called San Juan. The Spaniards later moved the capital to Santa Fe, establishing what is today the oldest continuing capital in the United States.

The Franciscan cried out. "Are you mad? Do not disturb yourselves. I will die a thousand deaths for you."

It wasn't long before these developments had thrown the traditional world of the peaceful and agricultural Pueblo Indians into chaos. The Spanish governors demanded food tributes and labor, and they responded to Indian resistance with beatings, mutilations, or death. European diseases, such as smallpox and measles, devastated the native population, claiming more than one-third of the estimated 25,000 Indians that inhabited the Southwest.

*The Pueblo Indians'
decades of resentment
finally erupted as they
burned the Spaniards'
missions, murdered
priests, and defiled altars.
"Now God and Santa
Maria were dead," the
Indians said.*

Some cultural exchanges, however, proved beneficial. European irrigation techniques helped the Pueblo farmers, and the Spanish absorbed local Indian lore about herbal remedies. The colonists brought livestock and useful crops, such as peaches, to add to the Indian staples of corn, melons, and beans. But even these advantages brought difficulties, as the bounty made the Pueblo villages all the more attractive to raids by nomadic bands of Apaches. Traditionalists among the Pueblo Indians complained that the new God of the Spanish and His representatives were not taking care of the people.

Of all the Native Americans' grievances, however, the greatest was the Franciscans' determination to stamp out all vestiges of the Indians' religion. The priests found the elaborate performances by masked dancers representing the manifold spirits of nature, called *kachinas,* particularly offensive. The Indians performed the dances in underground chambers called *kivas,* which the Spanish ridiculed as *estufas,* or stoves, for the smoke that issued forth from their roof entrances. The Spanish clergy saw such rites as works of the devil and witchcraft.

As the years passed, circumstances and Spanish intolerance worked to feed the Pueblos' resentment. Prior to the Spaniards' arrival, the Indians withstood the Southwest's periodic droughts by storing reserves and bartering with other pueblos. But the Spanish took all surplus as tribute, monopolized the Indian labor force, and prohibited trade between pueblos, so the Indians had nothing to sustain them when a four-year drought struck in 1666. According to Brother Juan Bernal, "For three years now no

crops have been harvested. In the past year, 1668, a great many Indians perished of hunger, lying dead along the roads, in ravines, and in their huts. There were pueblos where more than 450 died of hunger." Then in 1671 a new epidemic broke out, possibly anthrax, killing thousands of Indians and creating the psychological havoc that only a totally mysterious catastrophe can cause. Thus weakened, the province became even easier prey for marauding tribes. The resentments smoldered.

In addition to roughly 100 celestial and temporal officials and soldiery, by the 1670s the Spanish population included more than 1,000 settlers who lived among 17,000 Pueblo Indians. Although drastically outnumbered, the Spanish colonial government continued to crack down on native resistance, even stepping up its programs against native religion by outlawing it altogether and destroying many *kivas.* When Governor Juan Francisco de Treviño heard rumors in 1675 of Pueblo Indians practicing witchcraft, he rounded up 47 of their religious leaders, hauled them to the provincial capital of Santa Fe, and had them publicly whipped. The governor sentenced four to hang. In response, 70 warriors stormed Treviño's private rooms and threatened to kill him and lead a revolt unless he released the remaining 43 prisoners. Treviño relented.

Among those released was a man named Popé, from the northern pueblo of San Juan. Popé was said to have remarkable powers, including the ability to communicate directly with a revered deity called Po-Se-Ye-Mo. Fleeing further Spanish harassment, Popé retreated to a *kiva* in the northernmost Pueblo of Taos and communicated with Po-Se-Ye-Mo, who demanded nothing less than total eradication of the Spanish invaders. Various pueblos began to set aside some of their traditional isolation from each other and listen to this prophet's talk of rebellion.

Since the arrival of the Spanish colonists, the Pueblo Indians had attempted several revolts. Typically they had involved only a few pueblos, which were ultimately betrayed by Indians loyal to the Holy Church and the Europeans. The Spanish publicly hanged rebellion

leaders, so Popé became a fanatic about secrecy. He supposedly executed his own son-in-law when the man fell under suspicion.

Popé found a growing number of pueblos who were willing to work together against their mutual enemy. Achieving such unity among the Indian villages—historically independent, spread out over hundreds of miles, and speaking different languages and dialects—was one of Popé's most astonishing feats. Planning took place over several years, and in 1680 the auspices appeared good. Snowfall in the mountains along the Rio Grande had been heavy and the spring especially cool, delaying snowmelt. Popé knew that the snow would melt quickly in the summer heat, and the rivers would run unusually high. As a result, the triennial pack train—would be unable to ford the waterways. With their stores and ammunition running low, the Spanish in the province would be vulnerable.

The plotters chose August 12, 1680, for the day of the uprising and dispatched runners to spread the word. The messengers delivered a knotted string to all the rebel Pueblo leaders. They were to untie one knot each day. On the day they untied the last knot, it was time to strike. But rumors of the revolt reached the new governor, Antonio de Otermín, in Santa Fe on August 9. He immediately sent troops to search out and capture the Indian runners. Two youths were brought to the capital and tortured until they revealed that August 12 was the date of the uprising. They were then executed. The province of New Mexico was rife with intrigue and hidden allegiances, so Popé and the other leaders learned almost immediately that their plans had been discovered. They sent word around the pueblos that the date of the revolt had been changed to August 10, the very next day. With surprise on their side, the Indians of Tesuque killed Brother Pío, while other Pueblos overran haciendas from Taos to Santa Fe, killing European men, women and children. Taking horses and whatever weapons they could find, the attackers moved on. At missions Indian bands killed the priests, vandalized icons, befouled altars, and set the churches on fire in ferocious retribution for the stolen *kachina* masks and the other depredations the friars had wrought on their ceremonial ways for more than 80 years.

The Spanish finally submitted to the inevitable and left New Mexico after more than 80 years of colonization. However, the Pueblo alliances that made the Spanish defeat possible soon fell apart.

A handful of Spanish settlers escaped to Santa Fe with word of the uprising's progress. Otermín ordered all settlers in and around Santa Fe to congregate in the governor's palace for safety. By noon, the palace's plaza was jammed with settlers, soldiers, and livestock. Messengers brought word of Indian claims that "God and Santa Maria were dead," and that their own god had never died.

To the south, Indians sympathetic to the Europeans gathered together with the settlers under the command of Lieutenant Governor Alonso García in the Isleta Pueblo. A few rebellion Indians brought "news" to García that all the Spanish to the north—including Governor Otermín—were dead. A standing Spanish order forbade anyone, even the lieutenant governor, from leaving the province without the governor's permission. But believing Otermín dead and his own position untenable, García ordered those assembled to head south in the hope of meeting up with the triennial pack train and reinforcements.

Thanks to this disinformation campaign, Otermín remained isolated in Santa Fe for three more days as reports of death and destruction poured in. On August 13, the governor received word that many pueblos that had professed loyalty to the Spanish government were now joining the rebellion. According to Brother Francisco Gómez, Otermín, "foreseeing that all the nations [of the province] will join together and destroy this villa," ordered Gómez to "consume the most holy sacrament, and take the

images, sacred vessels, and things appertaining to divine worship, close the church and convent, and bring everything to the palace."

Two days later, as small armies of Indians assembled outside the capital to lay siege, Otermín was astonished to see his former manservant, an Indian he called Juan, arrive on horseback for a parley at the governor's palace. Juan wore as a sash one of the cloth bookmarks from the altar of a nearby convent and carried two crosses, one red, the other white. He offered Otermín a choice—take the white cross and the Spanish could leave the province without further harm. If the Spanish governor chose the red cross, more blood would flow.

Otermín chose neither, but instead offered amnesty to the Indians if they would go home after swearing fealty to Spain and the Holy Church. The Indians simply jeered at this and began setting fire to Santa Fe's outlying buildings. Otermín ordered all his soldiers—who numbered less than 100—into battle formation outside the government buildings. According to Spanish records, in a day of fighting "many of the enemy were killed and they wounded many of our men, because they came with the harquebuses and the arms which they had taken from the religious and Spaniards, and were well provided with powder and shot." Despite their losses, the Indians held fast until more warriors arrived and forced the Spanish back into the plaza of the governor's palace. During the next three days, the Indians' ranks swelled to some 2,500, and they rained arrows into the plaza, adding to the panic that was rapidly growing as food supplies ran out and sanitary conditions grew desperate in the heat.

Then August 18 the Indians cut off Santa Fe's water supply by damming the river that ran through the plaza. Two days later, deciding that "it would be a better and safer step to die fighting than of hunger and thirst," Otermín and his remaining soldiers charged the Pueblo Indians. In the melee, the Spanish claimed to have killed some 300 Indians and captured another 47. They herded their captives into the plaza for interrogation and execution. The remaining warriors temporarily withdrew, but every Spanish

soldier bore at least one wound, including Otermín, who had three.

By August 21, Otermín recognized that the situation in the plaza was hopeless. He believed that from north to south "all the people, religious, and Spaniards have perished.... For which reasons, and finding ourselves out of provisions, with very few horses, weary, and threatened by the enemy, and not being assured of water, or of defense" Otermín decided to "withdraw, marching [south] from this villa in full military formation until reaching the Pueblo of La Isleta." There he expected to find Lieutenant Governor García. The Spanish said Mass, then Otermín and approximately 1,000 others filed out of the plaza. Most were on foot.

The Pueblo warriors simply watched as the hated invaders finally left.

They feared the Indians would attack once they left the shelter of the plaza, but no assault occurred. Instead, the Pueblo warriors simply watched as the hated invaders finally left. All along the dreary road south the Spanish saw the burned buildings and grisly remains of the revolt's victims, while the Indians monitored their progress from the surrounding high ground. On August 26, just a day away from Isleta and the much-needed provisions they expected to find there, Otermín learned from a captured rebel Indian that García had taken his people away to the south.

Otermín sent scouts to overtake the lieutenant governor, and García immediately rode north to meet the governor. Otermín arrested his lieutenant governor for desertion and began court proceedings. In his defense, García argued that all intelligence from the north reported everyone there dead, and he claimed never to have received Otermín's orders to send aid to Santa Fe. Otermín acquitted García, and together they resumed their journey south.

They reached El Paso del Norte in early October. There, in what are today the slums of Ciudad Juarez, a few Indians and the Spanish refugees settled uncomfortably, some for good. Otermín estimated that 380 settlers had died in the uprising, and of that number only 73 had been adult males. Twenty-one out of 40 Franciscans had been martyred.

Although their victory proved temporary, in the history of Indian-white relations in North America the Pueblo Indians were the only Native Americans to successfully oust European invaders from their territory. A few years earlier in New England, eastern woodlands tribes had battled against colonists in King Philip's War, but they were defeated and driven to near extinction. Other great Indian leaders such as Pontiac and Tecumseh later organized their people into rebellions against encroaching Europeans, but they too were beaten. The Sioux would win the Battle of the Little Bighorn in 1876, but they ultimately lost the war for the Plains. Apart from the Pueblos, only the Seminoles were able to retain some of their homeland for any length of time, by waging war from the swamps of the Florida Everglades (see "The Florida Quagmire," October 1999).

For the Pueblo Indians, victory was short-lived. Popé demanded complete eradication of all things Spanish, including the valuable crops, such as peaches, they had introduced. He became something of a dictator, and the Pueblo alliance began to unravel soon after the Spanish exodus. Leadership changed hands, old feuds resurfaced, and the pueblos reverted to their normal quarreling. Popé apparently died in disgrace.

The lesson of the revolt was clear—the Pueblo people would rather die than relinquish their religious practices.

In January 1681 the Spanish government issued an order that the New Mexican province was to be reestablished as soon as possible. But it wasn't until 1693 that the Spanish staged a successful return under a new governor, Diego de Vargas. As before, the Europeans met resistance with force, literally obliterating some pueblos. Not for another three years would an uneasy peace again reign in New Mexico. The success of the Pueblo revolt continued to affect the regions beyond New Mexico, however, for years afterward. Word spread south into the tribes of Mexico and encouraged rebellions and resistance that plagued the colonists for decades. Plains Indians gained access to Spanish horses and began to breed them, transforming tribes such as the Cheyenne, Sioux, Apache, and Comanche into some of the finest light cavalry the world has ever seen.

There was lasting change in New Mexico too, as demonstrated by the returning Spanish, in particular the Franciscan friars. They now had an odd respect for the natives. The lesson of the revolt was clear—the Pueblo people would rather die than relinquish their religious practices. The friars, thus chastened, made no further attempt to stamp out the pagan religions of the Pueblos, but instead allowed them and the Catholic rites to co-exist. Pueblo people today attribute the persistence of their cultures to the 1680 uprising.

On a given Pueblo Indian feast day, the people assembled at night in the mission church for Mass and at dawn they carry the patron saint's statue from the church to the plaza. Enshrined there, the saint watches the new day unfold as hundreds of Pueblos dance through the day in a performance that both celebrates and reinforces their own unique heritage and culture.

Jake Page and his photographer wife, Susanne, have produced two books on the Hopi and Navajo Indians, along with numerous other books and articles on Indian affairs. Page is currently writing a popular history of the Pueblo rebellion.

Penning a Legacy

Imprisoned and vilified for his religious views, William Penn, a member of the Society of Friends, sought to establish a colony in the New World where people of all faiths could live in mutual harmony.

By Patricia Hudson

ON A CHILL WINTER DAY in 1668, 24-year-old William Penn paced back and forth in a cramped chamber in the Tower of London. Arrested for blasphemy after publishing a pamphlet that questioned the doctrine of the Trinity, Penn was being held in close confinement. The Bishop of London had decreed that if Penn didn't recant publicly he would remain imprisoned for the rest of his life. Penn's reply was unequivocal: "My prison shall be my grave before I will budge a jot, for I owe my conscience to no mortal man."

WILLIAM PENN WAS born on October 14, 1644, just a stone's throw from the Tower where he would one day be a prisoner. His father, William, Sr., was an ambitious naval officer who rose to the rank of admiral. Knighted by King Charles II, the elder Penn formed a friendship with the royal family that would play a major role in his son's future.

The Penn family's next-door neighbor on Tower Hill was the diarist Samuel Pepys, who noted in his journal that Admiral Penn was "a merry fellow and pretty good-natured and sings very bawdy songs." Pepys also recorded instances of William, Jr., playing cards with his father, going to the theater, and carelessly leaving his sword in a hired coach and then racing across London to retrieve it.

One incident from Penn's youth foreshadowed his later preoccupation with religious matters—at 17 William was expelled from Oxford University for daring to criticize certain Church of England rituals. Appalled, Admiral Penn packed his overly serious son off to France, hoping that he would grow more worldly amid the glitter of Paris.

When William returned to England after two years abroad, Pepys described him as "a most modish person, grown a fine gentlemen, but [having] a great deal, if not too much, of the vanity of the French garb and affected manner of speech and gait." The admiral, well-pleased with his fashionable son, sent William to Ireland to attend to family business, but it was there, in 1667, that the younger Penn embraced the Quaker faith.

The Society of Friends—dubbed Quakers by their enemies because they admonished listeners to "tremble at the word of the Lord"—had been founded in 1647 by George Fox, a weaver's son-turned-preacher who spoke of the Inner Light and believed that there was "that of God in every man." According to Fox, all people, regardless of their status here on earth, are equal in God's eyes. It was a challenge directed at the very heart of England's class-conscious society, and though all religious dissenters were subject to fines and imprisonments, the establishment singled out Quakers with particular ferocity.

When Penn again returned to London, his family was aghast at the change in him. Not only did young William insist on attending the outlawed Quaker meetings, he also ignored common courtesy by refusing to take off his hat in the presence of his "betters," just one of several methods Friends used to illustrate their belief in equality. In the eyes of acquaintances and family, William had betrayed not only the religious principles of the Church of England but also his social class. Noted Pepys in his diary: "Mr. Will Penn, who is lately come over from Ireland, is a Quaker... or some very melancholy thing."

Better educated than most of the early Friends, Penn quickly became one of their most outspoken advocates, taking part in public debates and writing pamphlets that he published at his own expense. One respected London minister, enraged by the conversion of two female members of his congregation to Quakerism, stated that he would "rather lose them to a bawdy house than a Quaker meeting" and then went on to denounce the group's theology.

When Penn responded to the attack in print, the pamphlet became the talk of the city and led to his imprisonment in the Tower. "Hath got me W. Pen's book against the Trinity," Pepys wrote. "I find it so well writ, as I think it too good for him ever to have writ it—and it is a serious sort of book, and not fit for everybody to read."

Despite the threat of life imprisonment, the cold confines of the Tower failed to dampen Penn's crusading spirit. He spent his time there writing a rough draft of *No Cross, No Crown*, one of his most enduring works. After nine months in custody, William was released, perhaps in part as a favor to Admiral Penn, who had loaned the cash-hungry King Charles II a great deal of money over the years.

In 1672, William married Gulielma Maria Springett. During their more than 21 years of marriage, the couple became the parents of seven children. Family responsibilities, however, did not keep Penn from again risking imprisonment by speaking at Friends' meetings, writing political and religious pamphlets, and refusing to take an oath of allegiance.

By the late 1670s, after more than a decade of clashes with the nation's authorities, Penn had grown pessimistic about the likelihood of religious and civil reforms in

England and so turned his thoughts to the New World. Although the colonies were heavily populated with dissenters from England, many colonial authorities exercised no more tolerance for Quakers than their English counterparts. In Puritan-controlled Boston, for example, two Quaker women were hanged when they refused to stop preaching in public.

Having experienced firsthand the horrors of forced religious conformity, Penn dreamed of showing the world that peaceful coexistence among diverse religious groups was possible and that a single, state-supported religion was not only unnecessary but undesirable. "There can be no reason to persecute any man in this world about anything that belongs to the next," he wrote.

When Admiral Penn died without collecting the money owed to him by the king, William saw a way to make his dream a reality. In 1680, he petitioned King Charles for a grant of land in America to retire the debt. Acceding to his request, the king conferred upon Penn an enormous tract of land, the largest that had ever been granted to an individual. William proposed calling the colony New Wales, it being "a pretty hilly country," but King Charles insisted on calling it "Pennsylvania"—Penn's Woods—in honor of his old friend, the admiral.

At the age of 36, Penn suddenly faced the enormous task of designing a government from scratch. The constitution he created, with its provisions for religious freedom, extensive voting rights, and penal reform, was remarkably enlightened by seventeenth-century standards. Despite the vast power it conferred on him as proprietor, Penn had been careful to leave "to myself and successors no power of doing mischief, that the will of one man may not hinder the good of an whole country...."

Before he set sail for Pennsylvania himself, Penn appointed three commissioners and charged them with establishing the new colony. While William saw nothing wrong with Europeans settling in the New World, he was among the few colonizers of his time who recognized the prior claims of the indigenous people. Thus, he gave the commissioners a letter, dated October 18, 1681, addressed to the people of the Lenni Lenape tribe who inhabited his proprietorship. The letter stated that King Charles had granted him "a great province; but I desire to enjoy it with your love and consent, that we may always live together as neighbours and friends, else what would the great God say to us, who hath made us not to devour and destroy one another but to live soberly and kindly together in the world?"

When he finally arrived in the colony in October 1682, Penn made a treaty with the Indians, in effect purchasing the land he had already been given by the king. Truly wishing to live in peace, he tried to be fair in his dealings with the Lenni Lenape, unmindful that they—like their Delaware kinsmen who "sold" Manhattan Island to Peter Minuit—did not understand the concept of exclusive ownership of the land and believed that the white men simply sought to share its use.

Penn had intended to settle permanently in Pennsylvania, but within two years a boundary dispute with neighboring Maryland required him to return to London, where a web of troubles awaited him. As a result, nearly 16 years passed before he again set foot in his colony. During his long absence, the colonists had grown resentful of his authority, and in 1701, less than two years after his second voyage to Pennsylvania, a disillusioned Penn sailed back to England, never to return. All told, he spent less than five years in America.

From his return to England until his death 16 years later, Penn continually struggled to stave off financial disaster. Never an astute businessman, he discovered, to his horror, that his trusted business manager had defrauded him, leaving him deeply in debt. At the age of 63, Penn was sent to a debtor's prison. Marveled one friend, "The more he is pressed, the more he rises. He seems of a spirit to bear and rub through difficulties." Before long, concerned friends raised enough money to satisfy his creditors.

Prior to his death in 1718 at the age of 73, Penn attempted to sell Pennsylvania back to the Crown, hoping to forge at least a modicum of financial security for his six surviving children. In making the offer, Penn sought to extract a promise from the English Crown that the colony's laws and civil rights would be preserved. But while the negotiations were still in progress, Penn suffered a debilitating stroke, and the transaction was never completed. Penn's descendants thus retained control of the colony until the American Revolution.

Despite imprisonment, vilification, and financial ruin, Penn had labored unceasingly to establish the principle of religious freedom in both his homeland and in America. He espoused such "modern" concepts as civil rights, participatory government, interracial brotherhood, and international peace.

Yet, despite the rich legacy that the founder of the colony of Pennsylvania left to Americans, William Penn remains a shadowy figure in our popular consciousness. For most people, his name conjures up little more than a vague picture that is remarkably similar to the bland, beaming face that adorns boxes of Quaker Oats cereal. The reality, however, was quite different; Penn was an extremely complex individual, whose life was filled with triumph and tragedy and was marked by startling contrasts.

In 1984, more than 300 years after the founding of Pennsylvania, the United States Congress posthumously granted Penn U.S. citizenship. "In the history of this Nation," the proclamation read, "there has been a small number of men and women whose contributions to its traditions of freedom, justice, and individual rights have accorded them a special place of honor... and to whom all Americans owe a lasting debt." The man who pursued his "Holy Experiment" on the shores of the New World was, indeed, one of those men.

Patricia Hudson is a freelance writer from Tennessee and a former contributing editor of Americana *magazine.*

BLESSED AND BEDEVILED

Tales of Remarkable Providences in Puritan New England

Helen Mondloch

On October 31, 2001, Massachusetts Gov. Jane Swift signed a bill exonerating the last five souls convicted of witchcraft during the infamous Salem witch trials of 1692. Rectifying a few of history's wrongs on this Halloween day, the governor's conciliatory gesture was arguably ill-timed, given the frivolous revelry associated with this annual celebration of superstition and frights. In the real-life horror of the witch scare, at least 150 people were imprisoned, including a four-year-old girl who was confined for months to a stone dungeon. Twenty-three men and women, all of whom have now been cleared of their crimes, were hanged or died in prison, and one man was pressed (crushed) to death for his refusal to stand trial.

In probing the underpinnings of this tragic and incredible chapter of American history, New England observers past and present have agreed that the nascent Massachusetts Bay Colony provided a fertile ground for the devil's plagues. Among others, folklore scholar Richard Dorson, author of *America in Legend and American Folklore*, has argued that the frenzy culminating in the witch-hunt was fueled by legends that flourished among the Puritans, a populace that imagined itself both blessed and bedeviled. Of key importance was belief in phenomena called "providences" (more commonly called "remarkable providences"). These were visible, often terrifying, signs of God's will that forged themselves onto the fabric of daily life.

As Dorson explains, "Since, in the Puritan and Reformation concept, God willed every event from the black plague to the sparrow's fall, all events held meaning for errant man." The providences brought rewards or protection for the Lord's followers (generally the Puritans themselves) or vengeance upon His enemies. Sprung from European roots and embraced by intellectuals and common folk alike, they became the subject of a passionate story tradition that enlarged and dramatized events in the manner of all oral legends.

The pursuit of providences was greatly reinforced by those who felt compelled to record their occurrence, including John Winthrop, longtime theocratic governor of Massachusetts Bay Colony. Two prominent New England ministers, Increase Mather and his son Cotton, became the most zealous popularizers of such tales. In 1684 the elder Mather set forth guidelines for their documentation in *An Essay for the Recording of Illustrious Providences*, a study that Cotton Mather would later extend in his own works. The Essay defined "illustrious" providences as the most extraordinary of divinely ordained episodes: "tempests, floods, earthquakes, thunders as are unusual, strange apparitions, or whatever else shall happen that is prodigious." The directives for recording the providences—a duty over which the elder Mather would preside in order to preserve the stories for all posterity—are likened by Dorson to methods observed by modern folklore collectors.

The flip side of the providences were the witchcrafts of the devil, who poised himself with a special vengeance against this citadel of God's elect. Where faith and fear converged, the tales of remarkable providences heightened both.

A 'City Upon a Hill'

In his *Book of New England Legends and Folklore in Prose and Poetry* (1901), Samuel Adams Drake called New England "the child of a superstitious mother." Dorson acknowledges that folk legends in the colonies were "for the most part carbon copies of the folklore in Tudor and Stuart England." But in grafting themselves onto a New World setting, says Dorson, the old beliefs took on a special intensity in the realm of the Puritans.

Many have credited the Mathers with projecting and magnifying this Puritan zeal. Writing at the turn of the last century, historian Samuel McChord Crothers, quoted in B.A. Botkin's *Treasury of New England Folklore*, captured the fervency of the younger Mather, who became a principal driver of the witch-hunt:

> Even Cotton Mather could not avoid a tone of pious boastfulness when he narrated the doings of New England …
>
> … New England had the most remarkable providences, the most remarkable painful preachers, the most remarkable heresies, the most remarkable witches. Even the local devils were in his judgment more enterprising than those of the old country. They had to be in order to be a match for the New England saints.

Perhaps we can gain the proper perspective on the Puritans' passion when we consider the enormous pains they undertook to escape persecution in England and establish their new covenant across the sea. Upholding that covenant was now critical, as evidenced in the lofty proclamations of a sermon delivered in 1630 by John Winthrop. Excerpted in Frances Hill's *Salem Witch Trials Reader*, the governor's words resound with poignant irony given the events that rocked Salem sixty-two years later: "We shall be as a City upon a Hill, the eyes of all people…upon us; so if we shall deal falsely with our God in this work we have undertaken and to cause Him to withdraw His present help from us, we shall be made a story…through the world…and…we shall shame the faces of…God's worthy servants, and cause their prayers to be turned into curses upon us."

Clearly, the task of maintaining this sinless "City Upon a Hill" wrought insecurity among the Puritans, and so, says Dorson, they "searched the providences for continued evidence of God's favor or wrath." As he reveals, popular legends spurred their confidence: "Marvelous escapes from shipwreck, Indian captivity, or starvation reassured the elect that the Lord was guarding their fortunes under His watchful eye."

Cotton Mather recorded many such episodes in his 1702 chronicle titled Magnalia Christi Americana: *The Ecclesiastical History of New England*. In one renowned tale, a spectral ship appeared to an ecstatic crowd of believers in New Haven harbor in 1647. Six months earlier the heavily freighted vessel was presumed lost, after it had sailed from that harbor and never returned. According to Mather's account, quoted by Botkin, the community lost "the best part of their tradable estates…and sundry of their eminent persons." Mather quotes an eyewitness who believed that God had now "condescended" to present the ship's ghostly image as a means of comforting the afflicted souls of the mourners, for whom this remarkable providence affirmed not only their fallen friends' state of grace but also their own.

The Puritans also gleaned affirmation from providences in which the Lord exacted harsh punishments on the enemies of His elect. According to Dorson, the Puritans apparently relished most these tales of divine judg-

ment. Those scourged in the tales included Indians, Quakers, and anyone else deemed blasphemous or profane. In the *Magnalia*, Cotton Mather correlates providential offenses to the Ten Commandments. He cites the destruction of the Narragansett Indian nation by a group of white settlers as retribution for the Indians' foul contempt for the Gospel. Oral legends also relayed the fate of Mary Dyer, a Quaker who was sent to the gallows around 1659; Dyer was said to have given birth to a monster, a common curse meted out to nefarious women. Even members of the elect might be struck down by plague or fatal lightning bolts for lapses ranging from the omission of prayer to adultery and murder. The *Magnalia* narrates the doom suffered by various "heretics" who quarreled with village ministers or voted to cut their salaries.

In addition to these ancient themes of reward and punishment, the providence tales incorporated a host of familiar spectacles from an Old World tradition, including apparitions, wild tempests, and corpses that communicated with blood—all magnanimous instruments of an angry but just Lord. Like the spectral ship, apparitions offered hope and solved mysteries; the apparition of a murder victim often disclosed the identity of his killer, a belief that came into play during the witch trials. The age-old notion that a corpse bleeds at the murderer's touch also surfaced abundantly in the tales.

Increase Mather devoted a whole chapter of his *Essay* to thunder and lightning, perceiving in them signs of God's consternation over the advent of secularism in Massachusetts Bay Colony. Mather declared that thunder and lightning had been observed ever since "the English did first settle these American deserts," but warned that only in recent years had they wrought "fatal and fearful slaughters … among us." In the *Magnalia*, Cotton Mather, too, expounded on thunder, a phenomenon that the Harvard scholar and scientist, quoted in Dorson, astutely attributed to the "laws of matter and motion [and] … divers weighty clouds" in collision; lightning, he postulated, derived from "subtil and sulphureos vapours." Like his erudite father, however, Cotton maintained that God was the omnipotent "first mover" of these and other natural forces.

Tales of witchcraft

Dorson explains that "providences issued from God and witchcrafts from the devil, and they marked the tide of battle between the forces of Christ and the minions of Satan." Tales of witchery had their own illustrious elements, including menacing poltergeists, enchantments, and innocent creatures who became possessed and tormented by wicked sorcerers.

He and others have argued that the widely circulated tales of remarkable providences, wherein the Puritans sealed their identity of chosenness, created a fertile climate for witch tales and the witch-hunt. According to

Dorson, "Other Protestants in New York and Virginia, and the Roman Catholics in Maryland, spoke of witchery, but the neurotic intensity of the New England witch scare…grew from the providential aura the Puritans gave their colonial enterprise."

Cotton Mather himself, quoted in Dorson, described the devil's vengeful plot to "destroy the kingdom of our Lord Jesus Christ" in this region that had once been "the Devil's territories" (that is, inhabited by Indians). Both Mathers were implicated as early as the mid-eighteenth-century for promoting bloodlust over witchcraft with their recordings of providence tales. Thomas Hutchinson, governor of Massachusetts Bay in 1771–74, lamented the witch debacle in his *History of the Colony of Massachusetts Bay* (1765). According to Hill, who refers to the governor as a "man of the Enlightenment," Hutchinson's chronicle suggests "that there was widespread disapproval of hanging witches until the *Illustrious Providences and Memorable Providences* [Cotton's later work]…changed the climate of opinion."

Providence lore undoubtedly played a part in the actions of those who spearheaded the witch scare with their clamorous cries of demonic possession. The trouble began in January 1692 when two girls, Betty Parris, the nine-year-old daughter of Salem Village minister Samuel Parris, and her cousin Abigail Williams, age eleven, began experiencing spells of bizarre behavior. In these alarming episodes, the girls convulsed and ranted incoherently. Within a month other neighborhood girls began having similar spells; soon they all began accusing various members of the community of bewitching them.

The cause of these disturbing bouts—which would continue for ten months, until the last of the condemned was pulled down from the gallows—has been the topic of much scholarly speculation and simplistic analysis. Some have theorized, at least as an initiating factor, that the girls suffered from temporary mental illness engendered by eating ergot-infected rye (a theory to which the growing conditions and agricultural practices of the time lend credence, according to Hill). Others have postulated a conspiracy theory incorporating the fierce factionalism that emerged in large part over arguments related to the Reverend Parris' salary and living arrangements.

The most prevalent theory suggests that the girls' hysteria grew from feelings of paranoia and guilt at having dabbled in fortune-telling and other occult practices with Tituba, a native of Barbados who served as the Parris family's slave (and who later confessed, albeit under dubious circumstances, to having engaged in such activities with her young charges). Perhaps one falsehood led to another as the girls struggled to cover up their forbidden deeds; perhaps one or another girl actually believed, for a period, that she had been bewitched; perchance the girls also were pressured by their elders, who were eager to avoid scandal, to reveal the cause of their afflictions. Quite possibly, too, some combination of these factors set into motion the outbursts and subsequent accusations. In any case, as Hill argues, the girls very likely started out as victims of "human suggestibility" and at some point later became perpetrators of fraud.

This view is supported by the fact that the girls had been reared abundantly on tales of providences and demonic possession. In his popular *Memorable Providences*, quoted by Hill, Mather provided a detailed description of four children who suffered "strange fits, beyond those that attend an epilepsy," as a result of a wicked washerwoman's sorcery. In addition, Hill reveals that Puritans young and old "devoured" sensational pamphlets describing similar demonic episodes, a fact that is hardly surprising, she says, since secular reading was prohibited. In his account of the witch trials, Governor Hutchinson charges that the similarities between these well-known accounts of demonic possession and those of the "supposed bewitched at Salem…is so exact, as to leave no room to doubt the stories had been read by the New England persons themselves, or had been told to them by others who had read them."

One case in particular demonstrates the far-reaching influence of the providence legends: that of Giles Corey, who suffered an excruciating death by pressing for his refusal to stand trial for witchcraft. According to Dorson, as the executions mounted with dreadful fury, the fatal torture of this "sturdy, uncowed farmer" aroused the people's sympathy. Some wondered whether his only crime had been his stubborn silence. Public opinion shifted, however, thanks to the actions of Thomas Putnam, a prominent citizen and the father of twelve-year-old Anne Putnam, one of the principal accusers.

The elder Putnam wrote a letter to Samuel Sewall, one of the trial judges who would later become a famous diarist. The letter reported that on the previous night, Anne had witnessed the apparition of a man who had lived with Giles Corey seventeen years earlier. This "Natural Fool"—perhaps a mentally disabled man—had died suddenly in Corey's house; his ghost now claimed that Corey had murdered him by pressing him to death, causing "clodders of blood about his heart." The apparition reported, moreover, that Corey had escaped punishment for his crime by signing a pact with the devil, whose protective powers were now being usurped by a God who meted out His just desserts—that is, a ghastly punishment precisely matching the crime. Hence, Putnam's letter, now filed by Cotton Mather as an official court document, helped sanctify Corey's execution in the eyes of the citizenry.

By the fall of 1692 the witch crisis had begun to die down. Hill explains that the girls had apparently "overreached themselves by naming as witches several prominent people, including Lady Phipps, the wife of the governor." As the executions began drawing public criticism, Phipps dissolved the witch court and later granted reprieves to the remaining accused. Twelve years later, a sullen Anne Putnam, now twenty-four years old, stood before the congregation in Salem Village Church while the minister read aloud her apology, quoted in Hill, for the "great delusion of Satan" that had caused her to "bring upon…this land the guilt of innocent blood."

A dark legacy

With his strangely circular reasoning, Mather, reflecting on the witch crisis in a 1697 chronicle excerpted by Hill, shaped the tragedies into one great remarkable providence. Oblivious to any possibility of delusion or fraud, he attributed the calamities to God's wrath on New England, ignited by the "little sorceries" practiced by its youth as well as the "grosser" witchcrafts of those condemned: "Although these diabolical divinations are more ordinarily committed perhaps all over the world than they are in the country of New England, yet, that being a country devoted unto the worship and the service of the Lord Jesus Christ above the rest of the world, He signaled His vengeance against such extraordinary dispensations, as have not often been seen in other places."

While post-Enlightenment scholars have generally dismissed Mather's arguments as the rantings of a self-righteous fanatic, his thoughts and actions have left their mark on us. In 1953, the "Red Scare" of the McCarthy era inspired playwright Arthur Miller to re-create the Salem witch-hunt in *The Crucible*. Miller remarked in a 1996 *New Yorker* article, quoted by Hill, that the play's enduring relevance lies in its core subject: "human sacrifice to the furies of fanaticism and paranoia that goes on repeating itself forever."

In our own time, such furies seem painfully present. The era of remarkable providences leaves as its dark legacy a number of lessons not easily reckoned. Now, as the world grapples with the bane of terrorism, Hill's analysis of the Salem trials strikes a contemporary nerve: "The more a group idealizes itself, its own values, and its god, the more it persecutes both other groups and the dissenters in its midst."

Today the American government is repeatedly challenged to implement policies that will prevent the current conflict from turning into a witch-hunt. Moreover, our democratic principles still face the perennial threat of an arrogant religious impulse that has never totally died out. Even now, those among us who boldly stake their claim to the mind of God—like the self-appointed prophets who construed the events of last September 11 as a kind of remarkable providence—risk the resurrection of demons similar to the forces that once ravaged a New England community. The calamities of 1692 entreat us to conquer those demons by loving our neighbor and consigning the will of Providence to the realm of mystery. ■

Additional Reading

B.A. Botkin, ed., *A Treasury of New England Folklore*, Crown Publishers, Inc., New York, 1967.

Richard Dorson, *American Folklore*, University of Chicago Press, Chicage, 1967.

——, *America in Legend: Folklore from the Colonial Period to the Present*, Pantheon Books, New York, 1973.

Samual Adams Drake, *A Book of New England Legends and Folklore in Prose and Poetry*, Little, Brown, 1901.

Frances Hill, *The Salem Witch Trials Reader*, DeCapo Press, Boston, 2000.

Increase Mather, *An Essay for the Recording of Remarkable Providences*, Scholars' Facsimiles and Reprints, Inc., Delmar, N.Y., 1977. Reprint of the 1684 edition printed by J. Green for J. Browning, Boston.

Helen Mondloch is a freelance writer and frequent contributor to the Culture section.

Roots of Revolution

The Royal Navy wanted exclusive use of New England's tall white pines for its ships' masts. That didn't go over too well with colonial lumbermen, so they decided to retaliate.

By Dick Conway

ONE APRIL EVENING in 1734 the door to Captain Samuel Gilmans inn in Exeter, New Hampshire, suddenly burst open. Startled from their drinking and carousing, the revelers at one of the tables looked up to see a mob of 30 or so angry men descending on them. War whoops, shouts, curses, and threats filled the smoke-laden air. The mob appeared to be Indians, wrapped in blankets, their faces blackened and painted. But they were not Indians, and the quickly sobering agents of the king began to fear for their lives. They knew perfectly well why the disguised men were there—it was because of the hated mast tree laws.

Mast trees were the giant white pines that once grew in seemingly limitless abundance in northern New England and as far south as Connecticut and Rhode Island. The huge trees grew straight and tall, sometimes reaching 200 feet in height and seven in diameter. Britain's Royal Navy eventually realized the value of these giants. Trimmed of its limbs—which didn't appear until a height of 75 feet or so—and properly sided, a single tree made for a perfect ship's mast. In contrast, when they used trees from the Baltic region of Europe, Britain's shipbuilders had to piece masts together from several trees.

Yet the colonists valued the trees too. They harvested white pine for building of all kinds, and logging had become a major industry in northern New England. Sawmills dotted the land, and lumber exports provided an important source of income. The Royal Navy and the local lumbermen were headed for a collision. Eager to protect this rich source of masts and to keep it out of the hands of potential enemies, in 1691 Britain passed the first of a series of laws designed to ensure that the majestic trees would be cut solely for the use of the Royal Navy. The law reserved all trees not on private land that measured 24 inches in diameter at a height of a foot from the ground. The penalty for illegally cutting down a mast tree was £100—a considerable sum at the time.

To enforce the law, Britain created the position of surveyor general of the woods. The surveyor general selected deputies to search out the best white pines and mark them with three slashes of a hatchet. Shaped like an arrowhead or a crow's foot, the mark indicated that a tree was designated for the Royal Navy. The law became known as the Broad Arrow policy.

Colonists essentially ignored the policy from the beginning. The roughhewn men who made their living off the woods had little respect for laws and authority, especially when those laws threatened their livelihood. The illegal cutting of the towering trees was rampant, and the often-abusive actions taken by those attempting to enforce the king's laws only deepened the settlers' enmity toward them. The situation worsened when Britain passed even more restrictive legislation and insisted on better enforcement, leading to what may have been the colonies' first recorded instance of armed insurrection against the Crown.

In 1730 David Dunbar, an Irish-born soldier in the British army, was appointed surveyor general of the woods for New Hampshire. He was also the province's lieutenant governor. An ambitious man, Dunbar was determined to make a name for himself and to undermine Governor Jonathan Belcher, with whom he was always at odds. Dunbar vigorously enforced the Broad Arrow laws and quickly became despised in the woods of New Hampshire. "His spy system, his high-handed seizures, and the rich feathering of his nest in the Sagadahoc region drew unusual antipathy from the colonists," noted a history of the Royal Navy's timber trade.

In April 1734, Dunbar heard rumors that workers at the Copyhold Mill were illegally cutting mast tree lumber. The mill was on the line between what are now the towns of Fremont and Brentwood, but was then part of Exeter. Dunbar saw his chance. Exeter was a stronghold of Belcher's political support. If the lieutenant governor could prove that illegal cutting was taking place there, he could blame it on Belcher's lack of commitment to enforcing the king's policy. Dunbar believed this would strengthen his own claim to be the true guardian of His Majesty's laws, and so he set out from Portsmouth to assess the situation in person.

Word of the surveyor general's approach preceded him, however, and before Dunbar reached the mill, an angry mob confronted him on the road, shouting warnings and threats, brandishing weapons, and discharging firearms into the air. Dunbar knew that these men would not hesitate to attack him, regardless of his position of authority, so he returned to Portsmouth. There he gathered 10 men to return to Exeter with him and inspect the Copyhold Mill for illegal lumber and confiscate any they found.

Dunbar and his party reached Exeter by sailboat in the late afternoon of April 23, 1734, and took lodging for the night at Captain Samuel Gilman's inn on Water Street. The rum flowed freely and the men began to boast of their mission. It didn't take long for word to spread that Dunbar had returned, still determined to shut down the mill.

Men from Exeter and its outskirts assembled at Zebulon Giddinge's tavern on Park Street to make their plans. The group numbered about 30 and included several of the town's leading residents. In an early instance of what was to become a rather common means for disaffected colonials to conceal their identities, the men disguised themselves as "Natick In-dians," blackening and painting their faces and wrapping themselves in blankets. Around 10:00 that night, they made their move.

The mob attacked the startled king's agents in Gilman's inn, beating, clubbing, and kicking them. The "Indians" found those who had already gone to bed, roused them, threw them downstairs, and tossed them out of windows into the street. Their point made, the attackers disappeared into the night.

Dunbar's men made for their boat, but found that the mob had slashed the vessel's sails and rigging. The beaten and bruised king's agents pushed off anyway, only to find that their attackers had punched holes in the bottom of the boat. Luckily, the men managed to scramble ashore not far downstream, where they spent a cold night hiding in the woods. The next morning, they began the 15-mile walk back to Portsmouth, some wearing little more than their bedclothes.

Dunbar was outraged by this clear act of open rebellion. Governor Belcher was absent, so Dunbar called a meeting of the province's council. He wanted Exeter's justices of the peace, whom he believed had knowledge of the affair, brought before the council for questioning. He also wanted a proclamation issued offering a reward for information leading to the arrest and conviction of those responsible for the attack.

The council was not about to oblige the unpopular lieutenant governor, however. Its members claimed that he had to take the matter before Exeter's justices of the peace, and that only the governor could issue the requested proclamation. Belcher finally made the announcement on behalf of his subordinate, but he worded it vaguely, saying only that "whosoever shall detect the offenders above mentioned, or any of them, shall receive all proper marks of the counte-nance and favor of this government." Belcher offered no reward.

Unable to identify any of the "Indians," Dunbar never received judicial satisfaction for the incident. But he continued his efforts to replace Jonathan Belcher as governor, and he traveled to England in 1737 to try to win royal favor there. Thwarted and humiliated in this also, he settled on an offer from the East India Company to become governor of the remote island of St. Helena.

The backlash against Dunbar was an early symptom of the discontent in the colonies, especially in New Hampshire, where the strongly independent settlers believed King George II had no right to interfere with their livelihood. Penalties for illegally cutting the great white pines may have been steep, but as time passed courts did little more than slap the wrists of those who were caught and convicted. In 1773 New Hampshire experienced another riot over mast trees, this time in the town of Weare. Other incidents against the king's agents took place in the woods of the other northern New England provinces, especially in Maine.

The Broad Arrow policy remained in effect until the beginning of the Revolutionary War, but all in all, it proved to be a failure. Available shipping records show that in the 84 years the policy was in effect perhaps some 4,500 masts were sent to England, but at the cost of increased anger in the northern colonies. The pine tree became a symbol of New England's growing defiance of what was believed to be ever more stifling acts of British oppression. At the Battle of Bunker Hill in 1775, as many as half of the patriot force hailed from New Hampshire—and one of the patriots' battle flags carried the symbol of the pine tree. ✪

Dick Conway is a freelance writer from Milan, New Hampshire.

UNIT 2
Revolutionary America

Unit Selections

Key Points to Consider

- Discuss the article "The American Self." Why does a sense of individualism sometimes threaten the needs of the community?

- Benjamin Franklin is popularly remembered as a plain-spun man who tinkered with bifocals and pot-bellied stoves. What were his contributions to science at the time?

- What purposes was the Declaration of Independence supposed to serve? How have perceptions of this document changed over the years?

- In what ways were the founders considered radical for the time? How did their beliefs make the Revolution possible?

- Why is the debate over the Second Amendment so emotional? Examine both sides of the issue. Does the amendment guarantee the unlimited possession of firearms or does it refer only to the establishment of militias?

 **Links: www.dushkin.com/online/**
These sites are annotated in the World Wide Web pages.

The Early America Review
http://www.earlyamerica.com/review/
House of Representatives
http://www.house.gov
National Center for Policy Analysis
http://www.public-policy.org/web.public-policy.org/index.php
Supreme Court/Legal Information Institute
http://supct.law.cornell.edu/supct/index.html
U.S. Senate
http://www.senate.gov
The White House
http://www.whitehouse.gov/
The World of Benjamin Franklin
http://www.fi.edu/franklin/

We live in an age of instant communication. Our call to complain about a credit card may be answered by someone in India. Television satellites permit the simultaneous viewing of events all over the world. Imagine what it was like in the 18th Century when it took weeks for a message to be delivered from London to one of the colonies, and weeks more to receive a reply. Under such circumstances the British understandably gave wide latitude to royal governors who were on the scene and who knew more about local conditions than could the bureaucrats at home. The fact that the American colonies were but part of the British world empire also discouraged attempts to micromanage their affairs.

According to economic theory at the time, an empire could be likened to an organism with each part functioning in such a way as to benefit the whole. The ideal of a colony, aside from helping to defend the empire when the need arose, was to serve as a protected market for the mother country's manufactured goods as a provider of raw materials for its mills and factories. Because imperial rivalries often led to war, particular emphasis was placed on achieving self-sufficiency. An imperial power did not wish to be dependent on another empire for materials—especially those of strategic value such as the shipbuilding materials mentioned in the previous unit—that might be cut off if the two came into conflict.

With regard to the American colonies, those in the South most nearly fit the imperial model. Southern colonies produced goods such as cotton and tobacco that could not be grown in Great Britain, and Southerners were disinclined to become involved in activities that would compete with British manufacturers. The New England and the middle colonies were another matter. Individuals in both areas often chafed at imperial restrictions that prevented them from purchasing products more cheaply from other countries or form engaging in manufacturing their own. What served to temper discontent among the colonists was the knowledge that they depended on the protection of the British army and navy against threats by other powers, most notably the French.

During the middle decades of the 1700's, London permitted the colonists to exercise a great deal of control over their own internal affairs so long as they played their designated economic role within the empire. This attitude, which came to be known as "benign neglect," meant that the colonies for all practical purposes became nearly autonomous. The passage of time and the great distances involved combined to make British rule more of an abstraction rather than a day-to-day relationship. Most colonists never visited the mother country, and they might go months or years without seeing any overt signs of British authority. They came to regard this as the normal order of things.

This casual relationship was altered in 1763 when what the colonists called the French and Indian war came to an end after seven years of fighting. The peace brought two results that had enormous consequences. First, British acquisitions of French possessions in North America meant that the military threat to the colonists had ended. Second, the war had been enormously costly to the British people who were suffering under staggering tax burdens. The government in London, taking the understandable view that the colonists ought to pay their fair share of the costs, began levying a variety of new taxes and enforcing shipping regulations that previously had been ignored.

The new British crackdown represented to the colonists an unwarranted assault on the rights and privileges they had long enjoyed. Disputes over economic matters escalated into larger concerns about rights and freedoms in other areas. Many colonists who regarded themselves as loyal subjects of the Crown at first looked upon the situation as a sort of family quarrel that could be smoothed out provided there was goodwill on both sides. When clashes escalated instead, more and more people who now regarded themselves as "Americans" began calling for independence from the motherland. The British, of course, had no intention of handing over portions of their hardwon empire to the upstart colonists. War became inevitable.

Throughout the colonial era, thoughtful individuals had debated the apparent contradiction between individual rights and the needs of the community. The first selection in this unit, Mark Richard Barna's "The American Self," explores this dilemma from colonial times to the present. He concludes that by the time of the Revolution, Americans were "simply too greedy and self-interested for communalism to work."

In many ways, Benjamin Franklin seems the most "approachable" of the founding fathers. In contrast with the admirable but aloof George Washington, for instance, Franklin comes across in illustrations and prose as a homespun "common" man with uncommon talents. Whether running up keys on kite strings, improving stoves, or inventing bifocal glasses, Franklin seems like the ultimate tinkerer. He was that, to be sure, but he was also a scientist of considerable achievement. "Ben Franklin's 'Scientific Amusements',", written by a Nobel Prize winner in chemistry, explores the man's vast gifts and suggests that his reputation in Europe helped attain America's diplomatic goals.

"Flora Macdonald" provides an account of a woman who had become a Scottish heroine in 1746 when she had helped "Bonnie Prince Charlie" escape British authorities. She was received with some fanfare when she moved to North Carolina in 1774, but her popularity vanished when she began recruiting men of Scottish descent to fight for the crown during the Revolution.

"Founding Friendship: Washington, Madison and the Creation of the American Republic" analyzes the extremely fruitful relationship between these two men before they parted ways. The Declaration itself is analyzed by author Pauline Maier in "Making Sense of the Fourth of July." She explains how the meaning and function of the Declaration has changed over the course of time.

Two essays deal with the conduct of the Revolutionary War. "Hamilton Takes Command" shows how the 20-year-old Alexander Hamilton's intelligence and courage propelled him into rapid advancement and, most important for his future, brought him to the attention of George Washington. Washington, a towering figure in this nation's history, was almost single-handidly responsible for keeping the colonial armies intact during the extremely difficult times. His leadership came under increasing criticism during the darkest days, however, and "Winter of Discontent" describes how something called the "Conway Cabal" nearly led to his resignation.

The last two essays in this unit treat the American Constitution. In "Founders Chic: Live from Philadelphia" author Evan Thomas argues that those who led the American Revolution and helped consolidate the new government were truly radical for the times despite their powdered wigs and knee britches. "Your Constitution is Killing You" discusses the changing interpretations of the Second Amendment. The issue continues to be hotly debated between those who believe the amendment guarantees the unconditional right to own guns, and those who believe it was originally intended primarily to provide for the arming of militias.

The American Self

Mark Richard Barna

The Founding Fathers understood the self to be a place of dark and forbidding passions. They were not interested in granting Revolutionary Americans the personal liberties espoused by Britain, and they scoffed at many thinkers of the French Enlightenment for claiming humankind was innately good. One of the founders, John Witherspoon, summed up in 1776 the pervading attitude toward the self: "Others may, if they please, treat the corruption of our nature as a chimera; for my part, I see it everywhere, and I feel it every day."[1]

The founders knew that the self could not be trusted; the selfish ambition overtaking Europeans and the self-knowledge of personal whims and passions were for them persuasive evidence. But being intellectuals, they needed precedent, and found it in ancient Greek and Roman political tracts, where the hegemony of the community was promulgated as a trump to selfish individualism. "Individual liberty," explains one historian, "could not exist" in the ancient Greek and Roman city-states, for the "citizen was subordinate in everything, and without reserve to the city; he belonged to it body and soul."[2] The national elite found this theory, commonly called republicanism, again in Renaissance works and in the writings of Enlightenment rationalists like John Locke.

Locke did not honor the individual's right to think as he pleased but only "his right to think as he must." Concurring with Plato and Aristotle, the philosopher believed we must control our passions by reason; otherwise, we become as beasts. A reasonable person has one choice—to think as he must, which is honoring the public good over private interest.

The national elite wanted a public-centered, selfless government. Not coincidentally, this was also the governmental philosophy of the New England Puritan colonials, who, rather than invoke as justification reason and historical precedent, like the Founding Fathers based their government on the need to thwart the innate sinfulness of humankind caused by Adam and Eve's transgression in the Garden of Eden.

The early Puritans owed their conception of original sin to Augustine, a fourth-century Christian saint who formulated his ideas after leaving and then renouncing the Manichaean heresy. The creation of a third-century twenty-six-year-old named Mani, Manichaeism soon became the most popular Gnostic religion. Its main tenet was that the earth is ruled by the devil and is separate from God, who is ensconced outside the universe. Salvation is gained by renouncing the evil world in favor of the divine spark within.

Augustine considered this view flawed because it projected evil outside the self. He knew this degenerates into people believing that the world—whether it be your neighbor or culture in general—is the problem, causing persons to lose the self-awareness of the sly tempters, like pride and ambition, within. Following Augustine, the early Puritan colonials considered the failure to love and honor a brother a sin, which could be as subtle as feeling hesitation to help someone in need. Sin was elusive, sly like the serpent in Eden, and almost never, at least in the early colonies, conceived of outside the self.

John Witherspoon summed up in 1776 the pervading attitude toward the self: "Others may, if they please, treat the corruption of our nature as a chimera; for my part, I see it everywhere, and I feel it every day."

It is commonly known that the New England Puritans were theocratic—the highest authority was the minister, and by law only church members were allowed to vote for community officials. At the center of the culture, says American Puritan scholar Perry Miller, was the "hypothesis of original sin" and the need for "a coercive state to restrain evil impulses."[3] Because of the innate depravity of humankind, nobody, not even authorities of the community, was trusted to act selflessly for the public good. Members of society were responsible for keeping each other in line. This was practical as well, for the Puritans knew that selfish, arrogant, ambitious persons upset the fragile equipoise of isolated, agrarian communities.

Raised in a pious society, the Founding Fathers were bound to be influenced by church doctrines. Deist John Adams combined Enlightenment thought and Christian theology when he declared, "Although reason ought always to govern individuals, it certainly never did since the Fall, and never will till the Millennium."[4] In a speech given in 1787, Ben Franklin, truly a product of the Enlightenment, said, "The longer I live, the more convincing proofs I see of this truth—that God governs in the affairs of men."[5]

Whether by belief in original sin (mostly the mass populace) or belief in reason and republicanism (mostly the elite), distrust of the self was irrefragable in Revolutionary America. This also explains Revolutionary Americans' abhorrence of monarchical governments and, in part, their break from Britain: for the monarch was depraved like his subjects and destined to become a tyrant. The founders tried to strike a balance between a monarchical and a democratic government to avoid the extremes of tyranny and anarchy. By allowing communities to be self-governing, and with the federal government monitoring from a distance, the national elite hoped to build a model republic.

CHANGING VALUES

It was a failure from almost the beginning. Throughout the 1700s, communal living competed with an emerging individualistic ideology that, in truth, actually began in the lives of the first Puritan settlers.

One may first think the Protestant celebration of freedom of religious conscience was a factor in the growth of individualism. By giving sanction to religious leaders' idiosyncratic interpretations of Scripture, Protestantism gave birth to manifold Christian sects; it also indirectly helped bring about the economic individualism that gripped America in the nineteenth century. But this does not tell the whole story.

Religious conscience is the non-Arminian Protestant response to Judaism's Law and Catholicism's sacramental rituals, which Jews and Christians believe will save them if practiced. The Puritans thought this was silly; they demanded more than obeisance to external rules and forms. A person must make a private choice to follow Christ, then submit to the will of the community for his glory. This is freedom to choose Christ, not freedom to think arbitrarily about him.

In the early seventeenth century, Anne Hutchinson and Roger Williams led rebellions against the Puritans' interpretation of religious conscience. While Hutchinson was banished from the Massachusetts Bay Colony for her antinomian views, Williams slipped off to Rhode Island and founded his own colony, Providence. Those of Baptist and Quaker persuasion soon formed colonies of their own, with the Quakers especially ridiculed by the Puritans for their "naive" and "dangerous" belief in the Inner Light. Nonetheless, heterodox interpretations of religious conscience were for the most part controlled by the Puritans' intrusive social structure, keeping the creed as the prevailing orthodoxy until the Second Great Awakening in the 1790s.

The immediate problem the Puritans countenanced was not abuse of religious conscience but high affluence. With abundant land and resources and no feudal system to limit ambition, the Puritans felt a zeal for acquisition and gain; indeed, ministers were among the most active land speculators. Their strong work ethic to glorify God resulted in an overload of produce that was shipped off to Europe for profit. And though they rested on the Sabbath, the sermons attended that day usually mixed in business concerns (creditors' obligations, the need for written contracts in land deals) with biblical exegesis.

Ambitous, proud, and rich, the self-made man was for millions of Americans the quintessence of success; sacrifice for the public good was a fatuous dream.

At the same time, these modern-day Zionists were aware that the exodus from Europe was to fulfill God's covenant. What is a just price, they sincerely asked, to charge a neighbor in need of grain in times of scarcity? What rule must we observe in lending and in the forgiving of unpaid loans? The Puritans wrestled with right and wrong, God and Satan, to a degree unimaginable today, with declining religious morals, modernist relativity, and waning affluence having leveled the playing field. Thus, ministers thundered from the pulpit warnings to their flock about the deceiver Satan, who swells the soul with the Augustinian sins of pride and ambition.

As the eighteenth century progressed, however, ministers no longer preached the rhetoric of honoring the public good exclusively for the greater glory of God; it also had utility in maintaining an economically strong society. And pride and ambition shifted from "sins" to "virtues," being qualities Americans now championed as requisites for the successful businessman.

By the Revolutionary era (1760–1790), Americans were simply too greedy and self-interested for communalism to work as the Founding Fathers envisioned. Moreover, during the 1780s, forward thinkers led by James Madison questioned the intrusive practices communities were enacting toward individuals. It was not uncommon for a child to be taken from parents by public officials who felt the youngster was not being raised under a strict moral code. If a new settler without a family entered a town and did not adhere to the community's religious and social dogma, he was in danger of being banished from the area, and sometimes tarred and feathered for good measure.

Research has shown that communalism was not unique to the North; autonomous county self-government in the South, says historian W.H. Nelson, was "as typically colonial as the towns of New England." And by the 1780s both the North and the South were "intensely local, dominated by a fierce suspicion of any active central government."[6] Communities were too parochial, elites grumbled, and, as Alexander Hamilton often pointed out, dangerous to the preservation of the Union.

COMPROMISE AND REBELLION

In 1787 John Adams wrote, "There is no man so blind as not to see that to talk of founding a government upon a supposition that nations and great bodies of men, left to themselves, will practice a course of self-denial is either to babble like a new-born infant or to deceive like an unprincipled imposter."[7]

Quite an admission, especially since throughout the 1770s Adams and the national elite had held such expectations. It was now time to be realistic, or in the words of historian Martin Diamond, a time to lower "the aims and expectations of political life, perhaps of human life generally."[8]

Giving up on the public's ability to live selflessly, political actors promulgated in its place the need for selfless leaders to carry out the common good. With the ratification of the Constitution in 1787 and the power it entrusted to the federal government, the national elite hoped to unite the country, something desperately needed in such an expansive state peopled by isolated, self-governing townships. For a political entity to survive, say political scientists, the governed need a relationship to something apart from themselves; otherwise the state risks fractures and dissolution. The elite hoped to accomplish this by the behavior codified in the Constitution.

Two proto-parties, represented by the political views of James Madison and Alexander Hamilton, emerged from the apologetics of the Constitution. Avid readers of Renaissance republican tracts, Madison and Hamilton used Renaissance ideas to remedy the effects of the people's self-centeredness. Many Renaissance thinkers were weary of the negative medieval understanding of human nature and turned instead to the works of antiquity, such as the Hermetic texts, which posit the potential divinity of humankind. "The human is a godlike living thing," says the Greek *Corpus Hermeticum*, "not comparable to the other living things of the earth but to those in heaven above, who are called gods."[9] Renaissance political theorists emphasized to a greater degree than the ancient Greek and Roman authors the need for godlike men to live selflessly. For such men, desire for fame and honor were noble passions that empowered them to renounce private interest for the commonwealth. In this way ambition for fame and honor, which Renaissance republicans agreed all great men share, would indirectly benefit the public. Ambitious in the republican sense, many eighteenth-century political actors (including Madison, Hamilton, and Thomas Jefferson) believed it was up to them to make the decisions that were in the best interest of the country.

On paper republicanism makes sense. It admits that most people are incapable of living for anything but themselves. It attempts to redirect private ambition to the public. It tries to protect the fights of the individual from hostile and intrusive communities. And by forming "societies" to collect the will of the people, argued Madison and Jefferson, it preserves the democratic majoritarianism on which this country was based. But in practice there were stumbling blocks: (1) the self-interest of political actors (beyond the allowed passions of fame and honor); (2) the town rebellions against government intrusiveness; and (3) the

Federalist opposition led by Hamilton, who feared the results of bestowing individual liberties on depraved Americans.

> *In the nineteenth century, "success" was wholly a private affair, and it created the dog-eat-dog world for which America is known.*

Thus entered the Federalist era (1790–1800), epitomized by Republicans accusing Federalists of tyranny and Federalists accusing Republicans of unwittingly perpetrating anarchy. During this era there were several major instances of resistance to government authority. Near the end of the century, Virginia and Kentucky threatened to secede from the Union and were supported by Jefferson, a Virginian who revealed his inherited communal ethos by calling the federal government "a foreign jurisdiction." Yet, as political actors debated and societies rebelled, Americans generally lived a peaceful, though less religious and more self-interested, form of communalism, gradually imbibing what would be the cohesive agent of the nation: not religious piety, not the articles of the Constitution, but the myth of success and the self-made man.

AGE OF TRANSITION

Historians agree that early in the nineteenth century a cultural shift occurred in America. Political and social theories of the last century suddenly seemed effete, naive, impracticable. Puritan hallmarks such as diligence in work, religious conscience, and cultivation of virtuous habits were exploited for secular gain. America was redefining itself as the land of opportunity, where success could be had by anyone with a strong work ethic and good habits. Ambitious, proud, and rich, the self-made man was for millions of Americans the quintessence of success; sacrifice for the public good was a fatuous dream.

In preindustrial America, "success" was defined as a harmonious community functioning for the glory of God. By the 1790s it was the man who attained glory and fame for dedicating his life to the commonwealth. In the nineteenth century, "success" was wholly a private affair, and it created the dog-eat-dog world for which America is known. "I don't know what people are meant for," says a character in a Henry James novel. "I only know what I can do with them."[10]

Change was not without a price—loss of personal identity and high anxiety were the by-products. When a person sets out to attain the putative notion of success, despite its contradistinction to private talents, life can become as meaningless as a corporate annual report is to a poet. Add to this a critique by Thomas Carlyle of the English that is also true of modern Americans. "What is it that the modern English soul does, in very truth, dread infinitely, and contemplate with entire despair? What is his hell? … The terror of not succeeding."[11] And most did not succeed. Historians point out that the real profiteers in

America were banks and railroads, not the diligent entrepreneur of legend, and certainly not the honest one.

The ratio of church members to total population in America nearly doubled between 1800 and 1835; however, people's connection to their creed was declining. Higher church attendance is indicative of confusion in an age of transition, a time when, said the English social critic John Stuart Mill, "mankind have outgrown old institutions and old doctrines, and have not yet acquired new ones."[12] Christianity had become an external religion—dogma and ritual—and as such could not adequately minister to the emptiness caused by obsession with the myth of success.

Nevertheless, clergymen of the early nineteenth century were still the leaders (though not the authorities) of the community. William Emerson, father of the poet and essayist, was one of these figures. "God preserve us," he wrote his sister in 1807, "in this howling and tempestuous world! ... One might almost as well be amidst the ... billows of the ocean, as to be over whelmed by the floods of democracy."[13] William Emerson was a Federalist; he believed democracy would lead to self-interest, license, and the eventual dissolution of the Union. Like many New England ministers, the reverend promulgated a return to the communal ethos of the Puritan colonies. This differed from Madison and Jefferson's republicanism in that the people's wishes would rarely be considered; it differed from Hamiltonian Federalism because it strove to preserve communalism. Many New Englanders supported a return to roots, since it offered an idealized hierarchical system that promised to remedy the anxiety of people caught in an age of transition.

Ralph Waldo Emerson, despite barely knowing his father, who died in 1811 when the boy was seven, was raised to be a leader of society in the Federalist/Puritan tradition. He was schooled at Boston Latin School, Harvard, and Harvard Divinity School; and he was ordained a Unitarian minister in 1826. In the first decades of the nineteenth century, New England Federalism seemed to be working. A visitor to Boston in 1811 wrote: "Here a man is not as in London, lost in an immense crowd of people, and thus hidden from the inspection of his fellowman; but is known, and is conscious that he is known."[14] But things soon changed. The enormous influx of immigrants turned the city into, as Emerson noted in 1822, "Boston Babylon." People entered and left the city without notice, making it easy for thieves and con men to avoid arrest, and many settlers did not join local churches. The preindustrial, sparsely populated, devoutly religious organism of the colonies was disappearing. Meanwhile, Emerson struggled to fit an anachronistic social scheme to a changing world.

Like his father, the young minister viewed democracy as the road to anarchy. People cannot govern themselves, because they too easily fall prey to whims and passions. But with religious sentiment and ministerial leadership in decline, how could one awaken the public?

Hamiltonian Federalists of the 1790s posited a strong national government to work selflessly for the public good. But with the change of power brought about by the election of the Republican Jefferson in 1801, the Federalists, many historians believe, were responsible for burning government buildings that housed documents that would have revealed their years of

corruption and lies. In the late 1820s and early 1830s, Emerson noted in his journal the political scandals reported in the press and was outraged by the "sham treaty" concocted by the government to remove the Cherokee people from their land. The election of Andrew Jackson by what Emerson considered the cajoling of the public led to this journal entry in 1827: "Public opinion, I am sorry to say, will bear a great deal of nonsense. There is scarce any absurdity so gross whether in religion, politics, science, or manners, which it will not bear."[15]

By 1834 Emerson concluded that neither New England Federalism, the church, nor the government could lead the country from gross self-interest. It was time to reconstruct the American self.

THE ABORIGINAL SELF

"I think no man can go with his thoughts about him into one of our churches, without feeling that what hold the public worship had on men is gone, or going," said Emerson in a speech to the Harvard Divinity School class of 1838. "It has lost its grasp on the affection of the good and the fear of the bad."[16] Though Emerson was raised a Calvinist, the youngster never truly believed humankind was unalterably depraved. "Evil is merely privative," he would write later, "not absolute."[17] Moreover, the New Englander was aware that "affection for the good" had eroded in the church and in the lives of Americans because attention was on exterior stimulants rather than on the inner life.

In his *Confessions*, Augustine tells how in youth he was a member of a debating team called the Subverters. A masterful and intelligent debater, the young man easily located and expounded the flaw of his opponents' arguments. But once cognizant of the pride he felt in his abilities, Augustine saw with clarity the cunningness of evil and the necessity for a probing self-awareness. It is unfortunate that John Calvin and other actors of the Protestant Reformation (which effectively ended in the West in normative circles the Renaissance emphasis on the godlike qualities of humankind) missed the saint's recondite conception of sin—which is not absolute but correctable and requires sober examination of the self.

People's accountability for their actions had been declining in the new land as early as the establishment of the Massachusetts Bay Colony in 1628. One of the leaders of the First Great Awakening, Jonathan Edwards, complained in 1754 that Americans never accepted blame for anything. Emerson watched his contemporaries cheat, lie, and steal with impunity for a piece of the American pie. It is as if the ideology of original sin had backfired: Having for so long feared the dark inner recesses, Americans no longer looked there, instead fixing their gaze outward—to pleasures, to riches, and to a titular religion.

Emerson resigned his Unitarian pulpit in 1832 because he no longer believed the church could sway Americans from the love of wordly things.

Emerson resigned his Unitarian pulpit in 1832 because he no longer believed the church could sway Americans from the love of worldly things. Employing an argument influenced by his reading of Quaker texts, the future Concord sage declared in his final sermon as minister of the Second Church in Boston that Christianity had become a place of antiquated rituals and ossified moral codes. "With whatever exception," Emerson told the divinity school graduates six years later, "it is still true that tradition characterizes the preaching of this country; that it comes out of the memory, and not out of the soul; that it aims at what is usual, and not what is eternal."[18]

By midcentury, communalism was hardly proffered as a viable social option by the American intelligentsia. At best it continued in small agrarian towns, and still does in the North, South, and Midwest; at worst it retrograded into narrow-minded, dangerous societies. The racism in these societies—evidenced most shockingly by the lynchings of the late nineteenth and early twentieth centuries—was not controlled until the federal government stepped in and the Supreme Court made important civil rights decisions from the 1950s through the 1970s.

Obsession with getting ahead was for Americans what was "normal," while those not so inclined, like Henry Thoreau, were oddballs.

Ironically, the rise of economic individualism in the nineteenth century did not create in Americans a corresponding ability to think in an individual manner. With so many pursuing the same goal—material success—the uniqueness of the individual was swept into the corner. Obsession with getting ahead was for Americans what was "normal," while those not so inclined, like Henry Thoreau, were oddballs. Furthermore, living in the midst of an increasingly immoral society, people were losing the ability to make individual moral judgments. Emerson perceived this and in 1834 moved from Boston Babylon to the country town of Concord, living there the remainder of his life. There is a maxim that a good man in a base crowd will descend to the baseness of his surroundings, not vice versa. I read recently an interview of a popular actor who bragged about his freedom of thought; yet his ideas were nothing new or out of the ordinary. It was the same baseness I have heard many times before.

Not by following the teachings of the church, not by seconding mass opinion, but by attention to the Self humankind can be saved. "In that deep force, the last fact behind which analysis cannot go, all things find their common origin," wrote Emerson. By connecting with the "aboriginal Self,"[19] the petty self concerned with selfish desires simply vanishes.

In an address given in 1837, Emerson declared: "There is One Man,—present to all particular men only partially, or through one faculty; and that you must take the whole society to find the whole man."[20] Emerson is expressing the Transcendentalist answer to uniting the country. Spiritual precepts—love thy neighbor, give to the poor, forgive a wrongdoer—are artificial constructs that do not become genuine in people's lives until the Self, the provenance of these precepts, is intimately known. Thus, each person must regularly seek seclusion from the noise of the world to hear the private whispers within. The more a person submits to these whispers—not those of the petty self but of the aboriginal Self—the greater his empathy for others and the benefit to society.

I WAS HUNGRY, I WAS THIRSTY

"Whoever degrades another degrades me, /And whatever is done or said returns at last to me."[21] This is Walt Whitman's version of a teaching by Jesus in Matthew's Gospel. "I was hungry and you gave me food, I was thirsty and you gave me drink," said Jesus. When the "righteous" asked Jesus when it was that they had performed these deeds for him, he responded, "Truly I say to you, as you did it to one of the least of these my brethren, you did it to me."[22] To question this teaching is to have waded only in the shallows of the petty self. In our cynical age it is easy to poke fun at our ancestors for thinking that members of a society and officers of a government could live selflessly for the commonwealth. Emerson's Self or One Man, which Jesus calls "me" (as does Whitman), may sound silly—but only if you have not experienced it.

As in Edward's and Emerson's America, people today skirt responsibility for their actions. Novelist Charles Baxter points this out by using the example of afternoon talk shows, which, he says, "have only apparent antagonists. Their sparring partners are not real antagonists because the bad guys usually confess and then immediately disavow.... The story is trying to find a source of meaning, but in the story, everyone is disclaiming responsibility. Things have just happened."[23] Denials by political actors caught in a lie, modernist theories of the relativity of morality, dead-beat dads, and abortion are further examples.

Then there is the twentieth-century version of Augustine's criticism of the Manichaean heresy—that of projecting evil outward, in other words, the blame game. Something else—culture, poor upbringing, circumstance—is at fault rather than the wrongdoer. Joyce Carol Oates says serial killers are a sign of our alienating social structure, making it easy for drifters to slip in and out of communities without detection. Oates is correct, but her analysis has a way of shifting blame away from the killer. Indeed, exterior factors (Oates' social structure) are consistently raised to ultimate meanings and tend to obscure the definitions of "good" and "evil"—a predictable outcome in a society losing its morality. "He laid the blame on fortune," wrote Plato of the worldly man, "on the decree of the gods, anything rather than himself."[24]

Where has neglect of the inner life gotten us? Thoreau discerned the "quiet desperation" of the mass; Kierkegaard said the specific character of despair is that it is unaware of being despair. A common phrase in conversation is "I've just been so busy." But I suspect this busyness is more by choice than necessity. To stop and think soberly about one's life is to open a pandora's box, something to be avoided at all cost. Inarticulated despair is always the most dangerous, for in trying to fill the gap a futile search begins that can last a lifetime. Egotism, ruthless business practices, promiscuity, workaholism—their overarching commonality is a sign of a forgotten inner life.

Emerson was soundly derided for proclaiming in his divinity school address the authority of the Self over the forms of the church. The fallout left him, he said in his poem "Uriel," with "a sad self-knowledge" that Americans may be doomed to facile interests. In the West the Self has been consistently misinterpreted. Whether by esoteric societies (Theosophical, Anthroposophical) or mainline Christian orthodoxy, the Self has been obscured by flaky teachers (Madame Blavatsky, Charles Leadbeater), tortuous intellectual systems (P.D. Ouspensky's, Rudolph Steiner's), spiritual materialism (Norman Vincent Peale, Robert Schuller), and nationalism (Billy Graham). Yet most of us have already experienced that moment when self-interest gives way to a feeling of overwhelming unity with and empathy for others.

Egotism, ruthless business practices, promiscuity, workaholism—their overarching commonality is a sign of a forgotten inner life.

To demand from Americans this level of consciousness is, I know, asking a lot. It requires tremendous inner attention and discipline to widen an ephemeral feeling into a bona fide lifestyle. But one thing is certain: America is still in an age of transition. Christianity remains the American religion, yet it is still unable to effect significant change in the lives of most of its followers. The words of Jesus quoted above present the vision; the words that follow, a much closer summation of America circa 1997, reflect the reality: "I was hungry and you gave me no food, I was thirsty and you gave me no drink," said Jesus. When the "cursed" ones asked Jesus when it was that they had failed to perform these deeds, he responded: "Truly, I say to you, as you did it not to one of the least of these, you did it not to me."[25]

America is not the first Western society to lose its religion. The ancient Greeks eventually replaced their pantheon of gods with a literalist belief in Christianity. During the transition, the Greeks fell into self-centered materialism, as Americans have for the last two hundred years. It is difficult to imagine Americans repudiating Christianity wholesale for, say, Buddhism or a farrago of ideas from the Eastern and Western faiths synthesized by New Age leaders. In the eighteenth century, the Germans Goethe and Herder suggested that societies eventually mature into a second phase of culture that considers sacred stories as myth yet retains them because of their figurative relevance to the culture. Yet this did not happen in ancient Greece. Indeed, asking American Christians to give up their literal interpretation of the resurrection of Christ for a symbolic one—that the Resurrection is the ultimate earthly experience of the Self—may be whistling in the dark. In his divinity school address, Emerson seems to suggest that orthodox Christianity shall be with

us a good while longer, so the wisest course is to incrementally change its emphasis to the cultivation of Self-knowledge.

Meanwhile, as this high-minded dialogue continues (albeit behind closed doors), signs of despair in the lives of Americans seem more prevalent every day. ∎

Notes

1. Quoted in Barry Alan Shain, *The Myth of American Individualism: The Protestant Origins of American Political Thought* (Princeton: Princeton University Press, 1994), 226.

2. Numa Denis Fustel De Coulanges, *The Ancient City: A Classic Study of the Religious and Civil Institutions of Ancient Greece and Rome,* 1864 (reprint, Baltimore: Johns Hopkins University Press, 1980), 211–12.

3. Perry G. Miller, *Errand into the Wilderness* (Cambridge, Mass.: Belknap Press, 1956), 129.

4. Quoted in Shain, *The Myth*, 227, from John Adams, "Defense," 1788.

5. Shain, *The Myth*, 196–97, from Franklin, "Speech," 28 June 1787.

6. W.H. Nelson, *The American Tory* (Oxford: Oxford University Press, 1961), 53.

7. John Adams, *A Defense of the Constitutions of Government of the United States of America* (reprint, New York: Da Capo Press, 1971), 3:289.

8. Martin Diamond, "Ethics and Politics: The American Way," in *The Moral Foundations of the American Republic*, ed., Robert Horowitz (Charlottesville: University Press of Virginia, 1986), 82–8.3

9. Brian P. Copenhaver, ed., *Hermetica* (Cambridge: Cambridge University Press, 1992), 36.

10. Henry James, *The Portrait of a Lady* (New York: New American Library, 1963), 356.

11. Thomas Carlyle, "Past and Present," *The Best Known Works of Thomas Carlyle* (New York: Blue Ribbon Books, 1942), 352.

12. Quoted in Walter E. Houghton, *The Victorian Frame of Mind*, 1830–1870 (London: Yale University Press, 1957), 1.

13. Quoted in Mary Kupiec Cayton, *Emerson's Emergence: Self and Society in the Transformation of New England, 1800–1845* (Chapel Hill: University of North Carolina Press, 1989), 8.

14. Cayton, *Emerson's Emergence*, 18.

15. Joel Porte, ed., *Emerson in His Journals* (Cambridge: Belknap Press, 1982), 65.

16. Ralph Waldo Emerson, "An Address," *The Complete Works of Ralph Waldo Emerson*, Edward Emerson, ed. (New York: Wm. H. Wise & Co., 1929), 44.

17. Emerson, "An Address," 38.

18. Emerson, "An Address," 44.

19. Emerson, "Self-Reliance," 144.

20. Emerson, "The American Scholar," 25.

21. Walt Whitman, "Song of Myself," *Leaves of Grass* (New York: Signet Classic, 1958), 67.

22. Matthew 25:35, 40.

23. Quoted in Mark Edmundson, "American Gothic," *Civilization: The Magazine of the Library of Congress*, May/June 1996, 54.

24. Francis MacDonald Cornford, trans., *The Republic of Plato* (New York: Oxford University Press, 1945), Book 10, 357.

25. Matthew 25:42, 45.

Mark Richard Barna is a freelance author who writes often on American spirituality. He lives in Berkeley, California.

BEN FRANKLIN'S
"SCIENTIFIC AMUSEMENTS"

*Although renowned for pragmatism, Franklin fathered
a scientific revolution by indulging his insatiable curiosity.*

by DUDLEY R. HERSCHBACH

As an American icon, Benjamin Franklin is often portrayed as wise and canny in business and politics, earnestly pursuing and extolling diligence, sensible conduct, and good works. Also legendary are some of his inventions, such as the lightning rod, bifocals, and an efficient wood-burning stove. All of this is usually taken to exemplify the virtues of his down-to-earth, pragmatic outlook. Today, however, surprisingly few people appreciate that, in his own time, Franklin was greatly esteemed throughout Europe as an intellectual. His work on electricity was recognized as ushering in a scientific revolution comparable to those wrought by Newton in the previous century or by Watson and Crick in ours. Moreover, by his own account, Franklin's studies of electricity and many other phenomena were prompted not by practical aims, but by his playful curiosity—which often became obsessive, even antic.

My first inkling of this side of Ben Franklin came in 1956, when I was a graduate student. To commemorate the 250th anniversary of Franklin's birth and the 200th of Mozart's, the American Academy of Arts and Sciences put on a concert that featured a glass harmonica specially constructed for the occasion, and intended to do justice to music that Mozart had composed specifically for that instrument. Like the "armonica" invented by Franklin in 1762, it consisted of glass bowls of increasing diameter mounted on a rotating spindle. Unlike the original models, which were played by pressing wet fingers against the rims of the bowls, this was a very large contraption with 37 glass bowls and a keyboard enabling it to be played like a piano. I remember that E. Power Biggs, after performing beautifully with simple musical glasses, had some difficulty with the armonica because several of the bowls had shattered, and more did as he played.

The concert included a live performance of the famous string quartet attributed to Franklin. Experts are unsure whether Franklin really composed it, but there are typically impish hints. The quartet is in the key of F. It employs three violins and a cello, with scordatura tuning such that each musician has to play only four notes, one on each of the open strings. The result is 16-tone music, vastly simplified for the performers. Indeed, the string

players had quizzical expressions on their faces; their left hands were used to fingering like mad but in this quartet had nothing to do. Certainly the piece, whether or not composed by Franklin, exhibits his yen for whimsical fun.

That concert left me intrigued with Franklin, and in the years since I have enjoyed looking into what he called his "scientific amusements." Like so much else he did, the scope of his work in science is amazing. (See "Chronology of Curiosity,") Fortunately, his experiments and observations are amply documented in his own writings, especially in letters to his friends and colleagues. While he was always alert for practical applications, in most of his scientific studies his style was that of an explorer, eager for adventure and insight rather than profit or utility. Many of his letters convey his zest for understanding and his joy in discovery; some ruefully admit an addiction to science akin to his indulgence in chess and magic squares.

Franklin's scientific work and engaging discussions of it are readily accessible to the general reader, but deserve to be better known. Much of this article draws on recent scholarship about him. The first part is based mostly on *Benjamin Franklin's Science*, by I. Bernard Cohen, Thomas professor of the history of science emeritus and surely the world's greatest authority on Franklin's science. The second part is drawn from *Ben Franklin Stilled the Waves*, by Charles Tanford, a distinguished biochemist and professor of physiology emeritus at Duke University. (For particulars about these and other pertinent books, see "A Shelf for Ben's Science,")

ELECTRICAL AMUSEMENTS: "HELP TO KEEP A VAIN MAN HUMBLE"

As Cohen emphasizes, in the early eighteenth century electricity was a greater mystery than was gravity a century earlier. Franklin, almost entirely self-educated and far from any center of learning, solved that mystery. He devised, executed, and correctly interpreted a series of simple, compelling experiments and formulated lucid explanations. Among his several major discoveries, foremost was his concept of

Chronology of Curiosity

When and where: Franklin was born in Boston on January 17, 1706, and died in Philadelphia on April 17, 1790. He lived in Boston until 1723, then in London (1724–26), Philadelphia (1726–57,1762–64; 1775–76), London (1757–62, 1764–75), Paris (1776–85),and Philadelphia (1785–90).

Franklin's world was much larger than ours: crossing the Atlantic took not a few hours but four to six weeks, a voyage he made eight times. To his perceptive eye the world bulged with challenging puzzles. His intellectual voyage extended more than 60 years, during which he recorded a host of fresh observations and interpretations and conducted many experiments. This sampling of his science includes annotations for a few choice items.

1726 Returning from his first trip to London, makes notes on ocean currents, temperature, weather—subjects that would continue to interest him all his life.

1729 While working hard to establish himself as a printer, performs his first recorded scientific experiments, on color and heat absorption, by laying squares of light- and, dark-colored cloth on snow on a sunny day and noting how deep they sank.

1730 Begins publishing his newspaper, *The Pennsylvania Gazette*, his own observations and those of others, indicating his wide range of interests. Writes about the effect of earthquakes on the color of rivers.

1732 Reports observations of the aurora borealis.

1739 Invents "Pennsylvania stove." (An amusing chapter of I. Bernard Cohen's *Benjamin Franklin's Science* points out that no genuine "Franklin stoves" exists today, for good reason: his clever design proved in practice to be a smoky fiasco. Ben was fallible!)

1742 Discusses behavior of comets.

1743 Reports observations on eclipse of the moon and motion of storms.

Attends electrical demonstrations by Archibald Spencer, becomes intrigued.

1745 Writes long critique of Cadwallader Colden's anatomical manuscript on perspiration and the bloodstream.

Receives from Peter Collinson an "electrical tube" apparatus and directions for its use; begins intensive series of electrical experiments.

1748 Retires from business at age 42, giving as a major reason his desire to concentrate on scientific experiments.

1750 Proposes use of lightning rods. Severely shocked while trying to electrocute a turkey.

1751 Collection of his letters to Collinson, read at the Royal Society, published in London as *Experiments and Observations on Electricity, made at Philadelphia in America*; additional work included in later editions of 1754, 1760, 1769, and 1774.

1752 Conducts kite experiment. Equips his house with a lightning rod. Invents flexible catheter (to aid brother John, who suffers from bladder stone).

1755 Writes *Observations Concerning the Increase of Mankind, Peopling of Countries, Etc.* Noting that the English population in North America was one million; but that only 80,000 had immigrated, Franklin calculated that population would double every 20 to 25 years, which it did until 1860, when immigration surged. This work also explicitly anticipated the limitations stressed by Thomas Malthus in his famous essay of 1798.

His major paper, *Physical and Meteorological Observations, Conjectures, and Suppositions*, read at the Royal Society.

1758 Performs experiments on evaporation at Cambridge University.

1773 Reports experiments on spreading of oil on water.

1775 On voyage to America, measures temperature of air and water to begin mapping of Gulf Stream.

1782 Witness early manned balloon ascensions; when asked by dubious observer, "What use is it?", replies "What use is a newborn baby?"

1784 Constructs bifocal eyeglasses.

1785 Serves as spokesman for a French royal committee that successfully discredits purported cures by "mesmeric fluid" generated from animal magnetism, which had become a craze in Paris. Appointed by Louis XVI, the committee included the famous chemist Lavoisier and the physician Guillotin. (A few years later the king and the chemist both lost their heads to another French craze via a means once publicly endorsed as humane by the physician.)

On last voyage home, at age 79, writes *Maritime Observations*, noting best form of rigging for swift vessels, proposing design of the sea anchor, and reporting further data about the Gulf Stream.

---

electricity as a single fluid, manifest as a "positive or negative" charge, depending on whether the fluid was present in excess or deficit relative to the neutral condition.

Franklin's book *Experiments and Observations on Electricity, made at Philadelphia in America*, consisting of the letters he had sent to Peter Collinson (who had supplied him with an electrical tube apparatus) was a sensation in Europe: it went through five editions in English and was translated into French, German, and Italian. It was read not only by scholars but by the literate public, including the clergy and aristocracy. All were as-

tonished that an amateur far off in America had been able to establish the nature of something as puzzling as electricity.

During the several years when he was chiefly occupied with his electrical studies, Franklin often confessed apologetically to friends that he had become obsessed with his experiments. He called them "philosophical amusements," which he pursued in hopes of gaining insight, despite what seemed then a total lack of prospects for practical applications. Three years before he conceived of the lightning rod, Franklin averred that electricity at least "may help to keep a vain man humble."

> **Franklin often confessed that he had become obsessed with his experiments, which he pursued despite what seemed a total lack of practical applications.**

Much that he did was for the sheer fun of it. For example, one of his favorite toys was an electrical spider; when charged up, it moved around like a real spider. In letters he mentioned the crowds that came to his house to see such things and how he liked to play tricks on them. He had an iron fence and would wire it up to make sparks leap along the rails to excite the onlookers. We can reproduce the effect with electrostatic machines such as those in the Harvard Collection of Historical Scientific Instruments. The machines have a glass globe that is rotated by a gear mechanism to rub the glass against silk and generate an electrical charge. Since antiquity, sparks have been generated this way, by rubbing suitable materials together. Often we do it inadvertently by walking across a carpet. Today we speak of knocking some electrons off by friction. But before Franklin established the nature of electricity, it was thought that different substances gave rise to various kinds of mystical particles.

A Shelf for Ben's Science

The two essential books on the scientific Franklin, both sprightly and nontechnical, are I. Bernard Cohen's superb *Benjamin Franklin's Science* (Harvard University Press, 1990) and Charles Tanford's *Ben Franklin Stilled the Waves* (Duke University Press, 1989). Also of much interest is another superb book just published by Cohen, *Science and the Founding Fathers: Science in the Political Thought of Jefferson, Franklin, Adams, & Madison* (Norton, 1995; see "Endpapers," page 118).

Foremost among the other books I particularly recommended is a fine anthology of Franklin's *Writings*, edited by J. A. Leo LeMay (Library of America, 1987). There are many biographies; my favorites are Catherine Drinker Bowen's *The Most Dangerous Man in America* (Little, Brown, 1974) and Ronald W. Clark's *Benjamin Franklin* (Random House, 1983). Both include some scientific episodes.

A rich lode of graphics is found in Louise Todd Ambler's *Benjamin Franklin: A Perspective* (Fogg Art Museum, 1975) and David P. Wheatland's *The Apparatus of Science at Harvard, 1765–1800* (Harvard University Press, 1968).

Striking material on lightning abounds; particularly vivid are accounts by James S. Trefil in *Meditations at Sunset* (Macmillan, 1987); by Ido Yaretz in "Lightning and the History of Science and Technology" (*News from the Burndy Library*, fall 1993); and by Dava Sobel in "Jove's Thunderbolts" (*Harvard Magazine*, July–August 1979).

In Franklin's day, the public became intensely interested in electrical phenomena. A very popular book of 1759, titled *Young Gentleman and Lady's Philosophy*, illustrated a parlor game that Franklin himself might well have pursued. Evidently the conversation did not go, "Would you like to see some fine etchings?", but "Would you like to see a fine electrostatic generator?" As a kid, I was puzzled to hear my parents speak of "sparking"; now I wonder whether that quaint usage derives from a higher level of scientific literacy 200 years ago!

The Lightning Rod

The concepts that Franklin established in several years of playful experiments were essential prerequisites to his invention of the lightning rod. In a 1750 letter he wrote:

> … may not the Knowledge of this Power of Points be of use to Mankind, in preserving Houses, Churches, Ships &c. from the Stroke of Lightning, by directing us to fix on the highest parts of those Edifices, upright Rods of Iron…and from the Foot of those Rods a Wire down the outside of the Building into the Ground, or down round one of the Shrouds of a Ship, and down her Side till it reaches the Water. Would not these pointed Rods probably draw the electrical Fire silently out of a Cloud before it came nigh enough to strike, and thereby secure us from that most sudden and terrible Mischief?

Nowadays this might be a grant proposal! It depends on his discovery that pointed conductors were very effective at drawing away the electrical fluid. We now say this happens because the "electrical field" is higher at a pointed conductor than at a rounded one, so some of the air is ionized and conducts better. Franklin's proposal further depends on his understanding that it is essential to ground the conductor (so the charge runs off into the vast reservoir of the earth or sea). Also fundamental, as revealed by his research, was the fact that the electricity would flow through a good metallic conductor instead of the poor conducting materials of the building or ship. Others had suspected that lightning is electrical, but an experimental test could not be devised until Franklin had created a sufficiently good intellectual conduit, connecting that conjecture to well-grounded concepts.

In the next paragraph of the letter, Franklin outlines his proposed experiment quite specifically:

> On the top of some high Tower or Steeple, place a kind of Sentrybox big enough to contain a Man and an electrical Stand. From the middle of the Stand, let an Iron Rod rise and pass bending out of the Door, and then upright 20 or 30 feet…

Cohen's book reproduces a diagram from Franklin's letter. In effect, the sentry would hold up the iron rod (or touch it with a wire) to draw off electrical current from the cloud, just as you might hold a key to a doorknob to discharge static electricity you've picked up in walking across the carpet. It was apt that Franklin specified a sentry, a disciplined person who doesn't flinch. Actually, as he correctly explained, if the sentry holds the rod via an insulated stick or wax bar, connected to a grounded conductor, he could do the experiment with perfect safety.

Franklin did not undertake this experiment because Philadelphia did not then have a suitably tall structure. Later he realized that by flying a kite he could accomplish his purpose much more simply. (That happens with research proposals in our day, too!) Meanwhile, his book, including the 1750 letter and others, caused particularly great excitement in France because Louis XV liked electrical parlor games. For instance, he would have 100 grenadiers line up holding hands, then connect them to electrical leads at each end, to see them all jump in unison. In one variant, the king had this done with 200 monks instead. The king requested that Franklin's experiments be performed for his edification. The proposed sentrybox experiment thus was first done in France, under direction of the translator of his book; it appears that Franklin heard of that only after his kite experiment.

We now know much more about lightning; *Meditations at Sunset*, by James S. Trefil, provides an excellent survey. In essence, Franklin's ideas hold up. Clouds contain some charged particles and, empirically, the positively charged particles tend to be somewhat lighter than negative ones. Thus, a cumulus cloud will often have excess negative charges along its bottom—say, at an altitude of 5,000 feet—and excess positive charges up above. As a result, a big potential difference can develop within the cloud. When the cloud floats over a tree or house, what matters is the charge near the earth. The negative bottom of the cloud repels some of the negative charges in the tree or house, pushing them into the ground. Things in the shadow of the cloud thus acquire a net positive charge, which drifts along the earth beneath the floating cloud. When the voltage difference between the negative cloud bottom and its positive shadow exceeds the capacity of the air to withstand it, lightning discharges via the most conductive available pathway.

High-speed photography has shown what Franklin couldn't see with his own eyes: the electrical breakdown usually ionizes the air for only a few hundred feet. Then there's another such breakdown, and another, until the cloud-ground gap is bridged when descending and ascending discharges meet. Franklin, simply by draining charge from a rod on his roof and finding it negative with respect to charge obtained from his electrostatic machine, did in fact infer that a lightning stroke typically goes up, not down.

Earthly Thunder

Soon after the kite and sentry-box experiments, Franklin installed lightning rods on the tallest public buildings in Philadelphia and placed an announcement in the 1753 edition of his best-selling book, *Poor Richard's Almanack*:

> It has pleased God in his goodness to Mankind, at length to discover to them the means of securing their Habitations and other Buildings from Mischief by Thunder and Lightning. The method is this: Provide a small Iron Rod [full construction details follow]....A House thus furnished will not be damaged by Lightning, it being attracted to the Points, and passing thro the Metal into the Ground without hurting any Thing.

From enlightened quarters there soon rained down on Franklin high honors, sparked by his invention of the lightning rod. These included the first honorary degree awarded by Harvard and the Copley Medal of the Royal Society, both in 1753. Further honors followed from a host of scholarly societies. In particular, in 1772 he was elected a foreign associate of the French Academy of Sciences (only eight are allowed); he was the first American elected—and the only one for another century.

Perhaps even more telling were what we might term low honors. The immense popularity Franklin enjoyed during his ministry to France stemmed from his fame as the tamer of lightning as well as a revolutionary patriot. Although T-shirts were not yet fashionable, Franklin's image appeared everywhere in Paris on medallions, engravings, and banners, often with the Latin motto coined by Turgot: *Eripuit coelo fulmen sceptrumque tyrannis* ("He snatched lightning from the sky and the scepter from tyrants"). Indeed, Louis XVI became so annoyed by this veneration that he gave his favorite mistress a chamber pot with a Franklin medallion at the bottom of the bowl.

The Local Connections

Crowns of lightning rods adorn most of the tallest buildings at Harvard, including William James Hall, the Science Center, Memorial Hall, and Holyoke Center, as well as the towers of several of the Houses. These crowns consist of short rods, 12 to 18 inches tall, spaced about 20 feet apart around the periphery of the highest portion of the roof. The rods are linked by half-inch-thick braided cables of copper wire, connected to a grounded bus bar. Some spires, such as the steeple of Memorial Church, are clad in a heavy copper sheath, directly connected to a grounded conductor. In effect, this makes the entire spire serve as a lightning rod.

All told, Harvard's lightning protection employs several hundred rods and many thousands of feet of copper cable. This is in the care of the Boston Lightning Rod Company; the firm's service extends back more than a century, during which Harvard has suffered almost no significant damage from lightning strokes.

An instructive exception occurred in August 1986. The building involved, Byerly Hall in Radcliffe Yard, had not been protected by lightning rods because its roof is much lower than surrounding trees. A bolt struck one of eight unused chimneys that had been capped by an ungrounded copper plates. The copper cap, about 5 feet square, was blown more than 50 feet into the Yard, together with several dozen bricks.

> **From enlightened quarters there soon rained down on Franklin high honors, including the first honorary degree awarded by Harvard.**

The Harvard Collection of Historical Scientific Instruments includes several versions of persuasive devices used by Franklin and many other lecturers to demonstrate the virtues of his lightning rod, both in classrooms and for popular entertainments. A fine example is the exploding "thunder house."

It's appropriate that the thunder house has a little steeple. Before Franklin's discoveries, lightning was generally seen as a supernatural phenomenon. If a house was struck by lightning, the fire company would douse the neighboring structures, but only pray over the struck one, not wanting to intrude on God's punishment. Such views also led to the custom of storing gunpowder in churches, where it might have divine protection. For example, in 1767 the authorities in Venice opted to store hundreds of tons of powder in a church vault. Lightning blew it up, killing 3,000 people and destroying a sizable portion of the city. After that, lightning rods became much more common in Italy.

Another long tradition, going back to the time of Charlemagne, was the ringing of consecrated church bells during thunderstorms to ward off lightning bolts hurled by diabolical spirits; church bells typically bore inscriptions extolling such powers. That made bell-ringing a hazardous occupation. A book published in Munich in 1784 recorded that in the previous 35 years, lightning had hit 386 churches in Germany and killed 103 bell-ringers. Cohen cites many other instances of lightning strikes on steeples and electrocutions of bell-ringers, some more than a century after Franklin had shown the down-to-earth efficacy of lightning rods.

Despite Franklin's astutely diplomatic assertion acknowledging divine beneficence ("It has pleased God…"), religious prejudice against his lightning rods was thunderous and sustained—understandably, perhaps, in the context of the times, since his science fundamentally challenged the supernatural. In 1756, when an earthquake hit Boston, ministers attacked Franklin for his audacity in stealing lightning from the Almighty. People feared that his rods would attract strikes that would not otherwise happen, and that draining electricity into the ground would cause earthquakes.

Political opposition also arose—particularly in England, from those angry with or suspicious of Franklin as the representative of rebel colonies. Some claimed the sharp-tipped rods he advocated were more likely than round knobs to attract strikes and thus become dangerous if the lightning did not meekly run down the rod to ground. (In fact, while this effect is marked in the lab, it is moot for lightning; to a cloud far aloft, any difference in the shape of a rod is imperceptible.)

For the most part, Franklin was unruffled by the opposition. But he was annoyed by the unsound attacks of the Abbé Nollet, a powerful French intellectual whose theorizing about electricity had been rendered void by Franklin's discoveries. Writing in 1753 to a friend, Franklin said:

> In one or two Places, [Nollet] seems to apply to the superstitious Prejudices of the Populace, which I think unworthy of a Philosopher. He speaks as if he thought it Presumption in man, to propose guarding himself against the Thunders of Heaven! Surely the Thunder of Heaven is no more supernatural than the Rain Hail or Sunshine of Heaven, against the Inconveniences of which we guard by Roofs & Shades without Scruple.

Gradually, of course, lightning rods became widely accepted, although that took roughly 40 years. A nineteenth-century illustration of a man with lightning-rod equipped umbrella offers a charming endorsement!

Franklin had a lightning detector of special design in his own house. The device had two parallel segments, one coming down from the roof beside his chimney, the other sunk in the ground and extending upward. Each segment led to a small bell; the two bells, a few inches apart, were connected by a silk thread carrying a little brass ball. When a cloud went over and induced some charge in the upper rod, the little ball would pick up the charge and rattle back and forth, ringing the bells. In the event of a lightning stroke, strong sparks would also leap between the bells. Franklin gleefully reported how the light from such sparks was sometimes strong enough that he could read a newspaper by it. (On the other hand, the rattling bedeviled his wife while he was away in London; he therefore suggested that she connect the balls by a metal wire, to conduct the current silently.)

OIL ON WATER: "THE LEARNED…ARE APT TO SLIGHT TOO MUCH THE KNOWLEDGE OF THE VULGAR"

Charles Tanford's *Ben Franklin Stilled the Waves* bears a subtitle in eighteenth-century style: *An Informal History of Pouring Oil on Water with Reflections on the Ups and Downs of Scientific Life in General.* He describes the context and consequences of a research odyssey that stems from one of Franklin's simplest experiments. It was done toward the end of his long sojourn in England as a trade representative, when ominous political waves were cresting. Here is Franklin's account, excerpted from a letter to William Brownrigg in 1773. It responds to Brownrigg's questions about the experiment, but begins by referring to an earlier experiment, of the culinary variety:

> …I suppose Mrs. Brownrigg did not succeed in making the Parmesan Cheese, since we have heard nothing of it….
> …I had when a Youth, read and smiled at Pliny's Account of a Practice…to still the Waves by pouring Oil into the Sea…it has been of late too much the Mode to slight the Learning of the Ancients. The Learned too, are apt to slight too much the Knowledge of the Vulgar…This art of smoothing the Waves with Oil, is an Instance of both.

…at Clapham I observed a large pond very rough with the Wind. I fetched out a Cryet of Oil, and dropt a little of it on the Water. I saw it spread itself with surprising Swiftness upon the Surface…the Oil tho' not more than a Tea Spoonful produced an instant Calm, over a Space several yards square, which spread amazingly, and extended itself gradually…making all that Quarter of the Pond, perhaps half an acre, as smooth as a Looking Glass.

…It seems as if a mutual Repulsion between its particles took Place.…The Quantity of this Force and the Distance to which it will operate, I have not yet ascertained, but I think it a curious Enquiry, and I wish to understand whence it arises.

This is one of my favorites among Ben's letters. Clearly, his always lively curiosity was excited. He devoted many pages to conjectures, reluctant to take leave of such intriguing phenomena, regardless of their practical import. That's something Franklin did all his life.

Later in his letter, Franklin writes:

…this is not a Chamber Experiment; for it cannot very well be repeated in a Bowl or Dish of Water on a Table. A considerable Surface of Water is necessary to give Room for the Expansion of a small Quantity of Oil. In a Dish of Water if the smallest Drop of Oil be let fall in the Middle, the whole Surface is presently covered with a thin greasy Film proceeding from the drop; but as soon as that Film has reached the Sides of the Dish, no more will issue from the drop, but it remains in the Form of Oil, the Sides of the Dish putting a Stop to its Dissipation by prohibiting the farther Expansion of the Film.

What Franklin could not understand in the eighteenth century is easy to picture today. Suppose you have a little pile of oil molecules on top of water. Oil and water molecules don't want to mix. So we imagine the pile of oil molecules tumbling down and spreading out, and continuing to spread until it's a monolayer.

Yet more must be said. Franklin knew that oil and water don't mix, and even considered matter to be composed of corpuscles. That was Newton's view in his *Opticks*, which exemplified for Franklin how to pursue experimental science. Why didn't Franklin suppose that oil corpuscles would spread out to form a cheek-by-jowl monolayer? Tanford suggests it's because the notion of corpuscles precluded recognizing a key property of molecules.

When Newton spoke of corpuscles, he imagined that they were the smallest indivisible units of matter, like the atoms of the ancient Greeks. But if corpuscles were indeed the smallest unit, they would all have exactly the same properties. That's why Franklin, who knew that like repels like, thought in terms of the mutual repulsion of oil corpuscles. The repulsion might spread them far apart, so there need be no relation between the corpuscles' size and their spacing in the oil film.

Franklin could have obtained the first fairly good estimates of molecular size and mass, had he not lacked an elementary molecular concept.

Molecules, as we now know, can have parts with very different properties, especially if they are big molecules—just as in human chemistry, large organizations often have antagonistic parts. In this case, one end of the olive-oil molecule loves water, but the other end hates it. This produces a monomolecular film, since the oil spreads until the water-loving ends are all submerged, while the water-hating hydrocarbon ends snuggle together, cheek-by-jowl.

If the molecules in the film form a cheek-by-jowl layer, one molecule thick, Franklin's experiment provides an extremely simple way to determine the size of a molecule and even its mass. He tossed on the pond a volume of one teaspoonful of oil (about 2 cubic centimeters—eighteenth-century teaspoons were smaller than ours) and estimated it spread over an area of half an acre (about 20,000,000 square centimeters). The ratio of volume to area gives the thickness of the film (roughly a hundred billionths of a centimeter). How small is that? I like Victor Weisskopf's favorite comparison: the width of a typical molecule is about one ten-thousandth of the thickness of a human hair. Another vivid answer was favored by John Strutt, Lord Rayleigh: the size of a molecule compares with the width of your thumbnail about as one-third of a second compares to a year. From the molecule's size we can estimate its volume; then the known density of the oil allows us to determine approximately the molecular mass. Franklin could have obtained the first fairly good estimates of molecular size and mass more than a century before anyone else, had he not lacked an elementary molecular concept. Elementary it seems now, but not so in historical context.

In fact, in 1890, Lord Rayleigh got the first quantitative estimates of the size and mass of a molecule from a scaled-down version of Franklin's experiment. The story is an illuminating one about both the continuity and the personality of science honorably conducted.

Rayleigh used a tub of water about 6 feet long (perhaps his Victorian bathtub) and repeatedly added oil drops to find out what sized individual drop would spread to cover the whole tub surface. He used little bits of camphor to tell how much of the surface the oil covered. On a clean water surface, bits of camphor will scoot around because camphor molecules dissolve somewhat in water, thereby causing the camphor bits to recoil much like the exhaust spewing from a mini-rocket. When oil covers the water, the camphor doesn't dissolve anymore, so the mini-rocket sits still.

Among other intriguing episodes traced by Tanford, we come now to the one I suspect would have pleased Franklin most. Soon after Rayleigh's paper about molecular size came out, he received a letter from a lady in Braunschweig, Germany, named Agnes Pockels. She was a housewife with no formal scientific education. For the past 10 years, as a hobby, she had been doing experiments in her kitchen to study surface tension and wetting phenomena. On reading Rayleigh's paper, she realized that her experimental technique was much better than his, and her insight at least comparable. So she wrote to tell him about her work.

Essentially, her apparatus was a rectangular baking dish, with a glass ruler across it. The ruler could be slid along to scrape the water surface clean. Franklin had said that his experiment wouldn't work on a small scale because he found a little smudge of grease from his finger was enough to contaminate the whole surface. The scraper employed by Pockels swept away that crucial difficulty, making it easy to clean the surface quickly and repeatedly. She had also devised an elegant way to measure surface tension: she hung a button from a thread and measured the force needed to barely raise the button from the surface.

To his credit, Rayleigh, with the help of his wife, translated Pockels's letter into English, wrote to her several times to clear up some points, and then submitted her paper to *Nature*, with this benediction:

> I shall be obliged if you can find space for the accompanying translation of an interesting letter which I have received from a German lady, who with very homely appliances has arrived at valuable results respecting the behavior of contaminated water surfaces. The earlier part of Miss Pockels' letter covers nearly the same ground as some of my own recent work, and in the main harmonizes with it. The later sections seem to me very suggestive, raising, if they do not fully answer, many important questions.

This letter was the first of a series of important papers by Pockels. Forty years later, the distinguished surface chemist Irving Langmuir would say that she had "laid the foundation for nearly all modern work with films on water."

I shall mention just one further descendant of Franklin's oil-on-water experiment. A line of work extending over 60 years finally established in the late 1960s the nature of cell membranes. This showed that the membranes are chiefly constructed from lipid molecules. These are akin to olive oil; they have a water-loving end and a fatty, water-hating end. In all living things, cells are packaged in a double layer of lipid molecules, termed a bilayer. This has the fatty ends of pairs of lipid molecules snuggled together, while the water-loving ends interact with the aqueous environment inside and outside the cell.

Bringing Franklin out from the shadow of his icon would at least add irony when confronting attacks now heard in Congress on "curiosity-driven" research as a luxury, as merely a hobby of professors, and even as an unpatriotic activity.

In his last years, Franklin—ever enthusiastic about science—liked to show visitors a glass model in his study that demonstrated the circulation of blood in the human body. He would have been delighted to learn that the packaging of the red blood cells is so simply related to the oil film he spread on the pond at Clapham. And, as Tanford says, he "would have enjoyed the unity of science that could make so marvelous a connection."

BEYOND THE ICON

As an icon, Ben Franklin has long been represented as the supreme utilitarian: striving always for what is useful and sensible, both in human affairs and in science. But this shortchanges his major role in science. The historical Franklin is far more instructive than the icon. In at least three respects, Franklin's work is pertinent to current debates about science policy and science education.

First, as both Cohen and Trefil emphasize, Franklin lived in an age even more eager for practical results than ours. Yet he lever limited his scientific studies to what he could anticipate would be useful. In current parlance, his research was "curiosity-driven." When he took up electricity, it was just an irresistible toy. He could not foresee that his work would establish a new field of physics, vital for understanding the nature of matter and radiation, key to myriad applications. The link Franklin made between leaping sparks and lightning bolts indeed resembles that which Newton made between falling apples and planetary orbits. Both exemplify the paradigm of Francis Bacon: advances in basic science inevitably create opportunities for practical applications. But neither the advances nor the applications can be foretold.

In making this case to public officials and the media, we should bring Franklin out from the shadow of his icon. That would at least add Franklinesque irony when confronting attacks now heard in Congress on "curiosity-driven" research as a luxury, as merely a hobby of professors, and even as an unpatriotic activity.

Second, we would do well to appreciate how Franklin's immense scientific reputation played a major role in the success of the American Revolution. His arrival in Paris coincided with the signing of a nonaggression pact between France and England, ending 20 years of conflict. Although the pact specified that France not aid any rebellion against the British, Franklin's stature helped him gain influence with the French court and thus obtain crucial arms and funds to aid the American colonies. Turgot's famous praise of Franklin might be recast as: "Snatching the lightning from the sky enabled him to take the scepter from tyrants."

A Franklinesque query: Now that America has become the leading debtor nation, might not respect for our science again be a significant factor in attracting vital foreign funds?

Finally, the historical Franklin can render unique service in our efforts to promote science education and literacy. In our society, science is regarded not as part of our general culture, but almost as the preserve of a distinct species.

This attitude, which greatly handicaps all aspects of education, is reinforced by the fact that we confine science to separate courses. The multifaceted Ben Franklin ought to appear throughout the curriculum, breaking down those barriers. He is so accessible and such fun! Everyone should repeat and enjoy some of his simple experiments, admire his descriptions and logic, trace the reception and legacy of his work. Doing so would not only show the rewards of inquiry pursued for its own sake. It would also help students and citizens understand how science reshapes human culture—in his time, in ours, and beyond.

Dudley R. Herschbach, Ph.D. '58, Baird professor of science, was awarded the Nobel Prize in chemistry in 1986 for developing techniques that enabled scientists to study the collisions that take place between pairs of molecules. This article is adapted from a lecture first presented at the American Academy of Arts and Sciences and repeated last March at Harvard's Science Center.

The author would like to thank Daniel Rosenberg, who for years has prepared the demonstrations in his freshman chemistry course, for the demonstratsions accompanying presentations of this lecture; and William Andrewes, curator of the Harvard Collection of Historical Scientific Instruments.

Flora MacDonald

By a twist of fate, the Scottish heroine who helped Bonnie Prince Charlie escape the British in 1746 immigrated to North Carolina in 1774, only to find herself allied with the Crown during the American Revolution.

By Jean Creznic

"… FLORA MACDONALD, a name that will be mentioned in history, and if courage and fidelity be virtues, mentioned with honour," wrote Doctor Samuel Johnson in *Journey to the Western Isles* after he and his friend James Boswell visited her in Scotland in September 1773. As Johnson predicted, her name is honored among her fellow Scots, and her life has become legend, a story that took this eighteenth-century heroine from the islands of Scotland to the colony of North Carolina, on the eve of America's Revolutionary War.

Flora MacDonald gained renown and the affection of her Scottish Highland countrymen when she helped Prince Charles Edward, the Stuart pretender to the British throne, escape capture in 1746. Her later association with America, though brief, placed her in the thick of the Revolutionary War.

Flora was born in 1722 in Milton, South Uist, one of the Hebrides Islands that lie off the western coast of Scotland.

Her father died when she was a child, and her mother remarried in 1728 and moved to the Hebridean Isle of Skye. Ever the independent thinker, six-year-old Flora declared that she would stay in Milton with her older brother, Angus, rather than go to her mother's new home. She said that she would be happier with him there than in a house that was strange to her. Later, an aunt and uncle took charge and sent her to school in Edinburgh, after which she lived as a member of a privileged family, spending her time in ladylike pursuits, frequently traveling to visit relatives and friends.

The adventure that brought Flora fame began as she was staying with relatives at Ormaclade, on South Uist. The talk in Scotland was all about Prince Charles Edward Stuart, known by the Scots as Bonnie Prince Charlie, and how he might reestablish the Catholic Stuarts as Great Britain's rightful rulers. The prince was the grandson of the Stuart King James II, who had reigned in Britain during 1685–88. English sentiment against Catholicism ran high during his reign, and James, whose sympathies leaned more and more toward Rome, fled to France in 1688 when the overthrow of the throne appeared imminent. His son, also named James, spent his life in France and Italy, plotting to regain his father's throne.

During the first half of the eighteenth century, the pressure on James's son, Charles Edward, to succeed to the throne

was enormous, but England under Protestant King George II had no intention of allowing the Catholic Stuarts to wear the crown. Despite the fact there was no encouragement for Prince Charles Edward from that quarter, agents of the exiled Stuarts traveled the Scottish Highlands, striving to enlist the support of the Highland clans. They succeeded in rallying a small band of Jacobites (supporters of the House of Stuart), most of them MacDonalds, to the cause.

Arriving in Scotland in August 1745, the prince and his followers launched their long awaited campaign. Although well begun, the effort was nevertheless doomed to failure and ended the next year on April 16, 1746, at the Battle of Culloden, where the prince and his five thousand Highland supporters were crushed by some nine thousand infantrymen led by George II's son, William, the Duke of Cumberland.

The English showed the weakened Scots no mercy, and this defeat sealed the fate of the prince and of the resurgence of the House of Stuart. Charles Edward fled for his life after the battle, hiding from the Duke of Cumberland's soldiers wherever he could, finally making his way to the western isles, and Flora MacDonald.

Some say that Flora's stepfather, Hugh MacDonald—a sympathizer of Prince Charles Edward despite his position as the commander of the government militia in South Uist—suggested her participation in the escape. Others credit the scheme to the prince's comrade and fellow soldier, Captain Felix O'Neill, who was acquainted with Flora and knew her to be a young woman of admirable common sense. Still other accounts say that her actions were entirely spontaneous. Whichever version of the events is accurate, the facts surrounding the plan that Flora devised and carried out have never been disputed.

With a bounty of £30,000 offered for his capture, the Bonnie Prince was hunted by British troops as well as local militia. Every traveler was suspect, and a passport was required of anyone wishing to leave the island or to come ashore. Careful planning would be required to effect the escape of such a notorious fugitive.

Flora, who already had her passport, built a scheme around her intended trip to see her sick mother at Armadale on the Isle of Skye. Once she succeeded in getting the prince to Skye, he would make his way to mainland Scotland and be picked up by a French naval vessel, which would transport him to safety in Europe.

Hugh MacDonald supplied the passports that Flora needed for the several boatmen, a manservant, and an Irish spinning maid who would help care for his ailing wife. According to the plan, Betty Burke, the Irish maid, would make the crossing bundled up against the wind and sea in a bonnet, cloak, and shawl, making it difficult for anyone to have a close look at her face—all for the best since "Betty," an ignorant and ungainly looking servant girl, would indeed be the Bonnie Prince.

Daylight lingers in June in the Hebrides, which increased the risk of the travelers being discovered by government scouts. The prince's party decided to hide themselves on shore until dark, when there would be less chance of being intercepted by British patrol vessels. In spite of high winds and stormy seas, they set out for the Isle of Skye on the night of June 28. En route, they narrowly avoided at least one British boat that passed so close they could hear the sailors' voices.

Landing on Skye the following morning, they made their way to Portree,

where friends hid the prince until he could exchange his female attire for kilt and plaid, then sail to the mainland, and on to France. At Portree, Prince Charles Edward and Flora parted, never to meet again.[1]

Flora spent a few days with her mother, then went to visit her brother at Milton. But word of the adventure got out. The authorities quickly apprehended Flora, and after questioning her, imprisoned her aboard a British sloop-of-war. In July, the ship made for Leith, just beside Edinburgh on the Firth of Forth, where it lay for several weeks.

By this time, all of Scotland seemed to have learned of Flora's part in the prince's escape, and many people, proclaiming her a heroine, came to visit her on the prison ship. November found her in the Tower of London, but she was soon paroled to the house of a Mr. Dick, an official Messenger at Arms in whose home prisoners of war who could pay for their keep were permitted to stay. Virtually free, Flora was allowed to visit friends, albeit always accompanied by Mr. Dick's daughters. She became something of a celebrity in London, and wealthy benefactors soon appeared with funds for her support at Mr. Dick's home.

Freed once and for all in July 1747, Flora headed straight for Scotland and home. She went to stay with her mother at Armadale, but her adventures had brought her such renown that she was a coveted visitor about Skye.

On November 6, 1750, Flora—reportedly dressed in a gown of Stuart tartan—married Allen MacDonald. But living happily ever after was not to be the lot of Flora and Allen. Hard times for the Highlanders increased after the short-lived campaign that had ended at Culloden, and those who had sided with Prince Charles Edward, especially the few who had given him shelter as he fled, seemed to face the most difficulties.

Over the years, the financial situation of Flora and Allen and their seven children steadily worsened. Feeling they had nothing to look forward to in Scotland but more oppression, the couple decided to leave for America. In 1774, they followed a growing number of their neighbors on Skye, including their married

daughter, Anne, to North Carolina.[2] Leaving their youngest son and daughter with friends in Scotland who would see to the youngsters' education, they took two of their older boys with them.

Flora and Allen were met in North Carolina with great fanfare and ceremony; friends held a ball in her honor at Wilmington. When the festivities subsided after several days, the new immigrants moved on to Cross Creek (now Fayetteville), where Flora stayed while Allen searched for a site on which to establish their new home. Near Rockingham, he found a place that would suit them and named it "Killiegrey." The property already had a dwelling and several outbuildings, so Flora, in her fifties by now, settled in, perhaps thinking she had found peace and security at last.

Their neighbors treated the famous Flora and her husband with great respect, and they came to occupy a prominent position in the community. Aside from one claim that Allen built and operated a grist mill on their land, almost nothing is known of their everyday life. J. P. MacLean's *Flora MacDonald in America*, published in 1909, does say, however, that "their influence was everywhere felt and acknowledged."

The peace that Flora was enjoying proved to be momentary; the American War for Independence erupted, and even remote Killiegrey soon became entangled in the troubles. At first it seemed that the North Carolina Scots would take up the American cause, urged on by a committee of patriots who conferred "with the gentlemen who have lately arrived from the Highlands in Scotland to settle in this province… to explain to them the nature of our unhappy controversy with Great Britain, and to advise and urge them to unite with the other inhabitants of America in defense of their rights.…"

But Josiah Martin, royal governor of North Carolina, did everything in his power to persuade the Highlanders to remain loyal to the Crown. In view of the treatment they had suffered at home at the hands of the British, it seemed unlikely they would ally themselves with the British cause in America. But threats, propaganda, and coercion from Governor Martin and his agents prevailed, and the

Scots, many of them MacDonalds, were won over. They organized a sizable army of volunteers, with Allen as a colonel.

In February 1776, events rushed toward a climax for the Highlanders. Word came that they were to meet a British fleet scheduled to land at Cape Fear and then nip the revolution in North Carolina in the bud. Although they were as secretive as possible, the difficulty inherent in concealing the movements of groups of armed men soon led to the patriots learning what was taking place.

An estimated 1,500 to 3,000 Highlanders assembled for the march, and Flora came out to cheer them on their way. Mounted on a white horse, she reviewed the troops, and then rode along for a short distance with Allen and their son-in-law, Alexander MacLeod, a captain in the regiment. With all attempts at maintaining secrecy apparently forgotten, the marching column made a dramatic departure, "drums beating, pipes playing, flags flying."

The Highlanders headed east to the coast, marching at night and criss-crossing creeks along the way in an attempt to evade opposing forces. They eluded Colonel James Moore, who, with about 650 troops from the First North Carolina Continentals, had been sent to head them off at Corbett's Ferry on the Black River.

When he realized that he had been outmaneuvered, Moore ordered Colonel Richard Caswell, commanding some eight hundred Parisan Rangers from New Bern, to cut the Scots off at Moore's Creek Bridge. Caswell and his men, along with 150 other troops commanded by Colonel Alexander Lillington, reached the bridge and quickly constructed earthworks on the west side of the creek. Deciding to abandon these works and meet the loyalist troops on the other side of the creek, they crossed the bridge, removing a section of flooring behind them as they went. After digging new entrenchments, they waited for the Scots to arrive.

Seeing the abandoned earthworks, the Highlanders assumed that their crossing of the bridge would be unopposed.

Nonetheless, Colonel Donald McLeod, the Scots' senior officer, led a charge, shouting "King George and Broadswords" as he ran toward the bridge. Shielded by breastworks, the Americans, who had two cannon to assist them, opened fire, almost immediately shattering the attack.

The first battle of the Revolution fought in North Carolina, "the Insurrection of the MacDonalds" left many Highlanders dead or wounded; a number of the loyalist troops drowned after losing their footing while trying to cross the section of the bridge where the flooring had been removed.[3] Many of the Highlanders were taken prisoner, among them Allen MacDonald and his son Alexander, a lieutenant in the loyalist regiment, who were jailed in the town of Halifax.

Things went badly for Flora after the Battle of Moore's Creek Bridge. Recognizing the part she had played in recruiting Highlanders and her influential role in the Scottish settlements, the revolutionaries were not about to allow her to escape punishment. She was viewed with suspicion by those who took the patriot side and deeply resented by the families who had lost men in the battle at Moore's Creek. Summoned to appear before the local Committee of Safety, Flora answered the charges against her with dignity and courage, defending her activities among her Scottish countrymen. Although the committee permitted her to return to Killiegrey, her property was confiscated a year later.

In August 1777, after having been moved several times by his captors, Allen was permitted to go to New York City to negotiate an exchange for himself and his son, Alexander. He was on his honor "not to convey to the enemy or bring back any intelligence whatever of a political nature, and to return [to Reading, Pennsylvania] in a certain time to be fixed by his parole or when called for, on behalf of the United States."

By November, he had succeeded in his mission and soon joined his battalion in Nova Scotia, where he was stationed

at Fort Edward, in Windsor. Flora, having first made her way to British-held New York City with her daughter and grandsons, arrived there the next year. Her health had suffered from her ordeal, and in late 1779, Flora, her daughter, and the children sailed for Scotland.

Home at last, Flora went to stay in a cottage on her brother's property in Milton. In 1784, the war over and his regiment disbanded, Allen returned home to Flora. The couple went back to Kingsburgh House on Skye, where they had started their marriage. Less than six years later, on March 5, 1790, Flora died. One of the bed sheets on which Prince Charles Edward had slept so many years before served as her shroud. She had kept the sheet with her during her North American sojourn and carried it back again to Skye, requesting that she be buried in it when the time came.

By all accounts, Flora's funeral was the grandest ever seen on the Isle of Skye. The procession to the cemetery stretched for more than a mile. People had traveled from all the islands and from the mainland to pay their last respects to the patriotic lady in whose heart Scotland was always first.

NOTES

1. Charles Edward Stuart spent the next twenty years in Europe, devising futile plots to establish his claim to the British throne. He returned to Rome, the city of his birth, at the time of his father's death in 1766. He remained there until he died in 1788. His remains are entombed in the vaults of St. Peter's Basilica in Rome.

2. More than 23,000 Highland Scots left their homeland for the American colonies between 1764 and '76.

3. The surviving loyalist troops claimed that the Americans had greased the wooden girders of the bridge with soft soap and tallow after removing the flooring, causing the attackers to slip while trying to cross.

Jean Creznic is senior editor of Early American Homes *magazine and a student of Scottish lore.*

Founding Friendship

WASHINGTON, MADISON AND THE CREATION
OF THE AMERICAN REPUBLIC

Stuart Leibiger looks at one of the most significant relationships behind
the politics that produced the American Constitution.

The friendships and political collaborations among America's founding fathers have long been a source of fascination. In fact, scholars have generated a whole literature about the critical roles these collaborations played in the American Revolution, for example, the John Adams–Thomas Jefferson friendship that produced the Declaration of Independence, and that of James Madison and Alexander Hamilton that yielded the *Federalist Papers*, perhaps the greatest American political commentary ever written. Historians have also studied the James Madison–Thomas Jefferson collaboration that brought about, in the words of the documentary editor Julian Boyd, 'the most extended, the most elevated, the most significant exchange of letters between any two men in the whole sweep of American history'. Yet all this scholarship neglects the most important founding father of all: George Washington (1732–99).

Washington has been called the Revolution's 'Indispensable Man'. If you took him out of the equation, then most likely the American Revolution would have failed. Yet, none of the so-called 'great collaborations' that historians have written about includes Washington, whose friendship with James Madison was the most important association in the founding of the United States.

The American Revolution is unusual among modern world revolutions because it produced not a dictatorship, but a republic. One of the main reasons for this outcome was Washington's careful use of power. By never abusing it, and by giving it away, his power increased: from commander-in-chief

of the Continental Army in 1775, he became president of the Constitutional Convention of 1787, and finally President of the United States for two terms in 1789 and 1793. In these roles, he resisted the temptation to use the army as his personal bodyguard and remained true to the ideals of American Republicanism.

When he was commissioned to portray Washington in 1785, the celebrated French sculptor Jean-Antoine Houdon (1741–1828) chose not to depict the General's glorious victories at Trenton or Yorktown, but instead Houdon's statue of 1788 shows Washington in the act of retiring from the army, returning his military cloak and sword to the state and resuming civilian life, represented by a walking stick and ploughshare. Houdon understood that Washington exhibited greatness by returning power to the people, and by going home to Mount Vernon.

Few people today realise that Washington and Madison were close friends. On the surface they had little in common. True, both men came out of the Virginia gentry, and thus shared a distinct political and social culture, but the similarities end there. George Washington was a military officer and a farmer, a large and athletic man of action. He possessed intelligence, but not a university education. Gracious and magnanimous, he was also taciturn, demanding and unforgiving. In contrast, Madison was small and sickly, perhaps even an epileptic. A bookworm, educated at Princeton University, Madison was highly intellectual and philosophical. Though shy and retiring in large social gath-

Bridgeman Art Library/Stapleton Collection/Getty Images, USA

'The resignation of General Washington, December 23rd, 1783' after a painting by John Trumbull. Madison was not actually present at the resignation, but Trumbull decided to include him in this work. He stands to the right of the left door frame.

erings, he was remarkably sweet-tempered and a wonderful conversationalist.

The relationship flourished because each man shared similar goals and possessed something the other needed. Both were committed to finalising the American Revolution by establishing an extremely republican and energetic federal government. Washington relied on Madison's advice, pen and legislative skill, while Madison manipulated Washington's prestige to achieve his own political goals.

The two first came face to face in August 1781, when Washington marched his army through Philadelphia on his way south to try to capture British troops under General Cornwallis in Virginia. Madison, at the time, was a member of the Confederation Congress. The relationship had actually begun, however, years before in 1777, when Madison became a member of the Virginia council of state under Governor Patrick Henry. In this role, Madison engaged in an extensive correspondence between the Virginia executive and Washington, commander-in-chief of the Continental Army. The correspondence dealt primarily with keeping Washington's troops manned and supplied. Through this communication, Madison developed a tremendous admiration for Washington. He also received a first-hand education in

civilian-military relations from the finest practitioner of that delicate art. As a result, Madison became more continental minded, and supportive of Washington's attempts to turn the American army into a paid, professional force.

By 1780, the calibre of delegates to Congress had declined precipitously, as talented men opted for state over federal service. Alarmed by this trend, Washington appealed to his native state to send men of the highest ability to Philadelphia. Virginia responded by electing four new delegates, including Madison. Thus Washington initiated Madison's advancement from state to federal service. During his years in Congress, Madison's political education continued. While in Philadelphia, he got to know Washington personally and their collaboration began.

The Newburgh Conspiracy exemplifies their association at this stage. In 1783, a faction of Congressmen (including Alexander Hamilton) and several Continental Army officers toyed with the idea of using a military *coup* led by Washington to scare Congress into raising revenue to pay the troops. At this moment the Revolution could have spun out of control. But the plan went nowhere, because Washington refused to have anything to do with it. During the crisis, he co-operated closely with a small group of moderate Congressmen, especially Madison.

While Washington pleaded with the army to have faith in Congress, Madison's forces worked feverishly on a plan to generate revenue, working within the republican ideals of the Revolution, rather than trying to scare Congress into raising money.

James Madison by Charles Willson Peale. The miniature was painted in 1783, the year Madison and Washington became allies over the Newburgh Conspiracy.

At the end of 1783, with the Revolutionary War over, both Washington and Madison retired to Virginia. Here they recognised something that few other Americans could see at this point: that the British Empire had been the glue that had held the thirteen colonies together. When Americans won their independence, the thirteen states started to spin off in separate directions, with new republics going their own ways. Washington and Madison believed that a new glue would have to be found to bind the states together again. They set about pushing for a stronger federal government.

In 1785, the two men launched a project to improve the Potomac River (making it navigable) deep into the Ohio country, then the western frontier. As the project grew beyond the borders of Virginia, more and more states participated—first Maryland, then Pennsylvania, and so on. The movement led to a series of conventions, first at Mount Vernon in 1785, then at Annapolis in 1786, and finally at Philadelphia in 1787, which of course produced the United States Constitution.

Between 1784 and 1787, the relationship between Washington and Madison developed as they became political confidants and intimate friends. The growth of their friendship is echoed in subtle shifts in the way they addressed each other and signed off in their letters. A typical eighteenth-century letter between two gentlemen might have closed with the words, 'your most obedient and humble servant'. At first, Washington's and Madison's letters ended in fairly generic terms. But after Madison made a three-day visit to Mount Vernon in 1785, Washington began adding the word 'affectionately' to the closings of his letters. Madison did not immediately reciprocate—not surprisingly considering he was nineteen years Washington's junior. But Madison visited Mount Vernon again in 1786. After this second visit, he, too, began closing his letters with the word 'affectionately'.

Exactly what went on during Madison's sojourns at Mount Vernon is hard to say. One hopes to find a detailed account in Washington's diary; instead, he writes only, 'home all day with Mr Madison'. Washington's reticence nevertheless speaks volumes. For him to forgo his daily ride to his farms to stay at home with a guest was truly remarkable. Clearly there was not only socialising, but serious business taking place. Madison visited Washington's plantation a total of ten times between 1785 and 1791. During the visits, which lasted up to a week, the two discussed important state affairs, such as Washington's decision to attend the Federal Convention and to accept the presidency.

Washington was reluctant to participate in the Federal Convention of 1787 because he did not want to waste his immense prestige on what could well turn out to be an abortive assembly (as the Annapolis convention had been which he had wisely not attended). Acting on his own, Madison, as a member of the Virginia legislature, nominated Washington as a delegate to the convention. When Washington insisted that his name be removed from the Virginia list, Madison persuaded him to leave it there. Even if Washington planned not to attend, Madison argued, the idea that he would participate would convince other states to send their best men. Madison's tactics worked. Washington's name secured a full turnout, allowing him to attend after all.

The fifty-five delegates to the Federal Convention met from May to September 1787 in Philadelphia's Independence Hall, then known as the Pennsylvania State House because it was the state capitol building. Washington and Madison stood out in their commitment to a government that was both very powerful and extremely republican. They voted alike nearly all of the time. The convention was often frustrating, especially for Madison, who failed to work many favourite details into the Constitution. On days that he suffered bitter defeats, such as the day the convention decided to grant two senators to each state instead of basing Senate representation on population, as Madison had hoped, he and Washington would dine together in the evening, Washington bucking up his dejected friend.

Individually, Washington and Madison played vital roles at Philadelphia, but their collaboration was also crucial in that together they constituted a bulwark within the Virginia delegation. Without Washington and Madison, the Virginia delegation as a whole might have opposed the Constitution. As a pair they offset fellow members George Mason and Edmund Randolph, who opposed the final document. Had the most influential state refused to endorse the Constitution at Philadelphia, ratification could never have been achieved.

During the ratification campaign, Washington—as the nation's inevitable choice for the presidency—maintained a low profile. Nevertheless, he collaborated closely with Madison to win approval of the Constitution. Together Washington at

Richmond Decr. 7. 1786

A page from a 1786 letter from Madison to George Washington, whom he had by now visited three times.

Mount Vernon in the south and Madison at Congress in the north helped co-ordinate the entire Federalist campaign. Madison secretly provided Washington with copies of his essays for the *Federalist Papers* and other propaganda to be reprinted in Richmond. Interestingly, Madison revealed his authorship of the essays to Washington, but not to Thomas Jefferson or even to his own father.

Madison had not planned to attend the Virginia ratifying convention because he thought that the authors of the Constitution should not pass judgement on it. But Washington, knowing that Madison alone could answer the Antifederalist objections of Patrick Henry, convinced him to seek election. At the Virginia Convention in June 1788, Madison delivered perhaps his finest performance, parrying Henry's every thrust until the Constitution won approval by a narrow margin. However, Madison became so stressed by the contest that he became ill. Back at Mount Vernon, Washington, as worried about Madison's health as he was about the Constitution, wrote pleading with him to take a few days vacation at Mount Vernon, where he could regain his strength. In closing, Washington wrote:

> I can assure you that no one will be happier in your company than your sincere & Affecte Servt, Go: Washington.

Not often did so exacting a man as Washington urge someone to take a break, especially with the country's fate at stake. But he could see that Madison's labours might take too heavy a toll on a man whose friendship he cherished and whose abilities he needed.

Washington's election as first president under the new Constitution was a foregone conclusion. However, Madison made sure that his friend did not waver about accepting the presidency. To ghostwrite his inaugural address, Washington turned to his collaborator. Washington provided him with an outline of major points, which Madison worked into a draft. Madison, in short, served much like a modern speechwriter—while Washington deserves credit for the ideas, both men deserve credit for

Bridgeman Art Library/Stapleton Collection/Getty Images, U.S.A.

The Pennsylvanian State House, scene of the 1787 Federal Convention. As a pair, Washington and Madison had a crucial bearing on the convention's outcome.

the language. Not only did Madison ghostwrite Washington's First Inaugural Address, as a member of the House of Representatives he wrote the House's reply to the Address, and, finally, the President's response to the House's reply. This dialogue with himself captures the central role Madison played in launching the federal government in 1789. Even though he held no official position, he acted as something of a prime minister, providing a bridge between the legislature and the executive.

When Washington took office, he and John Adams were virtually the entire executive branch of the federal government because it took months to create the executive departments. For example, Thomas Jefferson did not come aboard as Secretary of State for nearly a year. Not only was Washington initially alone, but virtually everything he did set important precedents that would be followed by his successors. Aware of this responsibility, Washington relied heavily on his right-hand man during these months. Madison provided advice on policy, appointments and presidential etiquette.

He also acted as Washington's 'hidden-hand' in resolving the fiasco over a title for the President. In 1789, the Senate, led by John Adams, voted to bestow on Washington the elaborate title 'His Highness, the President of the United States of America, and Protector of Their Liberties'. Washington, who realised that such a designation sounded too monarchical, was horrified. But he had to be careful not to offend or alienate the Senate. So he briefed Madison that the House must insist on the simpler title 'Mr President'. Madison convinced the House to hold firm, and eventually the Senate backed down.

Treasury Secretary Alexander Hamilton's financial programme is often seen as having driven a wedge between Wash-

ington and the emerging Republican Party, including Madison. But more important than the disagreements that arose between them over Hamilton's funding and assumption plan is the fact that all sides supported the Compromise of 1790. This bargain not only settled the national debt, but also permanently located the national capital on the Potomac River (after a ten-year stop in Philadelphia during the 1790s).

After 1790, with the cabinet finally in place, Madison stopped providing day-to-day advice, but he was still called in when precedent-setting situations arose. The best example is Washington's planned retirement in 1792. Concerned not to establish a tradition of dying in office that might allow his successors to serve for life, Washington hoped to retire at the end of one term. He turned to Madison for help in drafting a farewell message. Madison pleaded with the President to serve another term, warning that without Washington's stabilising influence, the emerging political parties might destroy the fledgling nation. Eventually, Washington agreed to serve a second term.

A year into this, Washington's Secretary of State, Thomas Jefferson, unhappy over constantly fighting Hamilton in cabinet meetings, decided to resign. Hoping to replace Jefferson with a Republican strong enough to balance the Federalist Hamilton, Washington invited Madison to succeed Jefferson. But Madison, equally reluctant to become locked in combat with Hamilton, declined. Madison's refusal to join the cabinet was a crucial turning point both in Washington's presidency and in the two men's friendship. Without a strong Republican in the cabinet, Washington's policies inevitably turned Federalist because virtually all his advisers were Federalists.

'View of Congress on the Road to Philadelphia'. Senator Robert Morris of Pennsylvania leads members of Congress to their new abode, temporary seat of the government from 1790 to 1800.

Despite their growing political differences, Washington and Madison remained close friends. Even as late as 1794, Washington and his wife, Martha, played a pivotal role on behalf of Madison in helping to arrange his marriage. Dolley Todd, a young Quaker widow, had lost her husband in the 1793 yellow fever epidemic that ravaged Philadelphia. Many suitors, including James Madison, came to court her. Finding that the forty-three-year-old Madison had been courting the twenty-six-year-old Dolley, Washington's wife Martha summoned Dolley to the President's house. Dolley's grand-niece recorded what happened:

> A report soon got about of their engagement; such unwonted attentions from Mr Madison excited comment...
>
> It reached the Presidential mansion, where General and Mrs Washington were much interested; and impatient to hear the truth, sent for Mrs Todd, who all unconscious obeyed the summons at once.
>
> 'Dolley', said Mrs Washington, 'is it true that you are engaged to James Madison?' The fair widow, taken aback, answered stammeringly, 'No', she 'thought not'. 'If it is so', Mrs Washington continued, 'do not be ashamed to confess it: rather be proud; he will make thee a good husband, and all the better for being so much older. We both approve of it; the esteem and friendship existing between Mr Madison and my husband is very great, and we would wish thee to be happy'.

And so, with a little encouragement from the Washingtons, Dolley married James, or, as she called him 'the great Little

Madison'. The ceremony took place on September 15th, 1794, at Harewood, the home of Washington's nephew George Steptoe Washington, near present Charles Town, West Virginia.

On the day he died Washington complained about having been betrayed by Madison.

Sadly, much of the goodwill generated by Madison's marriage was shattered by the Whiskey Rebellion of 1794 (in response to Hamilton's Whiskey Tax of 1791, which excited strong feeling from the backcountry where whiskey was the chief commodity, culminating in open rebellion in the four western counties of Pennsylvania). Unlike many Republicans, Madison supported Washington's decision to put down the Whiskey Rebellion by force. But he could not support his friend's decision to blame the rebellion on the Democratic Societies and political clubs that supported the Republican Party. Madison's act of defiance in this respect infuriated Washington, causing him to question the younger man's loyalty to him personally and to the nation. From this point onwards the friendship between the two men went downhill, as their politics polarised; Washington, increasingly Federalist, wanted to go further in his quest for a strong federal government. While Madison, staunch Republican, worried that the President's policies—political, financial, and industrial—threatened to restore

America's connection to Britain that had been severed during the Revolution.

The controversy over the 1795 Jay Treaty with Britain confirmed Washington's suspicions about Madison. Madison and the Republicans opposed the Jay Treaty because they believed that it neglected American interests, and that it virtually overturned the American Revolution by re-attaching the United States to Britain. When Republicans in the House of Representatives tried to block the appropriations necessary to implement the treaty, a major showdown between Washington and Madison ensued. The issue was whether the treaty power belonged only to the President and Senate, or whether the House could pass judgement on treaties as well by refusing appropriations. Not only did Madison loose this fight over the Jay Treaty, he lost his friendship with Washington as well. Convinced that Madison's behaviour had been virtually treasonous, Washington broke off their association once and for all.

HT Archive
Dolly Payne Todd (1768–1849), who married Madison in September 1794.

After they both retired to Virginia in March 1797, neither man saw or corresponded with the other again. Instead, they drifted further apart ideologically. On the day he died Washington complained about having been betrayed by Madison. On December 13th, 1799, Washington, suffering from a cold, spent the evening reading newspapers with Tobias Lear, his secretary. According to Lear, Washington

> requested me to read to him the debates of the Virginia Assembly... On hearing Mr Madison's observations... he appeared much affected and spoke with some degree of asperity on the subject, which I endeavored to moderate, as I always did on such occasions.

President Washington in evening dress, c. 1793.

The next night, the first president died of complications from an inflamed throat. One can't help wondering whether yelling about Madison had helped initiate his demise.

In many ways Washington and Madison have been misunderstood. Washington has been portrayed as a popular figurehead, a hands-off leader who reigned, but did not rule. His collaboration with Madison casts him in a new light, showing that he possessed a strong constitutional vision and always maintained control of his administration. Indeed, he was the central politician of his age. Conversely, the relationship with Washington shows that Madison richly deserves the attention historians have lavished on him as the Father of the Constitution. He was Washington's ideal collaborator in meeting the challenges posed by American independence: the need to design a government where the majority rules, but the minority is protected.

Why has the greatest partnership of the American founding, also been the most unheralded? Perhaps because Washington and Madison kept it a secret, with one or both partners working behind the scenes. Even at its zenith in 1789 and 1790, only the highest federal officials had an inkling of its existence, and few of them understood its true extent. The main evidence of their collaboration was their private correspondence, which each guarded carefully as long as he lived. Madison never wrote a tell-all book after Washington died, revealing his insider status in the first administration. Not only did Madison avoid enhancing his own reputation at Washington's expense, he (unlike John Adams) never became jealous of Washington's fame. Instead he quietly enjoyed knowing that he had been the Indispensable Man's 'Indispensable Collaborator'.

FOR FURTHER READING

Stuart Leibiger, *Founding Friendship: George Washington, James Madison, and the Creation of the American Republic* (University Press of Virginia, 1999); Lance Banning, *The Sacred Fire of Liberty: James Madison and the Founding of the Federal Republic* (Cornell University Press, 1995); Drew McCoy, *The Last of The Fathers: James Madison and the Republican Legacy* (Cambridge University Press, 1989); John E. Ferling, *The First of Men: A Life of George Washington* (University of Tennessee Press, 1988); Garry Wills, *Cincinnatus: George Washington and the Enlightenment* (Doubleday, 1984); Ralph Ketcham, *James Madison: A Biography* (Macmillan New York, 1971).

www.mountvernon.org

www.virginia.edu/gwpapers

www.virginia.edu/pjm

www.montpelier.org

Stuart Leibiger is Assistant Professor of History at La Salle University, Philadelphia.

Making Sense of the Fourth of July

The DECLARATION OF INDEPENDENCE is not what Thomas Jefferson thought it was when he wrote it—and that is why we celebrate it

By Pauline Maier

JOHN ADAMS THOUGHT AMERICANS would commemorate their Independence Day on the second of July. Future generations, he confidently predicted, would remember July 2, 1776, as "the most memorable Epocha, in the History of America" and celebrate it as their "Day of Deliverance by solemn Acts of Devotion to God Almighty. It ought to be solemnized with Pomp and Parade, with Shews, Games, Sports, Guns, Bells, Bonfires and Illuminations from one End of this Continent to the other from this Time forward forever more."

His proposal, however odd it seems today, was perfectly reasonable when he made it in a letter to his wife, Abigail. On the previous day, July 2, 1776, the Second Continental Congress had finally resolved "That these United Colonies are, and of right ought to be, free and independent States, that they are absolved from all allegiance to the British Crown, and that all political connection between them and the State of Great Britain is, and ought to be, totally dissolved." The thought that Americans might instead commemorate July 4, the day Congress adopted a "Declaration on Independency" that he had helped prepare, did not apparently occur to Adams in 1776. The Declaration of Independence was

one of those congressional statements that he later described as "dress and ornament rather than Body, Soul, or Substance," a way of announcing to the world the fact of American independence, which was for Adams the thing worth celebrating.

In fact, holding our great national festival on the Fourth makes no sense at all—unless we are actually celebrating not just independence but the Declaration of Independence. And the declaration we celebrate, what Abraham Lincoln called "the charter of our liberties," is a document whose meaning and function today are different from what they were in 1776. In short, during the nineteenth century the Declaration of Independence became not just a way of announcing and justifying the end of Britain's power over the Thirteen Colonies and the emergence of the United States as an independent nation but a statement of principles to guide stable, established governments. Indeed, it came to usurp in fact if not in law a role that Americans normally delegated to bills of rights. How did that happen? And why?

According to notes kept by Thomas Jefferson, the Second Continental Congress did not discuss the resolution on in-

dependence when it was first proposed by Virginia's Richard Henry Lee, on Friday, June 7, 1776, because it was "obliged to attend at that time to some other business." However, on the eighth, Congress resolved itself into a Committee of the Whole and "passed that day & Monday the 10th in debating on the subject." By then all contenders admitted that it had become impossible for the colonies ever again to be united with Britain. The issue was one of timing.

John and Samuel Adams, along with others such as Virginia's George Wythe, wanted Congress to declare independence right away and start negotiating foreign alliances and forming a more lasting confederation (which Lee also proposed). Others, including Pennsylvania's James Wilson, Edward Rutledge of South Carolina, and Robert R. Livingston of New York, argued for delay. They noted that the delegates of several colonies, including Maryland, Pennsylvania, Delaware, New Jersey, and New York, had not been "impowered" by their home governments to vote for independence. If a vote was taken immediately, those delegates would have to "retire" from Congress, and their states might secede from the union, which would seriously weaken the Americans' chance of realizing their independence. In the past, they said, members of Congress had followed the "wise & proper" policy of putting off major decisions "till the voice of the people drove us into it," since "they were our power, & without them our declarations could not be carried into effect." Moreover, opinion on independence in the critical middle colonies was "fast ripening & in a short time," they predicted, the people there would "join in the general voice of America."

CONGRESS DECIDED TO GIVE THE laggard colonies time and so delayed its decision for three weeks. But it also appointed a Committee of Five to draft a declaration of independence so that such a document could be issued quickly once Lee's motion passed. The committee's members included Jefferson, Livingston, John Adams, Roger Sherman of Connecticut, and Pennsylvania's Benjamin Franklin. The drafting committee met, decided what the declaration should say and how it would be organized, then asked Jefferson to prepare a draft.

Meanwhile, Adams—who did more to win Congress's consent to independence than any other delegate—worked feverishly to bring popular pressure on the governments of recalcitrant colonies so they would change the instructions issued to their congressional delegates. By June 28, when the Committee of Five submitted to Congress a draft declaration, only Maryland and New York had failed to allow their delegates to vote for independence. That night Maryland fell into line.

Even so, when the Committee of the Whole again took up Lee's resolution, on July 1, only nine colonies voted in favor (the four New England states, New Jersey, Maryland, Virginia, North Carolina, and Georgia). South Carolina and Pennsylvania opposed the proposition, Delaware's two delegates split, and New York's abstained because their twelve-month-old instructions precluded them from approving anything that impeded reconciliation with the mother country. Edward Rutledge now asked that Congress put off its decision until the next day, since he thought that the South

Carolina delegation would then vote in favor "for the sake of unanimity." When Congress took its final tally on July 2, the nine affirmative votes of the day before had grown to twelve: Not only South Carolina voted in favor, but so did Delaware—the arrival of Caesar Rodney broke the tie in that delegation's vote—and Pennsylvania. Only New York held out. Then on July 9 it, too, allowed its delegates to add their approval to that of delegates from the other twelve colonies, lamenting still the "cruel necessity" that made independence "unavoidable."

Once independence had been adopted, Congress again formed itself into a Committee of the Whole. It then spent the better part of two days editing the draft declaration submitted by its Committee of Five, rewriting or chopping off large sections of text. Finally, on July 4, Congress approved the revised Declaration and ordered it to be printed and sent to the several states and to the commanding officers of the Continental Army. By formally announcing and justifying the end of British rule, that document, as letters from Congress's president, John Hancock, explained, laid "the Ground & Foundation" of American self-government. As a result, it had to be proclaimed not only before American troops in the hope that it would inspire them to fight more ardently for what was now the cause of both liberty and national independence but throughout the country, and "in such a Manner, that the People may be universally informed of it."

Not until four days later did a committee of Congress—not Congress itself—get around to sending a copy of the Declaration to its emissary in Paris, Silas Deane, with orders to present it to the court of France and send copies to "the other Courts of Europe." Unfortunately the original letter was lost, and the next failed to reach Deane until November, when news of American independence had circulated for months. To make matters worse, it arrived with only a brief note from the committee and in an envelope that lacked a seal, an unfortunately slipshod way, complained Deane, to announce the arrival of the United States among the powers of the earth to "old and powerfull states." Despite the Decla-

ration's reference to the "opinions of mankind," it was obviously meant first and foremost for a home audience.

As copies of the Declaration spread through the states and were publicly read at town meetings, religious services, court days, or wherever else people assembled, Americans marked the occasion with appropriate rituals. They lit great bonfires, "illuminated" their windows with candles, fired guns, rang bells, tore down and destroyed the symbols of monarchy on public buildings, churches, or tavern signs, and "fixed up" on the walls of their homes broadside or newspaper copies of the Declaration of Independence.

BUT WHAT EXACTLY WERE THEY celebrating? The news, not the vehicle that brought it; independence and the assumption of self-government, not the document that announced Congress's decision to break with Britain. Considering how revered a position the Declaration of Independence later won in the minds and hearts of the people, Americans' disregard for it in the first years of the new nation verges on the unbelievable. One colonial newspaper dismissed the Declaration's extensive charges against the king as just another "recapitulation of injuries," one, it seems, in a series, and not particularly remarkable compared with earlier "catalogues of grievances." Citations of the Declaration were usually drawn from its final paragraph, which said that the united colonies "are and of Right ought to be Free and Independent states" and were "Absolved of all Allegiance to the British Crown"—words from the Lee resolution that Congress had inserted into the committee draft. Independence was new; the rest of the Declaration seemed all too familiar to Americans, a restatement of what they and their representatives had already said time and again.

The adoption of independence was, however, from the beginning confused with its declaration. Differences in the meaning of the word *declare* contributed to the confusion. Before the Declaration of Independence was issued—while, in fact, Congress was still editing Jefferson's draft—Pennsylvania newspapers announced that on July 2 the Continental Congress had "declared the United Colonies Free and Independent States," by which it meant simply that it had officially accepted that status. Newspapers in other colonies repeated the story. In later years the "Anniversary of the United States of America" came to be celebrated on the date Congress had approved the Declaration of Independence. That began, it seems, by accident. In 1777 no member of Congress thought of marking the anniversary of independence at all until July 3, when it was too late to honor July 2. As a result, the celebration took place on the Fourth, and that became the tradition. At least one delegate spoke of "celebrating the Anniversary of the Declaration of Independence," but over the next few years references to the anniversary of independence and of the Declaration seem to have been virtually interchangeable.

The Fourth of July was rarely celebrated during the Revolution and seems actually to have declined in popularity once the war was over.

Accounts of the events at Philadelphia on July 4, 1777, say quite a bit about the music played by a band of Hessian soldiers who had been captured at the Battle of Trenton the previous December, and the "splendid illumination" of houses, but little about the Declaration. Thereafter, in the late 1770s and 1780s, the Fourth of July was not regularly celebrated; indeed, the holiday seems to have declined in popularity once the Revolutionary War ended. When it was remembered, however, festivities seldom, if ever—to judge by newspaper accounts—involved a public reading of the Declaration of Independence. It was as if that document had done its work in carrying news of independence to the people, and it neither needed nor deserved further commemoration. No mention was made of Thomas Jefferson's role in composing the document, since that was not yet public knowledge, and no suggestion appeared that the Declaration itself was, as posterity would have it, unusually eloquent or powerful.

IN FACT, ONE OF THE VERY FEW PUBLIC comments on the document's literary qualities came in a Virginia newspaper's account of a 1777 speech by John Wilkes, an English radical and a long-time supporter of the Americans, in the House of Commons. Wilkes set out to answer a fellow member of Parliament who had attacked the Declaration of Independence as "a wretched composition, very ill written, drawn up with a view to captivate the people." Curiously, Wilkes seemed to agree with that description. The purpose of the document, he said, was indeed to captivate the American people, who were not much impressed by "the polished periods, the harmonious, happy expressions, with all the grace, ease, and elegance of a beautiful diction" that Englishmen valued. What they liked was "manly, nervous sense… even in the most awkward and uncouth dress of language."

ALL THAT BEGAN TO CHANGE IN THE 1790s, when, in the midst of bitter partisan conflict, the modern understanding and reputation of the Declaration of Independence first emerged. Until that time celebrations of the Fourth were controlled by nationalists who found a home in the Federalist party, and their earlier inattention to the Declaration hardened into a rigid hostility after 1790. The document's anti-British character was an embarrassment to Federalists who sought economic and diplomatic rapprochement with Britain. The language of equality and rights in the Declaration was different from that of the Declaration of the Rights of Man issued by the French National Assembly in 1789, but it still seemed too "French" for the comfort of Federalists, who, after the execution of Louis XVI and the onset of the Terror, lost whatever sympathy for the French Revolution they had once felt. Moreover, they understandably found it best to say as little as possible about a fundamental American text that had been drafted by a leader of the opposing Republican party.

It was, then, the Republicans who began to celebrate the Declaration of Independence as a "deathless instrument" written by "the immortal Jefferson." The Republicans saw themselves as the defenders of the American Republic of 1776 against subversion by pro-British "monarchists," and they hoped that by recalling the causes of independence, they would make their countrymen wary of further dealings with Great Britain. They were also delighted to identify the founding principles of the American Revolution with those of America's sister republic in France. At their Fourth of July celebrations, Republicans read the Declaration of Independence, and their newspapers reprinted it. Moreover, in their hands the attention that had at first focused on the last part of the Declaration shifted toward its opening paragraphs and the "self-evident truths" they stated. The Declaration, as a Republican newspaper said on July 7, 1792, was not to be celebrated merely "as affecting the separation of one country from the jurisdiction of another"; it had an enduring significance for established governments because it provided a "definition of the rights of man, and the end of civil government."

The Federalists responded that Jefferson had not written the Declaration alone. The drafting committee—including John Adams, a Federalist—had also contributed to its creation. And Jefferson's role as "the scribe who penned the declaration" had not been so distinguished as his followers suggested. Federalists rediscovered similarities between the Declaration and Locke's *Second Treatise of Government* that Richard Henry Lee had noticed long before and used them to argue that even the "small part of that memorable instrument" that could be attributed to Jefferson "he stole from *Locke's Essays.*" But after the War of 1812, the Federalist party slipped from sight, and with it, efforts to disparage the Declaration of Independence.

When a new party system formed in the late 1820s and 1830s, both Whigs and Jacksonians claimed descent from Jefferson and his party and so accepted the old Republican position on the Declaration and Jefferson's glorious role in its creation. By then, too, a new generation of Americans had come of age and made preservation of the nation's revolutionary history its particular mission. Its efforts, and its reverential attitude toward the revolutionaries and their works, also helped establish the Declaration of Independence as an important icon of American identity.

THE CHANGE CAME SUDDENLY. As late as January 1817 John Adams said that his country had no interest in its past. "I see no disposition to celebrate or remember, or even Curiosity to enquire into the Characters, Actions, or Events of the Revolution," he wrote the artist John Trumbull. But a little more than a month later Congress commissioned Trumbull to produce four large paintings commemorating the Revolution, which were to hang in the rotunda of the new American Capitol. For Trumbull, the most important of the series, and the one to which he first turned, was the Declaration of Independence. He based that work on a smaller painting he had done between 1786 and 1793 that showed the drafting committee presenting its work to Congress. When the new twelve-by-eighteen-foot canvas was completed in 1818, Trumbull exhibited it to large crowds in Boston, Philadelphia, and Baltimore before delivering it to Washington; indeed, *The Declaration of Independence* was the most popular of all the paintings Trumbull did for the Capitol.

Soon copies of the document were being published and sold briskly, which perhaps was what inspired Secretary of State John Quincy Adams to have an exact facsimile of the Declaration, the only one ever produced, made in 1823. Congress had it distributed throughout the country. Books also started to appear: the collected biographies of those who signed the Declaration in nine volumes by Joseph M. Sanderson (1823–27) or one volume by Charles A. Goodrich (1831), full biographies of individual revolutionaries that were often written by descendants who used family papers, and collections of revolutionary documents edited by such notable figures as Hezekiah Niles, Jared Sparks, and Peter Force.

Postwar efforts to preserve the memories and records of the Revolution were undertaken in a mood of near panic. Many documents remained in private hands, where they were gradually separated from one another and lost. Even worse, many revolutionaries had died, taking with them precious memories that were gone forever. The presence of living remnants of the revolutionary generation seemed so important in preserving its tradition that Americans watched anxiously as their numbers declined. These attitudes first appeared in the decade before 1826, the fiftieth anniversary of independence, but they persisted on into the Civil War. In 1864 the Reverend Elias Brewster Hillard noted that only seven of those who had fought in the Revolutionary War still survived, and he hurried to interview and photograph those "venerable and now sacred men" for the benefit of posterity. "The present is the last generation that will be connected by living link with the great period in which our national independence was achieved," he wrote in the introduction to his book *The Last Men of the Revolution.* "Our own are the last eyes that will look on men who looked on Washington; our ears the last that will hear the living voices of those who heard his words. Henceforth the American Revolution will be known among men by the silent record of history alone."

Most of the men Hillard interviewed had played modest roles in the Revolution. In the early 1820s, however, John Adams and Thomas Jefferson were still alive, and as the only surviving members of the committee that had drafted the Declaration of Independence, they attracted an extraordinary outpouring of attention. Pilgrims, invited and uninvited, flocked particularly to Monticello, hoping to catch a glimpse of the author of the Declaration and making nuisances of themselves. One woman, it is said, even smashed a window to get a better view of the old man. As a eulogist noted after the deaths of both Adams and Jefferson on, miraculously, July 4, 1826, the world had not waited for death to "sanctify" their names. Even while they remained alive, their homes became "shrines" to which lovers of liberty and admirers of genius flocked "from every land."

ADAMS, IN TRUTH, WAS MIFFED BY Jefferson's celebrity as the penman of Independence. The drafting of the Declaration of Independence, he thought, had assumed an exaggerated importance. Jefferson perhaps agreed; he, too, cautioned a correspondent against giving too much emphasis to "mere composition." The Declaration, he said, had not and had not been meant to be an original or novel creation; his assignment had been to produce "an expression of the American mind, and to give that expression the proper tone and spirit called for by the occasion."

Jefferson, however, played an important role in rescuing the Declaration from obscurity and making it a defining event of the revolutionary "heroic age." It was he who first suggested that the young John Trumbull paint *The Declaration of Independence.* And Trumbull's first sketch of his famous painting shares a piece of drawing paper with a sketch by Jefferson, executed in Paris sometime in 1786, of the assembly room in the Old Pennsylvania State House, now known as Independence Hall. Trumbull's painting of the scene carefully followed Jefferson's sketch, which unfortunately included architectural inaccuracies, as Trumbull later learned to his dismay.

> *Jefferson forgot, as the years went by, how substantial a role other members of the committee had played in framing the Declaration's text.*

Jefferson also spent hour after hour answering, in longhand, letters that he said numbered 1,267 in 1820, many of which asked questions about the Declaration and its creation. Unfortunately, his responses, like the sketch he made for Trumbull, were inaccurate in many details. Even his account of the drafting process, retold in an important letter to James Madison of 1823 that has been accepted by one authority after another, conflicts with a note he sent Benjamin Franklin in June 1776. Jefferson forgot, in short, how substantial a role other members of the drafting committee had played in framing the Declaration and adjusting its text before it was submitted to Congress.

INDEED, IN OLD AGE JEFFERSON FOUND enormous consolation in the fact that he was, as he ordered inscribed on his tomb, "Author of the Declaration of American Independence." More than anything else he had done, that role came to justify his life. It saved him from a despair that he suffered at the time of the Missouri crisis, when everything the Revolution had accomplished seemed to him in jeopardy, and that was later fed by problems at the University of Virginia, his own deteriorating health, and personal financial troubles so severe that he feared the loss of his beloved home, Monticello (those troubles, incidentally, virtually precluded him from freeing more than a handful of slaves at his death). The Declaration, as he told Madison, was "the fundamental act of union of these States," a document that should be recalled "to cherish the principles of the instrument in the bosoms of our own citizens." Again in 1824 he interpreted the government's re-publication of the Declaration as "a pledge of adhesion to its principles and of a sacred determination to maintain and perpetuate them," which he described as a "holy purpose."

But just which principles did he mean? Those in the Declaration's second paragraph, which he understood exactly as they had been understood in 1776—as an assertion primarily of the right of revolution. Jefferson composed the long sentence beginning "We hold these truths to be self-evident" in a well-known eighteenth-century rhetorical style by which one phrase was piled on another and the meaning of the whole became clear only at the end. The sequence ended with an assertion of the "Right of the People to alter or to abolish" any government that failed to secure their inalienable rights and to institute a new

form of government more likely "to effect their Safety and Happiness." That was the right Americans were exercising in July 1776, and it seemed no less relevant in the 1820s, when revolutionary movements were sweeping through Europe and Latin America. The American example would be, as Jefferson said in the last letter of his life, a "signal arousing men to burst the chains under which monkish ignorance and superstition had persuaded them to bind themselves, and to assume the blessings and security of self-government."

Others, however, emphasized the opening phrases of the sentence that began the Declaration's second paragraph, particularly "the memorable assertion, that 'all men are created equal, that they are endowed by their Creator with certain unalienable rights, and that to secure these rights, governments are instituted among men, deriving their just powers from the consent of the governed.'" That passage, the eulogist John Sergeant said at Philadelphia in July 1826, was the "text of the revolution," the "ruling vital principle" that had inspired the men of the 1770s, who "looked forward through succeeding generations, and saw stamped upon all their institutions, the great principles set forth in the Declaration of Independence." In Hallowell, Maine, another eulogist, Peleg Sprague, similarly described the Declaration of Independence as an assertion *by a whole people, of... the native equality of the human race,* as the true foundation of all political, of all human institutions."

AND SO AN INTERPRETATION OF THE declaration that had emerged in the 1790s became ever more widely repeated. The equality that Sergeant and Sprague emphasized was not, however, asserted for the first time in the Declaration of Independence. Even before Congress published its Declaration, one revolutionary document after another had associated equality with a new American republic and suggested enough different meanings of that term—equal rights, equal access to office, equal voting power—to keep Americans busy sorting them out and fighting over inegalitarian practices far

into the future. Jefferson, in fact, adapted those most remembered opening lines of the Declaration's second paragraph from a draft Declaration of Rights for Virginia, written by George Mason and revised by a committee of the Virginia convention, which appeared in the *Pennsylvania Gazette* on June 12, 1776, the day after the Committee of Five was appointed and perhaps the day it first met. Whether on his own inspiration or under instructions from the committee, Jefferson began with the Mason draft, which he gradually tightened into a more compressed and eloquent statement. He took, for example, Mason's statement that "all men are born equally free and independent," rewrote it to say they were "created equal & independent," and then cut out the "& independent."

Jefferson was not alone in adapting the Mason text for his purposes. The Virginia convention revised the Mason draft before enacting Virginia's Declaration of Rights, which said that all men were "by nature" equally free and independent. Several other states—including Pennsylvania (1776), Vermont (1777), Massachusetts (1780), and New Hampshire (1784)—remained closer to Mason's wording, including in their state bill of rights the assertions that men were "born free and equal" or "born equally free and independent." Unlike the Declaration of Independence, moreover, the state bills or "declarations" of rights became (after an initial period of confusion) legally binding. Americans' first efforts to work out the meaning of the equality written into their founding documents therefore occurred on the state level.

IN MASSACHUSETTS, FOR EXAMPLE, several slaves won their freedom in the 1780s by arguing before the state's Supreme Judicial Court that the provision in the state's bill of rights that all men were born free and equal made slavery unlawful. Later, in the famous case of *Commonwealth* v. *Aves* (1836), Justice Lemuel Shaw ruled that those words were sufficient to end slavery in Massachusetts, indeed that it would be difficult to find others "more precisely adapted to the abolition of negro slavery." White Americans also found the equality provisions in their state bills of rights useful. In the Virginia constitutional convention of 1829–30, for example, a delegate from the trans-Appalachian West, John R. Cooke, cited that "sacred instrument" the Virginia Declaration of Rights against the state's system of representing all counties equally in the legislature regardless of their populations and its imposition of a property qualification for the vote, both of which gave disproportional power to men in the eastern part of the state. The framers of Virginia's 1776 constitution allowed those practices to persist despite their violation of the equality affirmed in the Declaration of Rights, Cooke said, because there were limits on how much they dared change "in the midst of war." They therefore left it for posterity to resolve the inconsistency "as soon as leisure should be afforded them." In the hands of men like Cooke, the Virginia Declaration of Rights became a practical program of reform to be realized over time, as the Declaration of Independence would later be for Abraham Lincoln.

But why, if the states had legally binding statements of men's equality, should anyone turn to the Declaration of Independence? Because not all states had bills of rights, and not all the bills of rights that did exist included statements on equality. Moreover, neither the federal Constitution nor the federal Bill of Rights asserted men's natural equality or their possession of inalienable rights or the right of the people to reject or change their government. As a result, contenders in national politics who found those old revolutionary principles useful had to cite the Declaration of Independence. It was all they had.

THE SACRED STATURE GIVEN THE Declaration after 1815 made it extremely useful for causes attempting to seize the moral high ground in public debate. Beginning about 1820, workers, farmers, women's rights advocates, and other groups persistently used the Declaration of Independence to justify their quest for equality and their opposition to the "tyranny" of factory owners or railroads or great corporations or the male power structure. It remained, however, especially easy for the opponents of slavery to cite the Declaration on behalf of their cause. Eighteenth-century statements of equality referred to men in a state of nature, before governments were created, and asserted that no persons acquired legitimate authority over others without their consent. If so, a system of slavery in which men were born the subjects and indeed the property of others was profoundly wrong. In short, the same principle that denied kings a right to rule by inheritance alone undercut the right of masters to own slaves whose status was determined by birth, not consent. The kinship of the Declaration of Independence with the cause of antislavery was understood from the beginning—which explains why gradual emancipation acts, such as those in New York and New Jersey, took effect on July 4 in 1799 and 1804 and why Nat Turner's rebellion was originally planned for July 4, 1831.

Even in the eighteenth century, however, assertions of men's equal birth provoked dissent. As slavery became an increasingly divisive issue, denials that men were naturally equal multiplied. Men were not created equal in Virginia, John Tyler insisted during the Missouri debates of 1820: "No, sir, the principle, although lovely and beautiful, cannot obliterate those distinctions in society which society itself engenders and gives birth to." Six years later the acerbic, self-styled Virginia aristocrat John Randolph called the notion of man's equal creation "a falsehood, and a most pernicious falsehood, even though I find it in the Declaration of Independence." Man was born in a state of "perfect helplessness and ignorance" and so was from the start dependent on others. There was "not a word of truth" in the notion that men were created equal, repeated South Carolina's John C. Calhoun in 1848. Men could not survive, much less develop their talents, alone; the political state, in which some exercised authority and others obeyed, was in fact man's "natural state," that in which he "is born, lives and dies." For a long time the "false and dangerous" doctrine that men were created equal had lain "dormant," but by the late 1840s Americans had begun "to experience the danger of admitting so great an error… in the Declaration of Independence," where it had been inserted needlessly, Calhoun said, since separation from Britain could have been justified without it.

FIVE YEARS LATER, IN SENATE DEBATES over the Kansas-Nebraska Act, Indiana's John Pettit pronounced his widely quoted statement that the supposed "self-evident truth" of man's equal creation was in fact "a self-evident lie." Ohio's senator Benjamin Franklin Wade, an outspoken opponent of slavery known for his vituperative style and intense patriotism, rose to reply. Perhaps Wade's first and middle names gave him a special bond with the Declaration and its creators. The "great declaration cost our forefathers too dear," he said, to be so "lightly thrown away by their children." Without its inspiring principles the Americans could not have won their independence; for the revolutionary generation the "great truths" in that "immortal instrument," the Declaration of Independence, were "worth the sacrifice of all else on earth, even life itself." How, then, were men equal? Not, surely, in physical power or intellect. The "good old Declaration" said "that all men are equal, and have inalienable rights; that is, [they are] equal in point of right; that no man has a right to trample on another." Where those rights were wrested from men through force or fraud, justice demanded that they be "restored without delay."

Abraham Lincoln, a little-known forty-four-year-old lawyer in Springfield, Illinois, who had served one term in Congress before being turned out of office, read these debates, was aroused as by nothing before, and began to pick up the dropped threads of his political career. Like Wade, Lincoln idealized the men of the American Revolution, who were for him "a forest of giant oaks," "a fortress of strength," "iron men." He also shared the deep concern of his contemporaries as the "silent artillery of time" removed them and the *living history* they embodied from this world. Before the 1850s, however, Lincoln seems to have had relatively little interest in the Declaration of Independence. Then, suddenly, that document and its assertion that all men were created equal became his "ancient faith," the "father of all moral principles," an "axiom" of free society. He was provoked by the attacks of men such as Pettit and Calhoun. And he made the arguments of those who defended the Declaration his own, much as Jefferson had done with Mason's text, reworking the ideas from speech to speech, pushing their logic, and eventually, at Gettysburg in 1863, arriving at a simple statement of profound eloquence. In time his understanding of the Declaration of Independence would become that of the nation.

Lincoln's position emerged fully and powerfully during his debates with Illinois's senator Stephen Douglas, a Democrat who had proposed the Kansas-Nebraska Act and whose seat Lincoln sought in 1858. They were an odd couple, Douglas and Lincoln, as different physically—at full height Douglas came only to Lincoln's shoulders—as they were in style. Douglas wore well-tailored clothes; Lincoln's barely covered his limbs. Douglas was in general the more polished speaker; Lincoln sometimes rambled on, losing his point and his audience, although he could also, especially with a prepared text, be a powerful orator. The greatest difference between them was, however, in the positions they took on the future of slavery and the meaning of the Declaration of Independence.

Douglas defended the Kansas-Nebraska Act, which allowed the people of those states to permit slavery within their borders, as consistent with the revolutionary heritage. After all, in instructing their delegates to vote for independence, one state after another had explicitly retained the exclusive right of defining its domestic institutions. Moreover, the Declaration of Independence carried no implications for slavery, since its statement on equality referred to white men only. In fact, Douglas said, it simply meant that American colonists of European descent had equal rights with the King's subjects in Great Britain. The signers were not thinking of "the negro or... savage Indians, or the Feejee, or the Malay, or any other inferior or degraded race." Otherwise they would

have been honor bound to free their own slaves, which not even Thomas Jefferson did. The Declaration had only one purpose: to explain and justify American independence.

Lincoln believed the Declaration "contemplated the progressive improvement in the condition of all men everywhere." Otherwise, it was "mere rubbish."

To LINCOLN, DOUGLAS'S ARGUMENT left only a "mangled ruin" of the Declaration of Independence, whose "plain, unmistakable language" said *all* men were created equal. In affirming that government derived its "just powers from the consent of the governed," the Declaration also said that no man could rightly govern others without their consent. If, then, "the negro is a man," was it not a "total destruction of self-government, to say that he too shall not govern *himself?*" To govern a man without his consent was "despotism." Moreover, to confine the Declaration's significance to the British peoples of 1776 denied its meaning, Lincoln charged, not only for Douglas's "inferior races" but for the French, Irish, German, Scandinavian, and other immigrants who had come to America after the Revolution. For them the promise of equality linked new Americans with the founding generation; it was an "electric cord" that bound them into the nation "as though they were blood of the blood, and flesh of the flesh of the men who wrote that Declaration," and so made one people out of many. Lincoln believed that the Declaration "contemplated the progressive improvement in the condition of all men everywhere." If instead it was only a justification of independence "without the *germ,* or even the *suggestion* of the individual rights of man in it," the document was "of no practical use now— mere rubbish—old wadding left to rot on the battlefield after the victory is won,"

an "interesting memorial of the dead past... shorn of its vitality, and practical value."

LIKE WADE, LINCOLN DENIED THAT the signers meant that men were equal in *"all respects,"* including "color, size, intellect, moral developments, or social capacity." He, too, made sense of the Declaration's assertion of man's equal creation by eliding it with the next, separate statement on rights. The signers, he insisted, said men were equal in having "'certain inalienable rights....' This they said, and this they meant." Like John Cooke in Virginia three decades before, Lincoln thought the Founders allowed the persistence of practices at odds with their principles for reasons of necessity: to establish the Constitution demanded that slavery continue in those original states that chose to keep it. "We could not secure the good we did if we grasped for more," but that did not "destroy the principle that is the charter of our liberties." Nor did it mean that slavery had to be allowed in states not yet organized in 1776, such as Kansas and Nebraska.

Again like Cooke, Lincoln claimed that the authors of the Declaration understood its second paragraph as setting a standard for free men whose principles should be realized "as fast as circumstances... permit." They wanted that standard to be "familiar to all, and revered by all; constantly looked to, and constantly labored for, and even though never perfectly attained, constantly approximated and thereby constantly spreading and deepening its influence, and augmenting the happiness and value of life to all people of all colors everywhere." And if, as Calhoun said, American independence could have been declared without any assertion of human equality and inalienable rights, that made its inclusion all the more wonderful. "All honor to Jefferson," Lincoln said in a letter of 1859, "to the man who... had the coolness, forecast, and capacity to introduce into a merely revolutionary document, an abstract truth, applicable to all men and all times, and to embalm it there," where it would remain "a rebuke and a stumbling-block to the very harbingers of re-appearing tyranny and oppression."

JEFFERSON AND THE MEMBERS OF THE second contInental Congress did not understand what they were doing in quite that way on July 4, 1776. For them, it was enough for the Declaration to be "merely revolutionary." But if Douglas's history was more accurate, Lincoln's reading of the Declaration was better suited to the needs of the Republic in the mid-nineteenth century, when the standard of revolution had passed to Southern secessionists and to radical abolitionists who also called for disunion. In his hands the Declaration became first and foremost a living document for an established society, a set of goals to be realized over time, the dream of "something better, than a mere change of masters" that explained why "our fathers" fought and endured until they won the Revolutionary War. In the Civil War, too, Lincoln told Congress on July 4, 1861, the North fought not only to save the Union but to preserve a form of government "whose leading object is to elevate the condition of men—to lift artificial weights from all shoulders—to clear the paths of laudable pursuit for all." The rebellion it opposed was at base an effort "to overthrow the principle that all men were created equal." And so the Union victory at Gettysburg in 1863 became for him a vindication of that proposition, to which the nation's fathers had committed it in 1776, and a challenge to complete the "unfinished work" of the

Union dead and bring to "this nation, under God, a new birth of freedom."

The Declaration Lincoln left was not Jefferson's Declaration, although Jefferson and other revolutionaries shared the values Lincoln stressed.

Lincoln's Gettysburg Address stated briefly and eloquently convictions he had developed over the previous decade, convictions that on point after point echoed earlier Americans: Republicans of the 1790s, the eulogists Peleg Sprague and John Sergeant in 1826, John Cooke in the Virginia convention a few years later, Benjamin Wade in 1853. Some of those men he knew; others were unfamiliar to him, but they had also struggled to understand the practical implications of their revolutionary heritage and followed the same logic to the same conclusions. The Declaration of Independence Lincoln left was not Jefferson's Declaration, although Jefferson and other revolutionaries shared the values Lincoln and others stressed: equality, human rights, government by consent. Nor was Lincoln's Declaration of Independence solely his creation. It remained an "expression of the American mind," not, of course, what all Americans thought but what many had come to accept. And its implications continued to evolve after Lincoln's death. In 1858 he had written a

correspondent that the language of the Declaration of Independence was at odds with slavery but did not require political and social equality for free black Americans. Few disagreed then. How many would agree today?

The Declaration of Independence is in fact a curious document. After the Civil War members of Lincoln's party tried to write its principles into the Constitution by enacting the Thirteenth, Fourteenth, and Fifteenth Amendments, which is why issues of racial or age or gender equality are now so often fought out in the courts. But the Declaration of Independence itself is not and has never been legally binding. Its power comes from its capacity to inspire and move the hearts of living Americans, and its meaning lies in what they choose to make of it. It has been at once a cause of controversy, pushing as it does against established habits and conventions, and a unifying national icon, a legacy and a new creation that binds the revolutionaries to descendants who confronted and continue to confront issues the Founders did not know or failed to resolve. On Independence Day, then, Americans celebrate not simply the birth of their nation or the legacy of a few great men. They also commemorate a Declaration of Independence that is their own collective work now and through time. And that, finally, makes sense of the Fourth of July.

Pauline Maier is William Rand Kenan, Jr., Professor of American History at the Massachusetts Institute of Technology.

This article originally appeared in *American Heritage*, July/August 1997, pp. 54–65. *Adapted from American Scripture: Making the Declaration of Independence*, by Pauline Maier. © 1997 by Pauline Maier. Used by permission of Alfred A. Knopf, a division of Random House, Inc.

Hamilton Takes Command

In 1775, the 20-year-old Alexander Hamilton took up arms to fight the British. Soon the brash young soldier would display the courage and savvy that would take him to the apex of power in the new U.S. government.

"ALEXANDER HAMILTON is the least appreciated of the founding fathers because he never became president," says Willard Sterne Randall, a professor of humanities at Champlain College in Burlington, Vermont, and the author of Alexander Hamilton: A Life, *released this month from HarperCollins Publishers. "Washington set the mold for the presidency, but the institution wouldn't have survived without Hamilton."*

Hamilton was born January 11, 1755, on the island of Nevis in the West Indies, the illegitimate son of James Hamilton, a merchant from Scotland, and Rachel Fawcett Levine, a doctor's daughter who was divorced from a plantation owner. His unmarried parents separated when Hamilton was 9, and he went to live with his mother, who taught him French and Hebrew and how to keep the accounts in a small dry goods shop by which she supported herself and Hamilton's older brother, James. She died of yellow fever when Alexander was 13.

After her death, Hamilton worked as a clerk in the Christiansted (St. Croix) office of a New York-based import-export house. His employer was Nicholas Cruger, the 25-year-old scion of one of colonial America's leading mercantile families, whose confidence he quickly gained. And in the Rev. Hugh Knox, the minister of Christiansted's first Presbyterian church, Hamilton found another patron. Knox, along with the Cruger family, arranged a scholarship to send Hamilton to the United States for his education. At age 17, he arrived in Boston in October 1772 and was soon boarding at the Elizabethtown Academy in New Jersey, where he excelled in English composition, Greek and Latin, completing three years' study in one. Rejected by Princeton because the college refused to go along with his demand for accelerated study, Hamilton went instead in 1773 to King's College (now Columbia University), then located in Lower Manhattan. In events leading up to the excerpt that follows, Hamilton was swept up by revolutionary fervor and, at age 20, dropped out of King's College and formed his own militia unit of about 25 young men.

IN JUNE 1775, the Continental Congress in Philadelphia chose Virginia delegate Col. George Washington as commander in chief of the Continental Army then surrounding British-occupied Boston. Hurrying north, Washington spent a day in New York City where, on Sunday June 25, 1775, Alexander Hamilton braced at attention for Washington to inspect his militiamen at the foot of Wall Street.

Two months later, the last hundred British troops withdrew from Manhattan, going aboard the 64-gun man-of-war *Asia.* At 11 o'clock on the night of August 23, Continental Army Artillery captain John Lamb gave orders for his company supported by Hamilton's volunteers and a light infantry unit, to seize two dozen cannons from the battery at the island's southern tip. The *Asia's* captain, having been warned by Loyalists that the Patriots would raid the fort that night, posted a patrol barge with redcoats just offshore. Shortly after midnight, the British spotted Hamilton, his friend Hercules Mulligan, and about 100 comrades tugging on ropes they had attached to the heavy guns. The redcoats opened a brisk musket fire from the barge. Hamilton and the militiamen returned fire, killing a redcoat. At this, the *Asia* hoisted sail and began working in close to shore, firing a 32-gun broadside of solid shot. One cannonball pierced the roof of Fraunces Tavern at Broad and Pearl Streets. Many years later Mulligan would recall: "I was engaged in hauling off one of the cannons, when Mister Hamilton came up and gave me his musket to hold and he took hold of the rope.... Hamilton [got] away with the cannon. I left his musket in the Battery and retreated. As he was returning, I met him and he asked for his piece. I told him where I had left it and he went for it, notwithstanding the firing continued, with as much concern as if the [*Asia*] had not been there."

Hamilton's cool under fire inspired the men around him: they got away with 21 of the battery's 24 guns, dragged them uptown to City Hall Park and drew them up around the Liberty Pole under guard for safekeeping.

On January 6, 1776, the New York Provincial Congress ordered that an artillery company be raised to defend the colony; Hamilton, unfazed that virtually all commissions were going to native colonists of wealth and social position, leaped at the opportunity. Working behind the scenes to advance his candidacy, he won the support of Continental Congressmen John Jay and William Livingston. His mathematics teacher at King's College vouched for his mastery of the necessary trigonometry, and Capt. Stephen Bedlam, a skilled artillerist, certified that he had "examined Alexander Hamilton and judges him qualified."

While Hamilton waited to hear about his commission, Elias Boudinot, a leader of the New Jersey Provincial Congress, wrote from Elizabethtown to offer him a post as brigade major and aide-de-camp to Lord Stirling (William Alexander), commander of the newly formed New Jersey Militia. It was tempting. Hamilton had met the wealthy Scotsman as a student at Elizabethtown Academy and thought highly of him. And if he accepted, Hamilton would likely be the youngest major in the Revolutionary armies. Then Nathanael Greene, a major general in the Continental Army, invited Hamilton to become *his* aide-de-camp as well. After thinking the offers over, Hamilton declined both of them, gambling instead on commanding his own troops in combat.

Sure enough, on March 14, 1776, the New York Provincial Congress ordered Alexander Hamilton "appointed Captain of the Provincial Company of Artillery of this colony." With the last of his St. Croix scholarship money, he had his friend Mulligan, who owned a tailor shop, make him a blue coat with buff cuffs and white buckskin breeches.

He then set about recruiting the 30 men required for his company "We engaged 25 men [the first afternoon]," Mulligan remembered, even though, as Hamilton complained in a letter to the provincial congress, he could not match the pay offered by Continental Army recruiters. On April 2, 1776, two weeks after Hamilton received his commission, the provincial congress ordered him and his fledgling company to relieve Brig. Gen. Alexander McDougall's First New York Regiment, guarding the colony's official records, which were being shipped by wagon from New York's City Hall to the abandoned Greenwich Village estate of Loyalist William Bayard.

In late May 1776, ten weeks after becoming an officer, Hamilton wrote to New York's provincial congress to contrast his own meager payroll with the pay rates spelled out by the Continental Congress: "You will discover a considerable difference," he said. "My own pay will remain the same as it is now, but I make this application on behalf of the company, as I am fully convinced such a disadvantageous distinction will have a very pernicious effect on the minds and behavior of the men. They do the same duty with the other companies and think themselves entitled to the same pay."

The day the provincial congress received Captain Hamilton's missive, it capitulated to all his requests. Within three weeks, the young officer's company was up to 69 men, more than double the required number.

Meanwhile, in the city, two huge bivouacs crammed with tents, shacks, wagons and mounds of supplies were taking shape. At one of them, at the juncture of present-day Canal and Mulberry Streets, Hamilton and his company dug in. They had been assigned to construct a major portion of the earthworks that reached halfway across Manhattan Island. Atop Bayard's Hill, on the highest ground overlooking the city, Hamilton built a heptagonal fort, Bunker Hill. His friend Nicholas Fish described it as "a fortification superior in strength to any my imagination could ever have conceived." When Washington inspected the works, with its eight 9-pounders, four 3-pounders and six cohorn mortars, in mid-April, he commended Hamilton and his troops "for their masterly manner of executing the work."

Hamilton also ordered his men to rip apart fences and cut down some of the city's famous stately elm trees to build barricades and provide firewood for cooking. In houses abandoned by Loyalists, his soldiers propped muddy boots on damask furniture, ripped up parquet floors to fuel fireplaces, tossed garbage out windows and grazed their horses in gardens and orchards. One Loyalist watched in horror as army woodcutters, ignoring his protests, chopped down his peach and apple orchards on 23rd Street. Despite a curfew, drunken soldiers caroused with prostitutes in the streets around Trinity Church. By midsummer, 10,000 American troops had transformed New York City into an armed camp.

THE VERY DAY—July 4, 1776—that the founding fathers of the young nation-to-be were signing the Declaration of Independence in Philadelphia, Captain Hamilton watched through his telescope atop Bayard's Hill as a forest of ship masts grew ominously to the east; in all, some 480 British warships would sail into New York Harbor. One of Washington's soldiers wrote in his diary that it seemed "all London was afloat." Soon they had begun to disgorge the first of what would swell to 39,000 troops—the largest expeditionary force in English history—onto Staten Island. On July 9, at 6 o'clock in the evening, Hamilton and his men stood to attention on the commons to hear the declaration read aloud from the balcony of City Hall. Then the soldiers roared down Broadway to pull down and smash the only equestrian statue of King George III in America.

Three days later, British Vice Admiral Lord Richard Howe detached two vessels from his flotilla, the 44-gun *Phoenix* and the 28-gun *Rose*, to sail up the Hudson and probe shore defenses. The captain of the *Rose* coolly sipped claret on his quarterdeck as his vessel glided past the battery on Lower Manhattan—where an ill-trained American gun crew immediately blew itself up. The ships sailed unmolested up the river to Tarrytown as colonial troops abandoned their posts to watch. An appalled Washington fumed: "Such unsoldierly conduct gives the enemy a mean opinion of the army." On their return, the two British ships passed within cannon range of Hamilton's company at Fort Bunker Hill. He ordered his 9-pounders to fire, which the British warships returned. In the brief skirmish, one of Hamilton's cannons burst, killing one man and severely wounding another.

On August 8, Hamilton tore open orders from Washington: his company was to be on round-the-clock alert against an imminent invasion of Manhattan. "The movements of the enemy and intelligence by deserters give the utmost reason to believe that the great struggle in which we are contending for everything dear to us and our posterity, is near at hand," Washington wrote.

But early on the morning of August 27, 1776, Hamilton watched, helpless, as the British ferried 22,000 troops from Staten Island, not to Manhattan at all, but to the village of Brooklyn, on Long Island. Marching quickly inland from a British beachhead that stretched from Flatbush to Gravesend, they met little resistance. Of the 10,000 American troops on Long Island, only 2,750 were in Brooklyn, in four makeshift forts spread over four miles. At Flatbush, on the American east flank, Lord Charles Cornwallis quickly captured a mounted patrol of five young militia officers, including Hamilton's college roommate, Robert Troup, enabling 10,000 redcoats to march stealthily behind the Americans. Cut off by an 80-yard-wide swamp, 312 Americans died in the ensuing rout; another 1,100 were wounded or captured. By rowboat, barge, sloop, skiff and canoe in a howling northeaster, a regiment of New England fishermen transported the survivors across the East River to Manhattan.

At a September 12, 1776, council of war, a grim-faced Washington asked his generals if he should abandon New York City to the enemy. Rhode Islander Nathanael Greene, Washington's second-in-command, argued that "a general and speedy retreat is absolutely necessary" and insisted, as well, that "I would burn the city and suburbs," which, he maintained, belonged largely to Loyalists.

But Washington decided to leave the city unharmed when he decamped. Before he could do so, however, the British attacked again, at Kip's Bay on the East River between present-day 30th and 34th Streets, two miles north of Hamilton's hill fort, leaving his company cut off and in danger of capture. Washington sent Gen. Israel Putnam and his aide-de-camp, Maj. Aaron Burr, to evacuate them. The pair reached Fort Bunker Hill just as American militia from Lower Manhattan began to stream past Hamilton heading north on the Post Road (now Lexington Avenue). Although Hamilton had orders from Gen. Henry Knox to rally his men for a stand, Burr, in the name of Washing-

ton, countermanded Knox and led Hamilton, with little but the clothes on his back, two cannons and his men, by a concealed path up the west side of the island to freshly dug entrenchments at Harlem Heights. Burr most likely saved Hamilton's life.

THE BRITISH BUILT defenses across northern Manhattan, which they now occupied. On September 20, fanned by high winds, a fire broke out at midnight in a frame house along the waterfront near Whitehall Slip. Four hundred and ninety-three houses—one-fourth of the city's buildings—were destroyed before British soldiers and sailors and townspeople put out the flames. Though the British accused Washington of setting the fire, no evidence has ever been found to link him to it. In a letter to his cousin Lund at Mount Vernon, Washington wrote: "Providence, or some good honest fellow, has done more for us than we were disposed to do for ourselves."

By mid-October, the American army had withdrawn across the Harlem River north to White Plains in Westchester County. There, on October 28, the British caught up with them. Behind hastily built earthworks, Hamilton's artillerymen crouched tensely as Hessians unleashed a bayonet charge up a wooded slope. Hamilton's gunners, flanked by Maryland and New York troops, repulsed the assault, causing heavy casualties, before being driven farther north.

Cold weather pinched the toes and numbed the fingers of Hamilton's soldiers as they dug embankments. His pay book indicates he was desperately trying to round up enough shoes for his barefoot, frostbitten men. Meanwhile, an expected British attack did not materialize. Instead, the redcoats and Hessians stormed the last American stronghold on Manhattan Island, Fort Washington, at present-day 181st Street, where 2,818 besieged Americans surrendered on November 16. Three days later, the British force crossed the Hudson and attacked Fort Lee on the New Jersey shore near the present-day George Washington Bridge. The Americans escaped, evacuating the fort so quickly they left behind 146 precious cannons, 2,800 muskets and 400,000 cartridges.

In early November, Captain Hamilton and his men had been ordered up the Hudson River to Peekskill to join a column led by Lord Stirling. The combined forces crossed the Hudson to meet Washington and, as the commander in chief observed, his 3,400 "much broken and dispirited" men, in Hackensack, New Jersey.

Hamilton hitched horses to his two remaining 6-pound guns and marched his gun crews 20 miles in one day to the Raritan River. Rattling through Elizabethtown, he passed the Elizabethtown Academy where, only three years earlier, his greatest concern had been Latin and Greek declensions.

Dug in near Washington's Hackensack headquarters on November 20, Hamilton was startled by the sudden appearance of his friend Hercules Mulligan, who, to

Hamilton's great dismay, had been captured some three months earlier at the Battle of Long Island. Mulligan had been determined a "gentleman" after his arrest and released on his honor not to leave New York City. After a joyous reunion, Hamilton evidently persuaded Mulligan to return to New York City and to act, as Mulligan later put it, as a "confidential correspondent of the commander-in-chief"—a spy.

After pausing to await Gen. Sir William Howe, the British resumed their onslaught. On November 29, a force of about 4,000, double that of the Americans, arrived at a spot across the Raritan River from Washington's encampment. While American troops tore up the planks of the New Bridge, Hamilton and his guns kept up a hail of grapeshot.

For several hours, the slight, boyish-looking captain could be seen yelling, "Fire! Fire!" to his gun crews, racing home bags of grapeshot, then quickly repositioning the recoiling guns. Hamilton kept at it until Washington and his men were safely away toward Princeton. Halfway there, the general dispatched a brief message by express rider to Congress in Philadelphia: "The enemy appeared in several parties on the heights opposite Brunswick and were advancing in a large body toward the [Raritan] crossing place. We had a smart cannonade whilst we were parading our men."

Washington asked one of his aides to tell him which commander had halted his pursuers. The man replied that he had "noticed a youth, a mere stripling, small, slender, almost delicate in frame, marching, with a cocked hat pulled down over his eyes, apparently lost in thought, with his hand resting on a cannon, and every now and then patting it, as if it were a favorite horse or a pet plaything." Washington's stepgrandson Daniel Parke Custis later wrote that Washington was "charmed by the brilliant courage and admirable skill" of the then 21-year-old Hamilton, who led his company into Princeton the morning of December 2. Another of Washington's officers noted that "it was a model of discipline; at their head was a boy, and I wondered at his youth, but what was my surprise when he was pointed out to me as that Hamilton of whom we had already heard so much."

AFTER LOSING New Jersey to the British, Washington ordered his army into every boat and barge for 60 miles to cross the Delaware River into Pennsylvania's Bucks County. A shivering Hamilton and his gunners made passage in a Durham ore boat, joining artillery already ranged along the western bank. Whenever British patrols ventured too near the water, Hamilton's and the other artillerymen repulsed them with brisk fire. The weather grew steadily colder. General Howe said he found it "too severe to keep the field." Remming to New York City with his redcoats, he left a brigade of Hessians to winter at Trenton.

In command of the brigade, Howe placed Col. Johann Gottlieb Rall, whose troops had slaughtered retreating Americans on Long Island and at Fort Washington on Manhattan. His regiments had a reputation for plunder and worse. Reports that the Hessians had raped several women, including a 15-year-old girl, galvanized New Jersey farmers, who had been reluctant to help the American army. Now they formed militia bands to ambush Hessian patrols and British scouting parties around Trenton. "We have not slept one night in peace since we came to this place," one Hessian officer moaned.

Washington now faced a vexing problem: the enlistments of his 3,400 Continental troops expired at midnight New Year's Eve; he decided to attack the Trenton Hessians while they slept off the effects of their Christmas celebration. After so many setbacks, it was a risky gambit; defeat could mean the end of the American cause. But a victory, even over a small outpost, might inspire lagging Patriots, cow Loyalists, encourage reenlistments and drive back the British—in short, keep the Revolution alive. The main assault force was made up of tested veterans. Henry Knox, Nathanael Greene, James Monroe, John Sullivan and Alexander Hamilton, future leaders of America's republic, huddled around a campfire at McKonkey's Ferry the frigid afternoon of December 25, 1776, to get their orders. Hamilton and his men had blankets wrapped around them as they hefted two 6-pounders and their cases of shot and shells onto the 9-foot-wide, 60-foot-long Durham iron-ore barges they had commandeered, then pushed and pulled their horses aboard. Nineteen-year-old James Wilkinson noted in his journal that footprints down to the river were "tinged here and there with blood from the feet of the men who wore broken shoes." Ship captain John Glover ordered the first boatloads to push off at 2 a.m. Snow and sleet stung Hamilton's eyes.

Tramping past darkened farmhouses for 12 miles, Hamilton's company led Nathanael Greene's division as it swung off to the east to skirt the town. One mile north of Trenton, Greene halted the column. At precisely 8 in the morning, Hamilton unleashed his artillery on the Hessian outpost. Three minutes later, American infantry poured into town. Driving back Hessian pickets with their bayonets, they charged into the old British barracks to confront groggy Hessians at gunpoint. Some attempted to regroup and counterattack, but Hamilton and his guns were waiting for them. Firing in tandem, Hamilton's cannons cut down the Hessians with murderous sheets of grapeshot. The mercenaries sought cover behind houses but were driven back by Virginia riflemen, who stormed into the houses and fired down from upstairs windows. Hessian artillerymen managed to get off only 13 rounds from two brass fieldpieces before Hamilton's gunners cut them in two. Riding back and forth behind the guns, Washington saw for himself the brutal courage and skillful discipline of this youthful artillery captain.

The Hessians' two best regiments surrendered, but a third escaped. As the Americans recrossed the Delaware, both they and their prisoners, nearly 1,000 in all, had to stomp their feet to break up the ice that was forming on the river. Five men froze to death.

Stung by the defeat, British field commander Lord Cornwallis raced across New Jersey with battle-seasoned grenadiers to retaliate. Americans with $10 gold reenlistment bonuses in their pockets recrossed the river to intercept them. When the British halted along a three-mile stretch of Assunpink Creek outside Trenton and across from the Americans, Washington duped British pickets by ordering a rear guard to tend roaring campfires and to dig noisily through the night while his main force slipped away.

At 1 a.m., January 2, 1777, their numbers reduced from 69 to 25 by death, desertion and expired enlistments, Hamilton and his men wrapped rags around the wheels of their cannons to muffle noise, and headed north. They reached the south end of Princeton at sunrise, to face a brigade—some 700 men—of British light infantry. As the two forces raced for high ground, American general Hugh Mercer fell with seven bayonet wounds. The Americans retreated from a British bayonet charge. Then Washington himself galloped onto the battlefield with a division of Pennsylvania militia, surrounding the now outnumbered British. Some 200 redcoats ran to Nassau Hall, the main building at Princeton College. By the time Hamilton set up his two cannons, the British had begun firing from the windows of the red sandstone edifice. College tradition holds that one of Hamilton's 6-pound balls shattered a window, flew through the chapel and beheaded a portrait of King George II. Under Hamilton's fierce cannonade, the British soon surrendered.

IN THE WAKE of twin victories within ten days, at Trenton and Princeton, militia volunteers swarmed to the American standard, far more than could be fed, clothed or armed. Washington's shorthanded staff was ill-equipped to coordinate logistics. In the four months since the British onslaught had begun, 300 American officers had been killed or captured. "At present," Washington complained, "my time is so taken up at my desk that I am obliged to neglect many other essential parts of my duty. It is absolutely necessary for me to have persons [who] can think for me as well as execute orders.... As to military knowledge, I do not expect to find gentlemen much skilled in it. If they can write a good letter, write quick, are methodical and diligent, it is all I expect to find in my aides."

He would get all that and more. In January, shortly after the army was led into winter quarters at Morristown, New Jersey, Nathanael Greene invited Hamilton, who had just turned 22, to dinner at Washington's headquarters. There, Washington invited the young artillery officer to join his staff. The appointment carried a promotion from captain to lieutenant colonel, and this time Hamilton did not hesitate. On March 1, 1777, he turned over the command of his artillery company to Lt. Thomas Thompson—a sergeant whom, against all precedent, he had promoted to officer rank—and joined Washington's headquarters staff.

It would prove a profound relationship.

"During a long series of years, in war and in peace, Washington enjoyed the advantages of Hamilton's eminent talents, integrity and felicity, and these qualities fixed [Hamilton] in [Washington's] confidence to the last hour of his life," wrote Massachusetts Senator Timothy Pickering in 1804. Hamilton, the impecunious abandoned son, and Washington, the patriarch without a son, had begun a mutually dependent relationship that would endure for nearly 25 years—years corresponding to the birth, adolescence and coming to maturity of the United States of America.

HAMILTON WOULD BECOME inspector general of the U.S. Army and in that capacity founded the U.S. Navy. Along with James Madison and John Jay, he wrote the Federalist Papers, *essays that helped gain popular support for the then-proposed Constitution. In 1789, he became the first Secretary of the Treasury, under President Washington and almost singlehandedly created the U.S. Mint, the stock and bond markets and the concept of the modern corporation.*

After the death of Washington on December 14, 1799, Hamilton worked secretly, though assiduously, to prevent the reelection of John Adams as well as the election of Thomas Jefferson and Aaron Burr. Burr obtained a copy of a Hamilton letter that branded Adams an "eccentric" lacking in "sound judgment" and got it published in newspapers all over America. In the 1801 election, Jefferson and Burr tied in the Electoral College, and Congress made Jefferson president, with Burr his vice president. Hamilton, his political career in tatters, founded the New York Evening Post *newspaper, which he used to attack the new administration. In the 1804 New York gubernatorial election, Hamilton opposed Aaron Burr's bid to replace Governor George Clinton. With Hamilton's help, Clinton won.*

When he heard that Hamilton had called him "a dangerous man, and one who ought not to be trusted with the reins of government," Burr demanded a written apology or satisfaction in a duel. On the morning of Thursday, July 11, 1804, on a cliff in Weehawken, New Jersey, Hamilton faced the man who had rescued him 28 years earlier in Manhattan. Hamilton told his second, Nathaniel Pendleton, that he intended to fire into the air so as to end the affair with honor but without bloodshed. Burr made no such promise. A shot rang out. Burr's bullet struck Hamilton in the right side, tearing through his liver. Hamilton's pistol went off a split second later, snapping a twig overhead. Thirty-six hours later, Alexander Hamilton was dead. He was 49 years old.

Willard Sterne Randall is the Historical Scholar in Residence at Champlain College, Burlington, VT. Article from *Smithsonian*, January 2003, pages 64–71. This article is adapted from *Alexander Hamilton: A Life*, by Willard Sterne Randall. Copyright © 2003 by Willard Sterne Randall. Reprinted with permission of the author.

Winter of Discontent

Even as he endured the hardships of Valley Forge, George Washington
faced another challenge: critics who questioned his fitness to lead

BY NORMAN GELB

GEORGE WASHINGTON'S TROOPS could easily be
followed as they trudged through the wintry expanse of south-
eastern Pennsylvania in late December 1777. The soldiers,
many of them ragged and shoeless, left bloody footprints in the
snow, marking the grueling progress of this army of the American Revolution toward winter quarters at Valley Forge.

There was no shelter for the men when they reached the exposed, hilly landscape of that misnamed redoubt, actually a pla-
teau Washington chose largely for its defensibility. (A nearby
hollow had once been the site of a smithy hence the designation.) Tents provided their only barrier against frost and wind.
Their commander in chief insisted that he, too, would shelter in
a tent until his troops were able to cut down trees and construct
log huts for themselves.

Washington despaired for the fate of his army. "The whole
of them," said his comrade in arms, Gen. John Sullivan, were
"without watch coats, one half without blankets, and more than
one third without shoes … many of them without jackets … and
not a few without shirts." None had enough to eat: some had
gone hungry for days. Exhausted and ill, men were deserting in
great numbers, heading home to their families and farms. It was
a dark moment for the Revolution and for Washington. From
his makeshift headquarters, he wrote to warn Congress: "unless
some great and capital change suddenly takes place … this army
must inevitably… starve, dissolve or disperse."

At that instant, stays Revolutionary era historian Edmund
Morgan, Washington was indeed "giving Congress the facts of
life: you can't fight a war without an army. He was operating at
a big disadvantage; the state militias offered larger bounties
than Congress did for serving in the Continental army."

Yet even as Washington attempted to keep his army from
disintegrating, he found himself challenged on another front.
Prominent figures in the independence movement—most notably, some members of Congress—had begun to question his
very fitness to command. Over the course of the next several
months—until mid-March—Washington would be plagued by

a small but vocal contingent calling for his ouster. They engineered a very real distraction at a moment of grave crisis.

More than two years before, on June 15, 1775, Congress had
unanimously chosen the tall, 43-year-old Virginia plantation
owner and gentleman farmer "to command all the continental
forces, raised or to be raised, for the defense of American liberty." During the French and Indian War two decades earlier, he
had proved himself a courageous and levelheaded officer,
serving under British command and as a colonel in the Virginia
militia.

Washington had immediately justified the confidence placed
in him by bringing order to the hodgepodge of militia contin-
gents he led in what was becoming America's war of national
liberation. From disarray and muddle, he created an American
army and, in March 1776, orchestrated its first significant
achievement, besieging the British and causing them to withdraw from Boston, the principal redcoat base in America at the
time. "This was the moment," says historian John Ferling, author of the definitive Washington biography *The First of Men*,
"that George Washington first captured the imagination of the
American people."

But after Boston, his army suffered a series of serious re-
verses, including defeat at Brooklyn Heights on August 27,
1776, and the loss of New York. "At this point," says Ferling,
"Washington was on the run. He nearly got trapped two or three
times. During this period the British, under the command of
General Howe, could have defeated him."

Washington's daring strikes against the enemy at Trenton on
December 26 and Princeton on January 3, 1777, in New Jersey,
boosted morale, but otherwise had little lasting military importance. Then came Brandywine Creek, in Pennsylvania. on September 11, 1777, where Washington failed to stop the British
from advancing on Philadelphia, the capital of the Revolution.
Members of Congress, who faced execution if taken prisoner,
fled the city. This fiasco was followed by the Battle of Germantown, Pennsylvania, on October 4, where the Continental army

snatched defeat from the jaws of victory through blunders in the field. Washington's four-pronged attack for taking the city proved too complex for inexperienced troops to carry out. As his soldiers maneuvered in a dense fog, they accidentally fired on one another. Given this turn of events, few in Congress observed the progress of the war without growing anxiety.

In the small Pennsylvania market town of York, about 100 miles west of Philadelphia, where Congress reconvened, there was talk that the commander in chief was indecisive and overly dependent on the advice of his senior subordinates. Congressman Thomas Burke of North Carolina decried what he called the "want of abilities in our superior officers and want of order and discipline in our army." Pennsylvania's new attorney general, Jonathan Dickinson Sergeant, a former congressman, charged that Washington was responsible for "such blunders as might have disgraced a soldier of three months' standing." In a moment of despair, John Adams, although ever fearful that a tyrant might emerge to fill the gap left by the discarded British king, pleaded in his diary while en route from Philadelphia to York, "Oh, Heaven! grant Us one great Soul! … One leading Mind would extricate the best Cause, from that Ruin which seems to await it."

Suddenly, it seemed, that desperate prayer had been answered: a patriot paladin appeared on the scene. Less than nine weeks before Washington's troops retreated to Valley Forge—the main column arrived there on December 19—the Continental army had scored a decisive victory. On October 17, at Saratoga in eastern New York, American forces, under the command of Gen. Horatio Gates, inflicted the first major defeat of the war on the redcoats, their German mercenary auxiliaries and Indian allies. For Gates, the 49-year-old English-born son of a duke's housekeeper, it was a moment of both tactical and symbolic triumph. The dashing John Burgoyne, campaigning down from Canada to split the states and crush the Revolution, was ignominiously forced to surrender himself and his army to the gruff, battle-hardened American, himself a former British officer. "One cannot underestimate the importance of Saratoga," says Ferling. "It is this victory that induces France to come into the war."

Gates' success greatly lifted American spirits. But his victory also drew attention to the fact that Washington, his superior officer, could claim no equivalent battle honors. Within Congress, criticism of Washington's performance escalated. Perhaps, some legislators suggested, the victor at Saratoga would make a better commander in chief than the general who had not prevented the British from taking Philadelphia.

Massachusetts Congressman James Lovell was scarcely alone in his view, as he wrote Gates, "The army will be totally lost unless you…, collect the virtuous band who wish to fight under your banner." Dr. Benjamin Rush, a signer of the Declaration of Independence, contrasted Gates, "exulting in the success of schemes planned with wisdom and executed with vigor and bravery," with Washington, "outgeneralled and twice beaten."

Most of the delegates at York, however, along with the majority of the Continental army's officers and its ordinary soldiers, continued to esteem their commander in chief. They were well aware that it was Washington who had kept the army from dissolving, despite the paucity of resources provided by either the strapped and deeply shaken Congress or the newly independent states. When it was suggested to hulking Gen. Daniel Morgan, whose corps of riflemen had played a decisive role at Saratoga, that a handful of senior officers intended to resign unless Washington was removed, he unhesitatingly responded, "Under no other man than Washington as Commander-in-Chief would I ever serve."

Dr. Benjamin Rush, a signer of the Declaration of Independence, referred to Washington as "outgeneralled and twice beaten."

Washington knew well that he was blamed, in certain quarters, for the poor performance of his army. But he was fitted with far more pressing matters. He had troops to feed, clothe, prepare for battle—and, most important, inspire: he understood that he must rally his remaining troops—about 11,000 all told at Valley Forge—and dissuade them from deserting. The commander of the Continental army was, according to Philander D. Chase, editor of *The Papers of George Washington* at the University, of Virginia, "astute enough to take a longer view of things. He understood that criticism, fair or unfair, real or apprehended, was part of the price that he had to pay to remain an effective leader and to achieve the aims of the Revolution."

In addition, Washington was engaged in planning offensive campaigns against a powerful, well-supplied foe. "The British were indeed formidable," says Ferling. "They had defeated the French in the French and Indian War; they also had the best navy in the world."

To add to Washington's concerns, for months he had contended with an assortment of European military officers, most of them French, who had converged on America to volunteer their services. They were recruited in Paris by Silas Deane, America's first official diplomat.

Some of the officers Deane commissioned may have shared the principles that had sparked the American Revolution. But most had signed on to further their own military careers, hoping to leapfrog into higher ranks back in Europe. Washington welcomed some of those volunteers, who would prove of great value to the American cause. Notable among them were the Marquis de Lafayette, the 19-year-old French nobleman who became one of Washington's most trusted aides; Friedrich von Steuben, the German soldier who would transform Washington's ragged army into a disciplined fighting force at Valley Forge; and Tadeusz Kosciuszko, the Polish military engineer who contributed greatly to the American victory at Saratoga.

But some foreign officers who laid claim to senior command in the Continental army were a nuisance or worse—none more so than Col. Thomas Conway. He would figure prominently among Washington's detractors, whom history would come to designate the Conway Cabal. A French officer of Irish origin, the 42-year-old Conway, high browed, thin lipped and supercilious, made it plain that he had come to America "to increase my fortune and that of my family." He was a seasoned soldier who joined the French Army at the age of 14. Gen. John Sullivan, under whom he served in the ill-fated Battle of Germantown, believed "his knowledge of military matters in general far exceeds any officer we have."

Congress quickly awarded Conway the rank of brigadier general; his military background and charisma earned him many an admirer in York. When he threatened to return to France unless promoted to major general, more than a few congressmen, convinced that Washington needed experienced commanders, took up Conway's cause.

At first, Washington, too, had been impressed by Conway's credentials. Over time, however, he had come to believe that the French officer's "importance in this Army, exists more in his imagination than in reality." What troubled him most was Congress's readiness to promote Conway over the heads of Washington's own loyal brigadiers. Many of his officers, he warned, would refuse to serve under Conway and would simply go home. "I have been a slave to the service," Washington informed Virginia Congressman Richard Henry Lee on October 17, 1777. "But it will be impossible for me to be of any further service if such insuperable obstacles are thrown in my way."

While some in Congress would have welcomed Washington's resignation in favor of Gates, the prospect of sowing confusion in the ranks, or even of causing an already demoralized army to disband, was alarming. The Continental army embodied the Revolution.

At this juncture, during the fall of 1777, Washington prevailed and Congress failed to act on Conway's promotion. But Congress also, at this moment, reorganized its Board of War. That Congressional committee, charged with overseeing the struggle for independence, was in fact composed of members who possessed little understanding of military matters. Until then, the board had intervened only minimally when it came to the army. Now the committee would include senior officers; Washington, the commander in chief, was not consulted about whom they would be.

It was rumored that Conway might be among them. From the moment of his arrival in America in the spring of 1777, Conway had found that the organization of the Continental army clashed with his European understanding of how military units should be commanded, trained and deployed. He did not hesitate in express his deprecating views. After Congress, acting on the basis of Washington's firm intercession, had failed to support his promotion to major general, Conway stepped up his campaign to defame the commander in chief. He informed General Gates that he wished to serve under him because "the more I see of [Washington's] army the less I think it fit for general action."

Recognizing the delicacy of the situation, Congress did not name Conway to the board. But it did appoint Thomas Mifflin, the army's former quartermaster general. Once Washington's friend, Mifflin had differed sharply on strategy and was now among the general's most acerbic critics. He jealously asserted that the commander's "favourites … had an undue influence on

him" and told Gates that Conway's criticism of Washington contained "just sentiments."

But the most significant appointment to the board turned out to be none other than the hero of Saratoga himself: it was a decision bound to create problems. Ever since his victory only a matter of weeks earlier, Gates had behaved disdainfully toward Washington, his superior officer. He even failed to formally notify the commander in chief of the triumph at Saratoga. Instead, Gates reported directly to Congress, a gesture that implied he claimed equal status with Washington. He had been slow to respond to Washington's request that some of Gates' troops, no longer essential for much-reduced northern operations, be released to the south, where they were desperately needed. Now Gates emerged as the leader of the board that would superintend the operations of Washington and his ragtag army.

Conway informed General Gates that "the more I see of Washington's army the less I think it fit for general action."

Although Washington surely must have been offended by this high-handed treatment, he refused to engage in a squabble over the appointments. Whatever his complaints about Congress's shortcomings in providing supplies and pay for his men, he recognized the legislature's authority over the military wing of the Revolution.

Substantial changes, too, in the character of the Congress that had ringingly declared American independence more than a year earlier, on July 4, 1776, intensified the divisiveness. Many of the original founding fathers had already left the legislature or were soon to depart. Thomas Jefferson had returned to Virginia to assist its transition from a royal colony to an independent state. Benjamin Franklin was in Paris seeking French assistance for America in the war. John Adams was preparing to join him there. Twenty-one-year-old Lt. Col. Alexander Hamilton, Washington's aide-de-camp, angrily demanded, "The great men who composed our first council; are they dead, have they deserted the cause, or what has become of them?"

Among the new delegates, few were as gifted, or would prove as memorable, as their predecessors. Much time was wasted in futile bickering. Henry Laurens of South Carolina, president of Congress during much of its York exile, grumbled, "Some sensible things have been said [here], and as much nonsense as ever I heard in so short a space." Charles Carroll of Maryland complained, "We murder time, and chat it away in idle impertinent talk."

Meanwhile, detractors in Congress were becoming increasingly critical of Washington. After visiting York, Lafayette returned to Valley Forge and declared himself outraged by "stupid men who without knowing a single word about war, undertake to judge you."

The move to replace the commander in chief with Gates—or even, it was muttered, with Conway—came to a head early in

1778 after the Continental army had arrived at the glacial hell of Valley Forge. One of every four soldiers who wintered in that place would die there. Even hardened veterans, among them Albigence Waldo of Connecticut, an army surgeon who had served since 1775, were appalled by what they saw: "There comes a soldier," Waldo wrote, "his bare feet are seen thro' his worn-out shoes, his legs nearly naked from the tattered remains of an only pair of stockings, his Breeches not sufficient to cover his nakedness…. He crys … I am Sick, my feet lame, my legs are sore, my body covered with this tormenting Itch."

Reluctantly, Washington sent troops to seize food from nearby farmers. Already weighed down with dire anxieties, he suffered another blow. On December 13, he learned Congress had reversed itself and decided to appoint Conway to the Board of War, as inspector general of the army. What was more, Congress elevated Conway to the rank of major general—the promotion previously denied because of Washington's objections.

Conway wasted no time in presenting himself at army headquarters, where, predictably, he was received with cold formality. Washington informed Conway that the newly conferred rank—a promotion the commander in chief dryly referred to as "extraordinary"—would offend many senior officers; he then asked to see specific instructions Conway had received from the Board of War. When Conway failed to produce such a communique, Washington had him shown out.

Upon his departure from Valley Forge, Conway sent Washington a letter barbed with sarcasm and self-justification, complaining their meeting had been a reception "as I never met with before with any general during the course of thirty years in a very respectable [French] Army."

His patience exhausted, Washington decided to confront the Conway issue. He passed the new inspector general's comments on to Congress, along with a bitter rebuttal of each accusation. Washington denied that he had received Conway with anything less than "proper respect to his official character" as an appointee of Congress. Nevertheless, he concluded, "My feelings will not permit me to make professions of friendship to a man I deem my enemy."

All the while, despite reports from friends that members of Congress were maneuvering to install Gates in his place, Washington had not sought to clash with the victor of Saratoga. He refused to believe that the new president of the Board of War was conspiring against him. "Being honest himself," Joseph Reed, Washington's former military secretary wrote, "he will not readily suspect the virtue of others." However, recognition of the challenge to his position became unavoidable.

Washington's trusted friend Dr. James Craik, a senior army medical officer, wrote to inform him that although "they dare not appear openly as your enemies … the new Board of War is composed of such leading men as will throw such obstacles and difficulties in your way as to force you to resign." Without consulting Washington, Gates' board secured Congressional approval of a campaign to pursue the English into Canada (the plans were later aborted). Patrick Henry, the governor of Virginia, forwarded to Washington a disturbing anonymous letter warning that "unless a Moses or a Joshua are raised up in our behalf, we must perish before we reach the promised land."

Increasingly exasperated by such taunts, Washington told a friend he would be happy to resign his command. "There is not an Officer in the Service of the United States," he declared, "that would return to the sweets of domestic life with more heart felt joy than I should." But he would do so, he added, only if the will of the people ordained it: he feared destabilizing consequences if he stepped down.

"My Enemies take an ungenerous advantage of me," Washington wrote. "I cannot combat their insinuations."

The unkindest cut, however, came from those who suggested he had concealed the appalling condition of his army in order to deflect criticism of his command. "My Enemies take an ungenerous advantage of me," Washington protested to Henry Laurens. "They know I cannot combat their insinuations, however injurious, without disclosing secrets it is of the utmost moment to conceal." Had they known its state, the redcoats, a mere 18 miles away in Philadelphia, might well have launched an attack.

While Washington hoped that the British commander, Lord William Howe, remained ignorant of the extent of the patriot army's vulnerability as it bivouacked on frozen ground, members of Congress began arriving at Valley Forge to survey conditions for themselves. A shocked John Harvie of Virginia told Washington, "My dear General, if you had given some explanation, all these rumors [denigrating Washington] would have been silenced a long time ago."

Within Congress, a growing recognition of Washington's extraordinary leadership at Valley Forge—not only was he preventing the Continental army from dissolving, he was somehow inspiring his men under the cruelest of conditions— made a profound impression. Joseph Jones, a congressman from Virginia and a long-standing friend to Washington, wrote to offer his support: "The same equal and disinterested conduct, the same labor and attention, which you have manifested in the public service from the first of the contest, will shield and protect you from the shafts of envy and malevolence."

Still, Washington decided the time had come to take up the festering matter of a letter that Conway had written to Gates that autumn, which referred to a "weak general" who might prove the ruin of America.

He had learned of the letter when one of Gates' own aides had disclosed its contents to an officer loyal to Washington. When Gates discovered that the letter had been leaked to Washington, he wrote to him, demanding the identity of the "wretch" who had "stealingly copied" his private correspondence. Bent on dramatizing his challenge to the commander in chief's integrity, Gates sent a copy of this letter to Congress.

It would prove an enormous blunder. Washington was, quite rightly, able to take the high ground when he replied to the slander. Why, he inquired of Congress, would anyone want to add needlessly to the burdens on the beleaguered legislature, pestering it with details of a personal disagreement? He pointed out that he had learned of the malicious Conway letter to Gates through an indiscretion by one of Gates' own aides. Washington added that he had not previously gone public with the matter because he was "desirous … of concealing every matter that could give the smallest interruption to the tranquility of this army." In the end, the episode caused the hero of Saratoga, and Conway along with him, to appear small-minded and vindictive.

But what conclusively undermined Washington's critics was the recognition that, whatever his shortcomings, Washington remained the individual who most represented the cause of liberty in the minds of the American people and its army. Mercy Otis Warren reported to her husband, Continental Navy Board member James Warren, that "The toast among the soldiers" is "Washington or no Army." Thomas Paine, the conscience mad primary propagandist of the Revolution, expressed the fervent hope that he could "shame [Washington's critics]" or at least "convince them of their error."

Congressman Jones accurately foretold that whatever the conspirators had intended, "it will redound to their own disgrace." Men who had spoken belittlingly of the commander in chief would later deny they had ever held him in anything but the highest regard. Gates soon tried to effect a reconciliation with Washington, but his attempt was rebuffed. Congress later removed him from the Board of War and assigned him to a succession of field commands. His reputation as a military hero would soon come to grief in South Carolina where, at the Battle of Camden on August 16, 1780, his troops were routed by the British. During a hasty retreat, Gates' undisguised anxiety for his own personal safety made him an object of ridicule among his men. "The general's frantic dash from the scene," says historian John Ferling, "proved his ruination."

Mifflin also suffered a measure of disgrace. Charged with having contributed to the troops' hardships at Valley Forge through mismanagement of funds as quartermaster general, he was forced to resign from the Board of War. He denied conspiring against Washington, insisting he had always "dearly loved and greatly admired" him.

As for Conway, who was scarcely the most significant figure in the Conway Cabal—despite the name by which it became known—Congress acted with crushing decisiveness. Still denied a senior command in the army, he offered his resignation April 1778 and was surprised when it was accepted. Before returning to France, he wrote Washington "You are in my eyes the great and the good man. May you long enjoy the love, veneration and esteem of these States, whose liberties you have asserted by your virtues." In that, at least, his wish would be realized.

Historians disagree over the significance of the attacks on Washington. In his monumental biography of Washington, Douglas S. Freeman stated that "the imperative reason for defeating [the cabal] was to keep the Army and the country united in the hard battle for freedom." But Ferling tends to minimize its importance. "I don't really think the cabal existed as an organized conspiracy," he says. "It existed more in Washington's mind than in reality." Certainly, Washington was convinced that a "malignant faction" had conspired to remove him. So, too, was Patrick Henry, who, along with others, feared for the patriot cause if such efforts had succeeded.

Whatever the strength of those who considered Washington a liability, it is impossible to calculate the consequences for the Continental army, the American Revolution and the embryonic United States of America had their sentiments found greater resonance in Congress—and forced or provoked the man who would later be called the Father of the Country to resign his command.

NORMAN GELB, author of numerous histories, is currently working on a study of military leadership in the American Revolution.

From *Smithsonian*, May 2003, pages 65–72. Copyright © 2003 by Norman Gelb. Reprinted with permission of the author.

Founders Chic:
Live From Philadelphia

They cut political deals and stabbed each other in the back on the way to inventing freedom.
Why Jefferson, Adams and their brethren are suddenly hot again.

By Evan Thomas

GOOD THING THE FOUNDERS DIDN'T rely on pollsters. At the time of the Revolution, the American colonists, John Adams recalled, were "about one third Tories"—loyal to the British crown—"and [one] third timid, and one third true blue." Adams was true blue. "Sink or swim, live or die, survive or perish, I am with my country from this day on," he told a friend in 1774. "You may depend on it."

By the summer of '76, as Adams cajoled his fellow delegates to the Second Continental Congress in Philadelphia to declare independence from Great Britain, perishing was a distinct possibility. On the night of July 2, as the delegates were casting their first votes, word reached Philadelphia that a hundred British warships and troop transports had been sighted off New York.

The empire was striking back. The colonists had driven British forces from Boston in March, but now a vast armada—some 400 ships, packed with regiments of crack British redcoats and highly trained Hessian mercenaries—was arriving from the motherland to crush the upstart rebellion. By August there were more British soldiers in New York (32,000) than there were people (30,000) in Philadelphia, the largest Colonial city, a couple of days' march away. Between them stood George

Washington's Army of some 7,000 men, mostly untested, ill-equipped farmers.

The Founders were acutely aware that in signing the Declaration of Independence they were committing treason, for which the penalty was death

By affixing their signatures to the Declaration of Independence, the Founders were acutely aware that they were committing treason, the penalty for which was death. "We must all hang together, or most assuredly, we will hang separately," darkly joked Benjamin Franklin. On July 4, as the Declaration was being sent to the printers, one signer, Benjamin Harrison of Virginia, said to another, Elbridge Gerry of Massachusetts, "I shall have a great advantage over you, Mr. Gerry, when we are all hung for what we are now doing. From the size and weight of my body, I shall die in a few minutes, but from the lightness of your body you will dance in the air an hour or two before you are dead." Gerry was reported to have smiled, briefly. No one doubted the gravity of their actions. As he signed the document, Stephen

Hopkins of Rhode Island, who suffered from palsy, exclaimed, "My hand trembles, but my heart does not."

Two and a quarter centuries later, we have a new appreciation for the courage and the vision of the Founders (no longer called the Founding Fathers, for reasons of political correctness). As soon as this week, Congress is expected to authorize a national memorial to John Adams. David McCullough's new biography of Adams, published last month, went straight to No. 1 on the best-seller list, and historian Joseph Ellis's Pulitzer Prize-winning "Founding Brothers" has been a top seller for more than half a year. Why? "Partly, it's a desire for authenticity," McCullough told NEWS-WEEK. In an age of media-obsessed, poll-driven politicians who cannot, it sometimes seems, make a speech or cast a vote without hiring a consultant, many Americans are nostalgic for an earlier era of genuine statesmen. By humanizing the Founders, McCullough and others have rescued them from the sterility of schoolbooks and, vividly and often movingly, showed them overcoming their fears and flaws.

ADAMS, JEFFERSON, WASHINGTON and all the rest were the real thing, all right. They were an Even Greater Generation. While the World War II veterans deserve honor for preserving freedom in the world, in a real sense the Founders not only won freedom—they created it. The United States may seem inevitable today—a quasi-divine inspiration, schoolchildren were long told—but its genesis was painful and harrowing, and the nation was very nearly stillborn.

Washington's pickup Army could have been annihilated by the British in New York that summer of '76, had it not slipped away in the dead of night under the cover of some providential fog. The Continentals' victories over the course of the next few years were sporadic and small. General Washington was a genius at lifting morale and knowing when to retreat to fight again another day. But independence was not secured until France, Britain's global rival, intervened to bottle up the British Army at Yorktown, Va., in 1781. And America did not become a true nation until the Founders produced a constitution that was a blend of visionary foresight and careful compromise in 1787.

In an age of poll-driven politicians who cannot make a speech without hiring a consultant, Americans are nostalgic for an earlier era of genuine statesmen

---

It is hard to think of the Founders as revolutionaries. They seem too stuffy, too much the proper gentlemen in breeches and powdered wigs. But Jefferson, Adams, Madison et al. were, in fact, extreme radicals. They were far from pure. For all their high-minded rhetoric, the Founders were not above deal-cutting and backstabbing. They would have been right at home on "Hardball," had such a thing existed. It is certainly also true that they ducked the question that later split apart the nation and haunts us still—the moral obligation to free the slaves who made up almost a fifth of the Colonies' population. Yet "to focus, as we are apt to, on what the Revolution did not accomplish—highlighting and la-

menting its failure to abolish slavery and change fundamentally the lot of women—is to miss the great significance of what it did accomplish," wrote Brown University historian Gordon Wood, perhaps the leading scholar of the Revolutionary era, in his 1991 book, "The Radicalism of the American Revolution." "Indeed, the Revolution made possible the anti-slavery and women's movements of the 19th century, and in fact all our current egalitarian thinking."

Two men in particular stand out in the Revolutionary generation. Thomas Jefferson was lean, elegant, remote, spendthrift and a little devious. John Adams was stout, bristly, frugal and perhaps too honest about himself and everyone else. Jefferson had a great faith in improving mankind but "comparatively little interest in human nature," observes McCullough. "Adams," on the other hand, "was not inclined to believe mankind improvable, but believed an understanding of human nature was of utmost importance." Jefferson and Adams were in effect the perfect match for an undertaking that required equal parts dreaminess and hardheadedness, cunning and honor. Their rivalry, falling-out and later renewal of friendship offers a human template for understanding the depth and reach of the Founders' accomplishment, a creation so extraordinary that it surprised—and ultimately frightened—the Founders themselves.

IN HIS DRAFT OF THE DECLARATION OF independence, Thomas Jefferson wrote for all time, "We hold these truths to be self-evident, that all men are created equal…" Yet until that time equality had not been self-evident in the least. Since at least the days of ancient Rome, society had been divided into "the vulgar mob" and their "betters." In many places, an ordinary man had to take off his hat and step out of the street when a gentleman rode by, or risk being trampled with impunity. "Order is Heaven's first law; and this confest, / Some are, and must be, greater than the rest," wrote the 18th-century satirist Alexander Pope.

The Founders were creatures of a new "Enlightenment." They refused to accept that birth dictated place. "Virtue is not

hereditary," wrote Thomas Paine, whose "Common Sense" aroused egalitarian sensibilities in the 13 Colonies. The common man, the Founders believed, was not a beast to be kept tightly leashed; he was a blank slate upon which virtue and goodness could be written. "The mind once enlightened cannot again become dark," wrote Paine.

Jefferson was especially optimistic, even utopian. Heavily influenced by the French *philosophes*, who found benevolence to be man's natural state, Jefferson believed that the "will of the people" was inherently benign. Men (though, not yet, blacks or women) were fully capable of self-governance. Indeed, men behaved best, Jefferson argued, when governed least. From the luxury of his mountaintop farm in Virginia, filled with French furniture and worked by 200 slaves, the Sage of Monticello imagined a nation of honest and free farmers, laboring and living in harmony, lightly led by a natural aristocracy of virtue and talent.

Adams knew better. The Massachusetts lawyer had always been a self-declared student of the "labyrinth of human nature." Happily married, he listened closely to his wise wife, Abigail, who in 1775 wrote him, "I am more and more convinced that man is a dangerous creature, and that power whether vested in the many or few is ever grasping… The great fish swallow up the small fish." Adams replied: "I think you shine as a stateswoman." Adams used self-awareness as a tool of political science. He had only to look at his own vanity, his yearning for praise and distinction, to know that power needed to be checked. Forcefully, and as it turned out wisely, he insisted that the popular will of the legislature be balanced by a strong executive and an independent judiciary.

An irascible contrarian, Adams argued too hotly for his own good. Following George Washington as the nation's second president, he believed the chief executive should be called "His Majesty." His more democratically inclined colleagues in the fledgling republic accused Adams of wishing to restore the monarchy and mocked him as "Your Rotundity." Feeling surrounded and betrayed, Adams foolishly enacted the Alien and Sedition Acts so he could jail his critics, a terrible moment for free expression. Adams was not paranoid in suspecting that even his friends were conspiring against him. Stirring up trouble (though always from behind a veil) was Adams's own vice president, Thomas Jefferson. Using scandal-mongering journalists to spread vicious rumors about his revolutionary comrade, Jefferson helped ensure that Adams served only one term (1797–1801) as president—and was succeeded by Jefferson.

IN HIS MAGISTERIAL AND READABLE biography of Adams, McCullough clearly takes the side of his protagonist. In "John Adams," the hero is honest, if to a fault, and perceptive, while Jefferson is deceitful and naive. McCullough is perhaps too harsh on Jefferson. Great political leaders often need to be a little slippery and even self-delusional to survive factional struggles and balance irreconcilable interests. (In the 20th century Franklin Roosevelt and Ronald Reagan come to mind.) Unlike Adams, Jefferson was elected to a second term and accomplished much as president, most notably the Louisiana Purchase.

Adams sulked over Jefferson's perfidy for more than a decade, but he finally swallowed his pride and reached out to his fellow Founder. From their retirements—Jefferson's at Monticello, Adams's at his more modest farm in Quincy, Mass., which he self-mockingly dubbed "Montezito"—the two old statesmen repaired their friendship through 128 letters between 1812 and 1826. Writing with their eyes firmly fixed on posterity, Adams and Jefferson relived—and on occasion rewrote—the past. "I look back with rapture to those golden days," penned Adams to Jefferson in 1825, "when Virginia and Massachusetts lived and acted together like a band of brothers." In pungent, incisive prose (Adams) or with elegant, sometimes lyrical fluidity (Jefferson), the two men reflected, with growing apprehension, on the present and future of the republic they had helped create.

They bemoaned the rise of faction and interest in the political system, and crime and licentiousness in society. Freedom had brought their countrymen a measure of happiness, perhaps, but not, it seemed, greater virtue. America's capacity for alcohol consumption was staggering: by the 1820s Americans were downing spirits at the rate of five gallons per person per year, nearly triple today's levels and higher than Europe's.

Jefferson was bewildered and disillusioned. He had lived too long, longer than most of the Founders. "All, all dead," he wrote to a friend in 1825, "and ourselves left alone amidst a new generation we know not, and who knows us not." He was sick and, attached to French wines and furnishings as well as French philosophers, too indebted to free his 200 slaves.

Adams, too, was discouraged. He was bothered by the rise of evangelical societies and mob rule, which he linked to a streak of unreason unanticipated by even the most prescient Founders. "Where is now, the progress of the human mind?" he railed. "When? Where? and How? is the present Chaos to be arranged to Order?" he demanded as early as 1813. Yet Adams was also able to see beyond the tumult of the moment to appreciate that the new republic would stand for—he predicted—two centuries.

On July 4, 1826, the 50th anniversary of the Declaration of Independence, both Adams and Jefferson lay dying. Told that it was the Fourth, Adams stirred and said, "It is a great day. It is a good day." At Monticello, as bells celebrating Independence Day could be heard faintly ringing in the valley below, Thomas Jefferson died at around 1 p.m. At his home in Quincy, Adams could hear cannons, then natural thunder. Before he, too, died, he whispered, "Jefferson survives." Both Adams and Jefferson live on, newly remembered and praised. And so, 175 years later, does their legacy, the longest-lasting republic in the history of mankind.

Your Constitution Is Killing You

A reconsideration of the right to bear arms

By Daniel Lazare

A well regulated Militia, being necessary to the security of a free State, the right of the people to keep and bear Arms, shall not be infringed.

—Second Amendment to the Constitution of the United States

On June 17, in the aftermath of the massacre at Columbine High School and a similar, if less grisly, incident the following month in Conyers, Georgia, the House of Representatives passed a "juvenile crime bill" steadfast in its refusal to limit the ease with which juveniles can lay their hands on firearms. House Republicans, it was clear, were determined to avoid making any connection between the fact that there are an estimated 240 million guns in the United States, nearly one per person, a number that is increasing by some 5 to 7 million a year, and the increase of violence in our culture. Instead, the problem was that we had forgotten the importance of "family values," that our children had become "spoiled with material things," that we had given in to "liberal relativism." Guns weren't the problem; the problem was

"the abandonment of God" in the public sphere.

Representatives Henry Hyde (R., Ill.) and Tom DeLay (R., Tex.) were particularly enthusiastic in their efforts to look beyond guns for a solution. Hyde put the blame on the entertainment industry and tried to push through an amendment to the crime bill that would have made it a jailable offense to sell overtly violent or sexual material to minors. Even when 127 of his fellow Republicans voted against the measure, Hyde refused to let go. "People were misled," he said, "and disinclined to oppose the powerful entertainment industry." DeLay's approach was even more entertaining. At a "God Not Guns" rally, he read aloud an e-mail he claimed to have received that very morning: "The student writes, 'Dear God, Why didn't you stop the shootings at Columbine?' And God writes, 'Dear student, I would have, but I wasn't allowed in school.'" (So much for divine omnipotence.) An hour later DeLay was on the House floor, telling his colleagues that "our school systems teach the children that they are nothing but glorified apes who are evolutionized out of some primordial soup of mud." Other DeLay-isms: "We place our children in daycare centers where they learn their socializa-

tion skills... under the law of the jungle..."; "Our children, who historically have been seen as a blessing from God, are now viewed as either a mistake created when contraception fails or inconveniences that parents try to raise in their spare time." A proposal to allow the display of the Ten Commandments in public schools was subsequently voted into the bill.

Liberals cannot bear to admit the truth about gun control; the right wing is right. The second amendment confers an individual right

---

Among the further futile gestures housed in a second piece of crime legislation that failed the next day was a measure to reduce the Senate's proposed waiting time for purchases at gun shows and to limit the number of gun shows subject to any waiting period whatsoever. All this despite polls showing two-to-one support for stricter gun control even before Columbine. Two centuries ago, the great fear among the men who drew up the United States Constitution was of a popularly elected legislature falling all over itself to do the public's bidding; today we are witness to a popularly elected body falling all over itself not to carry out the democratic will. Why?

The standard liberal response is that the National Rifle Association made them do it. The NRA has used its immense campaign war chest to punish gun-control advocates and stifle dissent. It has twisted and distorted the Constitution. It has cleared a path for troglodytes like Hyde and DeLay. But the real problem is more disconcerting. The reason that Hyde and Co. are able to dominate the gun debate, the reason that the gun lobby is so powerful, is not the NRA but the basis on which the NRA's power rests; i.e., the Second Amendment. The truth about the Second Amendment is something that liberals cannot bear to admit: The right wing is right. The amendment does confer an individual right to bear arms, and its very presence makes effective gun control in this country all but impossible.

For decades liberal constitutional scholars have maintained that, contrary to the NRA, the Second Amendment does not guarantee an individual's right to own guns, merely a right to participate in an official state militia. The key phrase, they have argued, is "[a] well regulated Militia," which the introductory clause describes as nothing less than essential to "the security of a free State." A well-regulated militia is not just a goal, consequently, but *the* goal, the amendment's raison d'être. Everything else is subordinate. The right "to keep and bear Arms" is valid only to the degree that it serves this all-important end. There is therefore no *individual right* to bear arms in and of itself, only a *collective* right on the part of the citizens of the states to do so as members of the various official state militias. The right to own the assault weapon of one's choice exists only in the fevered imagination of the National Rifle Association. Its constitutional basis is nil. The only right that the Second Amendment confers is the right

to emulate Dan Quayle and join the National Guard.

This is the cheerful, anodyne version of the Second Amendment we're used to from the American Civil Liberties Union and other liberal groups. But as the gun issue has heated up since the Sixties and Seventies, constitutional scholars have taken a second look. The result has been both a renaissance in Second Amendment studies and a remarkable about-face in how it is interpreted. The purely "collectivist" interpretation has been rejected across the board by liberals and conservatives as ahistorical and overly pat. The individualist interpretation, the one that holds that Americans have a right to bear arms whether they're serving in an official state militia or not, has been more or less vindicated. In fact, some academics have gone so far as to compare the NRA's long campaign in behalf of an expansive interpretation of the Second Amendment to the ACLU's long campaign in behalf of an expansive reading of the First. As the well-known constitutional scholar William Van Alstyne put it, "The constructive role of the NRA today, like the role of the ACLU in the 1920s,… ought itself not lightly to be dismissed. Indeed, it is largely by the 'unreasonable' persistence of just such organizations in this country that the Bill of Rights has endured." Language like this is what one might expect at some Texas or Colorado gun show, not in the pages of the Duke Law Journal.

With day traders and students shooting citizens, the implications of an individual right to bear arms are profound

---

No less strikingly, the Second Amendment renaissance has also led to a renewed appreciation for the amendment's ideological importance. Previously, scholars were inclined to view the Second Amendment as little more than a historical curiosity, not unlike the Third Amendment, which, as almost no one remembers, prohibits the peacetime quartering of troops in private homes without

the owners' consent. Harvard's Laurence Tribe gave the Second Amendment no more than a footnote in the 1988 edition of his famous textbook *American Constitutional Law,* but a new edition, published this August, treats the subject much more extensively. It is now apparent that the amendment, despite its brevity, encapsulates an entire worldview concerning the nature of political power, the rights and duties of citizenship, and the relationship between the individual and the state. It *is* virtually a constitution-within-the-Constitution, which is undoubtedly why it fuels such fierce passions.

With crazed day traders and resentful adolescents mowing down large numbers of their fellow citizens every few weeks, the implications of this new, toughened-up version of the Second Amendment would seem to be profound. Politically, there's no doubt that it has already had an effect by encouraging the gun lobby to dig in its heels after Littleton, Conyers, the Mark Barton rampage in Atlanta, and the earlier shootings in Kentucky, Arkansas, and elsewhere. When Joyce Lee Malcolm, professor of history at Bentley College in Waltham, Massachusetts, and the author of a path-breaking 1994 study, *To Keep and Bear Arms: The Origins of an Anglo-American Right* (Harvard University Press), told a congressional committee a year later that "[i]t is very hard, sir, to find a historian who now believes that it is only a collective right… [t]here is no one for me to argue against anymore," it was just the sort of thing that pro-gun forces on Capitol Hill wanted to hear. If it wasn't a sign that God was on their side, then it was a sign that the Constitution was, which in American politics is more or less the same thing.

The judicial impact is a bit harder to assess. Although the Supreme Court has not ruled on the Second Amendment since the 1930s, it has repeatedly upheld gun control measures. But there is evidence that judicial sentiment is beginning to take heed of the academic change of heart. Two years ago, Supreme Court Justice Clarence Thomas indicated that he thought it was time to rethink the Second Amendment; Justice Antonin Scalia apparently thinks so as well. Then, just this past April, two weeks before Eric

Harris and Dylan Klebold shot up Columbine High School, a federal judge in a Texas gun case issued a ruling so enthusiastically "individualist" that it was virtually a brief in favor of what is now known in academic circles as the "Standard Model" of the Second Amendment. "The plain language of the amendment," declared Judge Sam R. Cummings, "shows that the function of the subordinate clause [i.e., the portion referring to a well-regulated militia] was not to qualify the right [to keep and bear arms], but instead to show why it must be protected." Rather than mutually exclusive, the collective right to join a state militia and the individual right to own a gun are, according to Cummings, mutually reinforcing. Although anti-gun groups predicted that the decision would soon be overturned, it is clear that a purely collectivist reading is becoming harder and harder to defend; the individualist interpretation, harder and harder to deny.

We have long been in the habit of seeing in the Constitution whatever it is we want to see. Because liberals want a society that is neat and orderly, they tell themselves that this is what the Constitution "wants" as well. This is a little like a nineteenth-century country vicar arguing that the Bible stands for moderation, reform, and other such Victorian virtues when in fact, as anyone who actually reads the text can see, it is filled with murder, mayhem, and the arbitrary vengeance of a savage god. By the same token, the increasingly sophisticated scholarship surrounding the Second Amendment has led to renewed respect for the constitutional text as it is rather than as we would like it to be. The Constitution, it turns out, is not neat and orderly but messy and unruly. It is not modern but pre-modern. It is not the product of a time very much like our own but reflects the unresolved contradictions of a time very different from our own.

Could it be that the Constitution is not the greatest plan on earth, that it contains notions that are repugnant to the modern sensibility? "When we are lost, the best thing for us to do is to look to our Constitution as a beacon of light and a guide to get us through trying times." So declaimed Representative Zoe Lofgren (D., Calif.) during the House impeachment debate last October. Considering how we've all been taught since childhood to revere this document, probably not one American in a thousand would disagree. But what if Zoe Lofgren is wrong—what if the sacred text is seriously, if not fatally, flawed? Could it be that constitutional faith is not enough to get us through trying times? In a faithbound republic like the United States, this is pretty heretical stuff. Yet one of the nice things about the Second Amendment renaissance is the way it forces us to grapple with such heresy. Instead of allowing us to go on blindly trusting in the wisdom of a group of tribal patriarchs known as the Founding Fathers, it compels us to think for ourselves.

Could it be that the constitution is not the greatest plan, that it contains notions repugnant to the modern sensibility?

The framers, as it turns out, were of two minds where the power of the people was concerned. The Preamble to the Constitution implies a theory of unbounded popular sovereignty in which "we the people" are so powerful that we can "ordain and establish" new constitutions and, in the process, abrogate old ones such as the disastrous Articles of Confederation. The rest of the document implies that "we the people" are so powerless that when it comes to an anachronism such as the Second Amendment, the democratic majority is effectively precluded from changing a Constitution made in the people's name. We the people can move mountains, but we cannot excise one troublesome twenty-seven-word clause. Because we have chained ourselves to a premodern Constitution, we are unable to deal with the modern problem of a runaway gun culture in a modern way. Rather than binding society together, the effort to force society to conform to the dictates of an outmoded

plan of government is tearing it apart. Each new crazed gunman is a symptom of our collective—one might say our constitutional—helplessness. Someday soon, we will have to emancipate ourselves from our eighteenth-century Constitution. The only question is how.

Americans tend to give history short shrift; after all, when your Constitution is a timeless masterpiece, who needs to bother with something as boring as the past? But in order to unlock the meaning of the Second Amendment, it is necessary to know a little about the world in which it was created. The most important thing to understand is the eighteenth century's role as the great transitional period. Capitalism, industrialism, the rise of the great metropolis, the creation of new kinds of politics—these were beginning to make themselves felt, and as they did so they were creating shock waves and counter shock waves from one end of the English-speaking world to the other. Urbanization fueled passionate defenses of the old agrarian way of life. A new system of government centered on a prime minister, a cabinet, and an all-powerful House of Commons provoked endless screeds in favor of the old system of checks and balances among a multitude of coequal governing institutions.

This is the source of the great eighteenth-century polarization between what was known as Court and Country— the powerbrokers, influence-wielders, and political fixers on one side, and all those who felt shut out by the new arrangement on the other. Since the 1960s, historians have made immense strides in reconstructing this Anglo-American ideological world. In essence, we now know that it was dominated by fierce controversy over the nature of political power: whether it was harmful or beneficial, oppressive or liberating, whether it should be concentrated in a single legislative chamber or distributed among many. The Country opposition believed passionately in the latter. As a couple of coffeehouse radicals named John Trenchard and Thomas Gordon put it in their hugely popular *Cato's Letters* in the 1720s, "Power is like fire; it warms, scorches, or destroys according as it is watched, provoked, or increased." The solution was to divide power among so many competitive institutions that politicians' "emulation, envy, fear, or interest, always made them spies and checks upon one another." Since power was growing, oppression was growing also. "Patriots," therefore, were continually fighting a rear-guard action against corruption and tyranny, which were forever on the increase.

Guns were a big part of the eighteenth-century Anglo-American debate, in which the popular militia represented freedom at its most noble

---

We can recognize in eighteenth-century beliefs like these such modern U.S. attitudes as the cult of checks and balances, hostility to "big gummint," and the Zoe Lofgrenesque conviction that everything will turn out well so long as we remain true to the constitutional faith of our forefathers. Guns, as it turns out, were also a big part of the eighteenth-century Anglo-American debate. "Standing armies," the great bugaboo of the day, represented concentrated power at its most brutal; the late-medieval institution of the popular militia represented freedom at its most noble and idealistic. Beginning with the highly influential Niccolò Machiavelli, a long line of political commentators stressed the special importance of the popular militias in the defense of liberty. Since the only ones who could defend popular liberty were the people themselves, a freedom-loving people had to maintain themselves in a high state of republican readiness. They had to be strong and independent, keep themselves well armed, and be well versed in the arts of war. The moment they allowed themselves to surrender to the wiles of luxury, the cause of liberty was lost.

Thus, we have Sir Walter Raleigh warning that the first goal of a would-be tyrant is to "unarm his people of weapons, money, and all means whereby they may resist his power." In the mid-

seventeenth century, we have the political theorist James Harrington stressing the special importance of an armed yeomanry of self-sufficient small farmers, while in the early eighteenth we have Trenchard and Gordon warning that "[t]he Exercise of despotick Power is the unrelenting War of an armed Tyrant upon his unarmed Subjects." In the 1770s, James Burgh, another writer in this long Country tradition, advised that "[n]o kingdom can be secured [against tyranny] otherwise than by arming the people. The possession of arms is the distinction between a freeman and a slave." A pro-American English radical named Richard Price added in 1784 that

> [T]he happiest state of man is the middle state between the *savage* and the *refined,* or between the wild and the luxurious state. Such is the state of society in CONNECTICUT, and in some others of the *American* provinces; where the inhabitants consist, if I am rightly informed, of an independent and hardy YEOMANRY, all nearly on a level—trained to arms,—instructed in their rights—cloathed in home-spun—of simple manners—strangers to luxury—drawing plenty from the ground—and that plenty, gathered easily by the hand of industry.

Not only were guns needed for self-defense but their widespread possession confirmed America's self-image as Homeland of Liberty

---

This was the Country myth in all its glory, the image of the roughhewn, liberty-loving "republican" as someone who called no one master, equated freedom and independence, and was not afraid to fight in defense of either or both. Joyce Lee Malcolm points out that where English patriots were content to pay lip service to the importance of arming the people, their cousins across the sea took the notion quite literally. A law

passed by the Plymouth Colony in 1623 required "that every freeman or other inhabitant of this colony provide for himselfe and each under him able to beare arms a sufficient musket and other serviceable peece for war." A 1639 law in Newport ordered that "noe man shall go two miles from the Towne unarmed, eyther with Gunn or Sword; and that none shall come to any public Meeting without his weapon." Measures like these were both practical and symbolic. Not only were guns necessary for self-defense but their widespread possession confirmed America's self-image as a homeland of liberty.

Ideas like these do not seem to have abated the least bit during the colonial period; indeed, by the 1770s they were at full boil. By the time British Redcoats faced off against heavily armed colonial irregulars at the Battle of Lexington and Concord in April 1775, it was as if both sides were actors in a political passion play that had been centuries in the making. It was the standing army versus the people's militia, the metropolis versus the hinterlands, centralized imperial power versus the old balanced constitution. Although the militias performed less than brilliantly in the Revolutionary War—Washington, professional soldier that he was, thought that the ragtag volunteer outfits were more trouble than they were worth—the myth lingered on. Americans needed to believe that amateur citizen-soldiers had won the war because their ideology told them that it was only via a popular militia that republican virtue could be established.

It is worth noting that even among those who were skeptical about the militias' military worth, the concept of a people in arms does not seem to have been at all problematic. Although Alexander Hamilton argued against separate state militias at the Constitutional Convention in 1787, for example, he seemed to have had nothing against popular militias per se. In 1788, he argued in *The Federalist Papers* that in the unlikely event that the proposed new national government used what was known at the time as a "select" militia—i.e., an elite corps—to oppress the population at large, the rest of the militia would be more than enough to fight them off. Such "a large body of citizens," he wrote, "little if at all inferior to them in discipline and the use of arms,… [would] stand ready to defend their own rights and those of their fellow-citizens." This is one reason why the argument that the Second Amendment confers only a collective right to join the National Guard is specious: today's National Guard is far closer to the eighteenth-century concept of a select militia than to the broad, popular militia the Framers clearly had in mind. And if the Second Amendment was nothing more than a guarantee of a right on the part of the states to organize state militias, it would imply that only the federal government was potentially tyrannical. Yet it is clear from James Madison's writings in *The Federalist Papers* that he saw state governments as potential sources of tyranny as well. Madison wrote that "the advantage of being armed" was one of the things that distinguished Americans from all other nations and helped protect them against abuse of power at all levels of government, federal and state. Antifederalists quite agreed. Their only quibble was that they demanded a Bill of Rights; they wanted the right to bear arms put in writing for all to see.

The meaning of what is now the Second Amendment becomes clearer still if we take a look at how its wording evolved. Madison's original version, which he drew up in 1789 as a member of the newly created House of Representatives, was on the wordy side but at least had the merit of clarity:

> The right of the people to keep and bear arms shall not be infringed; a well armed and well regulated militia being the best security of a free country; but no person religiously scrupulous of bearing arms shall be compelled to render military service in person.

By reversing the order between the right to bear arms and a well-regulated militia, Madison reversed the priority. Rather than a precondition, his original version suggested that a well-ordered militia was merely one of the good things that flowed from universal gun owner-

ship. A committee to which the amendment was referred, however, changed the order so that the amendment now read,

> A well regulated militia, composed of the body of the people, being the best security of a free State, the right of the people to keep and bear arms shall not be infringed, but no person religiously scrupulous shall be compelled to bear arms.

This was confusing but at least made plain that a militia was essentially synonymous with the people at large. Unfortunately, that notion, too, was lost when the Senate got hold of the amendment and began chopping out words right and left. The reference to "the body of the people" wound up on the cutting-room floor, as did the final clause. The effect was to deprive later generations of an important clue as to what a well-regulated militia actually meant. Although the final version was leaner and more compact, it was also a good deal less clear.

If the Framers were less than explicit about the nature of a well-regulated militia, it was because they didn't feel they had to be

Nonetheless, a few things seem evident. If the Framers were less than explicit about the nature of a well-regulated militia, it was because they didn't feel they had to be. The idea of a popular militia as something synonymous with the people as a whole was so well understood in the eighteenth century that it went without saying, which is undoubtedly why the Senate felt that the reference to "the body of the people" could be safely eliminated. It is also important to note that the flat-out declaration "[t]he right of the people to keep and bear arms shall not be infringed" remained unchanged throughout the drafting process. As Joyce Lee Malcolm has noted, the Second Amendment is a reworking of a provision contained in the English Bill of Rights of 1689. But whereas the English

Bill of Rights specified that subjects "may have arms for their defense suitable to their conditions, and as allowed by law," the American version avoided any such restrictions. Since all Americans (or, rather, members of the white male minority) were of the same rank, they possessed the same rights. They could bear arms for any purpose. And since the amendment was now part of the Constitution, the right was not limited by ordinary law but was over and above it. It was the source of law rather than the object. In this regard, as in virtually all others, Americans saw their role as taking ancient liberties and strengthening them so as to render tyranny all the more unlikely.

In the search for the meaning of the second amendment, we must recognize that "meaning" is problematic across the span of centuries

Although members of the legal academy assume that this is where the discussion ends, they're wrong: it's where the real questions begin. In attempting to nail down the meaning of the Second Amendment, we are therefore forced to recognize that "meaning" itself is problematic, especially across the span of more than two centuries. Once we have finished dissecting the Second Amendment, we are still left with a certain tension that necessarily exists between a well-regulated militia on the one hand and a right to bear arms on the other. One suggests order and discipline, if not government control; the other suggests voluntarism and a welling up from below. Eighteenth-century Country ideology tried to resolve this contradiction by envisioning the popular militia as a place where liberty and discipline would converge, where a freedom-loving people would enjoy the right to bear arms while proving their republican mettle by voluntarily rising to the defense of liberty. But although this certainly sounded nice, a harrowing eight-year war for independence had demonstrated the limits of such voluntarism. No-nonsense Federalists such as Washington and Hamilton recognized that there was no substitute for a professional army, not to mention a strong, centralized nation-state. But they also recognized that they had to get along with elements for whom such ideas were anathema. As a result, they felt they had no choice but to put aside their scruples and promise effective discipline from above and spontaneous self-organization from below, strong national government and states' rights, as contradictory as those notions might now seem.

The *meaning* of the Second Amendment, therefore, incorporates the contradictions in the Founders' thinking. But what's true for the Second Amendment is true for the Constitution as a whole. In June, William Safire rather naively suggested in his *New York Times* column that the solution to the problem of "the Murky Second" was to use the constitutional amending process to clarify its meaning. Did Americans have an unqualified right to bear arms or merely a right to enlist in the National Guard? Since the Founders had "botched" the wording, the solution was simply to fix it. This is indeed logical, but the problem is that the amending process is entirely useless in this instance. Because Article V stipulates that two thirds of each house, plus three fourths of the states, are required to change so much as a comma, as few as thirteen states—representing, by the way, as little as 4.5 percent of the total U.S. population—would be sufficient to block any change. Since no one would have any trouble coming up with a list of thirteen states in the South or the West for whom repealing the sacred Second Amendment would be akin to repealing the four Gospels, the issue is moot.

Since "we the people" are powerless to change the Second Amendment, we must somehow learn to live within its confines. But since this means standing by helplessly while ordinary people are gunned down by a succession of heavily armed maniacs, it is becoming more and more difficult to do so. As a result, politicians from President Clinton on down are forever coming up with ways of reconciling the irreconcilable, of reining in the gun trade without challenging the Second Amendment-fueled gun culture. The upshot is an endless series of ridiculous proposals to ban some kinds of firearms but not others, to limit handgun purchases to one a month, or to provide for background checks at otherwise unregulated traveling gun bazaars. Instead of cracking down on guns, the administration has found it easier to crack down on video games and theater owners who allow sixteen-year-olds to sneak into adult movies. The moral seems to be that guns don't kill people—fart jokes in the R-rated *South Park: Bigger, Longer & Uncut* do.

Why must we subordinate ourselves to a 208-year-old law that, if the latest scholarship is correct, is contrary to what we want?

This is the flip side of the unbounded faith of a Zoe Lofgren or a Barbara Jordan, who famously declared during Watergate, "My faith in the Constitution is whole, it is complete, it is total...." If one's faith in the Constitution is total, then one's faith in the Second Amendment is total as well, which means that one places obedience to ancient law above the needs of modern society. Once all the back-and-forth over the meaning of the Second Amendment is finished, the question we're left with is: So what? No one is suggesting that the Founders' thinking on the gun issue is irrelevant, but because they settled on a certain balance between freedom and order, are we obliged to follow suit? Or are we free to strike a different balance? Times change. From a string of coastal settlements, the United States has grown into a republic of 270 million people stretching across the entire North American continent. It is a congested, polluted society filled with traffic jams, shopping malls, and anomic suburbs in which an eighteenth-century right to bear arms is as out of place as silk knee britches and tricornered hats. So why must we subordinate ourselves to a 208-year-old law that, if the latest scholarship is correct, is contrary to what the democratic majority believes is in its best interest? Why can't *we* create the kind of society we want as opposed to living with laws meant to create the kind of society *they* wanted? They are dead and buried and will not be around to suffer the consequences. We the living will.

There is simply no solution to the gun problem within the confines of the U.S. Constitution. As the well-known Yale law professor Akhil Reed Amar put it recently, the Constitution serves to "structure the conversation of ordinary Americans as they ponder the most fundamental and sometimes divisive issues in our republic." In other words, the Constitution's hold on our society is so complete that it controls the way we discuss and debate, even the way we think. Americans are unable to conceive of an alternative framework, to think "outside the box," as the corporate strategists put it. Other countries are free to change their constitutions when it becomes necessary. In fact, with the exception of Luxembourg, Norway, and Great Britain, there is not one advanced industrial nation that has not thoroughly revamped its constitution since 1900. If they can do it, why can't we? Why must Americans remain slaves to the past?

Daniel Lazare is the author of The Frozen Republic: How the Constitution Is Paralyzing Democracy, *published by Harcourt Brace. His book about the prospects for re-urbanization in the twenty-first century,* America's Undeclared War, *was published on April 23, 2001.*

UNIT 3

National Consolidation and Expansion

Unit Selections

Key Points to Consider

- There is no provision in the Constitution for political parties. How and why did they arise when they did?

- Why can the Louisiana Purchase be considered "The Revolution of 1803?" Discuss the ramifications of this acquisition at the time and for the future course of American history.

- How did President Andrew Jackson succeed in removing the Cherokee Indians from Georgia? Why was the Indians' migration referred to as "The Trail of Tears?"

- The settling of the American West is presented in popular lore as the triumphant advance of civilization into the wilderness. What about those who were shunted aside in this process? What role did women play?

- Successive potato crops failures in Ireland forced many to emigrate. What reception did those who settled in the Unites States encounter? Are there similarities with attitudes toward more recent immigrants?

- Why did John Brown's raid on Harpers Ferry arouse such emotion in both the North and the South? How did he seem to symbolize the issues of the day?

 **Links: www.dushkin.com/online/**
These sites are annotated in the World Wide Web pages.

Consortium for Political and Social Research
http://www.icpsr.umich.edu

Department of State
http://www.state.gov

Mystic Seaport
http://amistad.mysticseaport.org/

Social Influence Website
http://www.workingpsychology.com/intro.html

University of Virginia Library
http://www.lib.virginia.edu/exhibits/lewis_clark/

Women in America
http://xroads.virginia.edu/~HYPER/DETOC/FEM/

Women of the West
http://www.wowmuseum.org/

The individuals who wrote the American Constitution could only provide a general structure that the government would work under. Those involved in actually making the system function had to venture into uncharted territory. There were no blueprints for which body had what powers, or what their relationships with one another would be. And, if disputes arose, which individual or group would act as arbiter? Officials during the first few years after 1789 were conscious that practically everything they did would be regarded as setting precedents for the future. Even such trivial matters as the proper form of addressing the president caused debate. From hindsight of more than 200 years, it is difficult to appreciate how tentative they had to be in establishing this newborn government.

The most fundamental difference over the Constitution arose over whether it should be interpreted strictly or loosely. That is, should governmental powers be limited to those expressly granted in the document, or were there "implied" powers that could be exercised as long as they were not expressly prohibited? Many of the disputes were argued on principles, but the truth is that most individuals were trying to promote programs that would benefit the interests they represented.

George Washington, as first president, was a towering figure who provided a stabilizing presence during the seemingly endless squabbles. He believed that he served the entire nation, and that there was no need for political parties (he disdainfully referred to them as "factions") which he regarded as divisive. Despite his disapproval, nascent political parties did begin to develop fairly early on in his first administration. Washington, first Secretary of the Treasury, Alexander Hamilton, almost invariably favored those measures that would benefit the commercial and manufacturing interests of the Northeast. Secretary of State, Thomas Jefferson and his ally James Madison just as often spoke for the rural and agricultural interests of the West and the South. These two groups frequently clashed over what the Constitution did or did not permit, what sources of revenue should be tapped to pay for government, and a host of other issues. The fact that Washington most often sided with Hamilton's views made him a partisan despite his wish to remain above the fray.

Washington's enormous prestige delayed the creation of formal political parties until he was out of office. In "The First Democrats," author Joseph J. Ellis shows how this changed after John Adams became president in 1797. It was not an edifying spectacle. As Ellis puts it, the two-part system arose "amid backroom deals, lying politicians, and a scandal-hungry press."

The United States already was a large country by 1803, stretching from the Atlantic Ocean to the Mississippi River. Some said it was too large. Propertied Easterners complained that the western migration lowered property values and raised wages, and they feared population shifts would weaken their section's influence in government. Other thought that the great distances involved might cause the system to fly apart, given the primitive means of communication and transportation at the time. When Thomas Jefferson had the unexpected opportunity to double the nation's size by purchasing the huge Louisiana Territory, as discussed in "The Revolution of 1803," he altered the course of American history. "Brains and Brawn: The Lewis and Clark Expedition" describes the Jefferson-sponsored effort to find out just what had been acquired.

Coverage of African-Americans in high school and college textbook is far more comprehensive than it was a few decades ago, according to Gary B. Nash, but some areas still merit greater concentration. "African Americans in the Early Republic" describes some of these, such as the rise of free Black communities and early abolitionism. More attention also should be paid to the treatment of Native Americans. "Andrew Jackson Versus the Cherokee Nation" tells of the forcible removal of the Cherokees from Georgia to west of the Mississippi. The trek had such awful consequences that it became known as "the trail of tears."

Accounts of settling the west also have changed over the years. Once presented in the relatively simplistic terms of "taming of the wilderness," the westward movement was far more complicated than the story of hardy pioneers overcoming obstacles. As shown in "New Horizons for the American West," recent examinations of the phenomenon emphasize other aspects such as the roles of women, the fates of minority groups that were shunted aside, and such unexciting but important subjects as water supplies.

Immigration, most notably from Asia and Latin America, has become a hot topic in recent years. Some welcome the diversity it affords, while others warn of dire consequences because of racial, linguistic, and cultural differences. To some extent such arguments echo past disputes over the impact of various waves of immigration would have on the American society. "The Great Famine" describes the treatment Irish immigrants received in this country when they fled the terrible potato crop failures in Ireland.

"James K. Polk and the Expansionist Spirit" discusses the election of 1844 and its aftermath. During the campaign, Polk called for the annexation of Texas and the "occupation" of the Oregon Territory. As president, he compromised with the British over Oregon but went to war with Mexico over Texas. During these years the vexatious question of slavery permeated every discussion over acquiring new territories. Polk left to his successors the problem of slavery in Texas.

As previously discussed with regard to African Americans, women have come to figure far more prominently than ever before in American history. "Little Women? The Female Mind at work in Antebellum America," explores a still neglected area, however, their intellectual lives. Louise Stevenson focuses particularly on the contributions of educated, middle-class women.

John Brown was a murderous fanatic to some, a noble martyr to others. In a nation already deeply immersed in controversy over slavery, Brown's raid on Harpers Ferry set off a firestorm. Brown had hoped his assault would lead to slave rebellions across the South, thereby destroying that barbaric institution. It did not do so, but the praise heaped upon Brown in some quarters of the North helped persuade Southerners that not only slavery but their entire way of life was threatened.

THE FIRST DEMOCRATS

*How the two-party system was born amid backroom deals,
lying politicians, and a scandal-hungry press*

BY JOSEPH J. ELLIS

As the party faithful gather in Los Angeles for their quadrennial festival, they are reenacting a ritual that goes back to Andrew Jackson and beyond. In 1828, Jackson became the first presidential candidate to run as the head of an organization that called itself the Democratic Party. When the Democrats wanted to renominate "Old Hickory" for a second term, they met in Baltimore for the first national convention of the Democratic Party.

But if you really want to recover the mother lode of inspiration for the Democratic Party, the seminal source for all the energy that will be expended this week amid the balloons, placards, speeches, and struttings, you have to go further back. You have to go back to the moment in 1797 when George Washington, that virtuoso of political exits, took his final leave from public office to retire beneath his "vine and fig tree" at Mount Vernon. You have to go back to Thomas Jefferson.

It was a smaller and tidier America, still living in the afterglow of the American Revolution. The total population of the emerging nation called the United States was about 5 million, far less than metropolitan Los Angeles today. Nothing remotely resembling the organized campaigns of modern American politics yet existed. There were no political primaries, no national conventions. The method of choosing electors to that odd inspiration called the Electoral College varied from state to state. And the very notion that a candidate, should openly solicit votes constituted a confession of unworthiness for national office.

Memories of "the Spirit of '76" were still warm, and the chief qualification for the presidency remained a matter of one's active role in the creation of American independence between 1776 and 1789. Only those leaders who had stepped forward at the national level to promote the great cause when its success was still perilous and problematic were eligible. Patriotism, not primaries, determined the viable candidates.

In 1796, the choice to succeed Washington had come down to John Adams and Thomas Jefferson. They were the odd couple of the American Revolution: Adams, the short, stout, candid-to-a-fault New Englander; Jefferson, the tall, slender, elegantly elusive Virginian. Adams, the highly combustible, ever combative, mile-a-minute talker whose favorite form of conversation was an argument; Jefferson, the forever cool and self-contained enigma who regarded an argument as dissonant noise that disrupted the natural harmonies he heard inside his own head. The list could go on—the Yankee and the cavalier, the orator and the writer, the bulldog and the greyhound. Abigail Adams called them "the oak and the willow." Choosing between them was like choosing between the words and the music of the American Revolution.

In the first contested presidential election in American history, Adams won a narrow electoral victory, 71 to 68. Before the passage of the 12th Amendment in 1804, the runner-up became vice president. As Jefferson assumed his understudy role, he grasped more firmly than anyone else what was to become the cardinal principle of modem American politics. And his insight is the reason that Jefferson deserves to be regarded as the Founding Father of both the two-party system and what would eventually call itself the Democratic Party.

While strolling around the grounds of Monticello with a French visitor, he explained his strategic sense of the new political realities: "In the present situation of the United States, divided as they are between two parties ..., this exalted station [the presidency] is surrounded with dangerous rocks, and the most eminent abilities will not be sufficient to steer clear of them all." Because of his Olympian status, Washington had been able to levitate above the partisan factions. But no one else would ever be able to repeat that bipartisan performance. No subsequent president would credibly claim to be above the fray. Jefferson was the first American leader to realize that the president must forever after be the head of a political party.

Adams, despite his considerable savvy and hard-earned political wisdom, could never grasp the point. He saw himself as Washington's successor, a statesman who harbored the same kind of towering defiance toward what might be called "the immorality of partisanship." In the spring of 1797, just before taking office, he saw to it that word was leaked to Jefferson's friends and supporters that he wished to create a bipartisan administration in which Jefferson would enjoy considerable influence over foreign and domestic policy, in effect recreating the famous Adams-Jefferson partnership that had performed so brilliantly in the Continental Congress during the heady days of 1776. Jefferson mulled the offer, even drafted a gracious letter of acceptance, but before sending it consulted James Madison, his chief political adviser.

Madison urged Jefferson not to send the letter. "Considering the probability that Mr. A's course of administration may force an opposition to it … there may be real embarrassments from giving written possession to him, of the degree of compliment and confidence which your personal delicacy and friendship have suggested." When Madison offered tactical advice of this sort, Jefferson almost always took it, even when it meant opposing the very administration he was officially serving as vice president.

The un-Republicans. This rather awkward posture was accompanied by several equally awkward historical facts that seem almost designed to confuse modern day students of American politics.

First, neither Jefferson nor his supporters called themselves "Democrats," since that word still carried the odor of an epithet, suggesting a person who panders to popular opinion rather than oversees the abiding public interest. The hallowed term of the day was "Republican," which was the label Jefferson adopted and the press used to describe the Jeffersonian camp. Anyone trying to trace the lineage of political parties in the United States must confront the messy fact that the nomenclature does not align itself with our modern political vocabulary. Indeed, some party designations, like the Federalists of the 1790s and the Whigs of the 1840s, have disappeared from our political lexicon altogether. Perhaps the most confusing coincidence of all is that the earliest version of the Democratic Party called itself by the name of its modern-day opponents, whose earliest origins date back to the 1850s and whose founding father was Abraham Lincoln.

Second, the translation problem applies to ideas as well as to names. The core conviction of the political party that Jefferson founded was that the federal government must be regarded as an alien force, an Evil Empire if you will, that had assumed powers over the domestic policy of the nation that were incompatible with the original goals of the American Revolution. In terms of its antigovernment ethos, Jefferson's political platform more closely resembles the agenda of 20th-century Republicans like Ronald Reagan than Democrats like Franklin Delano Roosevelt. Indeed, Roosevelt's New Deal was the epitome of everything that Jefferson opposed, even though Roosevelt did more than anyone else to claim Jefferson as the Founding Father of the Democratic Party. No merely logical rendering can capture clearly the historical convolutions from then to now, because of the flip-flop that has occurred in the meaning of liberalism and conservatism.

Finally, neither Jefferson nor his supporters ever acknowledged, even to themselves, that they were founding a political party, whatever the name. The very idea of a legitimate or loyal opposition did not yet exist in the political culture of the infant nation, and the evolution of political parties was proceeding in an environment that continued to regard the word *party* much like the word *democrat*, as an epithet. In effect, the leadership of the revolutionary generation lacked a vocabulary to describe the politics they were inventing. Jefferson, in fact, was on record as perhaps the staunchest opponent of the kind of partisan behavior associated with party politics: "I never submitted the whole system of my opinions to the creed of any party of men whatever," he insisted. "Such an addiction is the last degradation of a free and moral agent. If I could not go to heaven but with a party, I would not go there at all." It required herculean powers of denial for Jefferson to launch America's first political party while claiming to loathe the partisan mentality it required, but he was psychologically up to the task. After all, while Madison was orchestrating his chief's campaign for the presidency in 1796, Jefferson rather disingenuously claimed to be wholly oblivious to the wheelings and dealings, fully occupied with harvesting his vetch crop and making manure, completely unaware that he was even a candidate for public office.

Machine boss. What we might call Jefferson's interior agility also served him well in his behind-the-scenes campaign to undermine the Adams presidency from within. Adams refused to regard himself as the party leader of the Federalists, ignored the partisan advice of his supporters, and effectively made his beloved Abigail into his one-woman cabinet. Arrayed against the Adams team, which was completely dependent on personal trust, was the budding machinery of a political organization under the command of Madison (called "the General" by the Federalists) and Jefferson (called "the Generalissimo). Party politics in America began as a dirty and duplicitous business, which even included leaks from Jefferson to friends of the French government suggesting that they should ignore all diplomatic initiatives from the Adams administration, behavior that would be found treasonable in our own time.

In 1798, Jefferson secretly arranged to retain the services of James Callender, a talented but notorious scandalmonger who had recently become famous for his exposé of Alexander Hamilton's adulterous affair with the beautiful Maria Reynolds. Callender produced "The Prospect Before Us," a pamphlet that described Adams as a mentally unstable monarchist who, if reelected, intended to declare himself king and his son, John Quincy, his royal successor. When confronted with the charge that he had paid Callender to write these diatribes, Jefferson issued blanket denials, then seemed genuinely surprised when the incriminating letters that documented his complicity were published. All of which suggests that, for Jefferson, the deepest secrets were not the ones he kept from his enemies but the ones he kept from himself. (Callender subsequently displayed a flair for equal-opportunity scandalmongering. In 1802, enraged that Jefferson had not paid him sufficiently for his hatchet job on Adams, he broke the story of Jefferson's rumored liaison with the slave Sally Hemings. Jefferson denied that charge, as well, and was so adept at covering his tracks that it required nearly 200 years and the availability of improved DNA matching techniques to establish his paternity beyond a reasonable doubt.)

As these delectable morsels of scandal suggest, the birth of party politics coincided with the stunning significance of what we now call the media in influencing national elections. This was a truly novel development that followed logically from the core conviction of the American experiment with republican government. To wit, if all political leaders and their respective policies derived their authority from public opinion, then the chief conduit between the government and the electorate possessed unprecedented influence in mediating between candidates and their constituencies. Moreover, the increasingly powerful and plentiful newspapers—about 200 dailies or weeklies existed in 1800—had yet to develop established rules of conduct or standards for distinguishing rumors from reliable reporting. It was a recipe for making innuendo the main course in all campaigns, an early if rudimentary preview of our attack-ad politics.

Both Adams and Jefferson later claimed that they could have compiled massive, multivolume scrapbooks filled with libelous attacks on their character. In addition to being accused of emotional instability—Alexander Hamilton weighed in on this score with a 54-page diagnosis of Adams's volcanic eruptions—Adams was supposedly maneuvering to have his eldest daughter married into the family of George III in order to establish a royal bloodline. He also had purportedly arranged to smuggle a small bordello of London prostitutes across the Atlantic to satisfy his instincts for debauchery within the presidential mansion.

Jefferson, for his part, was described as a demonstrable coward who had avoided military service in the Revolutionary War and had fled rather precipitously while governor of Virginia at the approach of British troops. Though the Sally Hemings story did not break until after the election, the New England press accused him of monumental hypocrisy for wrapping himself in lyrical language about human freedom in the Declaration of Independence while owning 200 slaves. Selections from his *Notes on the State of Virginia*, the only book Jefferson ever published, were quoted back at him, especially his remarks on the inherent biological inferiority of blacks. But the chief criticism came from the New England clergy, which claimed that Jefferson denied the divinity of Jesus and was most probably an outright atheist. At the Yale commencement of 1801, the school's president, Timothy Dwight, invited all graduates to take an oath that they would never vote for Jefferson in their lifetimes.

There were no polls back then, but most political pundits predicted a race to the wire. New England's bloc of electoral votes were conceded to Adams. Most of the votes south of the Potomac were conceded to Jefferson. That left the Middle Atlantic region, with the largest number of swing votes in New York and Pennsylvania. Jefferson's operatives in Pennsylvania reported that their superior organization, especially in the ethnic enclaves around Philadelphia, promised to turn out a comfortable majority.

Buying votes. Meanwhile, in New York, Jefferson was taking no chances. The previous spring he had met with Aaron Burr, generally regarded as the most artful political operative in the entire country, a man whose only political principle was allegiance to his own ambition. In return for a place on the ticket with Jefferson, Burr was charged with delivering New York. He successfully lobbied and bribed enough powerful figures in New York City to produce a Jefferson sweep in the state. New York's 12 electoral votes put Jefferson over the top nationally by a margin of 73 to 65. The triumph included Republican control of the Congress, thereby achieving Jefferson's ultimate goal, as he put it, "to sink federalism into an abyss from which there shall be no resurrection of it."

One unforeseen problem delayed the final victory. When all the electoral votes were counted, Jefferson and Burr were tied. Although everyone knew that Jefferson headed the ticket and deserved the presidency, Burr refused to step aside. (Gracious acts of virtue were not parts of Burr's political repertoire.) The issue was thrown into the House of Representatives, which fell into a marathon of secret deals and backroom bartering. In the end, Jefferson triumphed on the 36th ballot. For his recalcitrance, Jefferson cast Burr into the political version of everlasting darkness.

On Inauguration Day, March 4, 1801, Jefferson walked from his boardinghouse down a stump-filled Pennsylvania Avenue toward the Capitol, which was still under construction. The roof was half-finished and the columns designed to support the front facade were lying flat on the lawn. Adams had taken the 4 o'clock stage out of town that morning.

The scene, which subsequent chronicles would describe in the "Mr. Jefferson Comes to Washington" mode, should more accurately be viewed as a metaphor for the transition from the old politics to the new. What died was the presumption that there was an overriding national interest that could be divorced from partisanship, that the chief duty of an aspiring president was to remain blissfully oblivious to the partisan pleadings of particular constituencies. What was born was the initial version of the modern Democratic Party and, more significantly, the party system itself.

Of course, few if any of the Democratic delegates gathered in Los Angeles would recognize themselves as the political descendants of Thomas Jefferson. He has become a mythical icon, a granite face on Mount Rushmore, a bronze statue on the Tidal Basin. In truth, Jefferson was a precociously modern politician who understood, earlier and more deeply than anyone else in the founding generation, the emerging ground rules for success in American politics. For better and for worse, he grasped the dynamics of party organization and discipline necessary to reach a mass electorate. In the history of American politics, he was the first natural.

Contributing editor Joseph J. Ellis won a 1997 National Book Award for his Jefferson biography, American Sphinx. *This article is drawn from his forthcoming book,* Founding Brothers: The Revolutionary Generation.

The Revolution of 1803

The Louisiana Purchase of 1803 was "the event which more than any other, after the foundation of the Government and always excepting its preservation, determined the character of our national life." So said President Theodore Roosevelt on the 100th anniversary of this momentous acquisition. As we celebrate the 200th anniversary, it's clear that the extraordinary real estate deal also shaped America's perception of its role in the world.

by Peter S. Onuf

If there was one thing the United States did not seem to need in 1803, it was more land. The federal government had plenty to sell settlers in the new state of Ohio and throughout the Old Northwest (stretching from the Ohio and Mississippi rivers to the Great Lakes), as did New York, Pennsylvania, and other states. New Englanders were already complaining that the westward exodus was driving up wages and depressing real estate prices in the East.

The United States then consisted of 16 states: the original 13, strung along the Atlantic seaboard, and three recent additions on the frontier: Vermont, which had declared its independence from New York during the Revolution, was finally recognized and admitted in 1791, and Kentucky and Tennessee, carved out of the western reaches of Virginia and North Carolina in 1792 and 1796, respectively, extended the union of states as far as the Mississippi River. The entire area east of the Mississippi had been nominally secured to the United States by the Peace of Paris in 1783, though vast regions remained under the control of Indian nations and subject to the influence of various European imperial powers.

Many skeptical commentators believed that the United States was already too big and that the bonds of union would weaken and snap if new settlements spread too far and too fast. "No paper engagements" could secure the connection of East and West, Massachusetts congressman Rufus King wrote in 1786, and separatist movements and disunionist plots kept such concerns alive in subsequent years. Expansionists had a penchant for naturalistic language: At best, the "surge" or "tide" of white settlement might be channeled, but it was ultimately irresistible.

Though President Thomas Jefferson and the American negotiators who secured the Louisiana Purchase in 1803 had not even dreamed of acquiring such a vast territory, stretching from the Mississippi to the Rockies, the expansion of the United States has the retrospective feel of inevitability, however much

some modern Americans may bemoan the patriotic passions and imperialistic excesses of "Manifest Destiny" and its "legacies of conquest." Indeed, it's almost impossible for us to imagine any other outcome now, or to recapture the decidedly mixed feelings of Americans about their country's expansion at the start of the 19th century.

Jefferson and his contemporaries understood that they were at a crossroads, and that the American experiment in republican self-government and the fragile federal union on which it depended could easily fail. They understood that the United States was a second-rate power, without the "energy" or military means to project—or possibly even to defend—its vital interests in a world almost constantly at war. And they understood all too well that the loyalties of their countrymen—and, if they were honest with themselves, their own loyalties—were volatile and unpredictable.

There were good reasons for such doubts about American allegiances. Facing an uncertain future, patriotic (and not so patriotic) Americans had only the dimmest sense of who or what should command their loyalty. The Union had nearly collapsed on more than one occasion, most recently during the presidential succession crisis of 1800-01, which saw a tie in the Electoral College and 36 contentious ballots in the House of Representatives before Jefferson was elevated to the presidency. During the tumultuous 1790s, rampant partisan political strife between Federalists and Jefferson's Republicans roiled the nation, and before that, under the Articles of Confederation (1781-89), the central government ground to a virtual halt and the Union almost withered away before the new constitution saved it. Of course, everyone professed to be a patriot, dedicated to preserving American independence. But what did that mean? Federalists such as Alexander Hamilton preached fealty to a powerful, consolidated central government capable of doing the people's will (as they loosely construed it); Republican oppositionists championed a strictly construed federal constitution that left power in the hands of the people's (or peoples') state governments. Each side accused the other of being subject to the corrupt influence of a foreign power: counterrevolutionary England in the case of Federalist "aristocrats" and "monocrats"; revolutionary France for Republican "Jacobins."

In Jefferson's mind, and in the minds of his many followers, the new Republican dispensation initiated by his ascension to power in "the Revolution of 1800" provided a hopeful answer to all these doubts and anxieties. Jefferson's First Inaugural Address, which the soft-spoken, 57-year-old president delivered to Congress in a nearly inaudible whisper in March 1801, seemed to his followers to herald a new epoch in American affairs. "We are all republicans, we are all federalists," he insisted in the speech. "Let us, then, unite with one heart and one mind." The president's inspiring vision of the nation's future augured, as he told the English radical Joseph Priestley, then a refugee in republican Pennsylvania, something "new under the sun."

While Jefferson's conciliatory language in the inaugural address famously helped mend the partisan breach—and, not coincidentally, helped cast Hamilton and his High Federalist minions far beyond the republican pale—it also anticipated the issues that would come to the fore during the period leading up to the Louisiana Purchase.

First, the new president addressed the issue of the nation's size. Could an expanding union of free republican states survive without jeopardizing the liberties won at such great cost by the revolutionary generation? Jefferson reassured the rising, post-revolutionary generation that it too had sufficient virtue and patriotism to make the republican experiment work and to pass on its beneficent legacy. "Entertaining a due sense of our equal right to the use of our own faculties" and "enlightened by a benign religion, professed, indeed, and practiced in various forms, yet all of them inculcating honesty, truth, temperance, gratitude, and the love of man; acknowledging and adoring an over-ruling Providence, which by all its dispensations proves that it delights in the happiness of man here and his greater happiness hereafter," Americans were bound to be "a happy and a prosperous people."

Jefferson congratulated his fellow Americans on "possessing a chosen country, with room enough for our descendants to the thousandth and thousandth generation," a vast domain that was "separated by nature and a wide ocean from the exterminating havoc of one quarter of the globe." Jefferson's vision of nationhood was inscribed on the American landscape: "An overruling Providence, which by all its dispensations proves that it delights in the happiness of man here and his greater happiness hereafter" provided this fortunate people with land enough to survive and prosper forever. But Jefferson knew that he was not offering an accurate description of the nation's current condition. Given the frenzied pace of westward settlement, it would take only a generation or two—not a thousand—to fill out the new nation's existing limits, which were still marked in the west

by the Mississippi. Nor was the United States as happily insulated from Europe's "exterminating havoc" as the new president suggested. The Spanish remained in control of New Orleans, the key to the great river system that controlled the continent's heartland, and the British remained a powerful presence to the north.

Jefferson's vision of the future was, in fact, the mirror opposite of America's present situation at the onset of the 19th century. The nation was encircled by enemies and deeply divided by partisan and sectional differences. The domain the president envisioned was boundless, continent-wide, a virgin land waiting to be taken up by virtuous, liberty-loving American farmers. In this providential perspective, Indian nations and European empires simply disappeared from view, and the acquisition of new territory and the expansion of the Union seemed preordained. It would take an unimaginable miracle, acquisition of the entire Louisiana territory, to begin to consummate Jefferson's inaugural promise.

Jefferson's expansionist vision also violated the accepted axioms of contemporary political science. In his *Spirit of the Laws* (1748), the great French philosopher Montesquieu taught that the republican form of government could survive only in small states, where a virtuous and vigilant citizenry could effectively monitor the exercise of power. A large state, by contrast, could be sustained only if power were concentrated in a more energetic central government; republicanism in an expanding state would give way to more "despotic," aristocratic, and monarchical regimes. This "law" of political science was commonly understood in mechanical terms: Centrifugal forces, pulling a state apart, gained momentum as territory expanded, and they could be checked only by the "energy" of strong government.

James Madison had grappled with the problem in his famous *Federalist* 10, in which he argued that an "extended republic" would "take in a greater variety of parties and interests," making it "less probable that a majority of the whole will have a common motive to invade the rights of other citizens." Modern pluralists have embraced this argument, but it was not particularly persuasive to Madison's generation—or even to Madison himself a decade later. During the struggle over ratification of the Constitution, Antifederalists effectively invoked Montesquieu's dictum against Federalist "consolidationism," and in the 1790s, Jeffersonian defenders of states' rights offered the same arguments against Hamiltonian High Federalism. And Jefferson's "Revolution of 1800," vindicating the claims of (relatively) small state-republics against an overly energetic central government, seemed to confirm Montesquieu's wisdom. Montesquieu's notion was also the basis for the popular interpretation of what had caused the rise of British tyranny in the colonies before the American Revolution.

At the same time, however, Montesquieu's logic posed a problem for Jefferson. How could he imagine a continental republic in 1801 and negotiate a land cession that doubled the country's size in 1803? To put the problem somewhat differently, how could Jefferson—who had, after all, drafted the controversial Kentucky Resolutions of 1798, which threatened state nullification of federal authority—overcome his own disunionist tendencies?

Jefferson's response in his inaugural was to call on his fellow Americans to "pursue our own federal and republican principles, our attachment to union and representative government," with "courage and confidence." In other words, a sacred regard for states' rights ("federal principles") was essential to the preservation and strength of a "union" that depended on the "attachment" of a people determined to secure its liberties ("republican principles"). This conception of states as republics would have been familiar and appealing to many Americans, but Jefferson's vision of the United States as a *powerful* nation, spreading across the continent, was breathtaking in its boldness. How could he promise Americans that they could have it both ways, that they could be secure in their liberties yet have a federal government with enough "energy" to preserve itself? How could he believe that the American government, which had only recently endured a near-fatal succession crisis and which had a pathetically small army and navy, was "the strongest Government on earth"?

Jefferson responded to these questions resoundingly by invoking—or perhaps more accurately, inventing—an American people or nation, united in devotion to common principles, and coming together over the course of succeeding generations to constitute one great family. Thus, the unity the president imagined was prospective. Divided as they might now be, Americans would soon come to realize that they were destined to be a great nation, freed from "the throes and convulsions of the ancient world" and willing to sacrifice everything in defense of their country. In Jefferson's vision of progressive continental development, the defensive vigilance of virtuous republicans, who were always ready to resist the encroachments of power from any and every source, would be transformed into a patriotic devotion to the transcendent community of an inclusive and expanding nation, "the world's best hope." "At the call of the law," Jefferson predicted, "every man ... would fly to the standard of the law, and would meet invasions of the public order as his own personal concern.

Jefferson thus invoked an idealized vision of the American Revolution, in which patriotic citizen-soldiers rallied against British tyranny, as a model for future mobilizations against internal as well as external threats. (It was an extraordinary—and extraordinarily influential—exercise in revisionist history. More dispassionate observers, including those who, unlike Jefferson, actually had some military experience, were not inclined to give the militias much, if any, credit for winning the war.)

Jefferson's conception of the American nation imaginatively countered the centrifugal forces, the tendency toward anarchy and disunion, that republicanism authorized and unleashed. Devotion to the Union would reverse this tendency and draw Americans together, even as their private pursuits of happiness drew them to the far frontiers of their continental domain. It was a paradoxical, mystifying formulation. What seemed to be weakness—the absence of a strong central government—was, in fact, strength. Expansion did not attenuate social and political ties; rather, it secured a powerful, effective, and affective union. The imagined obliteration of all possible obstacles to the enactment of this great national story—the removal of Indians and

foreigners—was the greatest mystification of all, for it disguised how the power of the federal state was to be deployed to clear the way for "nature's nation."

In retrospect, the peaceful acquisition of the Louisiana Territory, at the bargain-basement price of $15 million, seemed to conform to the expansionist scenario in Jefferson's First Inaugural Address. The United States bought land from France, just as individuals bought land from federal and state land offices, demonstrating good intentions (to be fruitful and multiply, to cultivate the earth) and their respect for property rights and the rule of law. Yet the progress of settlement was inexorable, a "natural" force, as the French wisely recognized in ceding their claims.

The threat of armed conflict was, nonetheless, never far below the surface. When the chilling news reached America in 1802 that Spain had retroceded Louisiana to France, under pressure from Napoleon Bonaparte, some Federalists agitated for a preemptive strike against New Orleans before Napoleon could land troops there and begin to carry out his plan for a reinvigorated French empire in the Western Hemisphere. As if to provide a taste of the future, Spanish authorities in New Orleans revoked the right of American traders to store goods in the city for export, thereby sending ripples of alarm and economic distress through farms and plantations of the Mississippi valley. Americans might like to think, with Jefferson, that the West was a vast land reserve for their future generations, but nature would issue a different decree if the French gained control of the Mississippi River system.

As Senator William Wells of Delaware warned the Senate in February 1803, if Napoleon were ensconced in New Orleans, "the whole of your Southern States" would be at his mercy; the French ruler would not hesitate to foment rebellion among the slaves, that "inveterate enemy in the very bosom of those States." A North Carolina congressman expected the French emperor to do even worse: "The tomahawk of the savage and the knife of the negro would confederate in the league, and there would be no interval of peace." Such a confederation—a powerful, unholy alliance of Europeans, Indians, and slaves—was the nightmarish antithesis of the Americans' own weak union. The French might even use their influence in Congress to revive the vicious party struggles that had crippled the national government during the 1790s.

Jefferson had no idea how to respond to the looming threat, beyond sending his friend and protégé James Monroe to join U.S. Minister to France Robert R. Livingston in a desperate bid to negotiate a way out of the crisis. At most, they hoped that Napoleon would sell New Orleans and the Floridas to the United States, perhaps with a view to preempting an Anglo-American alliance. Jefferson dropped a broad hint to Livingston (undoubtedly for Napoleon's edification) that if France ever took "possession of N. Orleans ... we must marry ourselves to the British fleet and nation." For the Anglophobe Jefferson this must have been a horrible thought, even if it was a bluff. But then, happily for Jefferson—and crucially for his historical reputation—fortune intervened.

Napoleon's intentions for the New World hinged on control of Saint-Domingue (now Haiti), but a slave revolt there, led by the brilliant Toussaint L'Ouverture, complicated the emperor's plans. With a strong assist from yellow fever and other devastating diseases, the rebels fought a French expeditionary force of more than 20,000 to a standstill. Thwarted in his western design and facing the imminent resumption of war in Europe, Napoleon decided to cut his losses. In April 1803, his representative offered the entire Louisiana Territory to a surprised Livingston. By the end of the month, the negotiators had arrived at a price. For $15 million, the United States would acquire 828,000 square miles of North America, stretching from the Mississippi River to the Rocky Mountains and from the Gulf of Mexico to the Canadian border. Over time 13 states would be carved from the new lands.

When the news reached America in July, it proved a great deal more than anyone had been contemplating but was met with general jubilation. There was widespread agreement that national security depended on gaining control of the region around New Orleans; and Spanish Florida, occupying the critical area south of Georgia and the territory that the state had finally ceded to Congress in 1802, was high on southern planters' wish list of territorial acquisitions. But it was hard to imagine any immediate use for the trans-Mississippi region, notwithstanding Jefferson's inspiring rhetoric, and there was some grumbling that the negotiators had spent more than Congress had authorized. A few public figures, mostly New England Federalists, even opposed the transaction on political and constitutional grounds.

The Lewis and Clark expedition, authorized before the Purchase was completed, testifies to Americans' utter ignorance of the West in 1803. The two explorers were sent, in effect, to feel around in the dark. Perhaps, Jefferson mused, the trans-Mississippi region could be used as a kind of toxic waste dump, a place to send emancipated slaves beyond harm's way. Or, a more portentous thought, Indian nations might be relocated west of the river—an idea President Andrew Jackson later put into effect with his infamous removal policy.

What gripped most commentators as they celebrated the news of the Purchase in 1803 was simply that the Union had survived another awful crisis. They tended to see the new lands as a buffer. "The wilderness itself," Representative Joseph Nicholson of Maryland exclaimed, "will now present an almost insurmountable barrier to any nation that inclined to disturb us in that quarter." And another congressman exulted that America was now "insulated from the rest of the world."

David Ramsay, the South Carolina historian and devout Republican, offered the most full-blown paean to the future of the "chosen country" as Jefferson had envisioned it. Echoing Jefferson's First Inaugural, he asked, "What is to hinder our extension on the same liberal principles of equal rights till we have increased to twenty-seven, thirty-seven, or any other number of states that will conveniently embrace, in one happy union, the whole country from the Atlantic to the Pacific ocean, and from the lakes of Canada to the Gulf of Mexico?" In his Second Inaugural, in 1805, Jefferson himself would ask, "Who can limit the extent to which the federative principle may operate effectively?" Gone were his doubts about the uses to which the new

lands could be put. "Is it not better that the opposite bank of the Mississippi should be settled by our own brethren and children, than by strangers of another family?"

Jefferson's vision of the American future has ever since provided the mythic master narrative of American history. In the western domains that Jefferson imagined as a kind of blank slate on which succeeding generations would inscribe the image of American nationhood, it would be all too easy to overlook other peoples and other possibilities. It would be all too easy as well to overlook the critical role of the state in the progress of settlement and development. When Americans looked back on events, they would confuse effects with causes: War and diplomacy eliminated rival empires and dispossessed native peoples; an activist federal state played a critical role in pacifying a "lawless" frontier by privatizing public lands and promoting economic development. In the mythic history of Jefferson's West, an irresistible westward tide of settlement appears to be its own cause, the manifest destiny of nature's nation.

Yet if the reality of power remains submerged in Jefferson's thought, it's not at any great depth. The very idea of the nation implies enormous force, the power of a people enacting the will of "an overruling Providence." In Jefferson's Declaration of Independence, Americans claimed "the separate & equal station to which the laws of nature and of nature's God entitle them." The first law of nature, the great natural law proclaimed by writers of the day, was self-preservation, and the defining moment in American history was the great mobilization of American power to secure independence in the Revolution. President Jefferson's vision of westward expansion projected that glorious struggle into the future and across the continent. It was a kind of permanent revolution, reenacting the nation's beginnings in the multiplication of new, self-governing republican states.

Born in war, Jefferson's conception of an expanding union of free states constituted a peace plan for the New World. But until it was insulated from Europe's "exterminating havoc," the new nation would remain vulnerable, unable to realize its historic destiny. By eliminating the clear and present danger of a powerful French presence at the mouth of the Mississippi, the Louisiana Purchase guaranteed the survival of the Union—for the time being, at least. By opening the West to white American settlers, it all but guaranteed that subsequent generations would see their own history in Jefferson's vision of their future, a mythic, nation-making vision yoking individual liberty and national power and promising a future of peace and security in a dangerous world. Two hundred years later, that vision remains compelling to many Americans.

PETER S. ONUF *is a professor of history at the University of Virginia. His most recent book is* Jefferson's Empire: The Language of American Nationhood (2001). *Copyright © 2003 by Peter Onuf.*

BRAINS AND BRAWN

The Lewis and Clark
Expedition

By Tom Huntington

It was one of American history's greatest adventures and a pioneering exercise in scientific observation. Two centuries ago a small band of explorers ventured into a land that no white man had ever seen. We now remember it as the Lewis and Clark expedition, after its two commanders, Meriwether Lewis and William Clark. It was also known as the Corps of Discovery. Following the instructions of President Thomas Jefferson, the expedition departed from St. Louis to travel up the Missouri River in search of that great waterway's source, and from there to find the best route west to the Pacific Ocean.

Much of the region Lewis and Clark traversed had only recently become United States territory. The vast interior of the North American continent, from the mouth of the Mississippi River to the headwaters of the Missouri, had belonged to Spain, until Spain transferred the land to France in 1800. The always ambitious Napoleon Bonaparte wanted to increase France's presence in the western hemisphere, but his plans suffered a setback when French troops failed to crush a slave insurrec-

tion in the French colony of Santo Domingo (now Haiti). Napoleon was also facing another war with Britain, so he decided to abandon his ambitions in North America and sell the Louisiana Territory to the United States. The government of President Thomas Jefferson acquired 800,000 square miles of territory for $15 million, a bargain that more than doubled the size of the United States. Jefferson championed limited government, but he made this unprecedented real estate deal despite its questionable constitutionality.

Jefferson possessed an insatiable curiosity, and he had long been itching for an opportunity to explore the continent's interior. When serving as secretary of state under President George Washington in 1792, Jefferson proposed an exploration of the west, and a young Virginian named Meriwether Lewis volunteered to conduct it. He came from a Virginia family of Jefferson's acquaintance and had experience fighting Indians. He did not get the assignment. Instead, it went to a Frenchman named André Michaux, who was recalled when it turned out he was a spy.

No doubt Jefferson kept Lewis's zeal for exploration in mind. In February 1801 the president-elect asked his fellow Virginian to serve as his private secretary. Lewis may have seemed an odd choice for the position, but we can assume the president had some other plans in mind for the young man. That became apparent in January 1803 after Jefferson sent a confidential message to Congress urging western exploration. The president informed Congress that an expedition could explore the Missouri and perhaps reach the Pacific for a mere $2,500 (in the end the costs were closer to $38,000). Congress gave its approval, and once again Lewis volunteered his services. "I had now had opportunity of knowing him intimately," Jefferson recalled. "Of courage undaunted, possessing a firmness & perseverance of purpose which nothing but impossibilities could divert from its direction, careful as a father of those committed to his charge, yet steady in the maintenance of order & discipline, intimate with the Indian character, customs & principles, habituated to the hunting life, guarded by exact observation of the vegetables & animals of his own country, against losing time in the description of objects already possessed, honest, disinterested, liberal, of sound understanding and a fidelity to truth so scrupulous that whatever he should report would be as certain as if seen by ourselves, with all these qualifications as if selected and implanted by nature in one body, for this express purpose, I could have no hesitation in confiding the enterprize to him."

Lewis requested that a friend from his army days, William Clark, serve as co-leader. Clark, too, was from a Virginia family, one with a distinguished military tradition. Three of his brothers were generals, and one of them was George Rogers Clark, a hero of the Revolutionary War with whom Jefferson had discussed a western expedition back in the 1780s. Lewis wrote a letter to Clark asking him to join the expedition and promising him equal rank as captain. Clark immediately accepted. The army refused Lieutenant Clark's promotion, but Lewis nonetheless considered Clark as his equal in every respect and referred to him as captain throughout the entire journey.

Now Lewis began his preparations in earnest. He went to Philadelphia to consult with scientific authorities for a tutorial on the subjects with which he would need to be familiar: navigation, medicine, botany, biology. He traveled to Harpers Ferry, Virginia, to get weapons and oversee the construction of a large iron boat of his own design. Lewis's plan was that his men would carry the boat, disassembled, to the upper Missouri, where they would assemble it for the rest of the river journey. (That scheme failed because the expedition members could not find enough pitch to seal the boat's animal-skin hull.) He gathered the myriad supplies he would need, including a large cache of gifts for the Native Americans he would meet on the way.

In June, Jefferson sent Lewis a letter with detailed instructions. "The object of your mission is to explore the Missouri River, and such principal streams of it, as, by its course and communication with the water of the Pacific ocean may offer the most direct and practicable water communication across this continent, for the purposes of commerce," the president wrote. He instructed Lewis to take careful navigational observations, and in a typical flight of Jeffersonian imagination, suggested that Lewis keep a second copy of this information on birch bark, "as less liable to damp than common paper." Jefferson stressed that the captain keep careful records of the Native Americans he met along the way and suggested that he bring along cowpox so he could teach the Indians how to inoculate themselves against smallpox.

We now realize that the Corps of Discovery had grave and unforeseen consequences for the Native Americans. Yet Jefferson, while recognizing the trade and diplomatic possibilities that good relationships with the Indian nations could bring, was also motivated by scientific curiosity. There was self-interest involved, but it was arguably an enlightened self interest. "It's hard to divorce diplomacy and commerce and ethnography from one another," says Gary Moulton, a professor at the University of Nebraska who spent 20 years editing the definitive, 13-volume edition of the expedition's journals. "They're all bound up in Lewis and Clark's relationships with Native Americans.

"Jefferson's instructions to Lewis about Indians are his most detailed instructions in that letter," Moulton continues. "He's always saying, 'if there's any threat of violence or difficulties, pull back instead of forcing ahead. If you have to give up the whole mission, it's worth it. Don't put yourselves or the Native peoples in danger.' I think that's a very laudable sentiment."

Lewis set out from Pittsburgh on August 31, 1803, for the long trip down the Ohio River. Clark joined him in Louisville, Kentucky. That winter the co-captains finished recruiting their men and preparing for the journey. The expedition set out from Camp Dubois near St. Louis on May 14, 1804, with a little fleet of a 55-foot keelboat and two pirogues (large canoes made from tree trunks).

From the perspective two centuries later, we may see the Corps of Discovery as a single unit with two heads, but it was in fact a many-footed beast. As is typical of such outfits, it required some early adjustments. The first major personnel problem came early in the journey, when Private Moses Reed deserted in August. The captains sent out a party to capture him, then had Reed court-martialed, flogged, and kicked out of the Corps. (He remained with the expedition until he could travel down the Missouri with the keelboat in spring.) Soon another private, John Newman, "uttered repeated expressions of a highly criminal and mutinous nature...." He too received the lash and a discharge. A third man, a French civilian named La Liberté, also deserted, but he managed to slip away from his pursuers and out of the pages of history. More seriously, on August 20 Sergeant Charles Floyd died and was buried in a lonely grave above the river. To replace him, the captains promoted Private Patrick Gass.

The expedition spent the bitterly cold winter of 1804-05 with the Mandan Indians in present-day North Dakota, then resumed its journey in the spring. With the explorers were three new additions to the party: Toussaint Charbonneau, his Shoshone wife Sacagawea, and their infant son Jean Baptiste. "Our vessels consisted of six small canoes, and two large perogues," Lewis wrote on the day they resumed their trek. "This little fleet altho' not quite so rispectable as those of Columbus or Capt. Cook were still viewed by us with as much pleasure as those deservedly famed adventurers ever beheld theirs; and I dare say with quite as much anxiety for their safety and preservation. [W]e are now about to penetrate a country at least two thousand miles in width, on which the foot of civilized man had never trodden...."

During the summer of 1805 the explorers followed the Missouri to its headwaters, battling grizzly bears, mosquitoes, rattlesnakes, and other trail hazards along the way. In September they faced hunger and miserable cold as they endured a brutal passage over the Bitterroot Mountains. With that hurdle behind them, the men knew they could reach their goal. Once again traveling by boat, the explorers made their way down the sometimes treacherous Snake and Columbia Rivers. On November 7, 1805, Lewis recorded in his journal, "Ocian in view! O! the joy!"

The Corps still had to make the return trip, and the men headed back east in March after a wet and uncomfortable winter at the outpost they named Fort Clatsop. But by then these travel-tested adventurers knew what to expect, although they did have one especially grave encounter on the return trip. Lewis and Clark were pursuing separate explorations, when Lewis and his men encountered a small band of Blackfeet. A scuffle over the expedition's guns left one Indian dead and another injured, perhaps fatally. It was a tragic foreshadowing of the bloodshed to follow during the development of the American West.

The explorers returned to St. Louis on September 23, 1806, bringing specimens of animals, minerals, and plants; maps of the west, and more than a million words in their journals. Unfortunately, the journals weren't published until 1814, and then in an edition that eliminated much of the scientific observation. As a result, the expedition's contributions have not always been fairly judged. "What the first generation of people interested in Lewis and Clark got was just the trip across the continent and not the deeper meaning of the expedition, which was a scientific endeavor," observes Moulton, who says the Corps' discoveries have enduring value. Scientists study the expedition's botanical specimens to learn about the environmental conditions from two centuries ago, while cartographers use its maps to determine the previous courses of the ever-changing Missouri and Columbia Rivers. Linguists use the language materials to gain insight into the native tongues of the time. "This goes on and on," says Moulton. "There's probably more intimate study being done now of Lewis and Clark materials than at any time in the past."

In some ways, the Lewis and Clark expedition was a failure. It did not find the most efficient route to cross the continent, and the men established poor relations with a few of the tribes they encountered, particularly the Blackfeet and Sioux. "I think a larger lesson is that Lewis and Clark succeeded in spite of their failures, that they were willing to push on," Moulton says. "They did get across the continent, they did establish an American presence in the Pacific Northwest, and they did come back with an incredible amount of material that is still being used by scientists today." They set out to explore uncharted territory, at a time when even someone as sophisticated as Thomas Jefferson believed that mammoths might still lurk in the North American wilderness, or that the Great Plains contained a huge mountain of salt.

Even after spending more than two decades immersed in the work of Lewis and Clark, Moulton has not grown tired of the expedition and its writings. "There's so much that's in that text," he says. "It's not just the amount of words, it's the depth and breadth of their study that just fascinates you. Plus, it's a great story. It's the story of getting across the continent, just the daily grind and the daily work of exploring. Which is, you just have to get up and pull that boat every morning." ✪

African Americans in the Early Republic

by Gary B. Nash

Any teacher using a textbook published before the 1980s would find virtually nothing on African Americans—slave or free, North or South—in the era of the American Revolution and the early republic. Though about 20 percent of the population, African Americans simply did not exist in the pre-1980s story of how the Revolution proceeded and how the search for "life, liberty, and the pursuit of happiness" affected those most deprived of these unalienable rights. Nor did textbooks take any notice of the free black churches, schools, and benevolent societies created by an emerging cadre of black leaders after the Revolution. A cursory examination of pre-1980s texts shows black history beginning when the first Africans arrived in Virginia in 1619 and then jumping magically over about two hundred years until the Missouri Compromise in 1820 produced heated arguments among white legislators over the spread of slavery. While older textbooks treat antebellum slavery and the rise of abolitionism after 1820 in some detail, they leave unnoticed the fast-growing free black communities of the North and upper South.

The outpouring of scholarship on African and African American history in the last third of this century, prompted by the civil rights movement and the opening up of the historical profession, has gradually remedied the astounding erasure of one-fifth of the American population in the nation's formative years. Yet many school textbooks today still lag a decade or more behind current scholarship on African Americans. Today, most students learn something about such figures as Olaudah Equiano, Crispus Attucks, and Richard Allen and have at least some notion that slaves and free blacks fought heartily in the American Revolution, began to throw off the shackles of slavery before the Emancipation Proclamation, and resisted slavery before Nat Turner's rebellion of 1831. Yet there is much still to be learned before the student graduating from high school can claim a basic grasp of both race relations during the nation's formative decades and the role of free and enslaved blacks in the nation's explosive growth. Five African American topics—some historians

might add more—ought to be essential parts of the history curriculum that young Americans learn as they study the years between 1760 and 1830.

The Black American Revolution

African Americans, most born in the colonies but many in Africa, were deeply involved in the American Revolution and were deeply affected by it. The earliest black historians, wanting to stimulate racial pride and counter white hostility, focused on the few thousand blacks who fought with white Americans to gain their independence. Crispus Attucks, Salem Poor, and James Forten were typical of those who made blood sacrifices for "the glorious cause." But now, in a latter era when we can be more realistic about the American Revolution, students will readily understand why ten to twenty times as many slaves (along with some free blacks) fought with the British as with the American patriots. While white Americans discouraged or forbade black enlistment in state militias and the Continental Army, the British promised to grant perpetual freedom to any slave (or indentured servant) who fled his or her master to join the British forces.

The wholesale flight to the British, Benjamin Quarles wrote in his mold-breaking *Negro in the American Revolution*, had "one common origin, one set purpose—the achievement of liberty." This book, first published in 1961 and republished with an introduction by this author in 1996, is still the best one-volume account of the African Americans' American Revolution. In ringing phrases, Quarles wrote of how the "major loyalty" of blacks "was not to a place nor a people, but to a principle" and "insofar as he had freedom of choice, he was likely to join the side that made him the quickest and best offer in terms of those 'unalienable rights' of which Mr. Jefferson had spoken." This little secret about African American history ought to become common knowledge, without embarrassment or anger.

Much scholarship since Quarles's book has deepened our understanding of the massive slave rebellion that occurred during the American Revolution and the effect of white rhetoric about unalienable rights and British oppression on early abolitionists, white and black. Teachers wanting to present heroic figures who stood with the Americans can bring alive figures such as James Armistead Lafayette, the double spy who helped win the climactic battle at Yorktown, and the men of Rhode Island's black regiment. But those who struggled for freedom with the British present equally heroic stories, and their travails after the war, as they sought refuge in Nova Scotia and then returned to Africa to join the Sierra Leone experiment, are remarkable examples of endurance and unextinguishable hopes for the future. Sidney Kaplan's *Black Presence in the Era of the American Revolution*, first published in 1976 and republished in an expanded edition with Emma Nogrady Kaplan in 1989, is a teacher's goldmine. Little-known black figures leap off the pages of this fine book, which is studded with short primary sources suitable for classroom use and includes nearly every image of African Americans in the revolutionary generation that has come to light. In addition, part two of PBS's new four-part television series, *Africans in America*, is available for classroom viewing. Accompanied by a teacher-friendly companion volume by Charles Johnson, Patricia Smith, and the WGBH Research Team, the episode is a surefire way to jumpstart classes in both middle schools and high schools[1]. For teachers with advanced students who want to pursue black involvement in the American Revolution, the third section of Ira Berlin's *Many Thousands Gone* provides a comprehensive view of the revolutionary generation of African Americans, free and slave, in all parts of North America.

The Rise of Free Black Communities

One of the big stories untold in most textbooks even today concerns the rise of free black communities after the American Revolution. Blacks released from slavery, and those who made good their flight from bondage, commonly sought new lives in urban centers. In the North, they gathered especially in the seaports, with Philadelphia and New York attracting the largest black populations. They congregated also in Baltimore, Washington DC, Charleston, and smaller southern towns. In these urban places they constructed the foundations of free black life in the United States.

Especially important was the creation of free black churches, which were originally under white ecclesiastical control, but which became autonomous by 1816. Black leaders such as Absalom Jones and Richard Allen in Philadelphia; Peter Spencer in Wilmington, Delaware; and Peter Williams in New York City became not only apostles to their flocks but political spokespersons, entrepreneurs, and teachers. Many mini-biographies of these black founders are included in Kaplan and Kaplan's *Black ·Presence in the Era of the American Revolution* and in the five-volume *Encyclopedia of African American Culture and History*, edited by Jack Salzman, et al.

Students need to study how much a generation of blacks accomplished in building free black communities organized around churches and schools. How, one might ask, could those recently emerging from slavery (which taught slaves not to think for themselves and not to think of themselves as capable) find the inner resources and external support to create new names, form families, learn to read and write, find employment, and create neighborhoods and social associations? One of the main themes of this quest for community was the notion that the only secure foundation of free black life was the construction of independent organizations embodying their sense of being a people within a people and relying on their own resources rather than on white benevolence. While coming to grips with this emerging sense of black autonomy and strength, students should recognize that mounting white hostility to free blacks complicated their struggle for family formation, work, education, respectability, civil rights, and justice before the law.

A torrent of scholarship in recent years traces how the Enlightenment ideals of the revolutionary generation crumbled by the early nineteenth century, how discrimination and violence against free blacks increased yet how the free black communities remained vibrant and enterprising. The three largest free black communities—Philadelphia, New York, and Baltimore—were studied respectively by this author in *Forging Freedom*, by Shane White in *Somewhat More Independent*, and by Christopher Phillips in *Freedom's Port*. Although too detailed for most students, they can be mined by teachers interested in explaining community building among free blacks. The surest way to capture the imaginations of students is to view part three of the PBS series *Africans in America* and read the parallel section of the companion book mentioned above.

Early Abolitionism

Most textbooks give only casual references to how the American Revolution fueled a prolonged debate over abolishing slavery. Nonetheless, this was a burning issue for the revolutionary generation and naturally a preoccupation of black American society. More than thirty years ago, Winthrop Jordan wrote, "It was perfectly clear that the principles for which Americans had fought required the complete abolition of slavery; the question was not *if*, but *when* and *how*"[2]. Twenty-four years ago, David Brion Davis wrote brilliantly on the rise of abolitionism—and on the exhaustion of it—in *The Problem of Slavery in the Age of Revolution, 1770-1823*. Both the rise and dissipation of abolitionist fervor ought to be understood in high school American history courses, and selected chapters of these two books can guide classroom discussions.

The North and upper South were the main theaters of abolitionism. Gradual legislated emancipation characterized northern attempts at eradicating chattel bondage while private (and limited) manumission characterized southern discomfort with the peculiar institution. Students need to understand how white economic interest and white abhorrence of the notion of freed slaves mingling on an equal standing with whites dashed revolutionary idealism, thus leaving the issue of slavery to another generation. This lesson of ideology facing off against economic interest and entrenched attitudes provides a weighty lesson for students to consider. The first two essays of this author's *Race and Revolution* discuss this and provide documents for classroom use on the rise and decline of abolitionism.

Two aspects of abolition ought to stick in students' minds. First, the freeing of slaves was not always benevolent, a simple case of morality transcending economic interest. Moreover, freedom came by degrees for emancipated slaves. They did not move from abject slavery to the light of freedom as if moving across the dark side of a river to the bright side. Legal emancipation did not confer full political rights, equal economic opportunity, or social recognition. All of that was denied and contested. Second, abolition was not engineered solely by high-minded whites. It was also produced, especially in the North, by slaves who made it their business to run away and perfect insolence to the point that their masters found slavery more trouble than it was worth.

Every American youngster studies the writing and ratification of the Constitution, but not all consider how the delegates to the 1787 convention in Philadelphia wrestled with the problem of slavery and the slave trade. Sparks will fly in classrooms where the teacher stages a debate pitting those who argue that the convention could—and should—have abolished slavery against those who argue that this was impossible at that point in time. The provocative essays in Paul Finkelman's *Slavery and the Founders* will help teachers construct lively classroom activities. Comparisons of how Washington and Jefferson—both professing to detest slavery and hoping to see it abolished in their own lifetimes—made their own decisions regarding their slave property can also be instructive. Available from the National Center for History in the Schools is a teaching unit utilizing primary documents and lesson plans to allow students to evaluate the positions taken during the congressional debates over slavery in the First Congress [3].

The Spread of Slavery

Many opponents of slavery (and some defenders of it) believed that the slave population would gradually wither after slave importations ceased. But the first state censuses after the Revolution showed that slavery was growing in spite of a wartime hiatus in importations. When Eli Whitney's invention of the cotton gin in 1793 gave a tremendous boost to the production of short-staple cotton, slavery acquired a powerful new lease on life. The cotton gin gave new incentives for reopening the slave trade and insured that slavery would spread rapidly into the deep South where the demand for field hands grew enormously between 1800 and 1830. Berlin's *Many Thou-*

sands Gone provides a fine account of how lawmakers in the lower South defended the expansion of slave society and how large slaveholders consolidated their power as the region's ruling class.

The growth of slavery amidst gradual emancipation needs to be understood. From about 470,000 slaves in 1770, the population grew to about 720,000 in 1790 and 1,200,000 in 1810 (while the population of free blacks grew from about 60,000 in 1790 to 185,000 in 1810). Also notable, the coming of King Cotton led to massive interregional transfers of slaves. The cotton revolution precipitated the widespread sale of slaves from the upper to lower South—a brutal process involving a kind of new Middle Passage that sundered thousands of slave families. Students can learn about this through Toni Morrison's poignant historical novel *Beloved* (which is also available in movie form).

Life under slavery is generally studied during the decades preceding the Civil War, but teachers may have time to delve into this as part of the curriculum that deals with the early republic. Some fine, accessible essays and excellent visual material are available in Edward Campbell's edited volume *Before Freedom Came*.

Black Resistance in the New Nation

If Congress did not listen to petitioners who urged the end of slavery; if hard-nosed economic realities about the profitability of slavery submerged idealistic hopes for a new nation cleansed of its most important cancer; if by the early nineteenth century it became clear that the new nation was to be defined as a white man's republic; then how would slaves and free blacks respond, and how would they carry on their lives? Several rich veins of scholarship have explored this question, and some of the new work ought to make its way into precollegiate classrooms.

One topic well worth discussing is the Haitian Revolution of 1791-1804, the long, slave-centered revolt against the powerful and brutal French slave regime in Saint Domingue. Textbooks hardly mention the prolonged revolution in Haiti, yet it was of signal importance. It was the first racial war to overthrow a European colonial power; the first instance of mass self-emancipation by a populous slave society; the first creation of a black republic in the Americas in the midst of the slaveholding West Indies; and the event that made the Louisiana Territory nearly useless to France, since its main importance was supplying the foodstuffs to feed the hundreds of thousands of French slaves in the Caribbean. Ironically, Jefferson's acquisition of the Louisiana Territory vastly extended the American domain suitable for enslaved labor.

Students can also explore how the Haitian Revolution spread the spark of black rebellion to the United States and how Haiti became a beacon of freedom and an inspiration for all who hoped for the overthrow of slavery. Students can also consider how it produced a morbid fear of black insurrection while dampening white manu-mitting instincts. Jefferson's personal inner conflict is il-luminating. As president, he encouraged the black overthrow of slavery in Saint Domingue and applauded black independence. But he refused to recognize the black government when it came to power in 1804 and worked to quarantine or neutralize Haiti commercially in deference to the interests of southern planters.

Another part of the continuing struggle of African Americans for freedom involved open resistance. Gab-riel's Rebellion of 1800 in Virginia and Denmark Vesey's plot in 1822 in South Carolina, both inspired in part by the Haitian Revolution, are well known; but many other smaller insurrections and plots deserve attention, partic-ularly the flight of slaves to the British forces in the War of 1812, paralleling the Revolutionary War attempts by blacks to cash in on British offers of freedom. Much of this resistance is captured in part three of the PBS video series *Africans in America* and in the companion book cited above.

Another aspect of the search for liberty and equality among free and slave, in both the North and South, is the remarkable growth of Afro-Christianity in the early nine-teenth century. A transformative process among African Americans living under slavery, it was a resistance move-ment in its own right, and it had much to do with their ability to endure captivity. Sylvia Frey and Betty Wood's *Come Shouting to Zion* is a rich treatment of this topic. The book pays particular attention to the role of women in fashioning black churches. The northern chapter of this quest for spiritual autonomy and the building of black churches as citadels of social, political, and psychological strength is movingly told by Vincent Harding in chapters three and four of *There is a River*. Many mini-biographies of black church leaders appear in Kaplan and Kaplan's *Black Presence in the Era of the American Revolution* and *The Encyclopedia of African-American Culture and History*.

One final aspect of black resistance that deserves at-tention involves emigrationist schemes. African Ameri-cans, led notably by the mixed-blood merchant and mariner Paul Cuffe, had toyed with immigrating to the African homelands since the 1780s and, after 1804, to Haiti and Canada. But the larger part of the story in-volves the launching of the American Colonization Soci-ety (ACS) in 1816. Historians have argued for many years about the strange mixture of northern clergy, southern slaveowners, and a few free black leaders who came together to promote the voluntary emigration of free blacks to what would become Liberia. The interest of African American leaders was centered in the belief that the rising tide of white hostility to free blacks made repatriation to Africa the only viable option. However, the mass of free blacks correctly understood that the ACS (notwithstanding the fact that some northern clergy who joined the ACS were sincere abolitionists who dwelled on the glory of African Americans return-

ing to their homelands to Christianize black Africa) was for southern leaders a deportation scheme that would remove incendiary free blacks from the United States and provide cover for slavery's expansion.

Most teachers will not have time to explore the mixed motives of the ACS and its limited success. However, at the least they can interest students in how the ACS's em-igrationist schemes reflected the crossroads at which the new republic stood. On the one hand, whites who were unwilling to give free blacks real equality and were eager to cleanse the country of them enthusiastically supported the ACS emigrationist efforts. On the other hand, this pas-sion to encourage a back-to-Africa movement galvanized free black leaders who now understood that a new mili-tance and a new inter-city league of black spokespersons were required to keep their revolutionary era hopes alive.

None of the five topics outlined above should be thought of as self-contained *African American* topics. Rather they are *American* history topics. Occupying vastly different social places, white and black Americans were linked together by a common quest for freedom, though freedom had many meanings and required various strat-egies to achieve. Their lives were intertwined whether on slave plantations, in cities, or on ships at sea. Their pro-ductive efforts were part of the development of the ex-panding nation. Great events outside the United States, such as the French and Haitian Revolutions, left imprints on everybody. While drawing attention to topics vital to the African American experience in the era of the Ameri-can Revolution and the early republic, this essay is a plea for restoring to memory African American topics that are indispensable elements of the larger American story.

Endnotes

1. Charles Richard Johnson, et al., *Africans in America: Amer-ica's Journey through Slavery* (New York: Harcourt Brace and Company, 1998); and *Africans in America: America's Journey through Slavery*, produced by WGBH Educational Foundation, 270 min., PBS Video, 1998, videocassette. Teaching kits are also available through WGBH. For more information or to order, write WGBH, 125 Western Ave-nue, Boston, MA 02134 or call (617) 300-5400.
2. Winthrop Jordan, *White over Black: American Attitudes To-ward the Negro, 1550-1812* (Chapel Hill: University of North Carolina Press, 1968), 342.
3. Copies of the teaching unit, *Congress Debates Slavery, 1790-1800*, are available for $12 from The National Center for History in the Schools, 6265 Bunche Hall, UCLA, 405 Hil-gard Avenue, Los Angeles, CA 90095.

Sources Cited

Africans in America: America's Journey through Slavery, produced by WGBH Educational Foundation. 270 min. PBS Video, 1998. Videocassette.

Beloved, produced by Harpo Films and Clinica Estetico. Directed by Jonathan Demme. 172 min. Touchstone Home Video, 1998. Videocassette.

Berlin, Ira. *Many Thousands Gone: The First Two Centuries of Sla-very in North America*. Cambridge: Harvard University Press, 1998.

Campbell, Edward D. C., Jr., ed. *Before Freedom Came: African-American Life in the Antebellum South.* Richmond, VA: Museum of the Confederacy, 1991.

Davis, David Brion. *The Problem of Slavery in the Age of Revolution, 1770-1823.* Ithaca: Cornell University Press, 1975.

Finkelman, Paul. *Slavery and the Founders: Race and Liberty in the Age of Jefferson.* New York: M. E. Sharpe, 1996.

Frey, Sylvia and Betty Wood. *Come Shouting to Zion: African American Protestantism in the American South and British Caribbean to 1830.* Chapel Hill: University of North Carolina Press, 1998.

Harding, Vincent. *There is a River: The Black Struggle for Freedom in America.* New York: Harcourt Brace Jovanovich, 1981.

Johnson, Charles Richard, et al. *Africans in America: America's Journey through Slavery.* New York: Harcourt Brace and Company, 1998.

Kaplan, Sidney and Emma Nogrady Kaplan. *The Black Presence in the Era of the American Revolution.* Amherst: University of Massachusetts Press, 1989.

Morrison, Toni. *Beloved.* New York: Knopf, 1987.

Nash, Gary B. *Forging Freedom: The Formation of Philadelphia's Black Community, 1720-1840.* Cambridge: Harvard University Press, 1988.

———. *Race and Revolution.* Madison, WI: Madison House, 1990.

Phillips, Christopher. *Freedom's Port: The African American Community of Baltimore, 1790-1860.* Urbana: University of Illinois Press, 1998.

Quarles, Benjamin. *The Negro in the American Revolution.* 1961. Reprint, Chapel Hill: University of North Carolina Press, 1996.

Salzman, Jack, et al., eds. *Encyclopedia of African-American Culture and History.* 5 vols. New York: MacMillan Library Reference, 1996.

White, Shane. *Somewhat More Independent: The End of Slavery in New York City, 1770-1810.* Athens: University of Georgia Press, 1991.

Gary B. Nash is a professor of history at the University of California, Los Angeles, and is the author of many books and articles on race, class, and society in the early republic, including Red, White, and Black: The Peoples of Early America *(1974, 4th ed. 2000). A Guggenheim Fellow, and finalist for the Pulitzer Prize for his book* The Urban Crucible, *Nash is a former president of the Organization of American Historians (1994-1995). He served as co-chair for the National History Standards Project and currendy directs UCLA's National Center for History in the Schools.*

From *OAH Magazine of History,* Winter 2000, pages 12–16. Copyright © 2000 by Organization of American Historians. Reprinted with permission.

Andrew Jackson Versus the Cherokee Nation

"Old Hickory" had been an Indian fighter, and he continued the struggle as president. His new weapon was the Indian Removal Act, which would force Eastern tribes to relocate west of the Mississippi.

By Robert V. Remini

The great Cherokee Nation that had fought the young Andrew Jackson back in 1788 now faced an even more powerful and determined man who was intent on taking their land. But where in the past they had resorted to guns, tomahawks, and scalping knives, now they chose to challenge him in a court of law. They were not called a "civilized nation" for nothing. Many of their leaders were well educated; many more could read and write; they had their own written language, thanks to Sequoyah, a constitution, schools, and their own newspaper. And they had adopted many skills of the white man to improve their living conditions. Why should they be expelled from their lands when they no longer threatened white settlements and could compete with them on many levels? They intended to fight their ouster, and they figured they had many ways to do it. As a last resort they planned to bring suit before the Supreme Court.

Prior to that action, they sent a delegation to Washington to plead their cause. They petitioned Congress to protect them against the unjust laws of Georgia that had decreed that they were subject to its sovereignty and under its complete jurisdiction. They even approached the President, but he curtly informed them that there was nothing he could do in their quarrel with the state, a statement that shocked and amazed them.

So the Cherokees hired William Wirt to take their case to the Supreme Court. In the celebrated *Cherokee Nation v. Georgia* he instituted suit for an injunction that would permit the Cherokees to remain in Georgia without interference by the state. He argued that they constituted an independent nation and had been so regarded by the United States in its many treaties with them.

Speaking for the majority of the court, Chief Justice John Marshall handed down his decision on March 18, 1831. Not sur-

prisingly, as a great American nationalist, he rejected Wirt's argument that the Cherokees were a sovereign nation, but he also rejected Jackson's claim that they were subject to state law. The Indians were "domestic dependent nations," he ruled, subject to the United States as a ward to a guardian. Indian territory was part of the United States but not subject to action by individual states.

When the Cherokees read Marshall's decision they honestly believed that the Nation had won the case, that Georgia lacked authority to control their lives and property, and that the courts would protect them. The Supreme Court, the Principal Chief told his people, decided "in our favor." So they stayed right where they were, and missionaries encouraged them to stand fast.

But they figured without Andrew Jackson—the man the Cherokees called Sharp Knife—and the authorities of Georgia. In late December 1830, the state passed another law prohibiting white men from entering Indian country after March 1, 1831, without a license from the state. This move was obviously intended to keep interfering clergymen from inciting the Indians to disobey Georgia law. Eleven such missionaries were arrested for violating the recent statute, nine of whom accepted pardons from the governor in return for a promise that they would cease violating Georgia law. But Samuel A. Worcester and Dr. Elizur Butler refused the pardon, and Judge Augustin S. J. Clayton sentenced them to the state penitentiary, "there to endure hard labor for the term of four years." They appealed the verdict and their case came before the Supreme Court.

On March 3, 1832, Marshall again ruled in *Worcester v. Georgia,* declaring all the laws of Georgia dealing with the

Cherokees unconstitutional, null, void, and of no effect. In addition he issued a formal mandate two days later ordering the state's superior court to reverse its decision and free the two men.

Jackson was presently involved in a confrontation with South Carolina over the passage of the Tariffs of 1828 and 1832. The state had nullified the acts and threatened to secede from the Union if force were used to make her comply with them. The last thing Jackson needed was a confrontation with another state, so he quietly nudged Georgia into obeying the court order and freeing Butler and Worcester. A number of well-placed officials in both the state and national governments lent a hand and the governor, Wilson Lumpkin, released the two men on January 14, 1833.

With the annoying problem of the two missionaries out of the way, both Georgia and Jackson continued to lean on the Cherokees to get them to remove. "Some of the most vicious and base characters that the adjoining states can produce" squatted on their land and stole "horses and other property" and formed a link with as many "bad citizens" of the Cherokee Nation "as they can associate into their club." Missionaries decried what was happening to the Cherokees. If only "whites would not molest them," wrote Dr. Elizur Butler in *The Missionary Herald.* They have made remarkable progress in the last dozen years and if left alone they can and will complete the process toward a "civilized life."

Ross resolutely resisted any thought of leading his people from their ancient land into a god-forsaken wilderness.

But allowing eastern Indians full control of their eastern lands was virtually impossible in the 1830s. There was not army enough or will enough by the American people to bring it about. As Jackson constantly warned, squatters would continue to invade and occupy the land they wanted; then, if they were attacked, they would turn to the state government for protection that usually ended in violence. All this under the guise of bringing "civilization" to the wilderness.

Even so, the Cherokees had a strong leader who had not yet given up the fight. They were led by the wily, tough, and determined John Ross, a blue-eyed, brown-haired mixed-blood who was only one-eighth Cherokee. Nonetheless he was the Principal Chief, and a most powerful force within the Nation. He was rich, lived in a fine house attended by black slaves, and had influence over the annuities the United States paid to the tribal government for former land cessions. His appearance and lifestyle were distinctly white; in all other respects he was Indian.

From the beginning of Jackson's administration Ross urged his people to stand their ground and remain united. "Friends," he told his people, "I have great hopes in your firmness and that you will hold fast to the place where you were raised. Friends if you all unite together and be of one mind there is no danger."

And the Cherokees cheered his determination. They approved wholeheartedly of his leadership and they took comfort in what he said. So, with the Nation solidly behind him, Ross resolutely resisted any thought of leading his people from their ancient land into a god-forsaken wilderness.

LIBRARY OF CONGRESS
John Ridge, a leader of the Treaty Party, was assassinated by opponents in 1839.

Still the Cherokees held out, even though even they had begun to feel the unrelenting pressure. A so-called Treaty Party emerged within the Nation, made up of chiefs and headmen who understood Jackson's inflexible will and had decided to bow to his wishes and try to get the best treaty possible. They were led by very capable, hard-headed, and pragmatic men, including the Speaker of the Cherokee National Council, Major Ridge; his son, the educated and politically ambitious John Ridge; and the editor of the Cherokee *Phoenix,* Elias Boudinot.

John Ridge took a leading role in the emergence of the Treaty Party, for when the *Worcester* decision was first handed down he instantly recognized that Chief Justice Marshall had rendered an opinion that abandoned the Cherokees to their inevitable fate. So he went to Jackson and asked him point-blank whether the power of the United States would be exerted to force Georgia into respecting Indian rights and property. The President assured him that the government would do nothing. He then advised Ridge "most earnestly" to go home and urge his people to remove. Dejected, the chief left the President "with the melancholy conviction that he had been told the truth.

From that moment he was convinced that the only alternative to save his people from moral and physical death, was to make the best terms they could with the government and remove out of the limits of the states. This conviction he did not fail to make known to his friends, and hence rose the *'Treaty Party.'*"

The members of this Treaty Party certainly risked their lives in pressing for removal, and indeed all of them were subsequently marked for assassination. Not too many years later, Elias Boudinot and John Ridge were slain with knives and tomahawks in the midst of their families, while Major Ridge was ambushed and shot to death.

John Ross, on the other hand, would not yield. As head of the National Party that opposed removal he was shrewd enough to recognize immediately that the President would attempt to play one party off against the other. "The object of the President is unfolded & made too plain to be misunderstood," he told the Nation. "It is to create divisions among ourselves, break down our government, our press & our treasury, that our cries may not be heard abroad; that we may be deprived of the means of sending delegations to Washington City to make known our grievances before Congress…and break down the government which you [Cherokees] have, by your own free will & choice, established for the security of your freedom & common welfare."

Under the circumstance, Ross decided to go to Washington and request a meeting with the President in order to try again to arrange some accommodation that would prevent the mass relocation of his people to what was now the new Indian Territory, which Congress had created in 1834 and which eventually became the state of Oklahoma. He was tormented by the knowledge that his people would be condemned to a "prairie badly watered and only skirted on the margin of water courses and poor ridges with copes of wood." Worse, districts would be laid out for some "fifteen or twenty different tribes, and all speaking different languages, and cherishing a variety of habits and customs, a portion civilized, another half civilized and others uncivilized, and these congregated tribes of Indians to be regulated under the General Government, by no doubt white rulers." The very thought of it sent shivers through Ross's entire body.

Since he had fought with Jackson at the Battle of Horseshoe Bend during the Creek War he reckoned that his service during that battle would provide him with a degree of leverage in speaking with the President. And, as Principal Chief, he could speak with the duly constituted authority of the Cherokee Nation as established under the Cherokee Constitution of 1827.

He had another reason for requesting the interview. He had heard a rumor that Jackson had commissioned the Reverend John F. Schermerhorn, an ambitious cleric who had assisted in the removal of the Seminoles from Florida, to negotiate with Ridge and his associates and see if a deal could be worked out that would result in a treaty. Definitely alarmed, Ross asked to speak with the President at which time he said he would submit his own proposal for a treaty.

Jackson never liked Ross. He called him "a great villain." Unlike Ridge and Boudinot, said Jackson, the Principal Chief headed a mixed-blood elite, and was intent on centralizing power in his own hands and diverting the annuities to those who

LIBRARY OF CONGRESS
Major Ridge, John Ridge's father, was also a member of the Treaty Party. He was killed in an ambush on the same day his son died.

would advance his authority and their economic self-interests. Real Indians were full-blooded Indians, not half-breeds, he declared. They were hunters, they were true warriors who, like Ridge and Boudinot, understood the President's concern for his red children and wished to prevent the calamity of certain annihilation that would ensue if they did not heed his pleas to move west. As for Ross's authority under the Cherokee Constitution, Jackson denied that it existed. He said that this so-called Constitution provided for an election in 1832 and it had not been held. Instead the Principal Chief had simply filled the National Council with his henchmen—another indication, claimed Jackson, of an elitist clique who ruled the Nation and disregarded the interests of the majority of the people.

Despite his feelings about the chief, Jackson decided to grant Ross's request for a meeting. Above all else he wanted Cherokee removal and if that meant seeing this "great villain" and hearing about his proposal for relocating the tribe then he would do it. As a consummate politician, Jackson understood the value of playing one party off against another, so when he granted the interview he directed that Schermerhorn suspend his negotiations with the Treaty Party and wait for the outcome of his interview with the Principal Chief.

Actually Jackson and Ross were much alike. They were both wily, tough, determined, obsessed with protecting the interests of their respective peoples, and markedly dignified and polite when they came together in the White House on Wednesday,

February 5, 1834. It was exactly noon when the Principal Chief arrived, and the Great Father greeted him with the respect due Ross's position. The chief returned the compliment. For a few minutes their conversation touched on pleasantries, then they got down to the question at hand and began playing a political game that involved the lives of thousands, both Native Americans and white settlers.

Unfortunately, despite his many talents and keen intelligence, Ross was no match for the President. He simply lacked the resources of his adversary.

The Principal Chief opened with an impassioned plea. "Your Cherokee children are in deep distress," he said, "… because they are left at the mercy of the white robber and assassin" and receive no redress from the Georgia courts. That state, he declared, has not only "surveyed and lotteried off" Cherokee land to her citizens but legislated as though Cherokees were intruders in their own country.

Jackson just listened. Then the Principal Chief acted imprudently and made impossible demands on the President. To start, he insisted that in any treaty the Nation must retain some of their land along the borders of Tennessee, Alabama, and Georgia, land that had already been occupied by white settlers. He even included a small tract in North Carolina. He then required assurances that the United States government would protect the Cherokees with federal troops in the new and old settlements for a period of five years.

Jackson could scarcely believe what was being demanded of him. Under other circumstances he would have acted up a storm in an attempt to frighten and cower the chief. But, on this occasion he decided against it. Instead, in a calm and quiet but determined voice, he told Ross that nothing short of an entire removal of the Cherokee Nation from all their land east of the Mississippi would be acceptable.

Having run into a stone wall, Ross headed in another direction. In view of the gold that had recently been discovered in Georgia and North Carolina, he wanted $20 million for all their eastern land plus reimbursement for losses sustained by the Nation for violations of former treaties by the United States. He also asked for indemnities for claims under the 1817 and 1819 Cherokee treaties. The total amount almost equaled the national debt.

On hearing this, Jackson also changed direction. His voice hardened, his intense blue eyes flared, and the muscles in his face tightened and registered his growing displeasure. Obviously the Principal Chief had not caught the President's meaning when he rejected the first demand. Jackson snapped at Ross, rejected the proposal as "preposterous" and warned him that the Great Father was not to be trifled with. If these demands were the best the chief could offer then there was no point in continuing the discussion.

That brought Ross up short. Completely surprised by Jackson's reaction he protested his sincerity, and to prove it he offered to accept any award the Senate of the United States might recommend. Apparently the chief was attempting to set up a bidding contest between the upper house and the chief executive. Surprisingly, Jackson accepted the offer and assured Ross that he would "go as far" as the Senate in any award that

might be proposed. And on that conciliatory note the interview ended.

In less than a week Ross received his answer about what the Senate would offer. John P. King of Georgia chaired the Committee on Indian Affairs that considered the question. That was bad enough. Then the committee came up with an offer of $5 million. The figure shocked the Principal Chief. Jackson probably knew beforehand what would happen and therefore agreed to Ross's suggestion. Now the Indian was faced with rejecting the money outright or accepting this paltry sum and thereby losing credibility with his people. Naturally he chose the former course. He claimed he had been misunderstood, that he could not possibly agree to such an amount, and that his reputation among the Cherokees would be shattered if he consented to it. He left Washington an angry and bitter man.

Having disposed of Ross, Jackson turned back to Schermerhorn and instructed him to renew the negotiations with the Treaty Party. With little difficulty the cleric managed to arrange a draft removal treaty signed on March 14, 1835, by Schermerhorn, John Ridge, Elias Boudinot, and a small delegation of Cherokees. After due notice the treaty was submitted to the Cherokee National Council at New Echota, Georgia, for approval and sent to the President for submission to the Senate. The draft stipulated that the Cherokees surrender to the United States all its land east of the Mississippi River for a sum of $5 million, an amount that one modern historian has called "unprecedented generosity." This cession comprised nearly 8 million acres of land in western North Carolina, northern Georgia, northeastern Alabama, and eastern Tennessee. A schedule of removal provided that the Cherokees would be resettled in the west and receive regular payments for subsistence, claims, and spoliations, and would be issued blankets, kettles, and rifles.

At approximately the same time this draft treaty was drawn up and considered at New Echota, a large delegation of Cherokee chiefs—in the desperate hope that their assembled presence would make a difference and prevent the treaty from going forward to the Senate—went to Washington and asked to speak to their Great Father. In contrast to his grudging granting of Ross's request, Jackson was anxious to meet the delegation and give the chiefs one of his celebrated "talks."

The Indians arrived at the White House at the designated hour, and Jackson treated them with marked respect, as though they really were dignitaries of a foreign nation. Yet he did not remotely say or do anything that would indicate an acceptance of their independence or sovereignty. Once the Indians had assembled they faced the President as he began his talk.

"Brothers, I have long viewed your condition with great interest. For many years I have been acquainted with your people, and under all variety of circumstances, in peace and war. Your fathers are well known to me…. Listen to me, therefore, as your fathers have listened…."

Jackson paused. He turned from side to side to look at and take in all the Cherokees standing around him. After a few moments he began again.

"You are now placed in the midst of a white population…. You are now subject to the same laws which govern the citizens of Georgia and Alabama. You are liable to prosecutions for offenses, and to civil actions for a breach of any of your contracts. Most of your people are uneducated, and are liable to be brought into collision at all times with your white neighbors. Your young men are acquiring habits of intoxication. With strong passions… they are frequently driven to excesses which must eventually terminate in their ruin. The game has disappeared among you, and you must depend upon agriculture and the mechanic arts for support. And yet, a large portion of your people have acquired little or no property in the soil itself.… How, under these circumstances, can you live in the country you now occupy? Your condition must become worse and worse, and you will ultimately disappear, as so many tribes have done before you."

They had two years—that is, until May 23, 1838—to cross over the Mississippi and take up their new residence in the Indian Territory.

These were his usual arguments, but he judged them essential for success.

You have not listened to me, he scolded. You went to the courts for relief. You turned away from your Great Father. And what happened? After years of litigation you received little satisfaction from the Supreme Court and succeeded in earning the enmity of many whites. "I have no motive, Brothers, to deceive you," he said. "I am sincerely desirous to promote your welfare. Listen to me, therefore, while I tell you that you cannot remain where you are now.… It [is] impossible that you can flourish in the midst of a civilized community. You have but one remedy within your reach. And that is to remove to the West and join your countrymen, who are already established there." The choice is yours. "May the great spirit teach you how to choose."

Jackson then concluded by reminding them of the fate of the Creeks, that once great and proud Nation. How broken and reduced in circumstances their lives had now become because they resisted. It was a not-so-subtle threat that also struck home. "Think then of these things," he concluded. "Shut your ears to bad counsels. Look at your condition as it now is, and then consider what it will be if you follow the advice I give you."

That ended the talk, and the Indians filed from the room more disappointed and depressed than ever. Jackson would not budge, and they knew their kinsmen were dead set against removal. It was a stalemate that could end only in tragedy.

Meanwhile Schermerhorn called "a council of all the people" to meet him at New Echota in Georgia during the third week of December 1835 to approve the draft treaty, making sure that a large contingent of Treaty Party members attended. Like Jackson, he had the temerity to warn other Cherokees that if they stayed away their absence would be considered a vote of consent for the draft.

Despite the threat and the warning, practically the entire Nation stayed away. As a consequence the treaty was approved on December 28 by the unbelievably low number of 79 to 7. The numbers represented only the merest fraction of the Nation. A vast majority—perhaps fifteen-sixteenths of the entire population—presumably opposed it and showed their opposition by staying away. The entire process was fraudulent, but that hardly mattered. Jackson had the treaty he wanted, and he did not hesitate to so inform the Senate.

The Treaty of New Echota closely, but not completely, resembled the draft treaty in that the Cherokees surrendered all their eastern land and received $4.5 million in return. They would be paid for improvements, removed at government expense, and maintained for two years. Removal was to take place within two years from the date of the treaty's approval by the Senate and President.

A short while later some 12,000 Cherokees signed a resolution denouncing the Treaty of New Echota and forwarded it to the Senate. Even the North Carolina Cherokees, in a separate action, added 3,250 signatures to a petition urging the Senate to reject it. But Jackson was assured by the Treaty Party that "a majority of the people" approved the document "and all are willing peaceable to yield to the treaty and abide by it." Such information convinced the President that the Principal Chief and his "half breed" cohorts had coerced the Cherokees into staying away from New Echota under threat of physical violence.

At New Echota the Treaty Party selected a Committee of Thirteen to carry the treaty to Washington and they were empowered to act on any alteration required by the President or the U. S. Senate. This Committee invited Ross to join the group and either support the treaty or insist on such alterations as to make it acceptable. "But to their appeal [Ross] returned no answer," which further convinced the President that the treaty represented the genuine interests and the will of the majority of Cherokees.

Militiamen charged into the Cherokee country and drove the Cherokees from their cabins and houses.

Although Henry Clay, Daniel Webster, Edward Everett, and other senators spoke fervently against the treaty in the Senate, a two-thirds majority of 31 members voted for it and 15 against. It carried by a single vote on May 18. Jackson added his signature on May 23, 1836, and proclaimed the Treaty of New Echota in force.

And they had two years—that is until May 23, 1838—to cross over the Mississippi and take up their new residence in the Indian Territory. But every day of that two-year period John Ross fought the inevitable. He demanded to see the President and insisted that Jackson recognize the authority of the duly elected National Council, but Sharp Knife would have none of him and turned him away. Back home the Principal Chief advised his people to ignore the treaty and stay put. "We will not recognize the forgery palmed off upon the world as a treaty by a knot of unauthorized individuals," he cried, "nor stir one step with reference to that false paper."

Not everyone listened to him. They knew Andrew Jackson better. Some 2,000 Cherokees resigned themselves to the inevitable, packed their belongings, and headed west. The rest, the vast majority of the tribe, could not bear to leave their homeland and chose to hope that their Principal Chief would somehow work the miracle that would preserve their country to them.

But their fate could not have been worse. When the two-year grace period expired and Jackson had left office, his hand-picked successor, President Martin Van Buren, ordered the removal to begin. Militiamen charged into the Cherokee country and drove the Cherokees from their cabins and houses. With rifles and bayonets they rounded up the Indians and placed them in prison stockades that had been erected "for gathering in and holding the Indians preparatory to removal." These poor, frightened and benighted innocents, while having supper in their homes, "were startled by the sudden gleam of bayonets in the doorway and rose up to be driven with blows and oaths along the weary miles of trail which led to the stockade. Men were seized in the fields, women were taken from their wheels and children from their play." As they turned for one last glimpse of their homes they frequently saw them in flames, set ablaze by the lawless rabble who followed the soldiers, scavenging what they could. These outlaws stole the cattle and other livestock and even desecrated graves in their search for silver pendants and other valuables. They looted and burned. Said one Georgia volunteer who later served in the Confederate army: "I fought through the Civil War and have seen men shot to pieces and slaughtered by thousands, but the Cherokee removal was the cruelest I ever saw."

In a single week some 17,000 Cherokees were rounded up and herded into what was surely a concentration camp. Many sickened and died while they awaited transport to the west. In June the first contingent of about a thousand Indians boarded a steamboat and sailed down the Tennessee River on the first lap of their westward journey. Then they were boxed like animals into railroad cars drawn by two locomotives. Again there were many deaths on account of the oppressive heat and cramped conditions in the cars. For the last leg of the journey the Cherokees walked. Small wonder they came to call this 800-mile nightmare "The Trail of Tears." Of the approximately 18,000 Cherokees who were removed, at least 4,000 died in the stockades along the way, and some say the figure actually reached 8,000. By the middle of June 1838 the general in charge of the Georgia militia proudly reported that not a single Cherokee remained in the state except as prisoners in the stockade.

At every step of their long journey to the Indian Territory the Cherokees were robbed and cheated by contractors, lawyers, agents, speculators, and anyone wielding local police power. Food supplied by the government disappeared or arrived in short supply. The commanding officer, General Winfield Scott, and a few other generals "were concerned about their reputation for humaneness," says one modern historian, "and probably even for the Cherokee. There just wasn't much they could do about it." As a result many died needlessly. "Oh! The misery and wretchedness that presents itself to our view in going among these people," wrote one man. "Sir, I have witnessed entire families prostrated with sickness—not one able to give help to the other, and these poor people were made the instruments of enriching a few unprincipled and wicked contractors."

And this, too, is part of Andrew Jackson's legacy. Although it has been pointed out many times that he was no longer President of the United States when the Trail of Tears occurred and had never intended such a monstrous result of his policy, that hardly excuses him. It was his insistence on the speedy removal of the Cherokees, even after he had left office, that brought about this horror. From his home outside Nashville he regularly badgered Van Buren about enforcing the treaty. He had become obsessed about removal. He warned that Ross would exert every effort and means available to him to get the treaty rescinded or delayed and that, he said, must be blocked. But the new President assured him that nothing would interfere with the exodus of the Cherokees and that no extension of the two-year grace period would be tolerated under any circumstance.

Principal Chief John Ross also shares a portion of blame for this unspeakable tragedy. He continued his defiance even after the deadline for removal had passed. He encouraged his people to keep up their resistance, despite every sign that no appreciable help would be forthcoming from the American people or anyone else; and he watched as they suffered the awful consequences of his intransigence.

Despite the obscene treatment accorded the Cherokees by the government, the tribe not only survived but endured. As Jackson predicted, they escaped the fate of many extinct eastern tribes. Cherokees today have their tribal identity, a living language, and at least three governmental bodies to provide for their needs. Would that the Yemassee, Mohegans, Pequots, Delawares, Narragansetts, and other such tribes could say the same.

Excerpted from *Andrew Jackson and His Indian Wars* by Robert V. Remini. Copyright © Robert V. Remini, 2001. Reprinted by arrangement with Viking Penguin, a division of Penguin Putnam, Inc.

Robert V. Remini is the author of a three-volume biography of Andrew Jackson as well as biographies of Daniel Webster and Henry Clay and many other books about Jacksonian America.

NEW HORIZONS FOR THE AMERICAN WEST

by Margaret Walsh

For many years and for millions of people on both sides of the Atlantic the American West was and still is the excitement, action and scenery of a John Ford-John Wayne Movie or of a Zane Grey dime novel. For others who have a different cultural approach to the West it is the magnificent landscape paintings of Albert Bierstadt or Thomas Moran or the backdrop to the classic literary works of James Fenimore Cooper or Mark Twain. For historians who studied North America the West was that part of the continent, usually the United States, which was unsettled at the time of the Revolution, or the area beginning at the Appalachian Mountains and stretching to the Pacific Coast. The process of settling this vast territory became the story of the West, often a saga of epic proportions filled with heroes who not only had major adventures but who brought civilisation in the shape of democracy and capitalism.

Such a West was popular for many years in the twentieth century, but then became unfashionable in the 1960s and 1970s when historians, popular culture and the media paid more attention to urban industrial settings and the issue of civil and equal rights. More recently, however, new currents have been flowing and the West has become a whirlpool of historical activity. Stirred in part by the concerns of residents to have a more realistic past and one which covered centuries other than the nineteenth, historians are busy uncovering the 'New West'. This West is a place or a region, rather than a process of development and it is a place which has possibilities as well as problems. Through discussing specific issues Western historians have not only reinterpreted and revitalised the traditional or 'Old' West, but they suggest ways in which the region may lead the nation into the twenty-first century.

Wild Bill Hicock and wagon trains—we all have familiar images of pioneer spirit and individual derring-do imprinted in our minds, but as **Margaret Walsh** explains here, historians are now presenting a more complex and less triumphalist view of how the American frontier moved West.

The traditional West which dominated the textbooks and media for much of the twentieth century had been given respectability through the pioneering work of Frederick Jackson Turner. His famous thesis 'The Significance of the Frontier in American History', first published in the American Historical Association, *Annual Report* of the Year 1893, (1894), set the framework for many of the ensuing historical outpourings. Writing that 'the existence of an area of free land, its continuous recession and the advance of American settlement westward explains American development' Turner hypothesised that abundant, available and cheap land ensured the triumph of American capitalism.

By utilising the resources of the West, pioneers contributed to raising American standards of living to the highest in the world. Equally if not more importantly the process of westward expansion meant that the nation was won for democracy and that the character of the American population was shaped by the struggle to win the environment. Turner and his followers, now called 'Old Western Historians' wrote optimistic history. Theirs was a story in which progress was the key feature. The American West had been won for the benefit of a wealthy democratic nation-state.

This traditional West, whether read in academically researched monographs, general textbooks or novels, or whether viewed on the large or small screens, was primarily a EuroAmerican male experience, often highlighted through the achievements of cowboys, homesteaders, fur traders or the United States' army. In Ray A. Billington's monumental classic (*Westward Expansion. A History of the American Frontier*, Macmillan, first edition, 1949, fifth edition, 1982) these men overcame obstacles like difficult terrain, drought, Indians, wild animals and distance through their perseverance, hard work, ingenuity and most of all through their use of technology. Such technology might be a Winchester repeating rifle, but it could also be a reaper, a windmill or the railroad. Though other people were present in the movement west, they were not the most important actors and could thus be either marginalised or stereotyped.

Modifications to this lopsided West came when these other people, women, Native Americans and Americans of colour became both visible and significant. The huge area west of the Appalachian Mountains was inhabited by numerous Indian or Native Americans long before Europeans arrived. The smaller area west of the Mississippi River had been El Norte or northwestern Mexico for Mexican Americans for many years before westward-moving settlers crossed that river. In addition to these antecedent settlers, Asiatic immigrants moved east across the Pacific ocean, Canadians ignored political boundaries and moved south while former black slaves from the American South moved west and northwest, all at a similar time to the mainstream migration. The 'New' West was a home for millions of diverse Americans, nearly half of whom were female by sex. Indeed it was a cosmopolitan area in which multiculturalism flourished.

Women's historians struck the first major blow at the Euro-American male framework in which women had been either invisible or were stereotyped as long-suffering, dauntless or deviant. For Sandra L. Myres (*Westering Women and the Frontier Experience, 1800-1915*, University of New Mexico Press, 1982) and Glenda Riley, (*The Female Frontier. A Comparative View of Women on the Prairie and the Plains*, University of Kansas Press, 1988) women were on many frontiers of settlement and were essential to survival and well-being. On the farms where most pioneers were to be found women as mothers raised children; as wives or partners they ran homes; as unpaid labourers they worked on the land and as entrepreneurs they 'paid their way' through 'butter and egg' money. A man could not farm successfully without a female helper. In the western towns women were essential parts of the community, running homes, establishing institutions like schools and churches or earning their living as teachers, hotel proprietors or prostitutes.

Women may have been fewer in number but they were also part of the arduous and adventurous male domains of fur trading, mining and army life. Where women were absent, as on some early logging frontiers or in the exploratory expeditions, Kathleen G. Morrissey ('Engendering the West' in William Cronon, George Miles and Jay Gitlin (eds) *Under An Open Sky. Rethinking the American West*, W.W. Norton, 1992) has suggested engendering such activities by considering how men still remained part of the wider world of two sexes. Relationships between men and women still existed although men were by themselves on the frontier.

The addition of women to the traditional westward process of frontier settlement required consideration of home-making. With the West as home families encountered other peoples and cultures with whom they competed, clashed and compromised. There are no outright winners or losers in this exchange, for much of what has become distinctive about New Western History is its mixed or multicultural nature. In a setting where everyone can contribute to a cosmopolitan experience, the majority, which are still male and female Euro-Americans, may be dominant, but their claim to authority has been seriously weakened. Their traditional 'winning of the West' is now politically incorrect. The so-called losers not only receive more sympathetic attention, but their encounter with the Euro-Americans is considered from their perspective.

The main losers in the conventional texts and pictures were the Indian Americans. Historians imbued with the ethos of 1960s liberalism like Angie Debo, (*A History of the Indians of the United States*, University of Oklahoma Press, 1970) sharply criticised the inefficiency of the federal government, the corruption of its agents and the greed of incoming settlers. Revisionist historians like F. Paul Prucha, (*The Great Father: The United States Government and the American Indians*, University of Nebraska Press, 1984) offered a defence on philanthropic and economic grounds. What else could the federal government, as guardian of the public domain, do other than remove Indian Americans in an era when they could not be accepted as equals and when the government did not have the resources to police the frontier effectively?

European ideas of efficiency earlier suggested that the land was not being utilised effectively by the indigenous dwellers. Given the later disasters which have occurred from over-use of resources some ethno-historians like Wilbur R. Jacobs ('The Indian and the Frontier in American History—A Need For Revision', *Western Historical Quarterly* vol. 4, 1979) and Indian Americans have responded that Indian Americans' land usage was more in harmony with the balance of nature and that their understanding of the environment could offer a better ecological balance. Furthermore their communal way of life, their religion and their culture were well worth appreciating on terms other than as an abberation from whiteness. Yet taking an Indian perspective on the peculiar ways of white people has not revised the disastrous impact of their arrival.

Other notable losers who were also displaced and dispossessed in their encounter with westward moving Euro-Americans were the Mexican and Hispanic Americans. In the early twentieth century Herbert E.

Bolton (*The Spanish Borderlands: A Chronicle of Old Florida and the Southwest*, Yale University Press, 1921) and his students acknowledged the impact of Spanish civilisation as a significant force in the history of the American southwest, but this civilisation did not make a major impact on the dominant Anglo-American frontier. Yet anyone visiting the borderlands of Texas, California, Arizona and New Mexico today cannot fail to notice Spanish names, architecture and language. While much of the language is a result of the inflow of millions of twentieth-century Mexican migrants, much of the other Spanish heritage dates back to earlier centuries.

In reappraising the historical dimensions of the frontier Southwest, social and cultural historians have moved beyond the traditional 'Borderlands School' to uncover sources and to use approaches and methodologies which acknowledge the importance of antecedent settlers. With newer categories of analysis like gender, race and culture at the centre, Antonia I. Castaneda ('Gender, Race and Culture: Spanish-Mexican Women in the Historiography of Frontier California', *Frontiers* Vol. 11, 1990) suggests that it is possible to ascertain how the lives of Spanish and Mexican settlers were changed by the later Euro-American arrivals and what the occupiers of the land offered to and thought of the incomers. Though this emerging scholarship is very sensitive to norms other than those of Anglo-American males, the theme of loss and conquest has not been eradicated from the Hispano-Mexican experience in the nineteenth century.

Other minority groups who were newcomers to the American West in its century of rapid development endured negative encounters on account of their colour. Traditionally they have been ignored or marginalised: now that colour has been given positive connotations by affirmative action programmes their contributions are being woven into, if not given prominence, in 'New' histories like those written by Patricia N. Limerick (*The Legacy of Conquest. The Unbroken Past of the American West*, W.W. Norton & Company, 1987) and Richard White ('*It's Your Misfortune and None of My Own*'. A New History of the American West, University of Oklahoma Press, 1991).

African Americans, moving from the American South, primarily as free persons after the Civil War, may have suffered less discrimination and harassment, but they still faced racial prejudice, as workers, as voters and in social settings. Asiatic immigrants too faced racial persecution as they were exploited as workers and were denied the vote. Furthermore social interaction was very limited as Chinese and Japanese were excluded from many meeting places by laws regulating their distinctive and inferior status. Though minority groups are now examined from the inside out rather than from the conventional Euro-American standards, the nineteenth-century West remains a negative terrain for people of colour. To be sure there is no longer a clear-cut division between triumphant white male pioneers and conquered or tragic Indians, but even with the presence of both sexes and several races and ethnicities the traditional 'majority' group retains its central presence and often dominates in establishing frameworks of analysis.

If the New West has become more complex and diverse in its human dimensions, its shape has also changed chronologically and geographically. The time-frame has been stretched and the area compressed. By looking at several centuries and a smaller region both the cultural historians who are interested in patterns of human behaviour and the environmental historians who are interested in the dynamics of place, whether natural, economic or political, have been able to concentrate on a history of continuity rather than one which has a turning point when the westward moving frontier ended about 1890. The New West thus does not begin either with the establishment of the American colonies in the seventeenth century or with the search for American independence in 1763. Nor does it end in the 1890s. The story of the West starts with an understanding of the many different groups of Indian Americans who have inhabited the land for centuries. More importantly for historians like Limerick and White, as distinct from anthropologists, it continues into the twentieth century, where diverse peoples live in an urban industrial and post-industrial society and economy.

Geographically this West is not a moving frontier. It is a region: indeed according to Donald Worster ('New West: True West: Interpreting The Region's History', *Western Historical Quarterly* vol. 18, 1987) it is one of the three great co-terminal regions, East, South and West, in the United States. The western boundary of this region is invariably the Pacific Ocean. Its eastern boundary is either a natural phenomenon, usually the Mississippi or Missouri Rivers or the political bounds encompassing either the seventeen or twenty-one states set off by those rivers. What best unites such a region is still a matter of contention.

It can be united by the problem of aridity. Late nineteenth-century explorers like John Wesley Powell (45 Congress 2nd Sessions, House Executive *Documents*, 73, 'Report on the Lands of the Arid Region', 1878) and historians like Walter Prescott Webb (*The Great Plains*, Grosset and Dunlap, 1931) had earlier pointed out that it would be very difficult to sustain European-style agriculture which depended on an adequate rainfall. The Great Plains was a grasslands area naturally suited to pastoral farming or to arable farming with irrigation. From the 98th meridian to the Pacific Coast, with the exception of the northwestern states of Washington and Oregon, the West was dry; in its most arid parts it was a desert. Indian Americans had been aware of establishing a delicate balance between man and nature in their patterns of land use. The Mormons early learned in the 1840s and

1850s that survival in Utah meant having a communal approach to harvesting and using water. Individualistic EuroAmerican farmers were much slower to come to terms with shortages of water and thereby suffered the consequences not only in the dry cycles of the late nineteenth century but periodically in the twentieth century.

If, following Donald Worster's example (*Rivers of Empire: Water, Aridity and the Growth of the American West*, Pantheon, 1985) the West is considered as a hydraulic region then its history can be organised round the theme of water, its location, amount and distribution. Water is not only essential to the production of farm crops: it is necessary to livelihood in urban places. The West has had an urban history since the mid-nineteenth century and urban residents too have encountered the problems of financing and engineering water supplies. Moving from activity at the local level in creating the dams, ditches and canals of irrigation districts to a demand for broader state government action, westerners lurched towards some solutions. Federal government intervention in the twentieth century has struggled to provide more satisfactory regional irrigation schemes, but these have often been caught up in bureaucracy and conflicting interest groups. Water and its shortage are essential to understanding the politics and economy of the region. They could form a central organising theme for studying the West systematically.

But can it be studied effectively? For some New Western historians, like Richard White, water is only one resource. In a broader environmental approach to the region it is also necessary to include animal, vegetable and mineral resources. The economic abundance of such resources drew many migrants westwards and their rapid exploitation created both urban growth and the possibility of a managed approach to the environment. The destruction of wildlife,

starting with the beaver in the Rocky Mountain streams and moving through the sea otters, the fur seal and most famous of all, the buffalo of the Plains in the 1870s and 1880s, has created endangered species which are now the concern of conservationists nationwide.

The depletion of precious minerals in California and the Rocky Mountains in the mid- and late-nineteenth century, the coal mining in the Plains and Mountain West and the oil drilling in California and Texas in the late nineteenth and twentieth centuries have left a legacy of waste and destruction as well as stimulating the boom and burst pattern of urban development. Ghost towns, corporate mining towns, commercial centres servicing mining ventures and railroad towns all feature in the New West. The felling of the magnificent strands of timber produced vast cutover districts in the Pacific Northwest. Here at least, however, it was possible to replant and conservationists, aided by government support, have made some progress in [reforestation]. As for the superb scenery and its relationship with tourism, this too has become a concern for conservationists. Naturalists and governments recognised the importance of 'set-asides' in the shape of national and state parks if the natural wonders were to be retained for the benefit of the people.

The West as a region is not the agrarian democracy envisaged by the older generation of historians who paid most attention to the settling of the frontier by farmers and the establishment of territorial and then state governments which would be the equals of the original thirteen states. The West had both an agrarian dimension and an urban dimension tied into the exploitation of non-land resources, and its political development came later chronologically. Its relationship with the federal government was thereby more problematic. Indeed some revisionists like Jack Eblen, (*First and Second United States' Empires: Governors and Territorial Gov-

ernment, 1784-1912*, University of Pittsburgh Press, 1968) and some of the New Western historians (in Gerald Nash and Richard W. Etulain (eds.) *The Twentieth Century West: Historical Interpretations*, University of New Mexico Press, 1989) have favoured an institutional framework of analysis for the region's history focused on the troublesome association between the West and Washington DC. Often using colonial or neo-colonial terminology they envisage the region as dependent upon, rather than interdependent with, national or even global affairs.

Traditionally the federal government was protector of pioneers through the defensive agency of the army, through the land office which distributed land cheaply, and through the territorial system of government which promised democracy and equality. Though settlement was not always fair it worked reasonably well for the majority of Euro-American migrants in the trans-Appalachian and mid-continental areas. Viewed from the Pacific Coast or from the Mountain West in the mid-late nineteenth century, the federal government was slow to provide for independence in the form of statehood and retained too much control over the land and other natural resources. Parts of the 'New West' thus lived under a system in which local political and economic decisions often needed the approval of outside officials. This 'colonial' heritage stimulated a dual reaction. Westerners resented a federal tyranny which frustrated their individualism. At the same time they became dependent and demanded increased federal spending to resolve regional problems and upgrade the quality of their lives. In the twentieth century the 'neo-colonial' tradition has continued with the federal government retaining ownership of large amounts of land and being regulator and subsidiser of major projects ranging from reclamation and conservation, through transportation to defence. Some New Western historians contend that it is impossible to look at the West without considering the significance of the bureaucracy of government.

What now is the history of the American West? Have the traditional stories of cowboys and Indians, the romantic yarns of lone Mountain Men or gold seekers or even of sturdy pioneer farmers disappeared? For some historians the adventurous and triumphal West rarely existed. For many others who moved steadily westwards with Turner's frontiering process, their analysis showed a realistic appreciation of its difficulties and successes. What the newer research and emerging frameworks like those discussed in the collection of essays, *Trails. Toward A New Western History* (Patricia N. Limerick, Clyde A. Milner II and Charles E. Rankin [eds.], University of Kansas Press, 1991) have done, is to shift the emphasis to the West as a region. Here all New Western historians want a longer time-frame and one which perhaps has a present perspective, but one which certainly calls for continuity. Many are concerned to focus on the human and cultural dimensions of settlement and the exchange between peoples of different race, ethnicity and sex. Many are more concerned with the problems and possibilities of the region's environment, whether defined in terms of natural and human resources or in a political sense. The New West is smaller geographically, but is more diverse and more complex than its traditional forerunner.

Margaret Walsh is Senior Lecturer in the Department of American and Canadian Studies at the University of Nottingham and author of The American Frontier Revisited *(Macmillan, 1981).*

This article first appeared in *History Today,* Vol. 44, No. 3, March 1994, pages 44–50. Copyright © 1994 by History Today, Ltd. Reprinted by permission.

THE GREAT FAMINE

WHEN A BLIGHT STRUCK THE IRISH POTATO CROP IN THE 1840S, IT PRECIPITATED A FAMINE THAT CAUSED MORE THAN A MILLION DEATHS AND THE EXODUS OF THAT MANY MORE TO AMERICA.

BY EDWARD OXFORD

"A MIST ROSE UP OUT OF THE SEA," a farmer said of the strange scene about him, "... then when the fog lifted, you could begin to see the potato stalks lying over as if the life was gone out of them. And that was the beginning of the great trouble and the famine that destroyed Ireland."

Something wicked had come Ireland's way in the somber summer of 1845, and the people of the land felt the touch of terror. While traveling from Dublin to Cork, Father Mathew, a well-known temperance apostle, beheld "the wide waste of putrefying vegetation.... In many places the wretched people were seated on the fences of their decaying gardens, wringing their hands and wailing bitterly the disaster that had left them foodless."

With terrifying suddenness, the countryside took on the countenance of annihilation. In field after field, Ireland's life-giving potatoes lay blackened, withered, and blasted. "The potatoes had been blighted, turned black and brown," Jeremiah O'Donovan Rossa recounted. "The air was laden with a sickly odor of decay. The hand of Death had stricken the potato fields."

Even after 150 years, accounts of the Irish sufferings strike deep at the heart: Mary St. Leger, sixty and blind, "died from want and hunger"... Mark Clancy, "died of starvation"... Mary Wright, dead from a fit "brought on by want of food"... 14-year-old James Foley "dead of cold on the road"... the widow Catherine McEvoy "died screaming in her hut".... Such was their losing struggle to get from one day to the next.

During its years of wrath, from 1845 to 1850, this scourge upon the land would prove to be the most stunning blow the Irish people ever received. More than a million of its estimated eight million men, women, and children perished—either from starvation or disease. As many as two million survivors fled the famine—and their native land—in sailing vessels weighted with human cargo. About 1.5 million Irish journeyed to America; others went to Canada, Australia, and England. The fungus was said to have reached Europe with a shipment of apparently healthy seed potatoes from America. The blight first took hold in Belgium, then spread to the Netherlands and France before crossing the Channel to England and, fatefully, Ireland.

The effects of the blight were first seen in Ireland in August 1845, and by November it was estimated that half the crop had been destroyed. Because the fungus reproduced in warm conditions, its effect was less noticeable during the winter months that followed. A heat wave the following summer, however, provided ideal conditions for the revival of the blight, and by late 1846, the potato crop was practically destroyed. It would be years before the cause of the blight was identified as an invisible fungus, *phytophthora infestans*, whose spores were carried on the wind.

The potato represented life to the poor of Ireland, who ate up to 12 pounds of potatoes each day. The nutrient-rich tuber was brought to Europe from the New World by the Spaniards in the late 1500s, and by the eighteenth century it had become Ireland's staple foodstuff, more commonly eaten than bread.

Although staggering in its sameness, the diet seems to have provided all that was needed for a healthy life. Travelers to Ireland noted the wholesome appearance of its people. They may have been regarded as the most wretched people in Europe, but the Irish were well nourished and physically robust.

Largely because of its importance within Ireland, the potato served as a convenient symbol of cultural disparagement. The British, who had for centuries held sway over Ireland, looked down upon the Irish potato as a "lazy root," grown in "lazy beds" by a "lazy people." But British antipathy toward the Irish went far beyond the inglorious "spud." The Anglo-Saxon held the Celt in disdain because he was of a separate race; and the Protestant disparaged the Catholic because he was of a different faith. Such feelings had, of course, long since become mutual.

Ireland's lot since its subjugation by England in the twelfth century had been one of woe. As early as 1729, Jonathan Swift, Dean of St. Patrick's Cathedral in Dublin, wrote a scalding satire—*A Modest Proposal*—in which he bitterly proposed that the Irish be taught to eat their own children as a solution to the ever-present food shortage. The African-American abolitionist Frederick Douglass—himself a former slave—wrote in 1845 that "of all places to witness human misery, ignorance, degradation, filth and wretchedness, an Irish hut is preeminent … the people [of Ireland] are in the same degradation as the American slaves."

Although there had been crop failures from time to time, the potato had never before truly failed the Irish poor. The less fortunate members of society could count on the potato as their staff of life. During the first half of the nineteenth century, however, an apocalyptic convergence of natural catastrophe, a slumping economy, and human enmities resulted in the Great Famine that laid siege to Ireland and whose horrors, declared one chronicler, "surpassed anything in the dismal chant of Dante."

Whole villages deserted, the dispossessed stalked about the countryside "scattering disease, destitution, and dismay in all directions." They would burrow among broken walls, or ditches, or bogs. The "haggard, sallow and emaciated figures, stricken down by fever," lay prostrate upon the streets.

The English Quaker James Hack Tuke called the scenes he witnessed in Ireland "the culminating point of man's degradation." A magistrate told of a dwelling-place in which "frozen corpses were found upon the mud floor, half devoured by rats," while a parish priest spoke of "a girl lying dead, with two others beside her just expiring. A famished cat got upon the bed and tried to gnaw the dead girl, but I struck it aside." Said a saddened physician, taking up a skeleton child in a cottage: "Here is the way it is with them all; their legs swing and rock like the legs of a doll."

"There is nothing for us to do," a forlorn woman told a passerby, "but to lie down and die." Which, with silent resignation, is what so very many did. Lying huddled in the darkened corners of their cottages, they waited for the end to come.

Landlords matter-of-factly drove the wretchedly poor, who were unable to pay their rent, out of their hovels. To be surely rid of the starving tenants, landowners tore down the ramshackle cottages and cabins that had sheltered them. An observer described one such eviction: "At a signal, the sheriff and the ruffian crowbar-brigade dragged the inmates of the cabin out upon the road. The thatched roof was ripped down and the earthen walls battered in by crowbars; the screaming mother, the half-naked children, the father and sons, the tottering elders were hauled out. So the villains plied their horrible trade." Local police saw to it that the peasants complied with the bidding of the landlords, one of whom stated that "The exuberance of the tree of Irish population must be cut off by extermination or death."

The numbers who died of fever far exceeded those who died of hunger. People became so fearful of contagion that they hesitated to bury the dead. At times, cabins were simply pulled down and the debris strewn over the corpses within them. When burial did take place, it was usually in unmarked graves on hillsides, in fields, or alongside roads.

Coffins with hinged-bottoms, which could be used over and over again, were put to widespread use by the destitute. The corpses, sometimes wrapped in sacks or straw mats, were carried to the grave-site for burial, whereupon the bottom of the coffin swung open, depositing the body in the earth.

At first, British efforts to relieve the Irish misery were vigorous, but they faltered as the famine persisted. Britain's Prime Minister at the outbreak of the famine, the Conservative leader Sir Robert Peel, took steps to alleviate the situation by purchasing Indian corn from the United States and having it shipped to Ireland for food.

But in 1846, the Whig party took over leadership of the government and was not so sympathetic to the plight of the Irish. Throughout the remainder of the famine years, British decision makers pursued that nation's traditional policy of *laissez faire*—a philosophy of non-interference by government in economic matters—which encouraged people to follow their own ideas free from government's meddling.

Ireland, they felt, should be left to "the operation of natural causes." And in fact, some of the populace did make economic headway under this system. But social philosophers turned a blind eye to the plight of Ireland's poor, who possessed ever-fewer resources with which to help themselves.

The government did set up hundreds of workhouses, not as much to save the Irish, as to keep them from fleeing to England. Thousands of Irish flocked to work-relief projects that paid them a pittance for doing such things as breaking stones for ten hours a day. More than 500,000 toiled at building roads, many of which, like the make-work schemes themselves, went nowhere in particular.

And Britain put its needs first. Rather than use Ireland's crops of oats, rye, wheat, and barley to feed the starving people there, the government saw to it that those grains continued to reach British markets unabated during the famine years. The Irish peasants sold their home-grown products even though their own families were hungry; the money earned from the sale of grain did pay the rent, thus keeping them from being evicted. Even so, many resented seeing crops, protected in transit by military escorts, leaving Ireland.

Some English citizens made private donations to the Irish poor, as did various charitable groups, most notably the Quakers—the Society of Friends—who set up relief committees in Dublin and in London and established soup kitchens in Ireland. The government also set up soup kitchens that served "stirabout"—a thin oatmeal-based soup—to as many as three million people a day during the worst of the famine.

In the main, however, the British government let God and the starving Irish work things out between themselves. To some British authorities, Ireland seemed cursed; her misfortunes were too frequent, too hopeless, and too vast to be solved by even the most magnanimous of human means. Others blamed the Irish themselves for many of their own troubles.

Some within the government at Westminster subscribed to the view that the famine confirmed that there was a natural superiority in the grand scheme of things, of rich over poor, of Anglo-Saxon over Celt, and of Protestant over Catholic. The Irish were perceived by these officials as the shiftless dregs of the earth, a "swinish multitude," whose plight was perhaps Nature's way of signifying their unworthiness. Since the Irish were meant to be born poor, such conjecture went, they also were meant to die poor.

Charles Edward Trevelyan, the Crown's official in charge of relief and a dominant figure throughout the famine years, wrote: "The Great Evil with which we are to contend is not the physical evil of the famine, but the moral evil of the selfish, perverse and turbulent character of the people." As the famine raged, one Irish Catholic priest charged British policymakers with having "made the most beautiful island under the sun a place of skulls."

For the downtrodden Irish, there was no staying. "Before the Famine, many emigrants *chose* to leave Ireland," explains Luke Dodd, Director of Ireland's Famine Museum in County Roscommon. "The Famine did away with the choosing. It had become a matter of leave or die."

So leave they did, by the tens of thousands. After the sad farewells and a final blessing by their priests, the wayfarers turned their backs upon their homes and the past they had known. Then, bearing their bundles of clothing, they headed by horse-cart or on foot for the coast, where they boarded cattle-boats for the trip across the Irish Sea to Liverpool. Few of them would ever again set eyes upon their native land.

For most, destiny pointed to America. The price of passage to U.S. ports was the equivalent of between $7.50 and $12.50 per person, roughly half of an Irish laborer's wages for an entire year. During the "Hunger Years," more than a million Irish men, women, and children came to America, many joining relatives already here who had paid their fares. It was one of the most massive and desperate migrations in human history.

The typical sea-going packet of the era was little better than a sealed box, with so little sail that the journey across the Atlantic Ocean could take six or more weeks. Known as "coffin ships," these vessels sailed without the legal quotas of food and water. But the desire to flee Ireland was so great—and the peasants' lack of knowledge of geography so poor, that they were eager to board the ships. Earl Grey, Britain's Secretary of State for the Colonies, noted that: "many of the emigrants are content … to submit to very great hardships during the voyage."

For most, the passage westward proved difficult; for those unfortunates in steerage, it was a horror-ridden experience. Hundreds, ranging in age from ninety years old to infants born aboard ship, huddled in a single, dark hold. Allotted scarcely more space than their bodies occupied, passengers kept their rag-tag

belongings by their sides; slept without bedding on pinewood shelves; and lived amid the scattered filth and human excrement that made the quarters below-deck a befouled, disease-ridden, noisome dungeon.

One Irish pauper who made the voyage in 1848 recalled that "Water was down to a cup a day per passenger. Of the four hundred who set out, sixteen died at sea—they were killed in fights for food, or died of fever."

Bodies of the dead were wrapped in old sails or placed in meal sacks. After some words of prayer by the living, the dead were dropped into the sea. It is estimated that more than 15,000 would-be Irish Americans perished during the Atlantic crossings. Wrote one U.S. official: "If crosses and tombs could be erected on the water, the whole route of the immigrant vessels from Ireland to America would long since have assumed the appearance of a crowded cemetery."

A doctor, clambering into the hold of the *Ceylon*, found "emaciated figures, eruptions disfiguring their faces … aboard were 115 cases of typhus." Peering into an open hatch on one vessel, a boarding officer saw "a mass of humans lying over each other, covered with sores." An inspecting official on another ship told of "oil lamps giving glimpses of forms, white faces looking up. It was a cavern of the damned."

Throughout the Famine years, the "coffin ships" loomed out of the ocean mists, bearing to New York, Boston, Philadelphia, and Baltimore, the living-dead of Ireland. As the immigrant-packets made their sullen way toward the landing piers, there was no rejoicing from harborside to bid them welcome.

Seven out of ten of the newcomers came ashore at New York. Denizens of the South Street waterfront—pickpockets, short-change artists, and assorted con men—did their best to bamboozle the newcomers. Unscrupulous touts called "runners" steered them to run-down boarding houses, where they were cheated out of their precious money and often had their baggage forcibly taken from them.

More than one million Irish emigrated to America during the famine years for reasons that extended beyond the fear of hunger to the desire to escape the justices and political persecution of life in their homeland. Their skills, hard work, and determination helped build cities, railroads, and road networks that laid the groundwork for much of the prosperity the United States later enjoyed. While the stories of most migrants faded into obscurity; a few—such as the six featured here—achieved great personal success and a permanent place in American history.

PATRICK AUGUSTINE FEEHAN
(1829-1902)

The first Catholic archbishop of Chicago was born in Killenaule, County Tipperary. While he was in training for the priesthood, his parents left famine-plagued Ireland for America. The young seminarian eagerly seized an opportunity to join them there and complete preparation for his 1852 ordination. As a curate in three St. Louis churches during the next few years, Father Feehan earned the title "priest of the poor" for his good works among those in need. During the Civil War, he tirelessly sought to comfort the wounded of all religions, and as Bishop of Nashville, Tennessee, in the postwar years, he reconstructed the war-torn diocese by rebuilding churches and establishing schools, a convent, and an orphanage for the children of soldiers who had died in the war. In 1880, Feehan was elevated to archbishop of the newly created Chicago arch-diocese, which thrived during his 22-year administration.

PATRICK ANDREW COLLINS
(1844-1905)

Born at Ballinafauna, County Cork, Collins and his family sailed to Boston in 1848, after his father's death. A laborer active in union matters in his younger years, Collins's ability as a public speaker led him into Democratic Party politics in 1867. He graduated from Harvard Law School in 1871 and successfully ran for Congress in 1882, serving three terms. Rewarded with a consulship in London for his party loyalty and support of President Grover Cleveland, Collins returned to the U.S. with a keen interest in Boston politics. In 1901, he was elected mayor of that city, where his fair-mindedness gained him much support.

MICHAEL CUDAHY
(1841-1910)

Michael and his parents left Callan, County Kilkenny in 1849. At the age of 14, he became employed at a meat-packing company in Milwaukee. During the next 25 years, he advanced rapidly within the business. His ability was rewarded in 1875 when he accepted a partnership in Armour & Company of Chicago. Cudahy's development of the summer curing of meats under refrigeration, which made fresh meat available throughout the year, was his singular contribution to the industry. He also was involved with the evolution of the refrigerator car that allowed perishable foods to be transported without spoiling. With his brother Edward, he formed the Cudahy Packing Company in 1890, continuing as its president until his death.

MICHAEL MORAN
(1833-1906)

A native of Killara, Westmeath, Michael emigrated with his family in 1850, settling in Frankfort, New York. At the age of 17, Moran worked on the Erie Canal, driving mules that pulled the cargo barges. In 1860, he moved to New York City, where he purchased a one-half interest in a tugboat. Eventually, he owned a fleet of tugs and operated the leading towing company in the port of New York. Moran's legacy continues today; the company he began remains one of the largest tugboat businesses in the United States.

KATE KENNEDY
(1827-1890)

Kate and her family were driven from their home in Gaskinstown, County Meath, in 1849 by the potato famine. Settling in New York City, she spent her spare time in preparation for a career in education. In 1856, she moved to San Francisco, where she became a teacher, well-known for her inspirational work. A fervent feminist who worked tirelessly for the woman suffrage and labor causes, Kennedy successfully campaigned for passage of a bill guaranteeing "equal pay for equal work" for teachers. In 1911, her memory was honored with the founding of the Kate Kennedy School women's Club of San Francisco; a public school in that city also bears her name.

MICHAEL CORCORAN
(1827-1863)

Corcoran, the son of a British army officer, was born in Carrowkeel, County Donegal, and at the age of 18 became a member of the Royal Irish Constabulary. In 1849, he resigned his commission in protest over the oppressive manner in which the police force treated the Irish people. He emigrated to the U.S., where he worked for the city of New York and served in the 69th New York Militia, rising by 1859 to the rank of colonel. Court-martialed for refusing to parade his regiment before the visiting Prince of Wales, he was released without a trial at the start of the Civil War to command his "Fighting 69th" for the Union army. Captured at the Battle of Bull Run, he was held prisoner for a year and threatened with execution. Upon his release, he was commissioned a brigadier general and raised the Corcoran Legion, composed mainly of Irish immigrants. He died in a riding accident in Virginia.

Diseased, worn, and penniless, most Irish remained close to the ports where they landed. Clinging together for companionship, they tried to eke out an existence. Bound by kinship of religion, politics, and custom, they mustered considerable communal fortitude to contend with the challenges they encountered. In Manhattan's notorious Five Points slum, where thousands of the famine refugees would settle, novelist Charles Dickens observed. "Leprous houses; lanes and alleys paved with mud knee-deep; underground chambers; hideous tenements, which take their name from robbery and murder; all that is loathsome, drooping, and decayed is here."

The beleaguered Irish crammed into mildewed, lice-infested rooms, from cellar to garret, in ramshackle lodging-houses. Such a room—serving as kitchen, living-space, and bedroom for five or more people—rented for about four dollars a week, close to a week's wages. Typhus, cholera, tuberculosis, and pneumonia took a heavy toll. Many who had fled for their lives from the old country came to grim endings in the almshouses, prisons, and gutters of the land where they sought safe haven.

The majority of immigrants arrived in the United States with few skills, and their knowledge of farming was usually limited to the planting and harvesting of potatoes. They were used to hard work, although famine and disease had left its mark. But the Irish had great powers of survival and through perseverance and often back-breaking toil, they proved their character and worth on just about every work-front.

Even so, American-born workers feared that the newcomers would drive wages down; a labor newspaper warned that they "will work for what Americans cannot live on." The "freedom" that many Irish experienced on their arrival in America bore a close resemblance to the subjugation they had suffered at the hands of the British in the world they thought they had left far behind.

"No Irish Need Apply" signs went up and were a long time in coming down. "We, as a people, are intolerant of ragged garments and empty stomachs," wrote one contemporary American observer of the famine arrivals. "The ill-clad and destitute Irishman is repulsive to our habits and our tastes."

Though still a new nation, America had begun to shape a distinctive national character. Like other nations, it formed its identity around the beliefs, customs, and experiences held in common by a majority of its people. The young republic had been fostered in the heritage of English law and the Protestant faith. With wave after wave of doom-ridden Irish, many of them devout Catholics, set upon America's shores by the famine, growing numbers of Americans feared a rending of their cultural and religious singularity.

By the mid-1800s, indeed, a mood of "nativism"— America for Americans—had taken hold. Even before the famine refugees reached the United States, Protestant antipathy toward Catholic immigrants had evidenced itself, sometimes violently. And newcomers responded in kind. The magnitude of the famine immigration only served to inflame such rancor. One American Protestant leader referred to the newcomers as "a massive lump in the community, undigested and indigestible."

"We were raised amidst ghosts of the Famine," Hannah Murphy, born into a tenant-farm family at the end of the nineteenth century, would say. Mother of the author of this article, she was to emigrate from Cork to New York just before World War I. In the new land, she met and married a man of English descent. "Even in America," she recalled, "those ghosts were with us. The famine was part of the Irish soul." "The Irish changed America," observes Rosa Meehan, Director of the American Irish Historical Society. "On just about every front—politics, unions, professions, the arts, among others—they made a significant difference in the quality of people's lives."

The potato famine was a tragedy that devastated Ireland, dishonored the British government, and changed the composition of the United States. But the Irish were ultimately strengthened by the hardships they encountered, their pride stirred by prejudice. They not only survived; in time, they and their descendants prevailed.

Ed Oxford is a frequent contributor to American History. *His most recent contribution— "TV's Wonder Years"—highlighted television's infancy during the early 1950s for our January/February issue.*

James K. Polk and the Expansionist Spirit

Harlan Hague

Only days after his inauguration in March 1845, President James K. Polk announced to Secretary of the Navy George Bancroft: "There are four great measures which are to be the measures of my administration: one, a reduction of the tariff; another, the independent treasury; a third, the settlement of the Oregon boundary question; and lastly, the acquisition of California."[1] It was the last two of his "great measures" that elected Polk, for he was swept into the White House by an expansionist fervor that peaked at his election. As President, Polk did not initiate a policy toward the West; he inherited one, based on the tenets of Manifest Destiny.

There was no doubt during the campaign where candidate Polk stood on the expansionist issue. In the spring of 1844, he called publicly for the annexation of both Texas and the Oregon country.[2] At the same time, Martin Van Buren, the assumed presidential candidate of the Democratic Party, announced his opposition to Texas annexation on grounds that it would mean war with Mexico.[3] Andrew Jackson, determined that the United States should have Texas, threw his support behind his fellow Tennessean for the Democratic Party nomination. In the end, Polk was nominated on the ninth ballot, as a compromise after the convention deadlocked on a choice between Van Buren, the lackluster ex-President whose political sun was setting, and Lewis Cass, an expansionist zealot who had won the support of many Westerners and Southerners and the enmity of multitudes. The Whig candidate, Henry Clay, had long opposed annexation of Texas, and the Whig platform ignored the issue. Polk's election assured the admission of Texas, and on 1 March 1845, the Lone Star Republic was invited into the Union by a joint resolution of Congress.

Upon his inauguration, the new President set to work on satisfying his campaign pledge. Polk was particularly concerned that the United States control important West Coast ports. He was not the first American leader to demand that a settlement of the Oregon question must give the United States control of Puget Sound, a region dominated by Britain's Hudson's Bay Company. A port on the Sound would be an American window on the Pacific, a jumping-off point for the Asian trade. Great

James K. Polk, 1795-1849. (Daguerreotype by Mathew B. Brady)

Britain was just as determined that it would surrender no land north of the Columbia River. Logic seemed to support the British view. British settlement, chiefly the works and farms of the Hudson's Bay Company, was located north of the Columbia in present-day Washington, while American settlement was located south of the river, chiefly in Oregon's Willamette Valley.

Since 1818, the United States and Britain, by agreement, had jointly occupied the Oregon country. During the negotiations that had established joint occupancy, the United States had proposed a division of Oregon at the 49th parallel, but Britain, preferring the Columbia River as a boundary, rejected the offer. The American claim was subsequently pushed northward until it rested at 54°40′, the southern limit of Russian claims which had been established by treaty between Russia and the United States in 1824.

By the early 1840s, interest in a settlement of the Oregon question had increased in both Great Britain and the United States. As presidential candidate in 1844, Polk accepted the demand of the Democratic Party leadership for a boundary at 54°40′ but only as a political expedient. Indeed in July 1845, after only a few months in office, he offered Richard Pakenham, the British minister in Washington, a boundary settlement at the 49th parallel. Privately, Polk acknowledged that American interests would be protected because the boundary would leave the United States in control of Puget Sound. Pakenham rejected the offer since it did not include free British navigation of the Columbia, a long-standing British condition. When London later showed interest, nevertheless, in the offer, Polk refused to renew it.[4]

The following December, the President explained rather weakly in a message to Congress that he had made the 49th parallel boundary offer only from respect for his predecessors, who had long favored that compromise. Perhaps, though unstated, he had also feared war with Britain. Now, in December, Polk vowed that he would make no other offer. Rather than accommodation, he recommended that notice of termination of joint occupancy be delivered to Britain. At the expiration of the agreement, he said, the United States would pursue its interests aggressively in the Oregon country. London favored accommodation and suggested that the issue be submitted to arbitration. Polk rejected arbitration on grounds that the British had no just claim to Oregon.[5]

The President's rhetoric was mostly bluff and bluster. It was directed as much at the British government and public as American. Polk's objective was more pacific than his words. He simply wanted to stimulate negotiations and to force the British to take the initiative. To Louis McLane, the American minister in London, Polk intimated that he would be receptive to a British restatement of his original proposal, that is, a 49th parallel boundary, though Britain could have all of Vancouver Island, but no free British navigation of the Columbia.[6] Polk expected that his belligerent posture would force the issue.

Many congressmen were alarmed at Polk's notice proposal, fearing that it could lead to war with Britain. Congress debated the proposal for over four months and finally, in April 1846, enacted a measure to give Britain notice to terminate joint occupancy.

In the end, the settlement of the Oregon question may be attributed less to belligerence than to a lack of zeal.[7] By the end of 1845, the British public and the larger part of the government were little interested in Oregon. They were preoccupied with the specter of famine at home because of the potato blight in Ireland and light harvests in Britain. Great Britain now needed American wheat, and trade relations in general improved in early 1846, leading many, including Polk, to hope for a lowering of tariffs. Furthermore, the fur trade was declining in Oregon, and British leaders were hard pressed to justify defense of a claim to the region below the 49th parallel at the risk of war. Finally, British leaders were convinced that sufficient British access to the sea would be secured if an agreement on a 49th parallel boundary left Britain all of Vancouver Island.

Accordingly, London tendered a proposal to Washington, and a treaty was concluded on these terms in June 1846. Both sides breathed a great sigh of relief. The signing came none too soon, particularly for the United States. Fighting had already begun on the disputed Texas border.

Polk's views on Oregon were contradictory at best. His obligation as leader of a party that was committed to having all of Oregon often conflicted with his own view. His involvement stemmed from political necessity, not personal interest, and he did what he had to do.

A Southerner, Polk was more interested in Texas and California. He was personally and passionately committed to American domination in the Southwest. The Oregon question settled, Polk turned to the Texas question.

Trouble between Mexico and the United States had been brewing since 1836 when Mexico blamed the United States for its loss of Texas. Mexico had never acknowledged the loss and warned the United States not to interfere, a warning that Polk ignored. He had no more sympathy for the arguments of anti-imperialists and anti-slavery leaders who spoke out against Washington's growing interest in Texas.

Polk dispatched agents to the Lone Star Republic in early 1845 to gather information and encourage Texans to call for annexation.[8] Following annexation in March, he sent William S. Parrott to Mexico City with instructions to convince the Mexican leadership to accept the finality of the American annexation of Texas and to resume diplomatic ties with the United States, which the annexation had ruptured. The shaky government of José Joaquín Herrera, mindful of the growing public clamor in Mexico against the American annexation of Texas, was noncommittal. Herrera preferred a British plan that included Mexico's recognition of Texas in return for the Lone Star Republic's rejection of annexation.[9]

Polk applied pressure. His administration accepted the Texas claim to the Rio Grande River boundary, and he moved to reinforce the claim. In mid-June, he ordered Zachary Taylor to move his troops from Louisiana to Texas where they installed themselves on the south bank of the Nueces River, thus inside the disputed territory between that river and the Rio Grande. Polk vowed that no invading force would be allowed to cross the Rio Grande.[10] In spite of the belligerent tone, he considered the Army's deployment a defensive move. Polk was an expansionist, but he was no fool. He did not shrink from the necessity of war, but he sought none, at least not until other measures were exhausted.

Mexico indeed appeared prepared to settle differences amicably. In August from Mexico City, Parrott notified Polk that the government seemed prepared to receive an American emissary. Polk appointed John Slidell his secret agent—during his presidency, Polk would appoint an abundance of secret agents—and instructed him to secure Mexico's acceptance of the Rio Grande boundary and a promise to pay the claims of American citizens against Mexico. And the pièce de résistance: He was to offer Mexico as much as $40 million for California and New Mexico. At the same time, Polk warned Mexico—and Britain and France, as well—against any plan for a European protectorate for California. The Monroe Doctrine would be enforced. Polk's prohibition of European protectorates, a new factor in American hegemony, in time became called the "Polk doctrine."[11]

The Slidell mission was doomed from the start. The Herrera government fell on 2 January to a new revolutionary movement under General Paredes y Arrillaga. Anticipating that the new administration would be no more stable than the former, Polk toyed with the idea of asking Congress for a secret fund of $500,000 to a $1 million which he would transfer to Paredes to strengthen his government during negotiations. He abandoned the scheme when he could not win sufficient support among Democratic leaders.[12]

In early 1846, Polk was intrigued by the possibilities suggested to him by one Alexander J. Atocha. A naturalized American citizen, Atocha was a friend of ex-President Antonio Lòpez de Santa Anna who was overthrown in 1845. Atocha had recently visited General Santa Anna in Havana. He believed that Santa Anna would soon be once again in power and that the general favored a treaty in which Mexico would cede New Mexico and California to the United States. Santa Anna, he said, had told him that $30 million would be a satisfactory sum to conclude the deal, but that the United States must take action to pose such an armed threat that Mexican citizens would be convinced that the cession was the only alternative to destruction.[13] Polk concluded that Atocha was probably not reliable, but the President continued to pursue the diplomacy-by-bribery scheme off and on. Nothing came of it.[14]

Polk's fears for the stability of the new government were well founded. He learned in early April 1846 that Arrillaga, certain that he would be removed from office by an angry citizenry if he agreed to negotiations, had refused to receive Slidell. War now seemed likely. That same day, Polk had told his cabinet that if Mexico rejected his envoy, the American leaders must "take the remedy for the injuries and wrongs we had suffered into our own hands."[15] He now "saw no alternative but strong measures towards Mexico."[16] Slidell counseled Polk that war now was probably the best course.[17]

War was not long in coming. By early May, Polk had decided that war would be necessary to achieve his objectives, which included California and New Mexico and perhaps additional northern Mexican states. He prepared a message for delivery to Congress on 12 May, a delicately worded message, for he was asking Congress for authority to initiate war. Three days before the scheduled delivery date, Polk learned that a Mexican patrol had crossed the Rio Grande and fired on American troops. In Polk's view, Mexico had invaded American soil. He changed his message, and on 11 and 12 May, Congress, by huge majorities, declared war.

Polk soon clarified his war aims, privately at least. Shortly after the declaration of war, he read a dispatch that Secretary of State James Buchanan planned to send to European governments to notify them of the declaration. Polk was not pleased; he ordered the Secretary to strike from the message a statement that the United States had no intention "to dismember Mexico or make conquests... [and] that in going to war we did not do so with a view to acquire either California or New Mexico or any other portion of the Mexican territory." Polk told Buchanan that we would seek indemnities, and Mexico had no other way of indemnifying the United States, save in territory. Buchanan said that unless the assurance that he recommended was included in the message, both England and France would join the war on the side of Mexico. Polk replied testily that before he gave this assurance, he would "meet the war which either England or France or all the Powers of Christendom might wage...." He would stand for no interference.[18] He had long since given his pledge to the American people, at least those of the public who counted, in Polk's estimation. Those who did not support his policy he branded as disloyal and hinted that such behavior was treasonous.

Polk had not forgotten that other prize that must come in a contest with Mexico: California. Polk's initial interest in the Mexican province was the same as his interest in Oregon; that is, its ports. For a while, it seemed that California might fall quietly to the United States. Thomas O. Larkin, American Consul to Mexican California, was making headway in convincing Californians that their destiny lay in an association, initiated by themselves, with the United States.[19] By the mid-1840s, however, there was reason for haste. American immigrants entering California overland were arguing belligerently for a "Texas solution" for California.

In 1845 affairs appeared to take an ominous turn in California. Larkin had written frequently to Washington from Monterey during the past year, telling of the revolutionary ferment among *Californios*. Some *Californio* leaders, said Larkin, favored associating a liberated California with the United States. On the other hand, the Consul warned of apparent British and French intrigues in the province and the interest of some California leaders in seeking protection from a European country.[20] Polk was convinced that Britain wanted California, and he was determined that the United States would not permit Britain or any other foreign power to possess it.[21]

The President was impressed by Larkin's revelations. In October 1845, Polk appointed him his confidential agent with instructions to inform the Californians that though the United States would not interfere in any conflict between California and Mexico, Americans would not permit California's becoming a colony of Britain or France. The United States would not leave its neighbor unprotected. Indeed, Larkin was to assure the Californians that an application for admission into the American union by a free California would be most welcome.[22]

Acting on Larkin's information, members of Polk's cabinet, unquestionably at the President's direction, strengthened American preparedness. Secretary of War George Bancroft ordered

Commodore John D. Sloat, commander of the American fleet off the Mexican coast, to be ready to blockade or seize California ports at the first sign of hostilities.[23] Secretary of State Buchanan alerted the American ambassador in London and briefed John Slidell on Larkin's correspondence.[24] Bancroft dispatched Commodore Robert F. Stockton to the West Coast to deliver the letters containing Sloat's new orders and Larkin's appointment. At the same time, Buchanan sent a copy of the appointment letter to Larkin by Marine Lieutenant Archibald H. Gillespie, who was to travel in disguise across Mexico. Gillespie, another of Polk's secret agents, also was ordered to deliver an informational copy of Larkin's letter to Brevet Captain John D. Frémont, who was exploring in California.

Frémont's role in California affairs was stormy, controversial, and contradictory.[25] Frémont had arrived in California with an expedition of 60 well-armed mountain men early in 1846. He soon offended California authorities and was ordered to leave. Instead, in March he erected barricades atop Hawk's Peak in the Gavilan Mountains near Monterey where he was besieged by a *Californio* force. Frémont soon withdrew, realizing that the affair was essentially personal and that his action could jeopardize Washington's plan to acquire California.[26]

Three months later in the Bear Flag affair, Frémont took a belligerent stance that angered *Californios* more than did the Hawk's Peak incident. He even arrested General Mariano Guadalupe Vallejo, who favored an association of California with the United States. By then, Frémont had seen the copy of Buchanan's letter to Larkin, and he was confident now that he was acting in the best interests of the United States. Questioned by Commodore Sloat in July 1846 about his part in the Bear Flag incident, Frémont replied that he "had acted solely on my own responsibility, and without any expressed authority from the Government to justify hostilities.'"[27]

Perhaps Frémont responded to a higher authority. "How fate pursues a man!" he had observed earlier, upon learning that Gillespie was on his trail.[28] Fate perhaps was on his side, but not his commander in chief. Polk later confided to his diary that Frémont had acted without authority.[29]

During the war in California, Frémont led his own men under the overall command of Commodore Stockton, who had replaced Sloat. When General Stephen Watts Kearny arrived from Santa Fé with an advance unit of his Army of the West, carrying orders that designated him governor of California, Frémont refused to recognize his authority.[30] A court-martial board in Washington the following January found Frémont guilty of mutiny and ordered him discharged from the service.

After a review of the court record and consultation with his cabinet, Polk concluded that the facts of the case did not prove mutiny. He dismissed that conviction, but let stand conviction on two lesser charges: disobedience of orders and conduct prejudicial to good order and military discipline. The President, influenced by the cabinet, also thought the sentence of dismissal from the Army too severe. Accordingly, he set aside the sentence and ordered Frémont to report for duty. The decision, he groaned, was "a painful and a responsible duty."[31] Frémont rejected Polk's clemency, for to accept would be to acknowledge guilt. He resigned from the Army and returned to California.

In the heated controversies between Kearny and Stockton and between Kearny and Frémont, Polk sided with Kearny. After a full examination of the correspondence in May 1847, Polk concluded that he was "fully satisfied that General Kearny was right, and that Commodore Stockton's course was wrong. Indeed, both he [Stockton] and Lieut.-Col. Frémont, in refusing to recognize the authority of General Kearny, acted insubordinately and in a manner that is censurable."[32]

At war's end, there was some concern in California that Washington would not insist in the peace treaty on retention of the province. Those that knew something of the origins of the New York Volunteer Regiment, which arrived in California in spring 1847, were less fearful. Polk had directed Colonel Jonathan D. Stevenson to recruit mechanics who would agree that they would, at war's end, accept their discharges and settle in California or the closest United States territory. The Eastern press, from the regiment's inception, guessed that its principal purpose was colonization rather than war.[33] Shortly before the end of the war, Polk confided in a letter to his brother that California indeed would be retained, and New Mexico as well, as war indemnifications. Furthermore, the longer Mexico continued hostilities by its "stubbornness," said Polk, the greater the indemnities.[34]

Publicly, Polk said little about California's destiny, for he did not wish to enter the debate on whether the United States intended to retain Mexican territory. He was no longer stating publicly, as he had before, that the United States had no intention to retain Mexican properties after the signing of a peace treaty.[35] His reluctance to make his position known baffled and angered the public. The public should have remembered that Polk at the outset of the war had similarly refused to clarify his war objectives.

At war's end, when it appeared that Polk might be forced to bow to powerful elements in the Democratic Party who were arguing for annexation of all of Mexico, Nicholas Trist signed the Treaty of Guadalupe Hidalgo for the United States, which established a boundary just south of San Diego Bay, virtually the same boundary that Polk had sought in the Slidell mission. The President's well-known quarrel with Trist would be overlooked, and the administration, according to the New Orleans *Picayune*, would be content to "swallow its disappointment, and California and New Mexico at the same time."[36]

Polk left to his successors the question of slavery which would become central to the issue of Westward Expansion for the next 15 years. During his presidency, Polk adopted a position that could have prevented sectional crisis if his successors had been so wise. He understood better than his contemporaries, and successors as well, the true nature of the issue of slavery in the Western territories. He assailed fellow Southerner John C. Calhoun for his extremist stance on the expansion of slavery. At the same time, he rejected the Wilmot Proviso which would have prevented slavery in any territory acquired from Mexico at the end of the war. Indeed, he favored the extension of the 1820 Missouri Compromise line of 36°30′ to the Pacific.

Polk saw no contradiction in his position. He was simply convinced that slavery would never exist in the territory south of the 36°30′ line.[37] A Southern man who wished to be president to all the people, he would permit slavery in the federal territories since he believed that it would never take hold there. If this view had prevailed, there might have been no Civil War.

Polk decided that he was going to enjoy retirement more than the presidency, and he left the office without regret. He was dismayed, however, to be succeeded by a Whig, especially by Zachary Taylor, whom he held in low regard. His opinion of Taylor undoubtedly reached rock-bottom during a coach ride to the Capitol on inauguration day. Polk was shocked when the President-elect, in the course of polite conversation, said that Oregon and California should establish an independent government, since they were so far removed from the United States. Polk, for some time, had been anxious that Congress form a government for California, fearing that otherwise the territory could be lost to the Union by the formation of a separate government, precisely the course the new President seemed to advocate. Polk concluded that Taylor was a "well-meaning old man," though uneducated and politically ignorant.[38]

If Polk's election in 1844 can be traced at least partly to the American people's expansionist spirit, then it can be argued that the voters' rejection of the Democrats in 1848 can be interpreted as a repudiation of the siren song of Manifest Destiny.[39] Yet, Polk's contributions, the fruit of the expansionist spirit, were embraced and defended. His "Polk Doctrine," which warned Europe not to interfere in the affairs of the North American continent, was subsequently embraced by the American people. During the four-year tenure, over one-half million square miles of territory were added to the United States, a number second only to Jefferson's Louisiana Purchase.[40] Even ill-gotten gains, like horse thieves and harlots in the family tree, can be accepted with resignation or amusement, even some pride, when separated by a sufficient lapse of time.

Notes

1. James K. Polk, *Polk: The Diary of a President, 1845–1849*, Allan Nevins, ed. (New York, 1952), xvii.
2. See, for example, Polk to Chase *et al*, 23 Apr. 1844, in James K. Polk, *The Correspondence of James K. Polk*, Wayne Cutler and James P. Cooper, Jr., eds. (Nashville, TN, 1989), 105–106.
3. Polk, *Diary*, xxiii.
4. Frederick Merk, *The Oregon Question: Essays in Anglo-American Diplomacy and Politics* (Cambridge, MA, 1967), 410; Jesse S. Reeves, *American Diplomacy under Tyler and Polk* (Gloucester, MA, 1967, a reprint of the 1907 publication of The Johns Hopkins Press), 252–253.
5. Merk, *The Oregon Question*, 219–220.
6. *Ibid.*, 343.
7. For an elaboration of the view following, see Merk, *The Oregon Question*, 415–416, and Norman A. Graebner, *Empire on the Pacific: A Study in American Continental Expansion* (Santa Barbara, CA, reprint, 1983), 137–140.
8. Commodore Robert F. Stockton, the most energetic among the agents, appeared bent on provoking a war with Mexico. See, generally, Glenn W. Price, *Origins of the War with Mexico: The Polk-Stockton Intrigue* (Austin, TX, 1967). Texas President Anson Jones, who later wrote an account of the intrigues of Stockton and his Texan and American cohorts, charged that Polk secretly sought to provoke war at the point, 112.
9. Charles Sellers, *James K. Polk: Continentalist, 1843–1846* (Princeton, NJ, 1966), 259.
10. Neal Harlow, *California Conquered: War and Peace on the Pacific, 1846–1850* (Berkeley, 1982), 55; Paul H. Bergeron, *The Presidency of James K. Polk* (Lawrence, KS, 1987), 62.
11. Polk, *Diary*, 10; Bernard DeVoto, *Year of Decision: 1846* (Boston, 1942), 16–17. Slidell's mission was to be kept secret to prevent foreign powers, particularly Britain or France, from interfering with it. Polk, *Diary*, 10.
12. Graebner, *Empire on the Pacific*, 121.
13. Polk, *Diary*, 50–53; Sellers, *Polk: Continentalist*, 401.
14. Polk, *Diary*, 53; Bergeron, *Polk*, 70–71, 83, 103; Sellers, *Polk: Continentalist*, 427–428, 430–431.
15. Polk, *Diary* (4-7-1846), 69–70. Polk believed that the British ambassador had influenced the Mexican government to reject Slidell *Ibid.* (4-18-1846), 71–72], perhaps assuming that the Mexican issue would be sufficiently irritating to the United States to encourage the settlement of the Oregon question.
16. Polk, *Diary* (4-18-1846), 71.
17. Graebner, *Empire on the Pacific*, 152.
18. Polk, *Diary* (5-13-1846), 90–92.
19. For Larkin's role in trying to persuade Californians, see Harlan Hague and David J. Langum, *Thomas O. Larkin: A Life of Patriotism and Profit in Old California* (Norman, OK, 1990), especially chapter 7.
20. Larkin's role in the approach to war with Mexico is told in *Ibid.*, chapter 7.
21. Polk, *Diary* (10-14-1845), 19. Spence and Jackson indeed conclude that Polk's concern about British designs on California became "one of the cornerstones of his foreign policy." John Charles Frémont, *The Expeditions of John Charles Frémont: The Bear Flag Revolt and the Court-Martial*, Mary Lee Spence and Donald Jackson, eds., vol. 2 (Urbana, 1973), xxi. If that is true, then Larkin's influence on American foreign policy during Polk's presidency looms large. Polk's fear of European interference would extend to the end of the war. As late as December 1847, he argued that a premature withdrawal of the American Army from Mexico might open the way to European intervention. Robert W. Johannsen, *To the Halls of the Montezumas: The Mexican War in the American Imagination* (New York, 1985), 304.
22. Buchanan to Larkin, 17 Oct. 1845, in George P. Hammond, ed., *The Larkin Papers: Personal, Business, and Official Correspondence of Thomas Oliver Larkin, Merchant and United States Consul in California*, 10 vols. (Berkeley, 1951–1968), 4: 44–46.

23. Bancroft to Sloat, 17 Oct. 1845, in Robert E. Cowan, ed., "Documentary," *California Historical Society Quarterly*, 2 (July 1923): 167–170.

24. Buchanan to McLane, 14 Oct. 1845, cited in Robert Glass Cleland, "The Early Sentiment for the Annexation of California: An Account of the Growth of American Interest in California, 1835–1846," *The Southwestern Historical Quarterly* (Jan. 1915), 243; Buchanan to Slidell, 10 Nov. 1845, cited in Howard William Gross, "The Influence of Thomas O. Larkin Toward the Acquisition of California," M.A. thesis, University of California, Berkeley, 1937, 112.

25. For an overview, see: Harlow, *California Conquered*, principally chapters 6–8; Hague and Langum, *Thomas O. Larkin*, 120–130, 136–139.

26. John Charles Frémont, *Memoirs of My Life* (Chicago: Belford, Clarke & Company, 1887), 460.

27. Frémont, *Memoirs*, 534. In later life, Frémont, probably influenced by Jessie, his wife, claimed that the letter from Buchanan that was shown him in spring 1846 was actually meant for *himself* not Larkin, that *he*, not Larkin, had been appointed Polk's confidential agent. The record does not support his claim. See Hague and Langum, *Thomas O. Larkin*, 128–130.

28. Frémont, *Memoirs*, 486.

29. Frémont, *Expeditions*, 2: xxix.

30. This tangled story is best told in Harlow, *California Conquered*, chapters 14, 15.

31. Polk, *Diary* (2-16-1848), 303. See also Frémont, *Expeditions*, 468n, 469n.

32. Polk, *Diary* (5-4-1847), 226.

33. Graebner, *Empire on the Pacific*, 156.

34. *Ibid.*, 158–159.

35. *Ibid.*, 161–162.

36. Quoted in *Ibid.*, 213–214.

37. Polk, *Diary*, xvi, 189–190, 376.

38. *Ibid.*, 389.

39. This argument is suggested in Graebner, *Empire on the Pacific*, 227.

40. Polk, *Diary*, xvii.

Harlan Hague is the author, with David J. Langum, of Thomas O. Larkin: A Life of Patriotism and Profit in Old California *(1990), winner of the Caroline Bancroft Prize. He is currently editing a collection of unpublished Larkin letters and working on a biography of Stephen Watts Kearny for the University of Oklahoma Western Biographies series. Recipient of a number of grants, including NEH, the Huntington Library, and the Sourisseau Academy, Hague is particularly interested in Mexican California, exploration and travel, and environmental history.*

Reprinted with permission from *Journal of the West*, Vol. 31, No.3 (July 1992), pp. 51–56. © 1992 by Journal of the West, Inc., 1531 Yuma, Manhattan, KS 66505-1009 USA.

LITTLE WOMEN?

THE FEMALE MIND AT WORK IN ANTEBELLUM AMERICA

Louise Stevenson argues that girls growing up in mid-19th-Century America were far more intellectually forceful and streetwise than often given credit for.

by **Louise Stevenson**

Most students pursuing an advanced degree of history before the 1970s would have thought women's intellectual life an unpromising subject. The classic works of American intellectual history seldom included women and rarely took their endeavours seriously. Intellectual historians did not recognise that they were defining 'intellectual' and 'intellectual life' in ways that excluded women. A sampling of the indices of surveys of American intellectual history reveal that none give women any sizable place. Ralph Henry Gabriel mentions four women in *The Course of American Democratic Thought* (1940, 2nd ed. 1956), Perry Miller one in the *Life of the Mind in America* (1965), Robert Skotheim none in *American Intellectual Histories and Historians* (1966), and Rush Welter three in *The Mind of America, 1820-1860* (1975).

The books published during the upsurge of women's history that began with Eleanor Flexner's *Century of Struggle* in 1959 offer little information about women's intellectual life. Historians of women from the sixties through to the late eighties mainly investigated political or social history. For political historians the struggle for the suffrage and other political rights and privileges was the central story of women's history. For social historians intellectual history seemed an elitist pursuit that ignored the many. For example, one of the path-breaking new social history books of those years, Nancy Cott's *The Bonds of Womanhood* (1977), described women's religious life and education as aspects of social life.

Not only did most women's historians ignore their subjects' intellectual lives, a few historians writing about women's cultural and intellectual history emphasised the limitations that women confronted when pursuing intellectual self-improvement and expression. The title of Susan P. Conrad's history of women intellectuals, *Perish the Thought* (1976), suggested this approach which Barbara Welter developed in 'Anti intellectualism and American Women'. She asserted that nineteenth-century American women could not be truly womanly if they were truly intellectual. For her Margaret Fuller's life told a story for all women intellectuals of opportunity denied.

Recently the historical profession has renewed its interest in intellectual and cultural history. On one front, women's historians are stepping beyond the focus on limitations that so occupied Conrad and Welter. Mary Kelley pioneered with *Private Woman, Public Stage* (1984) by showing how nineteenth-century authors contended with and used gender conventions to shape their lives and careers. Recent achievements include Charles Capper's biography of Margaret Fuller, the antebellum author and critic, and Joan D. Hedrick's *Harriet Beecher Stowe: A Life* (1994). These thoroughly researched biographies raise to serious scholarly consideration the domestic and quasi-public institutions that educated women, and through which women educated others. On another front, intellectual historians are borrowing from literary scholars and exploring new fields such as the history of books and reading. They are now conceiving of intellectual life in broad, embracing ways. David D.

Hall's *Worlds of Wonder: Days of Judgment* (1989), Janet Cornelius' *When I Can Read My Title Clear* (1991), and my own *Victorian Homefront: American Thought and Culture, 1860-1880* (1991) show how everyone has an intellectual life and participates in an everyday world of ideas.

For this article I have been working with a variety of sources from the years 1830-55 including advice books, diaries and letters, school records, commonplace books and albums. The commonplace book, student newspaper, and literary society records under consideration are typical of the written residue that survives as a source for investigation of antebellum middle-class women's intellectual lives. Their authors never will have biographers who record their literary talents or life achievements. Yet together these sources will prove their authors knowledgeable, in their own sense, and reveal how these women saw themselves as reforming womanhood.

These three sources originate in the great antebellum reform movement that inspired the founding of common school systems, academies, and seminaries. Many of the better known institutions of women's education were founded by women: to name a few, Mary Lyon's Mt. Holyoke, Massachusetts, Catharine Beecher's Hartford Female Seminary, Connecticut, and Emma Willard's Troy Seminary, New York. These institutions belong to a group comprising close to 6,000 academies that had enrolled 250,000 women by 1850 and had made attendance a usual occurrence for white middle-class women. Historians believe that graduates worked outside the home more often than other middle-class women. As many as one in four New England women taught before marriage, and academy graduates remained single more often than other women.

Sarah Jane Coates (b. 1820), a child from a large Quaker family prominent since Revolutionary War days, produced her commonplace book while she attended the Coatesville Academy that her relative

Moses Coates presided over from 1834 to 1838 in Coatesville, Pennsylvania. Her book consists of about eighty pages with one poem every page or two and shows us an active intellect that selected what ideas her book would preserve, even though she copied these poems mainly to practice and to demonstrate her handwriting and calligraphic abilities. Several poems have illuminated letters in the title, while others have small illustrations at their end suggesting that the commonplace book included drawing lessons as well. She wrote, 'To me, my tutor has disclosed his skill,/And here's the product of my hand and quill'. She cites no sources for her copied poems, which may have come from religious weeklies or monthlies, lady's magazines, printed broadsides and/or newspapers. The literary merit of some entries suggests that they may have been composed by Sarah or one of her friends in response to a current happening, such as 'Lines Written on the Death of Joshua and Milton Dance who was drowned in Abraham Hoopes's millpond ...'

The students of Sarah Porter's school in Farmington, Connecticut, (the school that became in the twentieth-century Miss Porter's School, a college preparatory boarding school for socially prominent young women like the late Jacqueline Kennedy Onassis) started a handwritten weekly newspaper, *The Revolver*, in November, 1859. Founded in 1847, the school drew its students from religiously liberal Congregationalists who expected the Millennium but eschewed the cataclysms of religious revivals as a means of preparing for it. Like most schoolgirl newspapers, *The Revolver* was short-lived, probably for only three months. The surviving two issues of the paper include articles on current events in the world and at the school. Girls wrote essays entitled 'Evening Hours' and 'The Past, Present, and Future', satirical descriptions of the modern young man and woman, and advertisements in which fictional men sought their ideal mates. As the editors

claimed, they 'loaded *The Revolver*' in hopes that its discharge would be 'for your amusement and (may we not hope it?) also for your instruction'. Students thus gave themselves power to reform themselves and their peers by adapting a conventionally male metaphor to show how they fired shots—persuasive words—to the hearts of their readers.

The Baptist town of New Hampton, New Hampshire, had a theological institute for men and a female seminary. A state history of 1857 touts the seminary as:

> Widely known and celebrated as one of the best institutions in the country, as well on account of its retired and healthy location as for the thorough and extended course of study pursued, including nearly all the various branches taught in our colleges.

The Young Ladies' Association of the New-Hampton (New Hampshire) Female Seminary for the Promotion of Literature and Missions met three times a month from 1833 to 1842 as a literary society and once a month as a missionary society and published their contribution in the annual seminary catalogue. The records contain titles of topics discussed at weekly meetings, excerpts of letters from former members and students at the school, and addresses from the association's members and president. For example, the women debated whether there was 'more in the life of Byron to admire or to detest' and whether it was 'deleterious for a young lady to support that side of a question which she believes to be wrong'.

While these sources represent different genres written by authors geographically distant from one another, of various ages from twelve to mid-twenties, and of different Protestant religions, these women belonged to one intellectual world. Though each source shows its creators' distinctive opinions on current events and literature, these differences spring from a shared understanding of a divine world.

Although their religious denominations' spokesmen differed over whether conversions were necessary for salvation and whether revivals promoted their god's second coming, in the women's writings, religious doctrine is absent. Present is a beneficent God. Their writings slide from consideration of everyday things to consideration of divine universals. For example, the subject of a poem might be the skylark, an American Indian, evergreen trees, a daisy, or a morning in spring, but each poem will evoke a divine, timeless world. When a little boy confronts the reality of his sister's burial in a poem copied by Sarah Coates, his mother reassures him that she will no longer need food or clothing in heaven because God will provide. Contemporary events, no matter how sorry, always recall that this world is probationary; the real world is universal. In another poem copied by Sarah Coates, a lover about to lose his beloved hears from a cupid who whispers 'You only part to meet tomorrow'. No morbid event, death brings ultimate happiness. In Coates' commonplace book, it is the event that occurs and reoccurs. While the poems mention the death of lovers, fathers, babies, brothers, and a sister, she writes of reassurance that death is a beginning not an end, a reconciliation not a parting.

Like mountains in a landscape, this divine world provides a distant and unchanging background for the current events and concerns of the young writers. Of the events that the girls foresee, the biological life cycle is always foremost. The girls deal with death as Coates does, by describing the transiency of human life and the cycles of change everywhere apparent in nature. One *Revolver* writer lets her thoughts go from the evening of a day to thoughts of the evening of life:

And, when the night of death shall come, and its deepening shadows shut out from our view the fast receding earth, may we be able to look beyond the 'dark valley', and behold the beams of everlasting morn.

The other foreground event that occupies the women is marriage, which loomed large for these women as it determined their social station and their future happiness. They had learned from popular literature, and family and friends too, that to botch this choice meant social ostracism and destitution. Despite the seriousness of the choice confronting them, the girls assumed that playfulness, even an occasional flirtation, would occur along the way to making it. For instance, *The Revolver* published a humorous advertisement stating that a pink necktie and a yellow glove had been found by a bridge, also known as the bridge of sighs, and the owner might reclaim them 'by applying to Miss Porter'. Whether with the humour of *The Revolver*, the sentimental poetry of Coates' commonplace book, or the serious essays of the New-Hampton literary association, all the sources describe the ideal woman and mate in terms that the other authors would embrace.

A young woman would make the correct choice of a mate if she were a certain type of woman that the school girls described in a backwards way. Infrequently they wrote about positives; frequently they wrote about negatives. In all sources, the woman to disdain was the fashionable lady who sought to win a mate through her looks. As Sarah Coates wrote in 'On Vanity':

Why should a weak and vain desire For outward show and gay attire, Engage our thoughts, employ our time, Wasting the precious hours of prime? … No dress can inward folly hide, Be virtue's garb our only pride; Her purity and taste refined Will teach us to adorn the mind.

The Revolver writers spoofed the young men and ladies who merely followed weak and vain desires by publishing a fictional advertisement from an Ohio man of six foot eight who was looking for a wife. He bragged that he had inherited $100,000 and sought a young lady 'neither too tall nor too short', of a good social position, and with a 25,000 [pounds] bank account. The mates whom the young women sought were educated, but not pompous about learning, and sufficiently prosperous, though they might not have inherited means. They rose early in the morning and attended to business. They did not spend time lounging in the vestibule of a hotel viewing 'the pretty foot, graceful figure, and imposing carriage of the modern young lady'.

The ideal man valued the sort of woman that these young women wanted to become. As an 1841 poem of the New-Hampton literary society proclaimed

'Be WOMAN; not a simple, simpering toy,/Made up of something, nothing, and alloy./Be WOMAN in all aims, and ranks, and stations,/Not a fantastic medley of flirtations'.

In eschewing a set of values described as material, childish, and superficial, the young women placed value on cultivation of their minds. A paper read at a New-Hampton meeting insisted:

We have imagination, we have taste, and we have reason. They are all susceptible of unlimited expansion. There are subjects adapted to call them forth, and we would apply ourselves to them for this specific purpose.

Attendance at academies furthered the students' aim of becoming the moral, tasteful, and intelligent women they wanted to be. They argued that the abstract knowledge learned in history, literature, and language classes was a means to this end.

These authors' claims for their intellectual selves countered critics of women's education. The New-Hampton members denied that learning might unfit a woman 'for the common duties of life' by making her genteel and 'superior to everyday duties'. They argued for the expansion of women's intellectual activities so that they could better perform their religious duties and domestic responsibilities. They wanted women to write, but not to pursue literary fame, and to play the piano and draw for 'the beneficial effects resulting to our own characters, and the increased power it gives us to apprehend and communicate the beautiful handiwork of God'. One member of the New-Hampton Association went so far as to:

> Consider it disrespectful to read in the presence of your husband, unless for his hearing, or when his attention is absorbed in concerns which will render your reading an aid to the prosecution of his wishes. Few are the moments, comparatively, he can pass in your society. These moments should leave an impress which would induce him to repeat them'.

By implication, reading might not encourage his return. Miss Porter's students and Sarah Coates also cautioned against unlimited intellectual expansion for women. A poem in the commonplace book cautions indirectly through the example of the skylark. It resembles 'the wise who soar but never roam,/True to the kindred points of heaven and home'.

Other foreground events show that school girls participated in a transatlantic literary heritage and were sufficiently culturally and politically literate to be engaged with their times. Of the three, the members of the New-Hampton literary association were the most discriminating readers. They stood ready to take on the literary giants of the past and popular authors of the present recommending the work of Hannah More, John Milton, Addison, Goldsmith, and Johnson, while criticising the works of Robert Burns and Shakespeare for demonstrating little 'permanency to principles'. They found current literature wanting. The fiction of Catherine Maria Sedgwick was 'an insult to the female mind', and much popular literature was dismissed as 'tin-foil' for its 'thoughts spread thin' and predictable endings.

The young women looked to historical figures for positive and nega-

tive role models. For example, Sarah Coates copied poems about the historical figures of Ann Boleyn, Benjamin Franklin, and George Washington. Boleyn stood as a negative role model whose figure could seduce while 'Her eyes could e'en more surely woo'. Washington was a model of the ideal father whether of his country or a family. A brave hero, accomplished soldier and statesman, he resembled the ideal man who might gain material success but also sought a greater reward. Washington 'felt a grandeur that disdained a crown'.

Current events might include happenings of local and personal importance as well as those of national significance. The drowning of two brothers leads Sarah Coates into thoughts of God's providence, while a student wearing such a bright coloured balmoral that a turkey supposedly chased her might suggest to the readers of *The Revolver* the false values of fashion that encouraged the young woman to wear such ostentatious colours.

The Revolver editors mocked the execution of abolitionist John Brown, who, they claimed, 'had attempted to sell all the United States south of the Mason and Dixon's line to Great Britain'. And another article in *The Revolver* displayed its author's verbal facility and knowledge of the worlds of publishing, business, and dry goods. With a zest for puns so often displayed in nineteenth-century periodicals, she wrote that rumours about 'several joint stock companies of conceited young ladies are decided by some pa(r), yet, strange to say, they have not gone off well on change, and few bidders have appeared with responsible endorses'.

These mentions of history and national politics show that the omission of lengthy disquisitions on these subjects did not occur out of ignorance but because these events may not have captured their imaginations with sufficient power to motivate an in-depth discussion or repetition. These preferences may have occurred because national politics seemed so distant and irrelevant

to the impending momentous personal decisions that the women thought they had to make. These women saw themselves as actors in a human story, but defined the story in personal, moral terms rather than in political or economic ones.

When the New-Hampton literary association members rephrased the Declaration of Independence to argue that woman possesses 'equally with man the sacred and inalienable right of pursuing her own happiness', they defined that happiness as intellectual improvement. It developed an individualism leading to greater connection with family, husband and the community. Education prepared women to care for the young, influence men, work through benevolent associations, and even write. Thus while participating in the gender conventions of the age that emphasised women's domestic role, the New-Hampton women modified these conventions to give themselves an intellectual life engaged with their times. These women saw themselves as having a biologically determined role over which they could exercise two important sources of control. They could decide the values on which to base their lives and marriages, and they could choose the proper husbands. By copying poems into a commonplace book, writing and reading articles in a school newspaper, or joining a literary association, women pursued an education that promised their destiny would result from choice and not chance. From individual will, not the dictates of fate or family.

These schoolgirl lesson's modify intellectual history textbooks which explicate works by the great men of American thought: Thomas Jefferson, Ralph Waldo Emerson, and William James to name a few. Professors lecture, often brilliantly, on their writings, often starting with a famous text such as Abraham Lincoln's Gettysburg Address and moving to the meaning of America or one of its geographical regions. These schoolgirls remind us that great texts may or may not reflect the larger culture. Education comes from school books and also from the self. Students learn more than text book lessons by transforming official lessons into ones individually applicable. We see this process of appropriation and self-education in the addresses and essays found in the records of the New-Hampton literary association, the pages of *The Revolver*, and the commonplace book of Sarah Coates.

While text books tell antebellum intellectual history in terms of the theological debates that separated Unitarians from Congregationalists, Boston from New Haven, and Old School from New School Presbyterians, these schoolgirl sources call us to a central fact of antebellum history. Doctrinal debates divided the few, while religious certainty united the many. From Coatesville Quaker Sarah Coates' 1830s commonplace book to the 1859 *The Revolver* of Farmington, Connecticut, the writers presume their relationship to the divine and destiny in a moral universe. The topic that they take care to elaborate upon, presumably because the understanding of their readers could not be taken for granted, is the

sort of woman that they wanted to be and the means they intended to pursue to bring her about. Thus their preoccupation with the ideal woman and her education. If these women taught intellectual history, they would agree with Emerson and Thoreau that theirs was the age of the first person singular. Their major concern is for the individual but for an individual who is female. Many historians have seen the mid-nineteenth century as a period of unlimited expansion. These women's vision reminds us that gender conventions bounded possibilities for the individual.

Yet, these women's sources do more than add a gender dimension to intellectual history. The texts reflect vast changes which themselves were producing more change. Nineteenth-century women belonged to a world of literacy unknown to their great grandmothers of pre-Revolutionary America who may have known merely how to read. The intellectual world these women occupied is novel because of its organisation. Antebellum academies provided women with social spaces for communal pursuit of their intellectual development,

while less than a century earlier, this activity was limited to the salons of the upper class and domestic prayer groups.

Finally, the women's embrace of gentility means that they were making educated womanhood a middle-class convention. For they eschewed other worldly piety on the one hand, and on the other aristocratic display of clothes and possessions. By claiming a place for education in the lives of middle-class women, these women were actively reforming womanhood and American culture through their intellectual self-development.

Louise L. Stevenson is Associate Professor of History and American studies at Franklin and Marshall College, Pennsylvania, and author of The Victorian Homefront: American Thought and Culture, 1860-1880 *(New York; Twayne-MacMillan, 1991). Her next book will be a history of American women's everyday intellectual lives.*

Grateful acknowledgments go the The Library Company of Philadelphia for a Mellon fellowship, and to the Spencer Foundation for a grant, both of which made possible the research and writing of this article.

A Violent Crusader in the Cause of Freedom

John Brown and his guerrilla force raided Harpers Ferry, Virginia, in hope of starting a slave uprising across the South.

by Ron Schaumburg

On the morning of Oct. 17, 1859, the people of Harpers Ferry, Virginia, awoke to discover that their town had been invaded.

During the night, a small band, led by a fiery antislavery crusader named John Brown, had occupied a gun factory and seized a federal arsenal stacked with thousands of muskets and rifles. The raiders—14 white and five black men—held dozens of prisoners at gunpoint and killed several people who got in their way.

Fierce and fearless, John Brown had conceived a bold plan: He hoped to incite black slaves throughout the South to rebel and take up arms against their masters. The guns from Harpers Ferry would give the insurrection the firepower it needed to spread, plantation by plantation, until all the slaves were freed.

Brown was convinced that an army of slaves would rush to join him after hearing of the Harpers Ferry raid. The throngs never came, but publicity surrounding Brown's subsequent trial and execution helped ignite the long-smoldering debate over slavery and moved the nation a step closer to the Civil War.

MAKING OF A RADICAL

By the time of the Harpers Ferry raid, Brown, at 59, was already known as a fanatical crusader against slavery. A few years earlier, in Kansas—where people were debating whether to become a slave state or free state—Brown's guerrilla gang, provoked by a bloody attack on abo-

litionist settlers, hacked to death five unarmed proslavery settlers.

Born in Connecticut, Brown hated slavery from his youth. As an adult, he worked as a farmer, tanner, and land speculator, but he was a poor businessman and had a hard time feeding his large family (two marriages had produced 20 children).

As a Calvinist, Brown practiced a strict form of Christianity. He believed the Bible contained God's law, which took priority over the laws of man. He deeply loved his country, but he had no qualms about breaking its laws if he felt they contradicted biblical morals. At his trial, he explained his beliefs by saying:

…[T]he New Testament…teaches me that all things whatsoever I would that men should do to me, I should do to them. It teaches me further to remember them that are in bonds, as bound with them.…

Brown especially despised the Fugitive Slave Act, which made it a crime to help escaped slaves. As a link in the Underground Railroad, he once led a group of 10 slaves to freedom in Canada, a journey that took three months and covered more than a thousand snow-covered miles.

To carry out his slave rebellion, Brown organized a private army, including three of his sons, and bought thousands of dollars in weapons with money supplied by Northern supporters. As Brown firmed plans for the Harpers Ferry raid, some who had pledged to take part backed out, con-

sidering the raid too risky. Even famed abolitionist and former slave Frederick Douglass, who admired Brown, considered the idea of attacking a federal arsenal a disaster. "You're walking into a perfect steel trap," he warned Brown.

The raiders hoped to capture the guns at the federal arsenal and escape before word reached Washington, D.C. They marched into Harpers Ferry (now part of West Virginia) late on Sunday night, Oct. 16, 1859, took the armory and several prominent local citizens as hostages. Brown's men cut telegraph lines to the town, but they allowed a train to pass after detaining it for five hours. When the train reached Baltimore, the conductor reported the siege to authorities.

On Monday, local militias surrounded the armory with Brown's band and prisoners inside, cutting off escape routes. Federal authorities dispatched marines commanded by Colonel Robert E. Lee, who would later lead Confederate troops in the Civil War.

Lee's men stormed the armory the next day, killing some of the raiders, and capturing or killing others who tried to flee. During the bloody battle, Mary Mauzy, a town resident, wrote a letter to her daughter describing the scene outside her window:

Our men chased them [Brown's followers] in the river just below here and I saw them shot down like dogs. I saw one poor wretch rise above the water and someone strike him with a club. He sank again, and in a moment they dragged him out, a corpse.

By 8 a.m. on the fourth day, the raid was over. Most of Brown's men, including two of his sons, lay dead. Brown was captured after being severely wounded with a sword.

A NATION SPELLBOUND

Brown's raid had failed to spark any slave uprising. But he had gotten the nation's attention. Just after the battle, as he lay bleeding in the armory's engine house, Brown was interviewed by reporters. The spellbound writers spread his abolitionist message to the shocked and curious nation.

Two weeks later, Brown's trial began. Still recovering from his wounds, Brown lay on a cot during the six-day proceeding. The jury convicted him of murder, treason, and insurrection. Before the judge pronounced a death sentence, Brown rose from his cot and delivered an impassioned speech, which appeared in the next day's newspapers:

> **Now, if it is deemed necessary that I should forfeit my life for the furtherance of the ends of justice, and mingle my blood with the blood of millions in this slave country whose rights are disregarded by wicked, cruel, and unjust enactments, I say let it be done.**

PURGED WITH BLOOD

Though some tried to brand Brown a madman bent on self-destruction, many Americans revered him as a hero who preached respect for all races and cherished the American ideal of freedom more than his life.

Douglass, the abolitionist, said, "His zeal in the cause of my race was far greater than mine.... I could live for the slave, but he could die for him."

Brown was hanged on Dec. 2, 1859, in Charlestown, Virginia (now Charles Town, West Virginia). As he mounted the wagon that would carry him to the gallows, he handed a message to a bystander. It read, in part:

> **I, John Brown, am now quite certain that the crimes of this guilty land will never be purged away, but with blood.**

In parts of the country, church bells rang to mourn the execution of Brown, whom many saw as a martyr for human liberty.

Just 15 months later, the Civil War erupted. As Brown predicted, the evil of slavery would be washed away in a torrent of American blood.

UNIT 4

The Civil War and Reconstruction

Unit Selections

Key Points to Consider

- How and why did the Civil War change from a limited conflict to almost total war? Why did Abraham Lincoln delay issuing the Emancipation Proclamation and why did he finally take the step?

- Black Northern troops performed valiantly in the doomed assault against Fort Wagner. What were they trying to prove to the world?

- At the end of the Civil War some people urged General Robert E. Lee to disband his troops so they could conduct guerilla warfare. Speculate on the possible results if he had done so.

- Analyze Lincoln's second inaugural address. Why does the author of the essay on it claim that it provides "the key to Lincoln's greatness?"

- How and why did Radical Reconstruction fail at the time? How can author Eric Foner claim that it nonetheless provided an "animating vision" for the future?

 **Links: www.dushkin.com/online/**
These sites are annotated in the World Wide Web pages.

The American Civil War
http://sunsite.utk.edu/civil-war/warweb.html

Anacostia Museum/Smithsonian Institution
http://www.si.edu/archives/historic/anacost.htm

Abraham Lincoln Online
http://www.netins.net/showcase/creative/lincoln.html

Gilder Lehrman Institute of American History
http://www.digitalhistory.uh.edu/index.cfm?

Secession Era Editorials Project
http://history.furman.edu/~benson/docs/dsmenu.htm

Sectionalism plagued the United States from its inception. The Constitutional proviso that slaves would count as three-fifths of a person for representational purposes, for instance, or that treaties had to be passed in the senate by two-thirds majorities grew out of sectional compromises. Manufacturing and commercial interests were strong in the North. Such interests generally supported high tariffs to protect industries, and the construction of turnpikes, canals, and railroads to expand domestic markets. The South, largely rural and agricultural, strongly opposed such measures. Southerners believed that tariffs cost them money that went to line the pockets of Northern manufacturers, and had little interest in what were known as "internal improvements." Such differences could be resolved because there were no moral issues involved, and matters such as tariffs aroused few emotions in the public.

The question of slavery added a different dimension. Part of the quarrel involved economic considerations. Northerners feared that the spread of slavery would discriminate against "free" farming in the west. Southerners just as adamantly believed that the institution should be allowed to exist wherever it proved feasible. Disputes in 1820 and again in 1850 resulted in compromises that papered over these differences, but they satisfied no one. More and more Northerners, as time wore on, came to regard slavery as sinful—an abomination that must be stamped out. Southerners, on the other hand, grew more receptive to the idea that slavery actually was beneficial to both blacks and whites and was condoned by the Bible. Now cast in moral terms, the issue could not be resolved in the fashion of tariff disputes by splitting differences. In what became an increasingly emotional atmosphere, John Brown's raid touched off an explosion of feverish charges and countercharges by both sides.

Moderates in the two national parties, the Whigs and Democrats, tried to keep the slavery question from tearing the country in two. Though suffering some defections, the Democrats managed to stay together until the elections of 1860. The Whigs, however, fell apart during the 1850s. The emergence of the Republican Party, with its strength almost exclusively based in the North, signaled the beginning of the end. Southerners came to regard the Republicans as the party of abolitionism. Abraham Lincoln, Republican presidential candidate in 1860, tried to assure Southerners that although he opposed the spread of slavery he had no intentions of seeking to abolish the institution where it already existed. He was not widely believed in the South. Republican victory in 1860 seemed to them, or at least to the hotheads among them, to threaten not just slavery but the entire Southern way of life. One by one Southern states began seceding, and Lincoln's unwillingness to let them destroy the union led to the Civil War.

The article "The Doom of Slavery: Ulysses S. Grant, War Aims, and Emancipation, 1861-1863," describes how the Civil War changed from a limited conflict to a concept of total war against Southern resources and morale. "Richmond's Bread Riot" shows how effective Northern efforts were. In 1863, thousands of women marched in the streets of Richmond, demanding food. Confederate President Jefferson Davis had to threaten to open fire on the protesters unless they dispersed.

In the article "The Civil War's Deadliest Weapons were not Rapid Fire Guns or Giant Cannon, but the Simple Rifle Musket and the Humble Minie' Ball" wars tend to be fought by young men and managed by old ones. All too often these old men re-fight the wars of their youth and are unable to adapt to more modern developments. The rifle musket, used by both sides, was so deadly as to render obsolete such tactics as head-on charges. Failure to appreciate this development resulted in hideous casualties.

There are two selections in this unit about the performance of African Americans in the war. "A Bold Break for Freedom" describes how an intrepid slave hijacked a Southern ship and turned it over to the North. He continued to pilot the ship during the war, and later returned to the South to work for black rights. "A Gallant Rush for Glory," provides an account of a courageous assault by a black regiment against a Southern stronghold in South Carolina. The attack failed with catastrophic losses, but showed that blacks could fight as courageously as whites.

"Between Honor and Glory" is about the final weeks of the war. Confederate General Robert E. Lee led his beleaguered Army of Northern Virginia on exhausting marches to avoid being captured, but in the end had to surrender. Some urged Lee to instruct his troops to disband and to carry on guerilla warfare. His refusal to do so spared the nation the agonies of protracted fighting and the resultant hatreds that would have radically changed the course of events.

"Absence of Malice" analyzes Abraham Lincoln's second inaugural address, made only weeks before his death. Author Ronald C. White, Jr., argues that this was his finest speech and provides the key to "understanding Lincoln's greatness." "America's Birth at Appomattox" also deals with the end of the war. Anne Wortham writes that ties of "friendship, battlefield comradeship, and shared nationality" helped to further reconciliation between the North and South.

A struggle took place after the war ended over how the South should be reintegrated into the Union. The most important issue was what status blacks would have in the postwar society. Moderates such as Lincoln wished to make Reconstruction as painless as possible even though this meant continued white domination of the Southern states. "Radical" or "advanced" Republicans wished to guarantee freed people the full rights of citizenship, using force if necessary to achieve this goal. Southern whites resisted "radical" Reconstruction any way they could, and ultimately prevailed when "Northern will" eroded. Eric Foner's "The New View of Reconstruction" argues that even though radical Reconstruction failed in the short run, it provided an "animating vision" for the future.

"The Doom of Slavery": Ulysses S. Grant, War Aims, and Emancipation, 1861–1863

Brooks D. Simpson

Like many northerners, Ulysses S. Grant went to war in 1861 to save the Union—and nothing more—in what he predicted would be a short conflict. By 1863, after two years of bloody struggle against a stubborn enemy, Grant came to understand that a war to preserve the Union must of necessity transform that Union. Central to that revolutionary transformation was the acceptance of emancipation as a war aim and the enrollment of ex-slaves in the bluecoat ranks. The intensity of Confederate resistance compelled Union commanders to accept this notion, while the influx of black refugees into Yankee camps helped to force a decision. In 1861 Grant believed that the Union should keep hands off slavery if a quick peace and rapid reconciliation was desired. By 1863 circumstances had changed. Notions of a limited conflict gave way to the concept of a total war waged against Southern resources and morale as well as manpower. New means were needed to attain victory. To save the Union one must destroy slavery. Grant's experiences as a field commander are illustrative of this process, suggesting the interaction between the progress of the war effort, the escalation of Southern resistance, and the transformation of war aims to encompass emancipation.

From war's beginning Grant realized that at the core of the dispute was the institution of slavery. His position on the peculiar institution was ambiguous, and he left no detailed explanation of his feelings for historians to examine. Marriage to the daughter of a slaveholder entangled him in slavery: he worked alongside slaves, his wife owned four house servants, and he was a slaveholder for a short period. Yet family slaves heard him speak out against the institution, he did not succumb to the blatant prejudices of his age, and he freed the slave he owned at a time when the money a sale might have brought could have been a great boon. He showed no interest in protecting slavery, let alone perpetuating it.[1]

Moreover, Grant understood that the advent of war in the spring of 1861 would affect slavery, no matter the outcome. Southerners were risking the foundation of their society even as they defended it. "In all this I can but see the doom of Slavery," he told his father-in-law. "The North do not want, nor will they want, to interfere with the institution. But they will refuse for all time to give it protection unless the South shall return soon to their allegiance." The disruption of the Southern economy by war would render it vulnerable to interna-

tional competition, reducing the worth of slaves "so much that they will never be worth fighting over again." Slavery would be destroyed as a consequence of prolonged conflict, a casualty of events rather than the target of Union policy.[2]

Nevertheless, a quick Northern victory, achieved before hatred could become deep-seated, might minimize the impact of the conflict upon slavery. And Grant believed that such a rapid triumph was possible. Startled by the vigorous reaction of Northerners in Sumter's aftermath, he ventured that if Southerners ever discovered what they had wrought, "they would lay down their arms at once in humble submission." Confidently he predicted a Northern triumph in a conflict "of short duration." With "a few decisive victories" by the North the "howling" Confederates would flee the field. "All the states will then be loyal for a generation to come, negroes will depreciate so rapidly in value that no body will want to own them and their masters will be the loudest in their declamations against the institutions in a political and economic view." If slavery was to suffer, it would be as a byproduct of the conflict, not because of deliberate policy decisions to eradicate it. Indeed, to take such steps might only prolong the conflict by engendering resistance born of bitterness.[3]

In June, Grant was commissioned colonel of the 21st Illinois. Soon his regiment was dispatched to Missouri to hunt down scattered rebel detachments. Grant kept a close eye on his men, making sure that they did not disturb citizens along the line of march. He reasoned that a well-behaved army would contradict rumors of a marauding bunch of Yankees bent upon plunder, eroding fears and enhancing the chances of a quick and easy peace. Such considerations were especially crucial in Missouri, where the population was nearly evenly divided between loyalists and secessionists. With the state still teetering on the edge of secession, it was of utmost importance that Grant maintain discipline among his new recruits. He did so, with good results. While there existed "a terrible state of fear among the people" when his troops arrived, he added that within a few weeks they discovered that the bluecoats "are not the desperate characters they took them for." He was convinced that "if orderly troops could be marched through this country… it would create a very different state of feeling from what exists now."[4]

Efforts to foster good feeling, however, met a serious obstacle in the stubborness of the local citizens. "You can't convince them but that the ultimate object is to extinguish, by force, slavery," he complained to his father. To his wife Julia he revealed concern that the war was getting out of hand. Not only were the citizens "great fools," but they "will never rest until they bring upon themselves all the horrors of war in its worst form. The people are inclined to carry on a guerilla Warfare that must eventuate in retaliation and when it does commence it will be hard to control."[5] Should the war transcend conventional limits, it would embitter both victor and vanquished, making it all the more difficult to achieve a lasting peace. Moreover, to abandon notions of a limited war fought between armies, in favor of a people's struggle, carried with it revolutionary implications. While both sides may have gone to war to preserve something—the North to save the Union, the South to protect a way of life—the resulting conflict, should it spill over its initial boundaries,

promised to transform American society whatever the result.

Signs of Confederate determination caused Grant to reconsider his earlier notions about a short war. "I have changed my mind so much that I don't know what to think," he told his sister. While he still believed that the rebels could be crushed by spring, "they are so dogged that there is no telling when they may be subdued." As resistance stiffened, Grant adopted a tougher policy toward secessionist sympathizers, arresting several to prevent them from relaying information, seizing a prosouthern paper, and warning businessmen not to trade with Confederates. If Southerners wanted to broaden the scope of the war, Grant was willing to respond in kind.[6]

Inevitably such a struggle affected the institution of slavery. While Grant did not go to war to free the slaves, he had maintained that Northerners would not prop up slavery while the South continued to fight. Eventually Union field commanders found themselves confronted with the problem of what to do about slavery in the war zone. Despite Grant's avowed disinclination to become involved in political questions, his actions toward civilians, property, and fugitive slaves inescapably carried with them political overtones. In August, General John C. Frémont ordered Grant to take command of troops concentrating in southeast Missouri. Arriving at Cape Girardeau on August 30, Grant observed "Contrabands, in the shape of negroes," working on the fortifications. "I will make enquiries how they come here and if the fact has not been previously reported ask instructions," he informed Frémont's headquarters at St. Louis. Grant was trying to avoid initiating policies which interfered with slavery.[7]

Unknown to Grant, Frémont, tired of harassment by Confederate sympathizers, struck at slavery the same day. His abolitionism, bolstered by a visit from Owen Lovejoy, and his ambition combined to convince him to issue a proclamation which imposed martial law on Missouri, confiscated the property of active Confederate supporters, and declared their slaves free. Local commanders wired Grant for instructions. "Protect all loyal Citizens in all their right[s]," Grant

replied, "but carry out the proclamation of Genl Fremont upon all subjects known to come under it." Frémont's order was soon countermanded by Lincoln, but it had alerted Grant to the possibility that the war could assume a wider scope and thus involve him in the very political questions he wished to avoid.[8] Lincoln's removal of Frémont several weeks later also reminded the new brigadier of the cost of violating established policy.

Grant's decision to invade Kentucky in September 1861 provided him with an opportunity to issue a proclamation outlining war aims, and the contrast with Frémont's missive was marked. Through August, Kentucky had managed to preserve a precarious neutrality in the sectional conflict. Neither side had set foot in the state, although it was obvious that sooner or later Union troops would have to violate its neutrality if they intended to launch an offensive to recapture Tennessee. Grant had been sent to southeast Missouri to plan for just such an invasion, but Confederate forces conveniently relieved him of the onus of disrupting the status quo first by invading Kentucky on September 3. The Rebel commander, General Leonidias Polk, had made a serious error, one on which Grant seized in moving his troops across the Ohio River into Paducah, Kentucky, on September 6.

Once installed at Paducah, Grant issued his own proclamation. He had invaded Kentucky, "not to injure or annoy,… but to respect the rights, and to defend and enforce the rights of all loyal citizens." It was a purely defensive move. "I have nothing to do with opinions. I shall deal only with armed rebellion and its aiders and abetors." Nothing was said about slavery. Grant issued special instructions "to take special care and precaution that no harm is done to inoffensive citizens."[9]

Grant's proclamation was as much a political statement as that issued by Frémont. Both were issued in states still technically loyal to the Union, and both reflected the lack of a declaration of overall war aims from Washington. Frémont, anxious to make a name for himself, had sought to place the war effort on advanced ground; Grant's announcement reflected his own belief that the war was one for reunion, not revolution. In contrast to Frémont, who saw his handiwork annulled by Lincoln, Grant's statement stood. It still remained for the Lincoln administration to make known its policy in order to guide military commanders in their actions.

Although Lincoln's action in countermanding Frémont's proclamation helped people understand what his policy was not, Grant was unsure of what government policy was, especially as it applied to black refugees. Within two weeks of the occupation of Paducah, blacks began entering Union lines, intent on making good their escape from slavery. Like Grant, Kentucky blacks knew that the presence of Union troops meant the disruption of slavery, regardless of the unwillingness of Union commanders to play abolitionist. And, if the Yankee army would not come to the blacks, they would go to it. The slaveholders followed, demanding the return of their property. They were willing to overlook the irony that they were asking the assistance of a government that many of them were rebelling against to protect their right to own slaves, when many of them had justified secession precisely because they had no faith that the same government would protect that right. Grant wired Washington for instructions. None came.[10]

Left on his own, and aware that fugitive slave legislation was still in force, Grant ordered the return of at least one slave. Some two months later he finally received definite guidelines on what to do. Major General Henry W. Halleck succeeded Frémont in November with orders to convince civilians in his command that the sole purpose of the war was to uphold "the integrity of the Union." The day after he assumed command Halleck issued General Orders No. 3, which closed Union lines to black fugitives.[11]

Grant received the order with mixed feelings. To be sure, he still held fast to his belief that the sole object of the war was to restore the Union. "My inclination is to whip the rebellion into submission, preserving all constitutional rights," he told his father. But Grant was willing to admit the possibility that this might not be possible. "If it cannot be

whipped in any other way than through a war against slavery," he continued, "let it come to that legitimately. If it is necessary that slavery should fall that the Republic may continue its existence, let slavery go." The general was willing to consider the possibility that slavery's demise might be a goal of Union war policy, instead of being merely the consequence of the disruptive impact of military operations. But he was not yet ready to take that step. Aware that many Northern newspapers had seized upon Halleck's order to renew their criticism of the narrow scope of Union war aims, Grant charged that such papers "are as great enemies to their country as if they were open and avowed secessionists." Adopting such broad goals would mean that the prospects for reunion and reconciliation would give way to a bitter struggle requiring the North to conquer the entire South.[12]

Despite his reaction to press criticism of Halleck's order, Grant was ambivalent about it. "I do not want the Army used as negro catchers," he explained in approving the return of a fugitive to a loyal master, "but still less do I want to see it used as a cloak to cover their escape. No matter what our private views may be on this subject there are in this Department positive orders on the subject, and these orders must be obeyed." While he still agreed that the army's mission did not include emancipation, he was not willing to endorse active support of slavery in all instances, especially in the face of growing resistance. Noting that it was not the military's policy "to ignore, or in any manner interfere with the Constitutional rights of loyal citizens," he denied the same protection to secessionist slaveholders when he refused to honor a Confederate master's demand for the return of a fugitive who had sought refuge in Grant's camp. "The slave, who is used to support the Master, who supported the rebellion, is not to be *restored* to the Master by Military Authority." The slaveholder might appeal to the civil authorities, but Grant did not "feel it his duty to feed the foe, or in any manner contribute to their comfort." This position, violating the letter of Halleck's order, went further in the direction of emancipation than existing congres-

sional legislation outlining confiscation policy, which concerned only those slaves actively employed in support of the rebellion.[13]

Grant let slip his growing antislavery convictions on other occasions. During the fall of 1861 his forces sparred with Polk's units, and the two armies met once in a pitched battle at Belmont, Missouri. Inevitably, prisoners were taken at these clashes, and Grant met with Polk several times on a truce boat to arrange exchanges and discuss other issues. At the conclusion of one meeting, drinks were served, and Polk offered a toast: "George Washington!" No sooner had Grant tipped the glass to his lips, however, when Polk added, "the first rebel." Chagrined, Grant protested that such sharp practice was "scarcely fair" and vowed to get even. The opportunity came several weeks later, at another truce boat conference. This time Grant proposed a toast: "Equal rights to all." Heartily assenting, Polk began to down the contents of his glass, when Grant quickly added, "white and black." A sputtering Polk admitted that Grant had achieved his object.[14]

Nor was Grant willing to tolerate actions which exceeded the bounds of conventional warfare. In January 1862, upon receiving reports that several of his pickets had been shot by civilians, he ordered that the surrounding area "should be cleaned out, for six miles around, and word given that all citizens making their appearance in within those areas are liable to be shot," thus establishing the Civil War version of a free-fire zone. These orders restored stability. A week later, he instructed the local commander to release all civilians captured under these orders and to allow all slaves to return to their masters.[15]

During early 1862 Grant remained uncertain about the correct policy to pursue toward fugitives, and his capture of Fort Donelson on February 16 added to the problem. Halleck wanted to consolidate Grant's gains by erecting fortifications to hold Donelson and its twin, Fort Henry, and instructed Grant to use slaves owned by secessionists to do the work. Grant sent division commander John A. McClernand out to capture slaves to increase the available work force. At least one expedition interpreted its orders liberally, seizing "mostly old men, women and children." The commander had violated Halleck's order, and the fugitives had to be returned. Grant finally halted McClernand, explaining, "It leads to constant mistakes and embarassment to have our men running through the country interpreting confiscation acts and only strengthens the enthusiasm against us whilst it has a demoralizing influence upon our own troops."[16]

The incident caused Grant a great deal of embarrassment. He reminded his troops that Halleck's order about returning fugitive slaves was still in force and must be observed. Union lines were flooded with slaveholders seeking to recover their slaves, proving that General Orders No. 3 continued to be a necessity. Halleck had issued a new order, reminding officers that civil courts, not military authorities, were empowered to rule on the status of slaves. Keeping fugitives out of camp would keep Grant out of trouble, or so he thought. But the image of Union soldiers returning "old men, women and children" to their masters was too much for many Northerners, and newspapers attacked Grant's action. "I have studiously tried to prevent the running off of negroes from all outside places," an exasperated Grant explained, "as I have tried to prevent all other marauding and plundering." It was not a matter of personal preference. "So long as I hold a commission in the Army I have no views of my own to carry out. Whatever may be the orders of my superiors, and law, I will execute." If Congress passed legislation "too odious for me to execute," he promised to resign. He enforced a strict observance of Halleck's order to avoid more trouble, including the arrest of any soldiers violating the order.[17]

Even when orders from Washington finally arrived, they did not ease Grant's mind. In March he received notification of new War Department guidelines which instructed soldiers not to return fugitives. One suspects that incidents in Grant's own command had contributed to the new directive. In response Grant pointed out the ramifications of such a policy. He had heard from former U.S. Representative J. M. Quarles that Con-

federate enlistments had risen around Clarksville, Tennessee, in reaction to the use of fugitives by a Union post commander. The post commander told Grant that "the return of those two negroes would do more good, & go further to cultivate a union sentiment in & about Clarksville than any other act." Grant forwarded the case, uncertain how to respond in light of the new directives, but expressed his opinion that the blacks should be returned.[18]

As Grant realized, federal policy toward fugitive slaves was intertwined with efforts at reconciliation. After Fort Donelson, he believed that one more Union victory would end the conflict, an impression made plausible by circumstances in his command. Many Tennesseans were declaring their loyalty to the Union; others were enlisting in Grant's regiments. Confederate deserters reported great discontent in rebel ranks. "With one more great success I do not see how the rebellion is to be sustained," Grant told his wife. He thought that the question of fugitive slaves would simply disrupt the reconciliation process at a time when the end seemed so near. But the bloodbath at Shiloh in April disabused Grant of these hopes. He later claimed that the battle changed his thinking about the conduct of the war. After Shiloh, "I gave up all idea of saving the Union except by complete conquest." Previous policies to "protect the property of the citizens whose territory was invaded, without regard to their sentiments," went out the door, and Grant began to make war not only on Confederate armies but the resources which sustained the war effort.[19]

But Grant's change in attitude was a little slower in coming than he liked to recall later. "This war could be ended at once," he told his wife in June, two months after Shiloh, "if the whole Southern people could express their unbiased feeling untrammeled by leaders. The feeling is kept up however by crying out Abolitionest against us and this is unfortunately sustained by the acts of a very few among us." He detailed instances where Tennesseans "inclined to Union sentiments" watched as soldiers encouraged their slaves to escape. This did little to assist reconciliation. Still, as Grant

took command of the District of West Tennessee in June, he expressed his confidence that as soon as his district was "reduced to working order" its residents would "become loyal, or at least law-abiding." Others were not so sure. Dr. Edward Kittoe, a friend of Grant's patron Congressman Elihu B. Washburne, complained, "We curry favour of these secessionists, and real Union men do not fare as well as they: we are obsequious to them, we feed them, we guard their property, we humble ourselves to gain their favor, and in return we receive insult and injury." Unionists were "disgusted," and both officers and men "feel outraged… and very naturally ask is this the way to crush this rebellion." To Kittoe the answer was obvious: "The iron gauntlet must be used more than the silken glove to crush this serpent."[20]

Grant's early hopes for reconciliation were dashed when he observed the temper of the people. Far from anxiously awaiting reunion, most west Tennesseans remained defiantly loyal to the Confederate cause, chafing under occupied rule. They cheered on the small bands of guerrillas who sought to disrupt and disturb Grant's operations. As Grant struggled to secure his lines from raiders, he began to reassess his beliefs about limited war in the face of escalating Confederate resistance. The intensity of the Southern attack at Shiloh, while alarming, remained within the bounds of conventional warfare: but when resisting citizens and marauding guerrillas expanded the scope of conflict beyond these limits, Grant had to meet the challenge. It was combatting a restive populace in occupied territory, stalking guerrillas, and absorbing black refugees, not merely Shiloh, that persuaded Grant to abandon limited war for total war. He did so with surprising speed. On July 1, he ordered the *Memphis Avalanche* to shut down after the paper had complained about the behavior of Union troops. Within days a Unionist paper, the *Bulletin*, replaced it. Two days later he took steps to halt guerrilla activities by ordering that property losses sustained by his army would be made up by assessments on the property of Confederate sympathizers. All captured guerrillas would not be treated as prisoners of war, leaving open the possibility of execution. The order provoked one Mississippian to protest Grant's "infamous and fiendish proclamation... characteristic of your infernal policy.... Henceforth our motto shall be, Blood for blood, and blood for property."[21]

Grant also tired of dealing with Confederate sympathizers in Memphis. On July 10 he issued a special order directing families of Confederate officers and officeholders to move south. Although the order was later modified to allow such families to remain in Memphis upon taking a pledge not to aid enemy operations, it outraged Confederate General Jeff Thompson, who promised revenge. In contrast, a local Unionist applauded the order: "I would suggest that all persons who *uphold,* and *preach* Secession in our midst be required to 'skedaddle' to the land of *'secession'.*"[22]

As Federal units probed southward across the Tennessee-Mississippi border, blacks continued to flood into Union lines. Their sheer numbers negated any further attempts at exclusion. If whites were "sullen" at the sight of the bluecoats, Kittoe told Washburne, "the darkies seemed joyous at our presence." Grant's soldiers realized that their mere presence destroyed slavery, "Where the army of the Union goes, *there slavery ceases forever,*" wrote a Wisconsin captain. "It is astonishing how soon the blacks have learned this, and they are flocking in considerable numbers already in our lines." Another officer noted, "All that came within our lines were received and put to work and supplied with clothing and subsistence. This policy was viewed by the soldiers with very general approbation."[23]

Grant moved slowly at first in responding to these new circumstances. "It is hard to say what would be the most wise policy to pursue towards these people," he wrote Washburne. He put blacks to work fortifying Memphis from Confederate attack, much as he had used blacks at Donelson. But he remained unsure of his responsibilities in other cases, and, rather than invite more criticism by acting on his own, he asked for instructions. After arresting Confederate sympathizer Francis Whitfield on July 17, 1862, Grant had to decide what to do

with Whitfield's slaves, who, since they were women and children, could not be used on fortifications. Whitfield, understandably, wanted the slaves sent south to relatives. Grant, preoccupied with enemy movements, asked Halleck what to do. The general-in-chief responded that if Grant had no use for or reason to detain the slaves, "let them go when they please."[24]

Halleck could have been more helpful to the befuddled Grant. On the day of Whitfield's arrest, Congress passed a second confiscation act which declared that slaves owned by rebels who came in contact with Union forces were free. Certainly Halleck should have been aware of this legislation, but he failed to pass policy directives down to his subordinates. Promulgation of a policy did not necessarily guarantee its immediate implementation and enforcement. Grant was not officially informed of the passage of the act for several weeks. Halleck finally instructed him to "clean out West Tennessee and North Mississippi of all organized enemies," eject civilian sympathizers, and confiscate rebel property. "It is time that they should begin to feel the presence of war on one side."[25]

Grant planned to make the war even more oppressive for Southern whites. He cracked down on the activities of Confederate sympathizers and guerrillas, following Halleck's advice to "handle that class without gloves." As William T. Sherman put it to Secretary of the Treasury Salmon P. Chase, "The Government of the United States may now safely proceed on the proper rule that all in the South are enemies of all in the North, and not only are they unfriendly, but all who can procure arms now bear them as organized regiments or as guerrillas." Grant also took steps to close down trade with the enemy, especially cotton speculators. To Chase he declared that such trade profited only "greedy" speculators and the enemy, failed to "abate [the] rancorous hostility" of Rebels, and hurt the war effort. Doubtless Grant's new toughness was due to his realization that the war had taken on a new character, but he was also frustrated with his present situation, holding territory while hunting down pesky guerrilla bands. If he could not attack the

South in battle, he would find another way to strike back.[26]

Washburne apprised Grant of the new attitudes in Washington. "This matter of guarding rebel property, of protecting secessionists and of enforcing 'order No. 3' is 'played out' in public estimation. Your order in regard to the Secessionists of Memphis taking the oath or leaving, has been accepted as an earnest of vigorous and decided action on your part.... The administration has come up to what the people have long demanded—a vigorous prosecution of the war by all the means known to civilized warfare." Such measures included striking at slavery. "The negroes must now be made our auxiliaries in every possible way they can be, whether by working or fighting." The general "who takes the most decided step in this respect," Washburne hinted, "will be held in the highest estimation by the loyal and true men in the country."[27]

Grant followed Washburne's advice, freed of the responsibilities of playing slave catcher. "I have no hobby of my own with regard to the negro, either to effect his freedom or to continue his bondage," he told his father. "If Congress pass any law and the President approves, I am willing to execute it." His headquarters established guidelines for the enforcement of the new confiscation legislation. Blacks would no longer be turned away: instead, they would be put to work. Manpower needs would be met by impressing the slaves belonging to Confederate masters. Uncertain as to the scope of the legislation, Grant excluded unemployed blacks from the lines, and prohibited soldiers "from enticing Slaves to leave their masters." The order had an immediate impact. "If the niggers come into camp for a week as fast as they have been coming for two days past," a Wisconsin private noted some two days after Grant issued his order, "we will soon have a waiter for every man in the Regt."[28]

The result pleased Grant. "The war is evidently growing oppressive to the Southern people," he told his sister. "Their *institution* are beginning to have ideas of their own and every time an expedition goes out more or less of them follow in the wake of the army and come to camp." The general employed them as teamsters, cooks, and hospital attendants, but there was not enough work for all. "I don't know what is to become of these poor people in the end but it [is] weakening the enemy to take them from them."[29]

With the approach of fall the black refugee problem assumed serious dimensions. Grant's troops, busy repelling Confederate offensives near Corinth, found the flood of fugitives obstructing movements and causing health problems. They described the blacks coming by the hundreds each night, "bearing their bundles on their heads and their pickaninnies under their arms." Chaplain John Eaton of the 27th Ohio recalled that the influx of refugees resembled "the oncoming of cities": once in camp, the bedraggled blacks produced "a veritable moral chaos." Sherman wrote his senator brother that "if we are to take along and feed the negroes who flee to us for refuge" on top of clothing and transportation shortages, military movements would bog down. "A perfect stampede of contrabands" confronted William S. Rosecrans, who was preparing to advance against enemy positions. Rosecrans sent them behind his lines to shield them from guerilias, complaining, "But what a burden what shall be done with them then."[30]

At first Grant tried to make use of the refugees, putting them to work in the Corinth fortifications. He sent the women and children to campsites east of Corinth and asked Secretary of War Edwin M. Stanton what he should do next. Some people in Chicago thought they would make excellent servants, a practice Stanton permitted for nearly a month until an adverse reaction in the Midwest, encouraged by electioneering Democrats, forced him to rescind the order.[31] Grant then decided to establish camps for the blacks and to let them bring in the cotton and corn crops under his supervision. They would live off the land, receive wages for their work, and strive toward providing for themselves. The Union authorities would exercise a form of guardianship over the refugees, for Grant did not believe that blacks fresh from slavery were prepared to take on the responsibilities of freedom immediately. He sought to provide them with some means of making the transition. His plan would allow him to provide for all blacks entering Union lines, not only the males able to work for the army.

Grant explained his reasoning to Chaplain Eaton, whom he had placed in charge of the project. Racial prejudice, Grant believed, was fundamentally a product of mistaken beliefs about behavior. One of those beliefs held by many whites was that blacks would not work of their own free will. Grant's plan would allow blacks to refute that stereotype. Once blacks assisting the military and working on the plantations had proved that they were responsible, whites would begin to accept the idea of handing a musket to a black man, and blacks could enlist in the Union army. And once blacks had fought for their freedom and demonstrated again that they were responsible and hard-working, whites could begin to entertain the idea of granting citizenship, even the ballot, to blacks. "Never before in those early and bewildering days had I heard the problem of the future of the Negro attacked so vigorously and with such humanity combined with practical good sense," Eaton recalled.[32]

Grant, who had once believed that the military should not interfere with slavery, now was pushing a plan of de facto emancipation, using military supervision to oversee the transition from slavery to freedom. It also reflected his belief that racial prejudice was best countered and conquered by actual demonstrations of its falsehoods. If his plan was paternalistic, at least it held out the prospect of progressive change. Of course, it also provided a solution to the problems of conducting military operations while disposing of a potential disaster by promising relief from the disease-ridden conditions currently confronting the freedmen. Grant took an active interest in Eaton's progress, ordering supplies and assistance whenever needed, and making sure that his subordinates followed suit.[33]

Perhaps the most notable aspects of Grant's solution to the refugee problem was that, for once, he acted without asking his superiors for advice. Not until four days after he had ordered Eaton's appointment did Grant tell Halleck what he was doing and ask for instructions. Halleck, too busy to be bothered by these problems, approved of Grant's policy, although he had only a vague idea of what his subordinate was doing. In fact, the Lincoln administration seemed more interested in taking steps which would halt Grant's plans in their tracks. On September 22, 1862, Lincoln had made public a preliminary version of the Emancipation Proclamation, promising that he would put it into force on January 1, 1863. He sought to take advantage of those hundred days to encourage Tennesseans to reenter the Union on their own, holding out the prospect that if the Volunteer State returned it could do so with slavery intact, since the proclamation applied only to areas under Confederate control. On October 21, 1862, Lincoln informed both Grant and military governor Andrew Johnson of his plan. He wanted them to hold elections for congressmen wherever they could do so. The President hoped that Tennesseans would rejoin the Union "to avoid the unsatisfactory prospect before them."[34]

Grant, who once had held high hopes for the prospect of a speedy reunion, was skeptical of Lincoln's plan. Months before he had heard reports of Unionist speakers such as Emerson Etheridge being mobbed by Rebels; certainly the actions of Memphis's residents struck a telling blow against stories of latent Unionism. Now guerrilla bands were firing on Union steamers with civilians on board. Sherman suggested various ways to punish the guerrillas; Grant approved the expulsion of secessionist families as adequate retaliation. Other policies suggested an intensification of the war effort. With fall came reports of families suffering from a lack of food and shelter. Grant, convinced that those "not actively engaged in rebellion should not be allowed to suffer" amidst plenty, decided that "the burden of furnishing the necessary relief… should fall on those, who, by act, encouragement or sympathy have caused the want now experienced." Some of the troops agreed. They were tired of guarding secessionist property: one private wrote that it made his regiment "squirm like a Sarpent." He concluded that there were "few if any Union men" in the area. Another veteran later remarked that the troops believed by now that "they did not go South to protect Confederate property."[35]

Nevertheless, Grant was not one to question presidential policy. On December 9, 1862, he issued a proclamation to the people of west Tennessee calling for elections in the 8th, 9th, and 10th Congressional districts. All "legal voters" as of 1860 were permitted to participate in the balloting, which would take place on Christmas Eve. Grant was more impressed with the sentiments displayed by the Mississippians, who "show more signs of being subdued than any we have heretofore come across." A reporter noted that many Mississippians wanted to reenter the Union "at whatever cost" before Lincoln's proclamation came into play.[36]

Confederate forces under Nathan Bedford Forrest and Earl Van Dorn had no intention of allowing the election to proceed. They launched an offensive that not only disrupted an attempt by Grant to take Vicksburg but also made it impossible to hold elections. Grant was too busy conducting military operations to take much notice. Attempts at reestablishing loyal governments were futile until military operations rendered territory secure from guerrillas. As the new year started, Grant instructed Brigadier General Stephen A. Hurlbut, commanding at Memphis, to transfer ten secessionist families to Confederate lines for every guerrilla raid launched by the enemy. The general's patience was wearing thin, and protecting his supply lines against cavalry thrusts and armed bands sapped too much energy, time, and men from offensive operations.[37]

But guerrillas proved to be only one of the problems disrupting Grant's control of his own lines. Despite Eaton's project, the flood of refugees threatened to overwhelm Union camps. As Grant reestablished his position around Corinth and Memphis, he sought help from Halleck. "Contraband question becoming serious one," he telegraphed the general-in-chief. "What will I do with surplus negroes?" He glimpsed one possible solution as he shifted his forces to the west bank of the Mississippi opposite Vicksburg in the aftermath of his failed December offensive. It had long been a

favorite belief of Union commanders that if the course of the river was diverted through the construction of a canal, Vicksburg, stripped of its western water barrier, would be rendered vulnerable. Grant, although somewhat skeptical, was willing to try the idea himself, using blacks to do the work. The project illustrated Grant's priorities. The problem presented by black refugees was first and foremost a military problem. Their presence obstructed military movements, disrupted camps, and promised to increase disease and disorder. Grant spared his soldiers of these risks as well as lessened the burden of digging trenches in the dirty swamps by employing black laborers. Military needs having been met, other concerns took over, as Grant worried about the conditions under which the blacks worked.[38]

But this solution was at best a stopgap measure. Nothing seemed to stop the influx of refugees. On February 12, 1863, Grant decided to issue an order excluding blacks from his lines. Soldiers were instructed to stop "enticing" blacks to enter Union camps; freedmen should remain on their plantations and work out a labor arrangement with the planters. "Humanity dictates this policy," he explained to Halleck. "Planters have mostly deserted their plantations taking with them all their able bodied negroes and leaving the old and very young. Here they could not have shelter nor assurances of transportation when we leave." The army was simply not equipped materially or mentally to take on any more freed men. As Grant told one subordinate, "the question is a troublesome one. I am not permitted to send them out of the department, and such numbers as we have it is hard to keep them in."[39]

Unfortunately for Grant, he was caught once more by a shift in administration policy. Halleck told Grant that reports had reached the War Department "that many of the officers of your command not only discourage the negroes from coming under our protection, but, by ill-treatment, force them to return to their masters." Obviously Grant's exclusion order had not gone over well with the top brass. "This is not only bad policy in itself," Halleck continued, "but is directly opposed to the policy adopted by

the government." In the wake of the Emancipation Proclamation, Washington decided to make war in earnest. Halleck—whose General Orders No. 3 in 1861 had epitomized the conservative attitude toward blacks—justified the new approach. "The character of the war has very much changed within the last year. There is now no possible hope of a reconciliation with the rebels. The union party in the south is virtually destroyed. There can be no peace but that which is enforced by the sword. We must conquer the rebels, or be conquered by them."[40]

With this acceptance of a total war approach against the Confederacy came new attitudes toward the treatment of black slaves by the Union army. It is the policy of the government to withdraw from the enemy as much productive labor as possible," Halleck explained, preaching with the passion of the recently converted. "Every slave withdrawn from the enemy, is equivalent to a white man put *hors de combat.*" Freedmen were to be used "so far as practicable as a military force for the defence of forts, depots, &c.… And it is the opinion of many who have examined the question without passion or prejudice, that they can also be used as a military force." Grant was instructed to assist this process by using his "official and personal influence to remove prejudices on this subject," and to assist General Lorenzo Thomas in efforts to organize black regiments."[41]

War had become revolution, taking the very path which Grant had outlined to Eaton the previous November. To arm ex-slaves was to make real the greatest fear of many a white Southerner by equipping blacks with the means to achieve revenge. Grant, who had grown weary of previous attempts at reconciliation, welcomed the change. "Rebellion has assumed that shape now that it can only terminate by the complete subjugation of the South or the overthrow of the Government," he informed Major General Frederick Steele, instructing him to provide for all the black refugees already in his lines and to "encourage all negroes, particularly middle aged males to come within our lines," obviously with an eye toward recruiting them. Then Grant welcomed Thomas to headquarters and did all he could to facilitate his mission. "At least three of my Army Corps Commanders take hold of the new policy of arming the negroes and using them against the rebels with a will," he told Halleck, adding: "You may rely on my carrying out any policy ordered by proper authority to the best of my ability." When several officers tendered their resignations over the new policy, Grant recommended that they be dismissed from the service instead.[42]

While Thomas proceeded with his mission, Grant embarked on yet another campaign against Vicksburg. Crossing the Mississippi below the city, Grant's army won five battles within three weeks, destroyed several factories at Jackson, and laid seige to Vicksburg itself in one of the most brilliant campaigns of the war. His troops took the war to the Southern people. Grant instructed commanders to make sure that their troops would "live as far as possible off the country through which they pass and destroy corn, wheat crops and everything that can be made use of by the enemy in prolonging the war. Mules and horses can be taken to supply all our wants and where it does not cause too much delay agricultural implements may be destroyed. In other words cripple the rebellion in every way."[43]

During the seige he received news that Thomas's recruits had engaged in their first battle at Milliken's Bend, some twenty miles upriver from Vicksburg. At first giving way, the blacks launched a vicious counterattack, spurred on in part by reports that Confederates were murdering blacks taken prisoner in the initial assault. Milliken's Bend proved blacks could fight, and many whites who were skeptical of black enlistment were won over when they heard accounts of the clash. Grant himself was pleased, endorsing the report of the Union commander at the battle with the comment that while the soldiers "had but little experience in the use of fire arms" they had been "most gallant and I doubt not but with good officers they will make good troops."[44]

But in the aftermath of the battle stories began to surface that the Confederates had executed captured black soldiers. Initially Grant was unsure

whether such acts had official Confederate sanction, or if they had been perpetrated by "irresponsible persons"; but additional reports suggested that Confederate General Richard Taylor had approved the measures. Grant told Taylor that if the Confederates were initiating a policy, "I will accept the issue. It may be you propose a different line of policy towards Black troops and Officers commanding them to that practiced towards White troops? If so," Grant added, "I can assure you that these colored troops are regularly mustered into the service of the United States," and all Union authorities "are bound to give the same protection to these troops that they do to any other troops." Such a statement had revolutionary implications, for now Grant was demanding that prisoners in blue uniforms be treated equally, whether their skin was black or white. While Taylor denied the stories, he pointed out that all black prisoners would be turned over to state authorities in accordance with Confederate policy. Grant, accepting Taylor's denial of responsibility, was not so gracious about Confederate policy toward black POWs, commenting that "I cannot see the justice of permitting one treatment for them, and another for the white soldiers." But the exchange proved Grant's willingness to accept the notion that equal treatment followed naturally from emancipation, an idea which promised to transform American society.[45]

By the summer of 1863 Ulysses S. Grant's thoughts on the relationship between slavery, war, and reunion had undergone a drastic change from the ones he voiced during his early weeks of field command. He had always assumed that slavery would be a casualty of the war, but his initial passivity toward "the peculiar institution," fueled by a desire to achieve a quick and painless peace based on reconciliation, had given way in the face of fierce Confederate resistance. Once it had become obvious that the war would be long, Grant grasped that Union military operations would help turn it into a social and economic revolution by disturbing the very foundation of Southern society. Moreover, he now welcomed that challenge. To Lincoln he explained that he was giving "the subject of arming black troops my hearty sup-

port." The enlistment of blacks, "with the emancipation of the negro, is the heavyest blow yet given the Confederacy.... By arming the negro we have added a powerful ally. They will make good soldiers and taking them from the enemy weaken him in the same proportion they strengthen us."[46]

Such measures signalled the death of slavery. "The people of the North need not quarrel over the institution of Slavery," Grant reassured Washburne. "What Vice President Stevens [Alexander H. Stephens] acknowledges the corner stone of the Confederacy is already knocked out. Slavery is already dead and cannot be resurrected. It would take a Standing army to maintain slavery in the South" now. Then Grant injected a personal note. "I never was an Abolitionest, [not even what could be called anti slavery," he admitted, "but... it became patent to my mind early in the rebellion that the North & South could never live at peace with each other except as one nation, and that without Slavery." To save the Union, one must first destroy slavery. Any other settlement would be flawed. With that in mind, he argued that no peace should be concluded "until this question is forever settled." War had become revolution, and Ulysses S. Grant had been both witness and participant in the process. As he told a committee of Memphis unionists, he, like they, had come to "acknowledge human liberty as the only true foundation of human government."[47]

Notes

1. On Grant and slavery see Brooks D. Simpson, "Butcher? Racist? An Examination of William S. McFeely's *Grant: A Biography*," *Civil War History* 33 (March 1987), 63–83.

2. Ulysses S. Grant to Frederick Dent, April 19, 1861, in John Y. Simon, ed., The Papers of Ulysses S. Grant, 16 vols. to date (Carbondale, Ill.: Southern Illinois University Press, 1967–88), 2:3–4.

3. Ulysses S. Grant to Mary Grant, April 29, 1861, ibid., 2:13–14; Grant to Jesse Root Grant, May 6, 1861, ibid., 2:21–22. In fact, Grant expressed some concern lest slaves rise up in insurrection against their masters.

4. Ulysses S. Grant to Julia Dent Grant, July 19, 1861, ibid., 2:72–73.

5. Ulysses S. Grant to Julia Dent Grant, August 3, 1861, ibid., 2:82–83; Grant to Jesse Root Grant, August 3, 1861, ibid., 2:80–81.

6. Ulysses S. Grant to Mary Grant, August 12, 1861, ibid., 2:105; Grant to John C. Kelton, August 14, 1861, ibid., 2:111; Grant to William H. Worthington, August 26, 1861, ibid., 2:139–40.

7. Ulysses S. Grant to John C. Kelton, August 30, 1861, ibid., 2:154–55.

8. Dudley Taylor Cornish, *The Sable Arm: Negro Troops in the Union Army, 1861–1865* (New York: Norton, 1966), 12–15; John Cook to Ulysses S. Grant, September 11, 1861, Simon, ed., *Grant Papers,* 2:220, and Grant to Cook, September 12, 1861, ibid., 2:243–44. Frémont issued a new proclamation on September 11 in line with Lincoln's policy.

9. Ulysses S. Grant, "Proclamation," September 6, 1861, and Grant to E. A. Paine, September 6, 1861. ibid., 194–95.

10. Ulysses S. Grant to Lorenzo Thomas, September 21, 1861, ibid., 2:291 and annotation.

11. Kenneth Williams, *Lincoln Finds A General,* 5 vols. (New York: Macmillan, 1949–59), 3:106–12.

12. Ulysses S. Grant to Jesse Root Grant, November 27, 1861, Simon, ed., *Grant Papers,* 3:227.

13. Ulysses S. Grant to John L. Cook, December 25, 1861, ibid., 3:342–43; William S. Hillyer (Grant staff officer) to L. F. Ross, January 5, 1862, ibid., 3:373–74; Charles F. Smith to Grant, January 4, 1862, ibid., 3:431.

14. James Grant Wilson, *Life and Public Services of Ulysses Simpson Grant* (New York: De Witt, 1885), 24.

15. Ulysses S. Grant to E. A. Paine, January 11, 19, 1862, Simon, ed., *Grant Papers,* 4:32, 68–69.

16. Henry W. Halleck to Ulysses S. Grant, February 8, 1862, and Grant to Halleck, February 11, 1862, ibid., 4:193–94; General orders No. 46, Department of the Missouri, February 22, 1862, ibid., 4:291; Grant to McClernand, February 18, 1862, ibid., 4:243; Grant to J. C. Kelton, February 22, 1862, ibid., 4:267–68; Grant to McClernand, February 22, 1862, ibid., 4:470.

17. General Orders No. 14, District of West Tennessee, February 26, 1862, ibid., 4:290–91; Grant to Elihu B. Washburne, March 22, 1862, ibid., 4:408; Grant to Philip B. Fouke, March 16, 1862, ibid., 4:377; Grant to Marcellus M. Crocker, March 17, 1862, ibid., 4:384; Grant to William T. Sherman, March 17, 1862, ibid., 4:382–83.

18. Ulysses S. Grant to Nathaniel H. McLean, March 31, 1862, ibid., 4:454; Philip B. Fouke to Grant, March 30, 1862, ibid., 4:454.

19. Ulysses S. Grant to George W. Cullum, February 23, 25, 1862, ibid., 4:276, 286; Grant to William T. Sherman, February 25, 1862, ibid., 4:289; Grant to Philip B. Fouke, March 16, 1862, ibid., 4:377; Grant to Nathaniel H. McLean, March 15, 30, 1862, ibid., 4:368, 447–48; Grant to Julia Dent Grant, March 18, 1862, ibid., 4:389; Ulysses S. Grant, *Personal Memoirs of U.S. Grant,* 2 vols. (New York: Charles L. Webster and Co., 1885–86), 1:368–69.

20. Ulysses S. Grant to Julia Dent Grant, June 12, 1862, Simon, ed., *Grant Papers,* 5:142–43; Kittoe to Washburne, June 24, 1862, Lloyd Lewis–Bruce Catton Research Notes, Ulysses S. Grant Association, Southern Illinois University.

21. Grant to Elihu B. Washburne, June 19, 1862, Simon, ed., *Grant Papers,* 5:146; Grant to William S. Hillyer, July 1, 1862, ibid., 5:181–82 and annotation; General Orders No. 60, District of West Tennessee, July 3, 1862, ibid., 5:190–91 and annotation.

22. "Union" to Grant, July 12, 1862, William S. Hillyer Papers, University of Virginia; see Simon, ed., *Grant Papers,* 5:192–94.

23. Seymour D. Thompson, *Recollections with the Third Iowa Regiment* (Cincinnati, 1864), 275; William P. Lyon, *Reminiscences of the Civil War* (San Jose, Calif.: Muirson and Wright, 1907), 53; Kittoe to Washburne, June 24, 1862, Lewis-Catton Research Notes, Ulysses S. Grant Association.

24. Ulysses S. Grant to Elihu B. Washburne, June 19, 1862, Simon, ed., *Grant Papers,* 5:146; Grant to Halleck, July 19, 1862, and Halleck to Grant, July 19, 1862, ibid., 5:218–19. See also Grant to Halleck, July 8[7], 1862, ibid., 5:199.

25. Herman Belz, *Emancipation and Equal Rights: Politics and Constitutionalism in the Civil War Era* (New York: Norton, 1978), 36–40; General Orders No. 72, District of West Tennessee, August 11, 1862, Simon, ed., *Grant Papers,* 5:273–74; Halleck to Grant, August 2, 1862, ibid., 5:243–44.

26. Grant to Halleck, July 28, 1862, and Halleck to Grant, August 2, 1862, ibid., 5:243–44; Grant to William W. Rosecrans, August 10, 1862, ibid., 5:282; Grant to Isaac F. Quinby, July 26, 1862, ibid., 5:238–41; Grant to Salmon P. Chase, July 31, 1862, ibid., 5:255–56; Grant to Rosecrans, August 7, 1862, ibid., 5:271; Sherman to Chase, August 11, 1862, quoted in John B. Walters, *Merchant of Terror: General Sherman and Total War* (Indianapolis: Bobbs-Merrill, 1973), 57–58.

27. Washburne to Grant, July 25, 1862, Simon, ed., *Grant Papers,* 5:226.

28. Grant to Jesse Root Grant, August 3, 1862, ibid., 5:264; General Orders No. 72, District of West Tennessee, August 11, 1862, ibid., 5:273–74; Stephen Ambrose, ed., *A Wisconsin Boy in Dixie: The Selected Letters of John K. Newton* (Madison. Wis.: The University of Wisconsin Press, 1961), 27–28.

29. Grant to Mary Grant, August 19, 1862, Simon, ed., *Grant Papers* 5:311.

30. Samuel H. M. Byers, *With Fire and Sword* (New York: Neale, 1911), 45; John Eaton, *Grant, Lincoln, and the Freedmen* (New York: Longmans, Green and Co., 1907), 2; William T. Sherman to John Sherman, September 3, 1862, William T. Sherman Papers, LC; Rosecrans to Grant, September 10, 1862, Simon, ed., *Grant Papers,* 6:32.

31. Grant to Thomas J. McKean, September 16, 1862, ibid., 6:54; James M. Tuttle to Edwin M. Stanton, September 18, 1862, ibid., 6:317; V. Jacque Voegeli, *Free But Not Equal: The Midwest and the Negro During the Civil War* (Chicago: University of Chicago Press, 1967), 60–61.

32. Eaton, *Grant, Lincoln and the Freedmen,* 9–15.

33. Ibid., 18–32. For additional discussion about Grant, Eaton, and the development of this policy at Corinth and at Davis Bend, Mississippi, which Grant hoped would become "a negro paradise," see Cam Walker: "Corinth: The Story of a Contraband Camp," *Civil War History* 20 (March 1974), 5–22; Steven J. Ross, "Freed Soil, Freed Labor, Freed Men: John Eaton and the Davis Bend Experiment," *Journal of Southern History* 44 (May 1978), 213–32; Louis S. Gerteis, *From Contraband to Freedman: Federal Policy Toward Southern Blacks, 1861–1865* (Westport, Conn.: Greenwood Press, 1973); and Janet Sharp Hermann, *The Pursuit of a Dream* (New York: Oxford University Press, 1981), 37–60.

34. Grant to Halleck, November 15, 1862, and Halleck to Grant, November 16, 1862, Simon, ed., *Grant Papers,* 6:315; Lincoln to Johnson and Grant, October 21, 1862, ibid., 7:3.

35. General Orders No. 4, Department of the Tennessee, November 3, 1862, ibid., 6:252–53; William W. Lowe to John A. Rawlins, August 18, 1862, ibid., 5:314; John W. Brinsfield, "The Military Ethics of General William T. Sherman: A Reassessment," *Parameters,* Vol. 12, No. 2 (1980), 42; Fred A. Shannon, ed., *The Civil War Letters of Sergeant Onley Andrus* (Urbana: University of Illinois Press, 1947), 25–26; Bruce Catton, *Grant Moves South* (Boston: Little, Brown, 1960), 336.

36. Ulysses S. Grant, "Proclamation," December 9, 1862, Simon, ed., *Grant Pa-*

pers 7:3–4; Grant to Halleck, December 14, 1862, ibid., 7:31–32; Thomas W. Knox, *Camp-Fire and Cotton-Field* (New York: Blelock and Co., 1865), 233.

37. Grant to Steven A. Hurlbut, January 3, 1863, Simon, ed., *Grant Papers,* 7:167–68.

38. Grant to Halleck, January 6, 1863, ibid., 7:186; Grant to George W. Deitzler, February 2. 1863, ibid., 7:278; Eaton, *Grant, Lincoln and the Freedmen,* 44.

39. Special Field Orders No. 2, Department of the Tennessee, February 12, 1863, ibid., 7:339; Grant to Halleck, February 18, 1863, ibid., 7:338, Catton, *Grant Moves South,* 401–2.

40. Halleck to Grant, March 30, 1863, Simon, ed., *Grant Papers*, 8:93n.

41. Halleck to Grant, March 30, 1863, ibid., 8:93n.

42. Grant to Frederick Steele, April 11, 1863, ibid., 8:49; Grant to Halleck, April 19, 1863, ibid., 91–92.

43. Grant to Stephen A. Hurlbut, May 5, 1863, ibid., 8:159–60.

44. Cornish, *The Sable Arm,* 144–45; Grant to Lorenzo Thomas, June 16, 1863, Simon, ed., *Grant Papers* 8:328.

45. Grant to Richard Taylor, June 22, 1863, ibid., 400–401 and annotation; Grant to Taylor, July 4, 1863, ibid., 468–69 and annotation. [Grant was unaware of Federal policy on the treatment of black prisoners of war, expressed in General Orders No. 100, issued April 24. Lincoln, perhaps because of this incident, issued an executive order on July 30, promising to retaliate in kind if Confederate officials mistreated black prisoners.] Cornish, *The Sable Arm,* 165–68.

46. Grant to Lincoln, August 23, 1863, Simon, ed., *Grant Papers*, 9:196.

47. Grant to Washburne, August 30, 1863, ibid., 9:217–18; Grant to Rue Hough and others, August 26, 1863, ibid., 9:203.

The author wishes to acknowledge the assistance provided by a research grant from Wofford College. He thanks Richard H. Sewell and Allan G. Bogue for their advice and counsel and John Y. Simon and David L. Wilson for their encouragement.

Richmond's Bread Riot

The women who marched through the streets of Richmond, Virginia, in April 1863 demanded food. Facing them, Confederate President Jefferson Davis was equally adamant: If the protesters did not disperse, they would be shot.

By Alan Pell Crawford

ON THE PLEASANT SPRING MORNING of April 2, 1863, a pretty young woman sat down on a bench at Capitol Square in Richmond, Virginia. Another woman on the bench later recalled that the girl had "delicate features" and "large eyes" and wore a clean, skillfully stitched calico gown that indicated she might have been a dressmaker's apprentice. When the girl reached up to remove her sunbonnet, her sleeve slipped, revealing "the mere skeleton of an arm."

As the two women sat together, several hundred people gathered on the grounds of the Confederate Capitol. The older woman, the wife of a former U.S. congressman who was then serving in the Confederate Army, wondered what was happening. "Is there some celebration?" she asked.

"There is," the girl said with great dignity. "We celebrate our right to live. We are starving. As soon as enough of us get together, we are going to the bakeries and each of us will take a loaf of bread. That is little enough for the government to give us after it has taken all our men."

The girl then made her way to the Capitol, where she disappeared into the crowd and from history. Within minutes, the crowd she had joined became a mob and moved noisily down Ninth Street toward the shops on Main Street. No one is sure of everything that happened during the next few hours, but the so-called Bread Riot resulted in dozens of arrests and numerous convictions, further demoralizing an already suffering city.

That conditions had become so dire in the Confederate capital was somewhat ironic. Ever since agricultural Virginia had been a state, and for many years before that, Richmond had been its commercial, if not industrial, center. Many Richmonders were lawyers, merchants, and tradesmen who tended to be Federalists and then Whigs, and therefore Unionists. Governor John Letcher, who took office in 1860, was a Unionist. Richmonders even organized a failed February 1861 "peace conference" at the Willard Hotel in Washington, D.C., and Virginia did not leave the Union until April 17, 1861, four months after South Carolina seceded and two days after President Abraham Lincoln called for 75,000 volunteers to put down the "insurrection" in the Southern states.

When General Robert E. Lee came to the city to accept command of the state's forces a week after Virginia joined the Confederacy, recruits from all over the South followed. With them, as Virginius Dabney wrote in *Richmond: The Story of a City*, came "adventurers, speculators, gamblers, prostitutes and every other type of person" who gravitates to the center of activity in wartime. After the engagement at First Manassas in July 1861, when Southern troops drove Union General Irvin McDowell's Yankees back to Washington, Richmond's population— 38,000 before the war—doubled, then tripled. It would reach 128,000 in 1864. Food that otherwise would be feeding the city's residents was by then being commandeered by the military. Almost constant warfare on Virginia's once-fertile farmland soon disrupted agricultural production. Before long, the military took over the railroads, further interrupting the transport of goods.

The momentum of early Southern victories at Manassas and at Ball's Bluff could not be sustained. In the late spring of 1862, Federal forces took Yorktown and Williamsburg in the Peninsular Campaign and then advanced to the outskirts of Richmond. There, spirits were sinking— and prices were rising. As soldiers on leave took advantage of the availability of alcohol and prostitutes, clogging the streets and dining in the gambling "hells" that cropped up near Capitol Square, the nature of the once-genteel city changed. Brawls had to be broken up, and in March, the Confederate Congress imposed martial law on Richmond and for an area 10 miles around the city. The new laws suspended habeas corpus, required passports for anyone leaving town, banned liquor sales without a physician's prescription, and ordered the closing of saloons and distilleries, although many continued to operate. The value of Confederate money declined, and corruption ran rampant.

In June 1862, after the Battle of Seven Pines, nearly 5,000 wounded soldiers came into Richmond, further straining the city's meager resources. A month later Lee's Army of Northern Virginia had driven the Federals away from Richmond and back to Washington, and at least 10,000 more bloodied men, plus thousands of Federal prisoners, poured into the city. And with them came still more prostitutes, who took over an entire block near Capitol Square, "promenading up and down the shady walks," Mayor Joseph Mayo complained, "jostling respectable ladies in the gutter." Venereal disease swept through the city. An outbreak of smallpox, from late 1862 to February 1863, contributed to anxieties against which even the staunchest of residents struggled.

At least 10,000 more bloodied men, plus thousands of Federal prisoners, poured into the city.

"We are in a half-starving condition," John B. Jones, a clerk in the Confederate War Department, wrote in his diary. "I lost twenty pounds and my wife and children are emaciated to some extent. Still I hear no murmuring." Rats ran amok. "Epicures sometimes manage to entrap them and secure a nice broil for supper, declaring that their flesh was superior to squirrel meat," reported Phoebe Yates Pember, a diarist who was the chief matron at one of the city's hospitals.

Food speculators, meanwhile, hoarded vast stores of flour, sugar, bacon, and salt, withholding them from market while prices soared. These speculators, President Jefferson Davis declared, were "worse enemies of the Confederacy than if found in arms among the invading forces." Governor Letcher said such profiteering "embraces to a greater or less extent all interests—agricultural, mercantile and professional." Military officials were also said to be hoarding food or, viewed in the most favorable light, making a botch of their commissary duties.

To make matters worse, nearly a foot of snow—rare in Richmond in any quantity—fell on the city in March 1863. Temperatures then rose quickly, melting the snow and turning roads into mud holes. These near-impassable roads made it difficult for farmers who had produce to sell to get their goods into town.

It was late in the month, apparently, that Mary Jackson, a "tall, daring, Amazonian-looking woman" who was married to a local housepainter, began to talk with her hungry neighbors in Oregon Hill about the need for them to take matters into their own hands. Oregon Hill was a working-class neighborhood where laborers from the Tredegar Iron Works, the largest cannon foundry in the South, made their homes.

Word quickly spread, and on the evening of April 1, Jackson and her female cohorts gathered at the nearby Belvidere Hill Baptist Church, where they decided they would demand food from the governor. The following morning, the women, led by Jackson, "who had a white feather standing erect from her hat," and Minerva Meredith, who carried a pistol, trooped over to the governor's office. Governor Letcher listened to their complaints, expressed his sympathy, and asked them to come back later. Then he might be able to help.

Unimpressed with the governor's response, the crowd moved on, gathering strength. Men and boys and more women—some carrying knives, hatchets, and guns—soon joined their ranks and made their way down Capitol Hill toward Main Street and the shops and the government commissary there. One black maid, seeing the rowdy procession, snatched her young charge away, fearing the child might "catch something from them poor white folks."

Governor Letcher ordered the bell rung in Capitol Square to call out the Public Guard (a state security force that protected the Capitol and other government buildings), as Richmond's small police force was no match for the advancing mob. When the rioters reached Main Street—shouting "Bread"—they broke into the commissary, smashed store windows, and grabbed food and anything else they could get their hands on. Some of them loaded their booty into carts and wagons they had seized for the occasion.

"Women were seen bending under loads of sole-leather, or dragging after them heavy cavalry boots, brandishing their huge knives, and swearing, though apparently well fed, that they were dying from starvation—yet it was difficult to imagine how they could masticate or digest the edibles under the weight of which they were bending," an author identifying herself only as "A Richmond Lady," wrote in *Richmond During the War: Four Years of Personal Observation*, published in 1867. "Men carried immense loads of cotton cloth, woolen goods, and other articles [but] few were seen to attack the stores where flour, groceries, and other provisions were kept."

"We do not desire to injure anyone," President Davis told the crowd, "but this lawlessness must stop."

Hurrying to Main Street, Mayor Mayo and Governor Letcher made fruitless appeals to the swelling crowd. When these attempts at persuasion failed, firemen turned their hoses on the mob. That too had little effect. Then the troops from the Public Guard arrived. They marched up Main Street, driving the looters before them, and then halted before a horseless wagon that had been turned sideways, blocking traffic in the street. The troops noticed some of their own wives among the rioters.

As the mayor and governor attempted to restore order, President Davis made his way from the Executive Mansion and through the crowd. The women hissed as he climbed onto a wagon and shouted for the crowd's attention. The president's widow, Varina, later wrote in her memoirs that he reached into his pocket and flung money into the crowd. The president told the mob that rioting was not the way to redress their grievances. Such disorder, Davis explained, would only make matters worse. It would discourage farmers from trying to bring their produce to town, further restricting access to food.

"We do not desire to injure anyone," he told the crowd, "but this lawlessness must stop."

Then, to back up his words, he announced: "I will give you five minutes to disperse, otherwise you will be fired upon."

No one budged. Davis pulled out his pocket watch. He glanced at the troops. Still none of the rioters moved. The commander of the Public Guard, Lieutenant Edward Scott Gay, Jr., ordered his troops to load their weapons and, when five minutes had elapsed, to shoot to kill. Again no one moved. The soldiers prepared their weapons, and Davis—steadying his hand—studied his watch. The seconds ticked away. Finally, the crowd began to disperse. Before long, the president, the mayor, the governor, and the soldiers were alone. The riot had ended.

Some contemporary versions of the peaceful end to the bread riot dif-

fer from Varina Davis's. Included in a series of newspaper articles were accounts that credit Letcher with quashing the riots, while others say Mayor Mayo played the prominent role. Some of the witnesses who gave their accounts to newspaper reporters were not familiar with one or more of the leaders and may have been mistaken when identifying them.

THE RICHMOND CITY COUNCIL met later that day. Members acknowledged that the residents faced hardships, but disputed their severity. Some of the council expressed anger that apparently well-fed residents had stolen dry goods. Some said Richmonders had not taken advantage of existing relief efforts. The council declared the riot to have been "in reality instigated by devilish and selfish motives" and that the city's "honor, dignity and safety" would be maintained, come what may. There was some discussion of requiring anyone who had lived in the city for less than a year to post bond for good behavior, but members dropped the idea.

Eager to contain the damage, President Davis told Secretary of War James A. Seddon to order telegraph operators to send "nothing of the unfortunate disturbance of today over the wires for any purpose," fearing the enemy would use the news to further demoralize the South. Seddon's subordinates also instructed Richmond newspapers to report nothing that would "embarrass our cause and encourage our enemies."

The editors complied. The next day's Richmond *Whig*, for example, reported nothing of the incident but noted that violence, even in response to "artificial wants" caused by "profligate commissaries" and "hoarding speculators," would "not be tolerated." These speculators, contemporary accounts indicate, were often assumed to be Jewish, though Jews had been solid citizens of the city for almost a century. Foreign-born Richmonders also came in for abuse. The *Southern Punch* blamed "the Jew-

Yankee, the Dutch-Yankee, French, Irish—in fact all breeds, who like the wild locust of Egypt, are devouring the substance of the land."

Authorities made as many as 47 arrests—accounts vary—and trials appear to have taken several weeks, during which "young men of the veriest rowdy class" as well as female defendants filled city hall. A woman from Oregon Hill said that Mary Jackson had threatened her if she did not participate in the riot, and a market clerk said Mrs. Jackson warned him before April 2 to stay off the street that day. Anybody who got in her way, she supposedly told the man, would be shot.

The city hospital reported the loss of 310 pounds of beef. One merchant lost more than $13,000 in stolen goods. The defendants' arguments did not impress Mayor Mayo. "Boots are not bread," he argued. "Brooms are not bread, men's hats are not bread, and I never heard of anybody's eating them."

> **President Davis told Secretary of War James A. Seddon to order telegraph operators to send "nothing of the unfortunate disturbance of today over the wires."**

Rioters received sentences of up to five years, but details about the incident have been lost to history. Many court records—including those of the circuit court where the bread-riot defendants were tried—were destroyed two years later, when the Yankees broke the defensive lines at Petersburg and headed toward Richmond. The Confederate government fled the city, and Southern troops, eager to prevent anything of value from falling into enemy hands, put much of the town to the torch—destroying, in the process, four-fifths of the city's remaining food supply.

No one knows exactly what happened to ringleader Mary Jackson. Michael Chesson, in *Richmond After the War*, reports that she refused bail and was held for felony trial, though her fate is "unknown." Richmond judge Douglas Tice, who researched the incident for several years, says felony charges against her were reduced to misdemeanors, but then the trail goes cold.

Richmonders' attention soon turned to new dangers. Shortly after Jefferson Davis urged Southern farmers to plant their fields "not in cotton and tobacco but exclusively in crops to feed man and beast," springtime military engagements resumed. At Chancellorsville in May, Lee's army defeated the Federals, but at great cost. The Army of Northern Virginia suffered more than 10,000 casualties at Chancellorsville, but one death hit the South particularly hard. That was the loss on May 10 of General Thomas J. "Stonewall" Jackson, mistakenly shot by his own troops. Jackson had become a hero not only in Virginia but throughout the Confederacy. Two months later, Lee again took his army north across the Potomac River into Maryland and then Pennsylvania, partly to find crops for his hungry troops. The Confederate defeat at Gettysburg in July, and the almost-simultaneous fall of Vicksburg, Mississippi, killed all rational hope for a Southern victory.

The 1863 Bread Riot had been one of the earlier signs that social stability was breaking down in the South. The riot dramatized how desperate matters had become in Virginia a full two years before General Lee surrendered to Union General Ulysses S. Grant at Appomattox and how unrealistic it was for the ill-prepared South to hope it could triumph in its rebellion.

Alan Pell Crawford is the author of Unwise Passions: A True Story of a Remarkable Woman and the First Great Scandal of Eighteenth-Century America *(Simon & Schuster).*

THE CIVIL WAR'S DEADLIEST WEAPONS WERE NOT RAPID-FIRE GUNS OR GIANT CANNON

BUT THE SIMPLE RIFLE-MUSKET AND THE HUMBLE MINIÉ BALL.

By Allan W. Howey

B<small>Y THE TIME THE SMOKE HAD CLEARED</small> and the veterans headed back to their homes, the American Civil War had exacted a terrible human cost. In four long years of bloody fighting, half a million of the three million men and boys in blue and gray had been wounded in combat. Two hundred thousand others had been killed.

These staggering figures may be less surprising after considering all the macabrely ingenious killing machines taken onto Civil War battlefields—rifled cannon, multi-shot arms, crude machine guns, and repeaters, to name a few. But it was not these spectacular weapons that drew the most blood during the Civil War. Ninety percent of the soldiers killed on the fields of battle owed their fate to a deceptively simple hand-held gun and its companion projectile: the rifle-musket and the minié bullet.

The rifle-musket and minié bullet together changed the face of warfare forever. For the first time in history, infantrymen could aim their weapons at a target a fair distance away and actually have a chance of hitting it. The days of successful frontal assaults by infantry and cavalry were over; defenders armed with the new rifle-musket could fire from a safe place and knock down attacker after attacker before they got close enough to do damage.

All this is quite a bit of notoriety for a humble-looking firearm with few visible characteristics to distinguish it clearly from its 1850s predecessor. But in many ways the Civil War rifle-musket was a brand new weapon that boasted the best features of its predecessors. It also had a more reliable ignition system and, more important, it fired a greatly improved projectile, the minié bullet.

The lineage of the Civil War rifle-musket reaches back to early-17th-century France. About 1610, the muzzleloading, smoothbore flintlock musket was invented as an improvement on the matchlock musket, a similar firearm that depended on a lit match for ignition. As the name muzzleloading, smoothbore flintlock musket suggests, the gun was loaded (with loose gunpowder and a round ball) at the mouth of its barrel. The bore, or inside of the barrel, was smooth; unlike the later rifle-muskets, it contained no spiral rifling grooves to force the projectile to spin evenly and thus travel rapidly in a straight line like a spiraling football. The ignition system featured a hammer—called a cock—that held a small piece of flint. When the shooter pulled the trigger, the cock fell and scraped the flint against a rough piece of metal know as the frizzen pan cover. This showered sparks into loose gunpowder in the frizzen pan, which then ignited the main powder charge inside the barrel, behind the projectile. The British army beat the French army to the punch and officially adopted the weapon in 1682. It eventually became the standard infantry firearm of Europe and America and remained so until the muzzle loading rifle-musket replace it in the 1850s.

What made the smoothbore flintlock musket so dominant an infantry weapon for so long was that it was easy to load; an experienced soldier could load and fire up to four times a minute, a rapid rate of fire for the time. Since the gun's barrel was not rifled—it had no grooves that a bullet needed to fit snugly against—the projectile could be cast slightly smaller than the bore diameter. That allowed the ball to fall to the bottom of the upturned barrel with little resistance. To load the weapon, a soldier pulled a paper cartridge containing both powder and ball from his cartridge box and tore off the powder end with his teeth. He primed the flintlock by pouring some of the loose gunpowder from the cartridge into the frizzen pan and closed the pan cover to keep the priming charge in place and dry. Next, he poured the remaining powder down the barrel and rammed the ball down on top of the powder down with a metal ramrod. Finally, he stuffed the empty cartridge paper down the barrel to serve as a plug, a stopper strong enough to keep the ball from rolling out by the force of gravity, but weak enough not to obstruct the travel of a fired ball.

The ease of loading the smoothbore musket allowed soldiers to fire quickly, but the shots were not likely to hit their targets. Accuracy and range were not the weapon's strengths. In fact, firing one of these guns would be similar to shooting a marble from a modern shotgun. The weapon did not even have a rear sight for precise aiming because aiming was a fruitless effort. The statistics boil down to this: at 40 yards, the flintlock smoothbore could usually hit a target measuring 1 square foot, but at 300 yards, only 1 shot in 20 would hit a target of 18 square feet. As Colonel George Hanger, a British officer who fought in the American Revolution, wrote in 1814:

> *A soldier's musket if not exceedingly ill-bored (as many are), will strike the figure of a man at 80 yards, perhaps even at 100; but a soldier must be very unfortunate indeed who shall be wounded by a common musket at 150 yards, providing his antagonist aims at him; and as for firing at a man at 200 yards with a common musket, you might just as well fire at the moon and have the same hope of hitting your object. I do maintain and will prove, whenever called on, that no man was ever killed at 200 yards by a common soldier's musket by the person who aimed at him.*

The chance of firing a smoothbore musket and hitting something beyond rock-throwing range was slim, but there *was* an alternative weapon: the rifle. The venerable Kentucky flintlock rifle, for example, the weapon favored by frontiersmen and by sharpshooters in the American Revolution, was extremely accurate at long ranges. Common practice targets were the head of a tack at 20 yards, the head of a turkey at 100 yards, and the body of a turkey at 200 yards—challenging targets even for today's sharpshooters with modern rifles and telescopic sights. At 400 yards, an American soldier with a Kentucky rifle could easily hit a target as large as a horse, a fact that made British cavalrymen very uneasy.

The problem with the rifle of the time was that loading it was a difficult and slow process. Because the ammunition had to fit inside the barrel tightly in order to fit in the spiral rifling grooves, soldiers had a tough job forcing it down from the muzzle, especially under combat conditions, when repeated firing quickly filled the grooves with the residue of burnt powder. Before long, the rifleman literally had to pound the tight-fitting bullet down the barrel. As a result, the rifle's rate of fire was only one-third of the smoothbore's, making the gun impractical for general military use. Soldiers were better off firing three or four shots a minute in the general direction of an approaching enemy unit than firing once a minute with pinpoint accuracy at individual targets.

What the infantryman needed was a firearm that combined the best of the smoothbore flintlock musket with that of the rifle—a gun that was easy to load *and* could hit a small target at 200 yards. That gun was the muzzleloading rifle-musket, and with it came the improved bullet that made it possible. Known to common soldiers as the minié ball (which they pronounced "minnie ball"), the conical bullet could be loaded quickly and easily down a rifle's muzzle and still fit the barrel's rifling grooves tightly when fired. But before all this came to bear, inventors and sportsmen were working to perfect a new ignition system. In 1807, the Reverend Alexander Forsyth, a Presbyterian minister from Belhelvie, Scotland, patented a new, more reliable ignition system than the flintlock system. Rather than have a shower of sparks ignite loose gunpowder, Forsyth employed a flat-nosed hammer to strike powdered fulminate of mercury, which detonated on contact, setting off the main charge of gunpowder inside the barrel. In 1814, Joshua Shaw of Philadelphia improved on Forsyth's system by packing the fulminate inside a small iron cap and placing it on a hollow nipple fixed to the gun barrel, and in 1816, he replaced the iron with copper. The copper percussion cap was easy to use and virtually impervious to water, and wind.

European and American armies embraced the new percussion, or caplock, system because of its reliability. The British army adopted it in 1834 after comparing the results of 6,000 test rounds fired from flintlock and percussion firearms. The flintlocks misfired 922 times (15 percent of the time), while only 36 (0.6 percent) of the percussion weapons misfired. The U.S. Army followed the British lead and adopted the percussion system in 1841. The following year, American armories began building smoothbore percussion muskets and converting older flintlocks to percussion weapons. Progress was slow, however, and the vast majority of American soldiers carried flintlocks in the Mexican War of 1846 to 1848. Even 13 years later, at the beginning of the Civil War, Union and Confederate authorities issued smoothbore flintlock muskets to thousands of unlucky soldiers.

The percussion ignition system made infantry weapons fire more reliably, but there remained the challenge of coupling easy loading with long range and accuracy. And it was here that the minié bullet entered the scene. Developed over a generation, its final design was the fruit of independent work by men from Great Britain, France, and the United States.

Great Britain took the lead. As early as 1818, Captain John Norton of the British 34th Infantry began experimenting with bullet design. Norton shaped the nose of his new bullet like a cone with a rounded point and made its cylindrical base hollow. The hollow base was the bullet's definitive feature. It allowed the bullet to be cast a bit narrower than the bore's diameter to allow easy loading, since when the gun was fired, the pressure expanded the base to fit the barrel's rifling grooves tightly. The inspiration for the bullet came to Norton while he was stationed in India and observed natives using blowpipes as weapons. He discovered that the base of the blowpipe arrow was made of elastic locus pith. When the natives blew, the pith expanded to form an airtight seal against the pipe's inner walls. It seemed a small jump from there to making a bullet with a base that would expand from the pressure of firing.

In 1836, a London gunsmith named William Greener found a way to improve Norton's design for expansion of the bullet base. He inserted into the hollow area a wooden plug that would push forward when the gun was fired and force the bullet's base outward. The result was that the bullet fit more uniformly inside the barrel, producing more reliable and accurate fire.

Norton's bullet with Greener's refinement eventually came before the British army for approval for use in the field, but the army's old-school officers rejected it. It was an overly conservative decision that squandered the opportunity to develop this innovative design into a truly remarkable weapon.

Several years after Norton had begun developing his hollow-base bullet, French weapons experts began working on a similar design. Eventually, three French army officers would share the credit for what would become the minié bullet: Captain Henri-

Gustave Delvigne, Colonel Louis-Etienne de Thouvenin, and Captain Claude-Etienne Minié.

Delvigne led the way when he designed a muzzleloading rifle to fire a new type of bullet. In 1826, Delvigne built a unique rifle barrel with an independent gunpowder chamber at its breech. This chamber was separated from the rest of the barrel by a strong lip, beyond which the powder could pass, but not the bullet. In the earliest models, after the chamber was filled with gunpowder, Delvigne rammed a standard soft, round lead ball down the barrel and pounded it against the lip with the ramrod until it flattened just enough to grip the rifling grooves. He soon discovered, however, that the pounding disfigured the ball and greatly reduced its accuracy, so he designed an elongated, cylindrical bullet with a flat base that would expand more evenly under the ramrod blows. In 1840, Delvigne even received a patent for an *explosive* bullet of this general design. (Imagine pounding *that* down a rifle barrel!) In time, Delvigne's design proved unsuitable for general military use; the powder chamber quickly became clogged, and the bullet still ended up too deformed for accurate flight.

RIFLE BULLETS, PRIMARILY THE MINIÉ BALL, CAUSED NINETY PERCENT OF ALL THESE CASUALTIES.

In 1828, Thouvenin modified and improved upon Delvigne's gun design. He replaced the lip and powder chamber inside the barrel with a hard metal post that screwed into the gun's breech. After loading, the flat base of the elongated, cylindrical lead bullet rested upon the post in a position to be easily and uniformly forced into the rifling grooves when compressed by the ramrod. The Thouvenin design was a moderate improvement over Delvigne's, and the French army selected it for trials in 1846. The gun and bullet combination was still not practical for widespread military use; the rifle breech was very difficult to clean, and the metal post was prone to breaking.

Delvigne's developments inspired Minié, who had served with the French Chasseurs in several African campaigns, to do further work toward making an efficient, effective bullet. In 1849, he came up with one that more closely resembled Norton's than Delvigne's. Like Norton's bullet, Minié's had a hollow cylindrical base and a rounded conical nose. Minié also incorporated a plug in the bullet's hollow base to assist expansion, just as Greener had done to Norton's design. Instead of a wooden plug, however, Minié used an iron cup, which in effect served the same purpose as Thouvenin's metal post. The explosion of the gunpowder would drive the iron cup forward and expand the bullet's base to fit the rifling grooves snugly.

By this point in the story, it should not be surprising to learn that the French army never adopted the new bullet. It took the British army to use it in their new 1851 Enfield rifles, paying Minié 20,000 pounds for his patent. The army also had to pay Greener 1,000 pounds, after he won a patent infringement lawsuit over the bullet's plug design. The bullet as it would be used by the soldiers in blue and gray was now virtually complete. It

had also acquired the name that stuck among English-speaking troops—minnie ball, even though the captain's French surname was properly pronounced *min*-YAY and his innovation was not a ball but a cone-shaped bullet.

In the early 1850s, James H. Burton, a master armorer at the U.S. arsenal at Harpers Ferry, Virginia, gave the minié bullet the form it would take into the Civil War. By lengthening the bullet slightly and thinning the walls of its hollow base, Burton was able to dispense with the iron plug. The base of the improved bullet expanded just as well as Minié's but was much easier and cheaper to mass-produce. By the mid-1850s, the fully evolved minié bullet made it possible to build an infantry weapon as easy to load as the old smoothbore musket but with the accuracy and range of a rifle. The term rifle-musket reflected the weapon's lethal combination of attributes.

U.S. Secretary of War Jefferson Davis, future president of the Confederacy, adopted the rifle-musket and minié bullet for the U.S. Army in 1855. An improved version of the rifle-musket—the 1861 model built by the federal armory in Springfield, Massachusetts—became the principal infantry weapon of Northern soldiers in the Civil War.

Hundreds of thousands of Union troops carried the 1861 Springfield onto the battlefields of the Civil War, and untold numbers of Confederates captured the weapon and used it themselves. Between 1861 and 1865, the Springfield armory manufactured nearly 800,000 of the guns; private contractors built 880,000 more; and slightly modified 1863 and 1864 models accounted for an additional 500,000. That put the total number of minié-bullet-firing Springfield rifle-muskets at more than 2 million.

The Springfield rifle-musket was a .58-caliber percussion weapon that weighed nearly 10 pounds and cost about $15. It was 58 inches long with a 40-inch barrel, and came with an 18-inch bayonet. On the negative side, bullets exited the Springfield's barrel at the relatively slow speed of only 950 feet per second (about the same as a modern .22-caliber rifle), but the gun's deadly accuracy at long ranges outweighed that shortcoming. Armed with a Springfield, a competent shooter could hit a 27-inch bull's-eye at 500 yards, the best performance to date for a standard-issue infantry weapon. A trained marksman could consistently hit a 4-inch target at 200 yards and a 6-by-6-foot target at 500 yards. At 1,000 yards, he could even hit an 8-by-8-foot target half of the time. That did not mean that the average Civil War soldier could hit anything at the more extreme distances, but improving the old smoothbore's 75 yard range by 125 yards dramatically increased the effectiveness of even the most inept infantryman.

On the Confederate side, the Enfield rifle-musket was perhaps the most common of a wide assortment of firearms. It was widely considered to be the equal of the Springfield. The Confederacy purchased about 400,000 of these 1853 model .577-caliber weapons from private manufacturers in England. (The Union imported a similar number for its troops.)

Studies done by weapons analysts from the U.S. Department of Defense 100 years after the Civil War proved that the rifle-musket was three times more deadly than the most lethal infantry weapon to that point in history. Taking into account factors such as range, accuracy, rate of fire, and battlefield mobility, the researchers awarded the rifle-musket a "lethality index" of 154. Its next closest competitor was the smoothbore flintlock musket, with an index of 47. That was followed by the flintlock rifle, with an index of only 36.

The deadly effectiveness of the rifle-musket loaded with a minié bullet was largely to blame for the Civil War's appalling casualty rates. During the nearly 10,500 skirmishes and battles of the war, more than 110,000 Union soldiers and 94,000 Confederates were killed, and an additional 275,000 and 194,000, respectively, were wounded. Rifle bullets, primarily the minié bullet, caused 90 percent of all these casualties. Artillery projectiles accounted for less than 9 percent, and swords and bayonets, less than 1 percent. Considering all this evidence, it is no exaggeration to conclude that the rifle-musket and minié bullet greatly affected the overall course of the Civil War and foreshadowed 20th-century warfare.

The rifle-musket and minié bullet revolutionized warfare by drastically altering the tactical balance between an attacking army and a defending one. Frontal assaults by infantry on a waiting enemy suddenly became suicidal. During the Napoleonic era, attacking infantry could safely approach to within 100 yards of an enemy line with little danger of being shot down. During the Civil War, however, because of the rifle-musket's accuracy at long ranges, stationary defenders could load and fire quickly *and* hit their attackers. Since advancing infantrymen could not easily stop to take aim in return, their losses were much heavier than the defenders'.

The combination of the rifle-musket and minié bullet also made the bayonet nearly obsolete. In earlier years, the bayonet was often the most decisive infantry assault weapon, because the smoothbore flintlock musket's short range allowed attackers to approach close enough for hand-to-hand fighting. In the Civil War, however, firepower almost always decided an assault's outcome before charging troops came within stabbing distance. In fact, very few Civil War surgeons reported bayonet wounds. During Lieutenant General Ulysses S. Grant's bloody campaign against Confederate General Robert E. Lee in the summer of 1864, for example, Union medical directors recorded only 37 bayonet wounds. Of the several hundred thousand wounded men treated in Union hospitals over the course of the war, surgeons noted only 922 bayonet wounds!

As they had done to the bayonet, the rifle-musket and minié bullet also reduced the effectiveness of field artillery. In the early 1800s, Napoleon often placed the artillery forward in his battle lines, even during advances, to provide direct fire in support of the infantry. During the Civil War, however, it was too easy to shoot down an exposed cannon crew operating in the front lines. The artillery was forced to seek protection in the rear, a position from which it was more difficult to hit enemy targets without endangering friendly troops in the front.

The cavalry was similarly ousted from its former role by the rifle-musket and minié ball. Napoleon often used his cavalry as a surprise offensive weapon, sending his horsemen on charges to trample infantrymen armed with smoothbore flintlock muskets. But the Civil War soldier armed with a rifle-musket and minié bullets could hit a man at 100 to 200 yards; a horse and rider made an even more inviting target. Consequently, the colorful cavalry charges of the Napoleonic era became all but obsolete. In fact, as the war continued, more and more cavalrymen fought as mounted infantry, using their horses for mobility and then dismounting to fight on foot. In effect, they became the forebears of today's mechanized infantry.

Unfortunately, it took most Civil War generals too long to realize that some critical tactics they had learned at West Point or from military manuals were obsolete, particularly the frontal assault. Generals on both sides continued to send their men on these suicidal attacks. In Pickett's Charge alone, almost 6,000 Rebels were killed or wounded as they advanced uphill over a mile of open ground toward entrenched Union positions at Gettysburg. The equations and formulas of warfare had been changed completely, mostly by a simple firearm and bullet: the rifle-musket and minié ball.

ALLAN W. HOWEY, *the director of the Air University Press at Maxwell Air Force Base in Alabama, has taught Civil War military history at the Air Force Academy and other military colleges.*

Almost 5,000 soldiers were killed or mortally wounded in the Battle of Antietam, the bloodiest single day of fighting in the whole war. Ninety percent of all Civil War soldiers who died in combat were killed by minié bullets fired from rifle-muskets. The minie bullet has a metal plug in its base that may have been a gun-barrel cleaner. Inserted randomly in bullets—one per cartridge pack—the soft zinc plugs scraped powder residue out of the rifling grooves as the bullet shot out of the barrel.

Library of Congress

A **Bold** Break for Freedom

Robert Smalls Made a Daring Escape from Slavery During the Civil War. His Real Battle, However, Came When He Tried to Preserve the Freedom He Had Won.

by Mark H. Dunkelman

The plot to steal the Confederate steamship *Planter* started with a joke. One spring day in 1862, Captain C.J. Relyea and the ship's other officers went ashore at their home port of Charleston, South Carolina, leaving the *Planter* in the hands of her African-American crewmen. With the white men gone, 23-year-old wheelman Robert Smalls amused his fellow slaves by trying on Relyea's distinctive broad-brimmed straw hat. The crew kidded Smalls about his resemblance to Relyea—both men were short and stocky—and suggested that from a distance it would be impossible to distinguish between the black slave and the white captain. Smalls cut short the ensuing laughter with a warning not to repeat the joke. He had an idea.

Later, at a secret meeting in Smalls' tiny East Bay Street room, he revealed his plan. On a night when the *Planter*'s officers were ashore, the crew would take the ship from her mooring, pick up family members hidden aboard another vessel nearby, and sail to the safety of the Union blockading fleet outside the harbor. Smalls would disguise himself as the captain and duplicate Relyea's usual routine so as not to arouse suspicion when the *Planter* steamed past the watchful sentries at Charleston's Confederate forts and batteries.

Smalls was up to the perilous task. Although he was referred to as the *Planter*'s wheelman, Smalls was in fact the ship's pilot in all but name—the title being reserved exclusively for white

men. He had been sailing aboard the *Planter* since before the Civil War began. Built in Charleston in 1860, the 300-ton, two-engine sidewheeler was about 150 feet long and could carry 1,400 bales of cotton or 1,000 troops. She was armed with a 32-pound pivot gun on her foredeck and a 24-pound howitzer on her afterdeck. Guided by Smalls, the *Planter* had navigated the harbor, rivers, and coast, making surveys, laying torpedoes, and delivering men and matériel to fortifications. Smalls knew the signals Relyea used to pass Confederate military installations, and the location of deadly underwater mines. He needed no supervision from a white man to sail the *Planter* safely.

ROBERT SMALLS WAS BORN on April 5, 1839, in the slave quarters of the home of his master, John McKee, on Prince Street in Beaufort, South Carolina. Smalls' descendants have claimed that McKee was Robert's father, but even white paternity would have made no difference for the newborn boy. Roberts mother, Lydia, was McKee's slave, and so her son was also a slave.

By slavery's standards, though, Robert led a pampered life. Lydia was one of McKees "Swonga people," as house servants were called in the Gullah dialect spoken by the local black population. Robert consequently grew up in the McKee household instead of toiling in the master's rice fields, and he enjoyed considerable independence. His mother had

spent her childhood as a field hand on the McKee's rice plantation, and she made Robert aware of his advantages—and that his situation could change instantly. She forced him to watch slaves being whipped and sold at auction, told him stories of their sufferings, and made him identify with less-fortunate blacks.

When McKee died in 1848, his son Henry inherited Lydia and Robert. In 1851, Henry hired Robert out in Charleston, and the 12-year-old moved to the city, where he waited tables and worked as a lamplighter. The boy, however, was drawn to the bustling waterfront, where he found work as a stevedore, a teamster, and a sailmaker and rigger. During the summers Smalls sailed aboard a coastal schooner, developing skills as a boat handler and navigator. He took control of his financial affairs by arranging to hire himself out and pay Henry McKee $15 per month. After his 1856 marriage to Hannah Jones, a hotel maid 14 years his senior, Smalls bought her time from her master for $7 a month. When the couple had daughter Elizabeth, he arranged to purchase Hannah and the baby for $800. He was still saving toward that end when he hatched his plan to escape with his family from slavery aboard the *Planter*.

ON AN APRIL SUNDAY Smalls reassembled the plotters at another clandestine meeting in his room to detail his plan. Then they waited for the right circumstances to spring the plot. The opportunity finally arrived on the evening of

May 12, 1862, when Captain Relyea ordered Smalls to ready the *Planter* for an early morning departure to deliver guns and ammunition to a battery. Smalls acknowledged the order and betrayed no excitement when Relyea and his white mate and chief engineer went ashore to spend the night—in violation of standing orders—leaving Smalls and eight black crewmen aboard the ship.

With the whites gone, Smalls notified his shipmates that the time had come. Presumably, one of the men assembled the women and children at their hiding place, a merchant ship berthed in the Cooper River. Meanwhile, Smalls and his crew waited and listened as a crier ashore called out the passing hours. At about 3:00 A.M. on May 13, Smalls donned the absent captain's coat and straw hat and ordered the crew to fire the boilers. Crewmembers hoisted the Confederate and South Carolina flags, cast off the hawsers mooring the ship to the wharf, sounded the required departure signal, and slowly backed the *Planter* away from the dock. A Confederate sentry, barely 50 yards away, paid the *Planter* no heed.

Imitating Relyea's gait and posture, Smalls ordered his crew to proceed to the North Atlantic Wharf in the Cooper River, where he made a brief stop to pick up his passengers—five women and three children. Among them were Smalls' wife and his children, four-year-old Elizabeth and newborn Robert, Jr. With everyone safely aboard, Smalls blew the steam whistle, eased into the inner channel, patiently kept the ship at her regular pace, and, as Confederate guards idly watched, sailed away from Charleston and slavery.

However, Confederate artillery of the harbor defenses still offered a threat. Fighting an impulse to hurry the pace, Smalls gave the traditional whistle salute as he passed Fort Johnson on James Island. Then he and his crew peered apprehensively as they approached their next obstacle—Fort Sumter, the brick pentagon looming 40 feet above the water on a man-made island, famous as the site where the war began. Situated near the center of the channel between Morris and Sullivan's Islands, Sumter com-

manded all entrances and exits from Charleston Harbor.

As the *Planter* labored against the incoming tide and daybreak began lighting the eastern horizon, some of the crew pleaded with their leader to alter course and make a run for it. Smalls refused and reportedly prayed to God to deliver the ship as He had delivered the Israelites from the Egyptians. Then, as the *Planter* passed beneath Sumter's walls, Smalls stood in the shadows of the pilothouse, his face shielded by Captain Relyea's hat, and gave two long and one short yanks on the whistle cord and waved to the sentinel atop the ramparts. A suspense-laden moment passed before the guard shouted, "Pass the *Planter!*" Completely fooled by Smalls' masquerade, the Confederate added, "Blow the damned Yankees to hell, or bring one of them in!" "Aye, aye," Smalls called back, and he put his ship to sea.

Now a new danger loomed. Ahead lay the Union fleet, and the Yankee sailors naturally thought that the Confederate steamer approaching at full throttle was either attacking or attempting to run the blockade. Aboard the USS *Onward*, Lieutenant J.F. Nickels hurriedly ordered his men to their duty stations and prepared to fire a broadside at the interloper headed in his direction. Aboard the *Planter*, Smalls ordered a white bedsheet run up the foremast. The Union lookouts saw the surrender signal, and Nickels allowed the *Planter* to come alongside. Quickly boarding her, the lieutenant and his men were astonished to discover Smalls and his all-black crew and passengers. "I thought the *Planter* might be of some use to Uncle Abe," Smalls reportedly said to the Union tars, and he formally surrendered the ship.

News spread quickly of the abduction of the *Planter* and of the brave slave who had masterminded the theft. Confederate newspapers bemoaned the incident and expressed indignation at the negligence of Relyea and his officers. Northern papers praised the bold act. *Harper's Weekly* printed a woodcut of the *Planter* and proclaimed the theft of the ship "one of the most daring and heroic adventures since the war commenced." In his *Naval History of the Civil War*, Union Admiral David Dixon later wrote, "The taking out

of the 'Planter' would have done credit to anyone, but the cleverness with which the whole affair was conducted deserves more than a passing notice."

The black hero was sent to Washington for audiences with President Abraham Lincoln and Secretary of War Edwin M. Stanton. Asked by the president why he had stolen the ship, Smalls gave a succinct answer: "Freedom."

With the shackles of bondage broken, Smalls grasped opportunity after opportunity as they arose. When President Lincoln signed a bill awarding the *Planter*'s black crew a monetary reward for their deed, Smalls, as the leader, received the largest amount, $1,500. At a tax auction in Beaufort in 1863, the former slave used part of the payment to purchase his birthplace, the Prince Street property of his former master. For the rest of the war, Smalls piloted vessels for the Union forces. He was aboard the ironclad *Keokuk* during the naval attack on Charleston on April 7, 1863, when the ship was hit 90 times. Smalls steered the crippled vessel out of range of the Confederate guns to a position off Morris Island, where she finally sank.

Most often, he piloted his old ship. On December 1, 1863, the *Planter* was carrying rations to Union forces when she came under crossfire from Union and Confederate artillery. The white captain panicked, ordered the ship beached and rushed below to hide. Smalls refused to obey the order and guided the *Planter* to safety. The cowardly captain was dismissed from the service; Smalls was appointed in his place.

For more than a year after the end of the war, Smalls worked aboard the *Planter* for the government. In September 1866, he made his last voyage in his beloved ship, sailing her to Baltimore, where she was decommissioned and Smalls was laid off.

WITH ONE WAR OVER, Smalls plunged into another one, a political struggle to preserve the freedom he had won aboard the *Planter*. South Carolina's blacks outnumbered whites by some 400,000 to 275,000, and most of the African-American population was concentrated in the coastal Low Country, where they made up more than 80 percent of the population. Robert Smalls was their hero, and they never tired of hearing his story of the *Planter*—and Smalls never tired of telling it. He proved to be an adept politician. He founded his own newspaper to promote his cause and organized a brass band to attract crowds to rallies and torchlight parades. And he literally spoke the language of the black population—Gullah. He was the "King of Beaufort County," according to the *Charleston News and Courier*.

Smalls disregarded politics in the immediate postwar period, concentrating instead on business ventures and the accumulation of large amounts of property. Political power was beyond the grasp of even a famous black war hero. Pardoned Confederate military and civil officers gained control of South Carolina's government, ratified a constitution, and enacted legislative "Black Codes" denying blacks social and political equality. But the Radical Republican triumph in the congressional elections of 1866 spelled doom for repressive white regimes in the former Confederate states. The new Congress passed Reconstruction acts establishing military rule in the South and stipulated that no state would be readmitted to the Union until it passed a new state constitution guaranteeing universal male suffrage and ratified the Fourteenth Amendment, which granted black men citizenship and voting rights. Here was an opportunity, and Robert Smalls grasped it.

Smalls was elected a delegate to the 1868 state constitutional convention, which drafted a document guaranteeing black suffrage. In subsequent elections the constitution was overwhelmingly endorsed despite the bitter opposition of reactionary whites. Smalls won a seat in the South Carolina House of Representatives on a Republican ticket that gained huge majorities in both houses, even with widespread intimidation and violence against black voters. South Carolina ratified the Fourteenth Amendment and was readmitted to the Union on July 9, 1868.

After spending time in the state senate, Smalls was elected to the United States House of Representatives in the 1874 election. His four South Carolina congressional colleagues were Republicans, but for the first time in 18 years, Democrats—among them a large number of Confederate veterans—held the majority in the House. Radical Republican influence was fading, a victim of corrupt Southern state administrations and a decline in support from Northerners. The stage was set for the climax of Reconstruction—and of Robert Smalls' political career.

As the election of 1876 approached, whites in South Carolina banded together in rifle and saber clubs, ostensible social organizations whose real purpose was the armed intimidation of blacks. By the summer of 1876, almost 300 such clubs numbered 14,000 members. Their uniform—a red shirt—gave a name to their white supremacist movement. Their politics made them diehard supporters of the Democrats, who in August nominated a slate of state officials composed entirely of Confederate veterans, headed by former general Wade Hampton for governor. The Republicans—at a convention chaired by Smalls—countered with the incumbent Daniel H. Chamberlain. The carpetbagger Chamberlain had been implicated in frauds over the years, but after winning the governorship as a reform candidate he proved to be hard-working and honest.

The campaign was marred by violence and threats—perpetrated by both sides. Whites terrorized blacks, Smalls reported, "by riding armed through the country, by day and night; by firing into the houses of republicans; by breaking up republican mass-meetings; ...by discharging employes [sic] who refuse to promise to vote the democratic ticket, etc." Smalls himself had a close call at a campaign stop in Edgefield on August 12, when a mob of howling Red Shirts prevented him from speaking and chased him to the safety of his railroad car, shouting, "Kill the damn son of a bitch! Kill the nigger!"

Hampton won the governorship in a disputed contest, and the Democrats gained control of the state government. Nationally, the compromise that settled the disputed Tilden-Hayes presidential election ended Reconstruction, and four million African Americans were abandoned to the mercies of white supremacy and Jim Crow. Smalls was reelected to Congress but was arrested before he left for Washington, D.C. The charge was that, while a state senator, he had accepted a $5,000 bribe to steer state contracts to Josephus Woodruff, the clerk of the senate, who was also president of a printing company. Smalls denied the charge. Democrats hoped to link Smalls to Republican corruption, to deflect attention from their own misdeeds, and to defame Smalls and delay him from taking his congressional seat while his Democratic opponent contested the election.

The principal witness against Smalls was Woodruff, who had stolen $250,000 in state funds and fled to Pennsylvania, from where he was extradited and granted immunity in exchange for his testimony against Smalls. Despite a weak case built on the testimony of an unreliable witness, Smalls was convicted and sentenced to three years in prison. Nevertheless, in a deal worked out between the state attorney general and the U.S. district attorney, the state dismissed the charges against Smalls while the federal government dropped charges against South Carolinians accused of violating election laws. Smalls, who was appealing the case, was unaware that such a deal was in the works. In the end, Democratic governor William Simpson granted Smalls a full pardon.

Smalls' political career never fully recovered from the taint of the conviction. He was elected to two more terms in Congress, but was also twice defeated and failed several times to win renomination. All the while, the white supremacists in control of the Democratic Party tightened their hold on South Carolina. "In South Carolina there is neither a free ballot nor an honest count," Smalls declared in 1890, "and since the election in 1874 the history of elections in the State is a history of a continued series of murders, outrages, perjury and fraud." In 1895 Smalls was one of only six black delegates to South Carolina's constitutional convention; 154 whites attended. In his last important political act, Smalls spoke passionately but in vain against the suffrage provisions of the new constitution, which effectively disenfranchised blacks. "My race needs no special defense," he declared, "for the past history of them in this country proves them to be the equal of any people anywhere. All they need is an equal chance in the battle of life."

TIME TRAVELER
Beaufort, South Carolina

Antebellum Beaufort was "the most cultured town of its size in America," according to a local historian. It was a time of "fabulous parties, beautiful women, ornamented coaches, fine wines and bourbon, hunting, fishing, boat racing, long cigars, duels, discussions of the cotton market, political talk, all too often, heated political talk." Until Yankee cannon brought their world crashing down, Beaufort's elite fully expected their high life would last forever.

Beaufort began as a colonial seaport in 1712 but suffered hard times when the indigo market collapsed after the Revolutionary War. Local planters sought salvation in the cultivation of long-fibered sea cotton, a commodity coveted by French and English mills. In 1860, prices were as high as any in living memory, and the crop of 1861 was the best in a decade.

Gullah slaves made it all possible. The Gullah (probably a corruption of Angola) were imported through Charleston in great numbers in the late 1700s. Isolated on remote island plantations, the Gullah retained a rich and cohesive culture despite 150 years of servitude.

Given land and freedom by the Union victors and educated by Quaker schoolmarms, the Gullah survived the chaos of Reconstruction and the whittling away of their rights during the Jim Crow era of the 1890s. The white genteel mindset survived too. Postwar political transitions were painful, but there were no race riots in Beaufort, and no Ku Klux Klan.

Beaufort's sudden capture by the Union fleet in November 1861 assured the survival of much of its antebellum architecture. In 1976 the Department of the Interior proclaimed much of the town a National Historic Preservation District. Robert Smalls' home at 511 Prince Street is a painstakingly restored private residence, but closed to the public. Smalls was buried at the Tabernacle Baptist Church at 911 Craven Street. A bronze bust in the churchyard commemorates his wartime bravery and lifetime of public service. You can contact the Greater Beaufort Chamber of Commerce and Beaufort Visitors Center at P.O. Box 910, 1106 Carteret Street, Beaufort, SC 29901, (843) 524-3163.

The Penn Center on nearby St. Helena Island, which helps preserve Gullah culture, contains a museum, archives, and an extensive photo collection. Call (803) 838-2432 for more information.
—Roger Pinckney

On the convention's final day each delegate was expected to sign the new constitution. Smalls refused, and when delegates then proposed to cut his travel expenses, he said he would rather walk home than endorse the document.

The 51-year-old war hero was appointed collector of customs at Beaufort by President Benjamin Harrison in 1890 and was repeatedly reappointed by succeeding Republican presidents. His political power had waned, but he continued to support the Grand Old Party—"the party of Lincoln which unshackled the necks of four millions human beings"—even after it acquiesced in the disenfranchisement and segregation of southern blacks. After his removal as customs collector following the 1912 election of Democrat Woodrow Wilson, Smalls spent much of his time in a rocking chair on his front porch, suffering from ill health. Part of his routine was lunch at a neighborhood drugstore, where he was the only black served. Smalls died on February 23, 1915. For a half-century, he had been the foremost African American in his native state and a champion of the political, social, and economic improvement of black South Carolinians.

Mark H. Dunkelman is the author of Gettysburg's Unknown Soldier: The Life, Death, and Celebrity of Amos Humiston *(Praeger, 1999).*

A Gallant Rush for Glory

For the men of the 54th Massachusetts, the assault on a Confederate fort outside Charleston was much more than just another battle. It was their chance to show the world that black troops could fight—and die—for the Union.

by William C. Kashatus

BEFORE UNION FORCES could capture Charleston, South Carolina, they first had to take Fort Wagner, a Confederate stronghold guarding the harbor's entrance. So shortly after 6:30 p.m. on July 18, 1863, Union Colonel Robert Gould Shaw readied 600 men of the 54th Massachusetts Regiment for an assault on the fort. Shaw, the 25-year-old son of Boston abolitionists, was white, as were all his officers. The regiment's men were black.

The 54 would spearhead a three-pronged attack aimed at capturing the necklace of heavily fortified islands that dotted Charleston harbor. If they could take Fort Wagner, the Federals would launch a major assault on nearby Fort Sumter. From there, it would only be a matter of time before Charleston fell. But capturing Fort Wagner would be no easy task.

At first glance, the fort appeared to be little more than a series of irregular, low sand hills. In fact, it was much more formidable than that. A timber and sandbag foundation beneath the sand-covered hills allowed the structure to absorb artillery fire without any significant damage. The fort had 11 heavy guns mounted in fixed positions behind the parapets, while smaller wheeled cannon could be quickly repositioned where needed. Defending it were 1,300 men from the 51st and 31st North Carolina Regiments as well as several companies of South Carolina artillerymen.

Fort Wagner sat in the middle of Morris Island's northern sandy peninsula. Four batteries at the island's northern tip

guarded the entrance to Charleston harbor. The largest of these batteries was Battery Gregg, whose guns faced the ocean and covered the harbor mouth. South of the batteries, a deep moat with a sluice gate and three guns bounded Fort Wagner along its northern sea face. To the east lay the Atlantic Ocean, and on its western boundary were the impassable marshes of Vincent's Creek. On its southern side the fort had guns and mortars for direct and flanking fire on any advancing troops. The only possible assault approach was east of the fort, along a slim stretch of sand, narrow even at low tide. Shaw and his troops would have to launch their attack on the seemingly impregnable fort from there.

Colonel Shaw readied his men on the beach. Tightly wedged together, elbow to elbow, the soldiers of the 54th began their gallant rush, determined to disprove the popular belief among whites that Negroes were an inferior race, lacking the courage and intelligence of combat-ready soldiers.

THE ONSET OF THE Civil War set off a rush by free black men to enlist in the U.S. military, but a 1792 law barred "persons of color from serving in the militia." Also, strong opposition in the North as well as a widespread prejudice that blacks were intellectually and socially inferior limited their involvement in the war to driving supply wagons, burying the battle dead, and building railroads.

USAMHI

Shaw came from a prominent New England anti-slavery family, but he was initially hesitant about accepting command of the 54th. Once in command of the black regiment, he encountered considerable scorn from other white officers.

Yet public opinion slowly began changing. Northern morale faltered after Union forces suffered a series of military defeats, and fewer white men were willing to join the army. Pressured by this turn of events, on July 17, 1862, Congress passed a Confiscation Act that declared all slaves of rebel masters free as soon as they came into Union lines, and a Militia Act that empowered the president to "employ as many persons of African descent" in "any military or naval service for which they may be found competent." Congress also repealed the 1792 law.

On August 25, 1862, the War Department authorized Brigadier General Rufus Saxton, military governor of the Union-controlled South Carolina Sea Islands, to raise five regiments of black troops for Federal service, with white men as officers. Volunteers came forward slowly at first, but by November 7 the regiment had reached its quota and was mustered in as the 1st South Carolina Volunteer Regiment under the command of Massachusetts abolitionist Colonel Thomas Wentworth Higginson. A second regiment followed, led by Colonel James Montgomery.

Still, President Abraham Lincoln refused to raise a large black army on political grounds. "To arm the Negroes would turn 50,000 bayonets from the loyal Border States against us that were for us," he told his abolitionist critics. Black leaders continued to urge the necessity of enlisting black troops, realizing that if the black man proved his patriotism and courage on the battlefield, the nation would be morally obligated to grant him first-class citizenship. No one expressed those sentiments more eloquently than Frederick Douglass, a former slave and the nation's most prominent black abolitionist. He insisted that "once the black man gets upon his person the brass letters 'U.S.', a musket on his shoulder and bullets in his pocket, there is no power on earth which can deny that he has earned the right to citizenship in the United States."

Debate continued within the Union command until January 1, 1863, when President Lincoln signed the Emancipation Proclamation. Having freed, by executive order, those slaves in the South, Lincoln could no longer deny the black man the opportunity to fight. Now the Civil War was being fought not only to preserve the Union, but for the freedom of all the American people, white and black. The success of the 1st and 2nd Carolina Colored Troops only reinforced that position. Higginson and Montgomery had already led their black troops on several successful raids into the interior of Georgia and Florida, and in March 1863 they captured and occupied Jacksonville.

On February 13, 1863, Senator Charles Sumner of Massachusetts introduced a bill proposing the "enlistment of 300,000 colored troops." Although the bill was defeated, abolitionist governor John A. Andrew of Massachusetts requested and received authorization from Secretary of War Edwin M. Stanton to organize a colored regiment of volunteers to serve for three years.

Massachusetts had a small black population, and only 100 men volunteered during the first six weeks of recruitment. Disillusioned by the turnout, Andrew organized a committee of prominent citizens and Negro leaders to supervise the recruitment effort. Within two months the committee collected $5,000 and established a line of recruiting posts from Boston to St. Louis, resulting in the recruitment of 1,000 black men from throughout the Union who became part of the 54th Regiment Massachusetts Volunteer Infantry, Colored, the first black regiment raised in the free states. Toward the end of the second recruiting month, volunteers arrived at the rate of 30 to 40 each day, and Andrew soon had enough men to form a second black regiment, the 55th Massachusetts.

For the 54th's commander, Governor Andrew turned to Robert Gould Shaw, captain of the Massachusetts 2nd Infantry. Charming and handsome, Shaw came from a wealthy and socially prominent Boston abolitionist family. His parents Francis and Sarah had joined the American Anti-Slavery Society in 1838, and by 1842 Francis was working with the Boston Vigilance Committee to help runaway slaves gain their freedom. Robert entered Harvard University in 1856 but abandoned his studies during his third year and moved to New York to work in his uncle's mercantile office. Shaw joined an exclusive militia regiment, the 7th New York National Guard, where he talked about what he would do if the South made trouble. Shaw did not possess the strong anti-slavery calling of his parents, but he was fiercely patriotic. When the Civil War began, he was primed to take revenge on the South. To Shaw, the South was the transgressor, and if it took the end of slavery to redeem the honor of America, then he was willing to fight for that. When the 7th disbanded, Shaw accepted a commission in the 2nd Massachusetts Infantry. During his 20 months there, Captain Shaw received a minor wound at Antietam, during the single bloodiest day of the war.

When Governor Andrew asked the young captain to lead a black volunteer infantry, Shaw was hesitant. The prospect of heading a regiment of armed blacks would not be popular among the white ranks. Nor did he want to abandon the men of the 2nd Infantry. Shaw initially refused the position but changed his mind after much discussion with his parents. In a February 1863 letter to his future wife, Annie Haggerty, Shaw wrote, "You know how many eminent men consider a negro army of the greatest importance to our country at this time. If it turns out to be so, how fully repaid the pioneers in the movement will be, for what they may have to go through…. I feel convinced I shall never regret having taken this step, as far as I myself am concerned; for while I was undecided I felt ashamed of myself, as if I were cowardly." Shaw received a promotion to major on April 11, 1863, and attained the rank of colonel the following month. Colonel Shaw would now have to navigate the turbulent forces of discrimination that existed within the Union Army.

The men of the 54th trained near Boston at Readville, under the constant scrutiny of white soldiers, many of whom believed black soldiers lacked the stomach for combat. Yet the negative perceptions seemed only to inspire a sense of unity within the ranks of the regiment and their white officers.

Contrary to recruitment promises, the soldiers of the 54th were paid only $10.00 per month, $3.00 less than the white troops. Shaw had become so committed to his men that he wrote to Governor Andrew, insisting that his entire regiment, including white officers, would refuse pay until his soldiers were "given the same payment as all the other

Massachusetts troops." Yet Congress did not enact legislation granting equal pay to black soldiers until June 15, 1864.

Shortly after the 54th was mustered into service, the Confederate Congress passed an act stating its intention to "put to death" if captured, "any Negro" as well as "white commissioned officer [who] shall command, prepare or aid Negroes in arms against the Confederate States." The directive only served to strengthen the resolve of the black soldiers.

On May 18 Governor Andrew traveled to the camp to present Shaw with the regimental flags. He made the trip with 3,000 other visitors, including such prominent abolitionists as Frederick Douglass, William Lloyd Garrison, and Wendell Phillips. Douglass had a strong personal link with the 54th—two of his sons, Lewis and Charles, had joined the unit. Andrew presented the flags to Shaw. "I know not, Mr. Commander, in all human history, to any given thousand men in arms, has there been committed a work at once so proud, so precious, so full of hope and glory as the work committed to you," the governor said.

Massachusetts Governor John A. Andrew advocated the enlistment of black men into the Union Army. After President Lincoln issued the Emancipation Proclamation on January 1, 1863, Andrew approached Secretary of War Edwin Stanton and obtained authorization to raise a black Massachusetts regiment.

Ten days later the 54th Regiment of Massachusetts Volunteer Infantry marched through the streets of downtown Boston, greeted by the cheers of thousands who assembled to see them off at Battery Wharf. It was an impressive spectacle. Shaw, atop his chestnut brown horse, led the way. Close behind marched the color bearers, followed by young black soldiers, handsomely clad in their sharp, new uniforms.

The dress parade gradually made its way to the wharf and boarded the *De Molay* bound for Port Royal Island, South Carolina. There the regiment reported to the Department of the South. Once the men arrived, however, reality set in when they were relegated to manual labor. Not until June 8, when Shaw and his men joined Colonel James Montgomery and the black troops of his 2nd South Carolina Colored Volunteers on an "expedition" to Georgia, did they see any action, and that was during a pointless raid on the small town of Darien. After plundering the 100 or so residences, three churches, the market-house, courthouse, and an academy, Montgomery ordered Darien set afire. Begrudgingly, Shaw directed one of his companies to torch the town. Fanned by a high wind, the flames eventually destroyed everything but a church and a few houses.

Afterward, Shaw wrote to lieutenant Colonel Charles G. Halpine, the acting adjutant general of the department, to condemn this "barbarous sort of warfare." Shaw knew his complaint could result in his arrest or even court-martial, but he felt compelled to express his feelings. He later learned that Montgomery had acted in accordance with the orders of his superior officer, General David Hunter. Soon after the Darien raid, President Lincoln relieved Hunter of his command.

The sacking of Darien and the manual labor his troops were compelled to do disheartened Shaw. "Our whole experience, so far, has been in loading and discharging vessels," he wrote to Brigadier General George C. Strong, commander of Montgomery's brigade. "Colored soldiers should be associated as much as possible with the white troops, in order that they may have other witnesses beside their own officers to what they are

capable of doing." That opportunity finally arrived on the morning of July 16, 1863. Fighting alongside white troops on James Island, Shaw's men acquitted themselves well in a sharp skirmish. That same night they ferried to Morris Island, where battle lines had already been drawn for the anticipated attack on Fort Wagner. Despite their exhaustion, hunger, and wet clothes, the men of the 54th were determined to fight on.

WHEN GENERAL STRONG, now Shaw's brigade commander, heard of the of the 54th on James Island, he asked the colonel if he and his regiment would lead the attack on Fort Wagner. Shaw and his men readily agreed and prepared to lead the charge across a narrow beach obstructed by felled branches, crisscrossed wire, and a deep moat—all of which were constructed to slow the attackers, making them vulnerable to enemy fire. Eight all-white units were to follow. All day long, Union artillery bombarded Fort Wagner in an effort to soften the Confederate defense and minimize the bloodshed that would inevitably follow. Late in the day Shaw arranged the 600 able-bodied men of his regiment into two wings of five companies each and moved them slowly up the beach. He assigned Company B to the right flank, using the surf as its guide. The other companies lined up on its left.

At dusk, General Strong addressed Shaw and his men. Pointing to the flag bearer, he said: "If this man should fall, who will pick up the flag?" Shaw stepped forward. "I will," he said. Addressing his troops with final words of inspiration, Shaw reminded them: "The eyes of thousands will look on what you do tonight." Then, drawing his sword, the young Boston Brahmin barked: "Move in quick time until within a hundred yards of the fort, then, double-quick and charge!" Quickstep became double-quick, and then a full run, as Confederate riflemen on the ramparts of the fort let loose a torrent of fire upon the Union soldiers. Men fell on all sides, but those who were able continued the charge with Shaw in the lead.

Company B passed through the moat to the base of the fort where canister, grenades, and small arms fire rained down

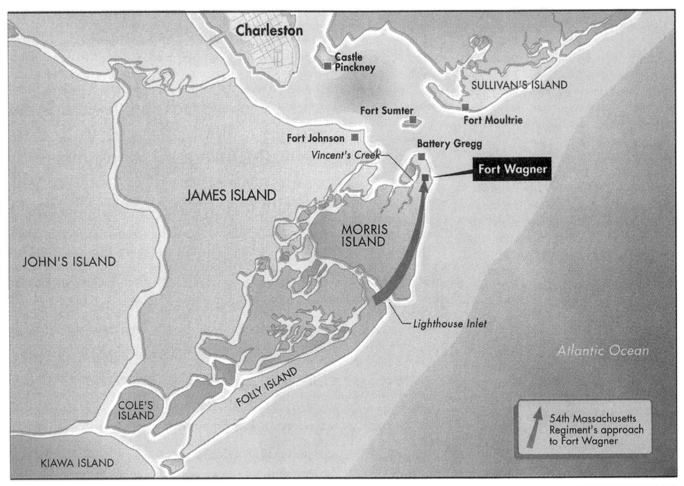

MAP BY RICK BROWNLEE

The 54th Regiment approached Fort Wagner along a narrow stretch of beach by the Atlantic Ocean.

on them. Surrounded by bloodshed, the 54th commander realized that he could not retreat, and he ordered the final assault on the fort. Shaw somehow managed to reach the parapet before a Confederate bullet pierced his heart.

"Men fell all around me," Lewis Douglass later wrote. "A shell would explode and clear a space of twenty feet, our men would close up again, but it was no use we had to retreat, which was a very hazardous undertaking. How I got out of that fight alive I cannot tell, but I am here."

The intense fire mowed down the color bearers. Sergeant William Carney, a barrel-chested 23-year-old, seized the national flag and planted it upon the fort's parapet. The men of the 54th fought gallantly for about an hour until Confederate guns forced them to abandon their position. Before retreating, Carney once again grasped the flag, and

despite bullets in the head, chest, right arm, and leg, he returned it to Union lines. His heroism earned him the distinction of being the first of 21 black men during the war to earn the Medal of Honor.

Subsequent waves of Federal troops tried for two hours to take the fort but failed, and casualties mounted by the hundreds. At the end of the assault, the Union had lost 1,515 killed, wounded or missing. Of that number, 256 were black soldiers from the 54th Massachusetts.

The following morning revealed a grisly scene. The dead lay in contorted positions along the beach, their fingers and legs stiffened from rigor mortis. The soft but painful cries and moans of the dying could be heard, begging for help.

A few days after the siege, a Union party under a flag of truce requested the return of Shaw's body. Brigadier General Johnson Hagood, Fort Wagner's

new commander, reportedly answered, "We buried him in the trench with his niggers." Learning of Hagood's reply, Colonel Shaw's father declared, "I can imagine no holier place than that in which he is, among his brave and devoted followers, nor wish for him better company."

From a military standpoint, the assault on Fort Wagner proved to be a costly failure. The blame rested on the shoulders of commanding general Quincy A. Gillmore and his commander in the field, Brigadier General Truman Seymour, who had not ordered the usual preparations for such an assault—no one sent out guides to check the terrain in advance or dispatched lines of skirmishers to soften the enemy. Nor had the 54th ever practiced storming a fort. Nevertheless, the assault proved to be a turning point for black soldiers, serving to dismiss any lingering skepticism among whites about the combat readiness of African Americans. "I have given the subject of arming the Negro my hearty support," General Ulysses S. Grant wrote to President Lincoln in August. "They will make good soldiers and taking them from the enemy weakens him in the same proportion they strengthen us."

When other Union generals remained recalcitrant, Lincoln responded swiftly.

"You say you will not fight to free Negroes," he said. "Some of them seem to be willing to fight for you. When victory is won, there will be some black men who can remember that, with silent tongue and clenched teeth, and steady eye and well-poised bayonet, they have helped mankind on to this great consummation. I fear, however, that there will also be some white ones, unable to forget that with malignant heart and deceitful speech, they strove to hinder it."

William C. Kashatus is a professional historian at Chester County Historical Society, West Chester, Pennsylvania.

Between Honor and Glory

By Jay Winik

…**To grasp the full horror** of the march it is necessary to make it yourself. The landscape constantly changes: open fields are exasperatingly punctuated by high hedges and dense windbreaks that are impossible to see through or over or around. On the other side, they seamlessly merge into swamps, or dense, claustrophobic woods, or undergrowth so thick as to be a second forest; or, conversely, they run into long, muddy tracts, known euphemistically as Virginia quicksand.

Once more, Lee pushed his men to the outer limits of human endurance. "I know that the men and animals are exhausted," he bluntly told one of his generals, "but it is necessary to tax their strength." And remarkably, once more, they complied. Damp from the day's rain, their senses numbed from too little nourishment, they stumbled along with scarcely a word of complaint. But by now they were fighting a second struggle, this one from within. The dreadful consequences were inevitable: without food and deprived of sleep, the body begins to feed on itself, consuming vital muscle, raping invaluable tissue, robbing itself of what little energy is left. Thoughts become woozy; some experience a light-headedness, others even hallucinate. And with each hour, the situation worsens: initiative is deadened, and judgment becomes impaired, giving many the mental capacity of a small child. The elements, too—the sun, the wind, and the rain—become merciless. So does thirst. Limbs struggle to obey the simplest motor commands. Yet somehow, Lee's men inched forward…

Davis had called on the Confederacy to shift to a guerrilla war to wear down the North under interminable sacrifice. Militarily the plan had merit.

To the contemporary mind, it is as difficult to contemplate the westward march of the Army of Northern Virginia as it is to step outside all the history that has come after. To us, an extended troop march appears an anachronism. Today, great military machines race across terrain in high-speed tanks and armored personnel carriers. Unless they are poorly equipped, or the battlefield has collapsed around them, they do not march on foot, and, if they do, they certainly do not expect grand victory. It is no accident that one of the most famous military marches of the twentieth century was neither a strategic retreat nor a tactical feint, both of which were part of Robert E. Lee's stock-in-trade, but a journey into captivity known as the Bataan Death March, made over ten days and seventy-five miles by 36,000 defeated American servicemen in the Philippines. Even now, Bataan, where upward of 10,000 men died of thirst, exhaustion, beatings, torture, or beheadings, is a march that skews the modern military imagination.

But Robert E. Lee was not of a twentieth-century mind. The marches he knew were not Bataan, but heroic efforts by Hannibal, Alexander the Great, and Napoleon, for whom the distinction between genius and insanity was often measured by the razor-thin line of success. People must have thought Hannibal especially crazy, setting out from Spain with 40,000 men and an ungodly number of elephants to traverse two hazardous mountain ranges—the Pyrenees and the Alps—and a deep, rushing river, the Rhône, and to endure landslides, blinding snowstorms, and attacks by hostile mountain tribes; they thought him crazy, that is, until he did it in fifteen days and swept down upon the unsuspecting Romans. Now Lee and his veterans, some 35,000 men, had a roughly 140-mile march to make and a solid twelve- to twenty-four-hour lead. Lee understood the odds, but ever the gambler, hadn't he bested them before? Hadn't he gotten to Cold Harbor first? To leave Grant behind now would enshrine him among history's great commanders and tacticians.

With little sleep and even less respite, the men continued to march under the cover of darkness. On and on, hour after hour, from hilltop to hilltop, for the better part of two solid nights and one continuous day, they struggled to keep their lead. By April 4, they were dirty, unwashed, mud-splattered, exhausted, and, most of all, desperately hungry. Still, after months of languishing in the trenches, their morale and élan were surprisingly strong; and at the thought of food in Amelia, so were their spirits. Once replenished, their lead over Grant solidified, they would complete their dash to safety. So what mattered now was each new stride, each new landmark, bringing them closer to the 350,000 rations they expected at Amelia Court House, and taking them a step farther away from Grant's huge force, eagerly trailing behind.

Lee's plans had called for his vast columns of men and material to cross over three separate bridges; but one of them, Bevil's Bridge, was washed out; at another, Genito Bridge, the materials to shore it up had never arrived. Lee improvised: in the first case, three separate corps—Gordon's, Longstreet's, and Mahone's—were densely wedged onto a single bridge; for the second, the Confederates found a nearby railway pass that they neatly planked over. But these delays, costing the Confederates in manpower, in stamina, and, most precious of all, in ticks of the clock, held up the completion of the crossing until the following evening.

The stoic Lee himself made it across the Appomattox River only on the morning of April 4, at 7:30 a.m. Like his men, he had scarcely slept since leaving Petersburg and Richmond. But this morning, his hopes—and theirs—rose at the stirring thought of the relief waiting for them in Confederate boxcars on the Danville line at Amelia. Several hours later, around midday, Amelia itself came into view—a sleepy village of unpaved streets, with houses neatly tucked behind tumbled roses and weathered fences, and a few small shops converging around a grassy square. Lee raced ahead. Upon locating the boxcars, he ordered them to be opened.

This is what he found: 96 loaded caissons, 200 crates of ammunition, 164 boxes of artillery harnesses. But no bread, no beef, no bacon, no flour, no meal, no hardtack, no pork, no ham, no fruit, no cornmeal. And no milk, no coffee, no tea, no sugar. Not one single ration. Lee was stunned.

His men had left Richmond and Petersburg with only one day of rations. That day had come and gone, and much

more hard marching lay ahead of them. Already, weakened men and animals were slowly dropping in their tracks. But to eat now meant halting the march to find food—which meant squandering his priceless lead over Grant. And in either case, there was no guarantee that he would secure food—that day, the next, or the next after that.

The general wasted little time, quickly giving the bad news to his division commanders and then writing out an appeal to "the Citizens of Amelia County" in which he called on their "generosity and charity" and asked them "to supply as far as each is able the wants of the brave soldiers who have battled for your liberty for four years."

Then he waited.

As dawn broke on April 5, he received his answer.

The citizens of Amelia County had already been cleaned out by Confederate impressment crews and the exigencies of war. Lee's forage wagons came back virtually empty: there were no pigs, no sheep, no hogs, no cattle, no provender. And there would be no breakfast that morning for the men. His only option now was a hard, forced march toward Danville—where a million and a half rations were stored. It was 104 miles by railroad; four grueling days by foot. But this time could be whittled down to only one day if rations were rushed forward by train to Burkeville, a mere eighteen miles down the line. Lee dispatched an order by wire. Would it work? Just as he could no longer wait in Amelia for rations, no longer could he wait for an answer. With the buffer of the Appomattox River gone and crucial hours lost, Grant's men were closing in. There was no time to waste.

Lee hastily mounted his horse, Traveller, and immediately ordered his men to move toward Burkeville. But it was worse than Lee realized.

Just outside Jetersville, itself a ragtag town consisting of little more than a collection of weathered wooden houses scattered alongside the rail line, Union cavalry had beaten the rebels to the

punch; earthworks were blocking the retreat path like a dam; battle flags had been raised; and well-fed bluecoats were peering over the lines. Dug in, "thick and high," the Federals were waiting.

Longstreet had already sought to dislodge them; convinced that it was only cavalry in the way, he briskly attacked. But Sheridan's horsemen were now backed by two Federal corps strung out between Lee and North Carolina. The road of escape—through Burkeville—had been cut off.

Riding down the retreat line, Lee cast a sidelong glance, lifted his field glasses, and gazed out at the freshly dug Union fortifications. For several tense moments, he considered one last massive and final assault. But the Union troops were too well entrenched, and his army was in no condition for an all-out battle. Instead, Lee set his men back in motion, again. This time due west, for Lynchburg.

Thus was delivered what many regimental commanders considered to be "the most cruel marching order" that they had ever given.

In every direction, the dead—men, mules, and horses—began to litter the roadside. Dense columns of smoke rose from exploding vehicles, and shells burst after being touched by flames. Following alongside, Lee learned from two captured Federal spies that the Union was gaining ground. He pushed his men that much harder.

Nighttime fell. It didn't matter. Morning now seamlessly intermingled with evening, darkness with sunset, the fifth of April with the sixth, two hours with eight hours, eight hours with sixteen hours, and eventually, twenty-four hours with forty hours. Hungry, with barely one night of rest in three days, many of the men wandered forward in a giddy, phantasmagoric state, slipping in and out of sleep and confusion as they walked. The evening was little better: as the long, black night wore on, more troops fell by the wayside; they would halt for a few moments' rest, and fail to rise, their dazed eyes gazing haplessly at Lee's line, still lumbering west.

Still outwardly calm, Lee's face nonetheless looked "sunken," "haggard." But there was suddenly the prospect of food to spur his men on. That afternoon, he had learned that more than 80,000 rations of meal and bread—and even such delicacies as French soup packaged in tinfoil along with whole hams—were definitively waiting in Farmville. Nineteen miles away.

So it was in that direction that the Confederates picked up their step and began again, in one long, snaking line, to move.

Grant wasted no time. This was the opportunity that he had hoped for. Sheridan's cavalry and three infantry corps continued to race alongside the retreating rebels, bludgeoning them with sledgehammer blows and quick, in-and-out lightning attacks that heightened panic and fatigue. Fueled by the prospect of victory, the Federals had at long last begun to show a fighting spirit that had been sorely lacking since the Grant-Lee slugfest began almost a year before: gone were the shock and dread of another Wilderness or Cold Harbor; no longer did they fear seeing "the elephant" of battle. It showed in their very stamina: Union men, despite their own obvious exhaustion, now seemed incapable of straggling, some handily marching upward of thirty-five miles per day.

The fighting would outdo much of the war in its savagery. After the methodical rebel order of "Fire!" the line of advancing bluecoats wavered and broke. Then the killing began.

"Lee's surely in a bad fix," he announced. "But if I were in his place, I think I could get away with part of the army." Then he added tantalizingly, "I suppose Lee will."

So meeting with Sheridan and Major General George Meade, he reiterated his central plan. He did not want to follow Lee; he wanted to get ahead of him. Playing for keeps, this time Grant refined his stratagem. At dawn the next day, April 6, he dispatched Sheridan on a northwest swing—no longer aimed at Lee's rear but intended to move ahead of him, directly positioning the hot breath of Union armies against Lee's face. For good measure, he ordered another infantry corps to join the push in the rear…

The skirmishing at Sayler's Creek, across three separate battle sites that would eventually merge into one, began early on April 6 and mounted as the sun climbed. The battle itself began in earnest by the first brush of afternoon, when two dangerous gaps appeared in Lee's lines. Deadly Federal horsemen, swinging sabers and led by the dashing, yellow-haired general, George Armstrong Custer, rushed in through the holes. Soon, three Union corps had cut off a quarter of Lee's army; their guns shattering the unearthly silence of the rolling hills. A row of artillery batteries followed, decking Confederates who had been lingering in the dank and muddy swale. "I had seldom seen a fire more accurate nor one that had been more deadly," one rebel noted. Off-balance from lack of food, dazed by lack of sleep, the rebels were at first stunned, then, as one Confederate put it, they "blanched," and finally, they were "awe-struck."

Sheridan wasted no time in capitalizing on their diminished state. "Go through them!" he shouted angrily. "They're demoralized as hell."

Not completely. At the sight of the Yankees, they rallied. Rebel batteries swung into position, anchored their lines, and trained their barrels on the advancing Federals, while infantry crouched and pointed muskets at the enemy. It was only a prelude to fighting that would outdo much of the rest of the war in its savagery. After the methodical rebel order of "Fire!" the line of advancing bluecoats wavered and broke. The first crisis was apparently over. But then, without warning, the conflict degenerated, and the insensate killing began. The hollow-eyed Confederates sprang to

their feet with empty muskets, starting after the retreating Yankees. Catching up to the Federals, they became entangled in vicious hand-to-hand combat. Men struck one another with bayonets, flogged one another with the butts of guns, and flailed at one another with their feet. "I well remember the yell of demonic triumph with which that simple country lad clubbed his musket and whirled savagely upon another victim," observed one commander. Grabbing one another with dirt-sodden fingers, callused, sweaty hands, and sharp fingernails, they rolled on the ground like wild beasts, biting one another's throats and ears and noses with their teeth. Officers dispensed with their guns, fighting with swords and, when they no longer worked, with fists. Astoundingly, in this jumble of conflict, they were no longer battling one another over territory or vital military advantage or even tactical gain, but out of sheer impulse: they were killing one another over battalion colors.

The Yankees kept coming, and the battered rebels, their assaults increasingly uncoordinated and disjointed, could not keep up the ferocity. By day's end, they were overwhelmed; the dead lay so close and dense that bodies had to be dragged away to let a single horse pass. It was the South's worst defeat of the entire campaign. All told, Grant's army had captured an astonishing 6,000 rebels—Lee's son Custis and the one-legged General Richard Ewell among them—and destroyed much of their wagon train. Adding up the killed and wounded, Lee had lost up to 8,000. Lee himself felt the sting of defeat sharply. Late in the afternoon, he rode out to a high ridge overlooking the battlefield. Sitting on Traveller, on this small rise, the general found the sight astonishing. Lee was a badly shaken man.

"My God!" he cried out. "Has the army been dissolved?"

Bill Mahone, the tall, bearded general, was there, riding at his side. Deeply touched, he took a moment to steady his voice, then quickly offered words of encouragement. "No general, here are troops ready to do their duty."

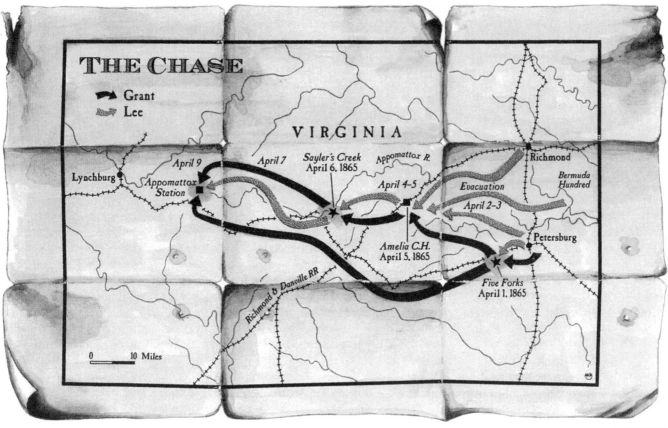

As Mahone and his men drew into a line to hold back the Federals, Lee's temper again flared; he, too, was drawn to the fight. Leaning forward in his saddle, he snatched a single battle flag, to rally fresh troops as well as retreating men. On this day, it was no idle gesture. Earlier in the fighting, one flag bearer had been brought down by an artillery shell, only to have his brother grab the standard and promptly be shot through the head. Another Confederate quickly reached for the colors and also fell. So did a fourth. And so did a fifth, until the flag was firmly planted by a sixth in a low bush. Now it was Lee who sought to cheat fate. Riding past Mahone's assembled troops, he held the flag staff high in one hand. At the top of the rise, he stopped and waited. The wind caught the flag, and it snapped and curled around his silver mane, flapping about him and draping his body in Confederate red. Mahone's men fell deathly silent, and then this collective hush was punctuated by a scattered, spontaneous cry emanating from the frenzied survivors stumbling back: "Where's the man who won't follow Uncle Robert!"…

After Sayler's Creek, Phil Sheridan tersely wired Grant: "If the thing is pressed, I think that Lee will surrender." When Lincoln read this, his melancholy spirits soared.

Lincoln bluntly telegraphed to Grant: "Let the thing be pressed."

It was now April 7.

Lee's remaining forces had again crossed the Appomattox to arrive in Farmville, where the first rations of the march awaited them. While the food was dispensed, campfires were hastily built; bacon sizzled; and corn bread was devoured. His troops, at last able to eat and rest, still had two options: try again to turn south toward Danville, or set out for Lynchburg and the sheltering protection of the Blue Ridge mountains. But inexplicably, one of Lee's generals had neglected to blast High Bridge—a massive steel and brick structure spanning a floodplain half a mile wide, at a spectacular height of 126 feet. Frantically riding back, an officer finally torched it, but the delay was fatal; a hard-marching Federal column reached the accompanying wagon bridge in time to stomp out the flames. Now there was no river between Lee and Grant's lead troops; indeed, the distance separating them was barely four miles. With Union soldiers approaching, Lee's army stood nearly naked to assault.

Lee was forced to quickly withdraw his men from Farmville and recross the Appomattox to escape the threat, even as Union cavalry drew so close that fighting broke out in the town's streets. The priceless supply train quickly rolled away, while thousands of starving soldiers, who had not yet drawn their rations, watched in agony. Bedlam

173

followed; haversacks still open, muskets in hand, men turned and raced across bridges that were already burning.

Once more, Federal and Confederate soldiers clashed. But now, the shards of Lee's army successfully fended off the Union, smashing the bluecoats along both their front and their flank, even taking some 300 prisoners, including a Union general—all under the direct eye of Lee himself. This time, the rebels inflicted more casualties than they suffered—in fact, the Union had lost some 8,000 men in just the last week alone—and by moonlight, the road west to Lynchburg now beckoned.

"Keep your command together and in good spirits," Lee reassured his son Rooney. "Don't let them think of surrender."

And he concluded: "I will get you out of this."

Shortly before dusk on April 8, as he dismounted to make camp for the night, Lee received a letter from Grant offering generous terms for the surrender of Lee's army and the only condition that he demanded was that the officers and men "be disqualified from taking up arms" until exchanged. Unknown to Lee, Grant had labored more than six hours to compose this letter. In a tactful combination of diplomacy and insight, he suggested that Lee could be spared the humiliation of surrendering in person.

Six straight days of the relentless march had not dimmed Lee's audacity, or his desire for victory.

Lee responded. Of all the sentiments it reflects, despair and surrender are not among them:

Genl

I received at a late hour your note of today. In mine of yesterday I did not intend to propose the surrender of the Army of N. Va.—but to ask the terms of your proposition. To be frank, I do not think the emergency has arisen to call for the surrender of this Army, but as the restoration of peace should be the sole object of all, I desire to know whether your proposals would lead to that and I cannot therefore meet you with a view to surrender... but as far as your proposal may affect the C.S. forces under my command & tend to the restoration of peace, I shall be pleased to meet you at 10 a.m. tomorrow on the old state road to Richmond between the picket lines of the two armies.

The letter was sealed, and the courier dispatched. Under a soft midnight sky, with a bright, nearly full moon overhead, Grant scanned Lee's letter, then handed it to his chief of staff to read aloud. The aide was furious at Lee's brash response, but Grant just coolly shook his head. "It looks as if Lee still means to fight."

With enemy artillery roaring in the background, that night Lee and his weary lieutenants gathered around a campfire in the woods near Appomattox Court House. The Confederates were almost entirely surrounded, outnumbered nearly six to one, with little food, little hope of resupply, little prospect for immediate reinforcement. But there was still the distinct prospect of escape. And before the opportunity slipped away, Lee hoped to turn the momentary lull to his advantage. Six straight days of Lee's relentless march westward had not dimmed his audacity, or his desire to avoid surrender and somehow salvage victory. He devised another plan for breaking through the enemy lines: his men would attack as soon as possible, attempting to slice a hole through Grant's slumbering army, and if successful, they would resume the march southward. General John Gordon, one of Lee's most daring officers, was chosen to lead the breakout. And, if necessary, there remained a fallback position: they could make their way to the Blue Ridge mountains, where, Lee had once said, he could hold out "for twenty years."

Before dawn on April 9, in the pitch black, the advance was to begin. It was Palm Sunday, the day that marked the start of the Holy Week and Jesus' arrival in Jerusalem. Neither the day nor its significance would have been lost on Lee or his men.

At 5 a.m., just beyond Appomattox Court House, a fog hovered over the landscape like a thick, sprawling ghost; the rolling hills soon echoed with the staccato rattle of artillery; and the Sunday stillness was again shattered by the piercing cry of the rebel yell. Gordon's men fought with a special fury. They drove Federal cavalry from their positions, captured several guns, duly cleared the road of bluecoats, and then swept forward to the crest of a hill. Suddenly, below them, concealed in the woodlands, lay the inexorable logic of the mathematics of war: a solid wall of blue, some two miles wide, was advancing—two Yankee infantry corps, with two other Union corps closing in on Lee's rear. Quipped one soldier at glimpsing this awesome sight: "Lee couldn't go forward, he couldn't go backward, and he couldn't go sideways."

Three hours later, around 8 a.m., a courier from Gordon hastily carried the apocalyptic message to Lee. "I have fought my corps to a frazzle," he wrote. "And I fear I can do nothing..."

Thus the ominous choice was finally set before Lee: surrender or throw his life on one last murderous fight—Lincoln's feared Armageddon. Lee summoned General Longstreet, who brought Mahone and Lee's chief of artillery, the twenty-nine-year-old brigadier general, E. Porter Alexander. All were expecting a council of war. Instead, the discussion turned to surrender. When a moment of vacillation came and an opening occurred, Alexander, one of the most talented and innovative men in Lee's command, took it. Pleading with his chief not to give up, Alexander saw another recourse: a third option.

"You don't care for military glory or fame," he protested, "but we are proud of your name and the record of this army. We want to leave it to our children... a little more blood more or less now makes no difference." Instead, Alexander suggested a Confederate trump card, in fact, the specter most dreaded by Lincoln,

Grant, and Sherman: that the men take to the woods, evaporate into the hills, and become guerrillas. "Two thirds" would get away, Alexander contended. "We would be like rabbits or partridges in the bushes," he said, "and they could not scatter to follow us."

A veteran of Fredericksburg and Gettysburg, Cold Harbor and Petersburg, Alexander was so valued by Lee that Jefferson Davis once noted, he is "one of a very few whom Gen Lee would not give to anybody." And Alexander was already prepared to take to the bush rather than surrender—and so, he later indicated, were countless other men. There were no more miracles to be performed, but there were indeed certainly still options. And this option—guerrilla warfare—was not one to be lightly ignored. During the Revolutionary War, Lee's own father had fought the British as a partisan. Moreover, on April 4, a fleeing President Jefferson Davis had issued his own call for a guerrilla struggle. Yet it was Lee's judgment—and not Davis's—that would be most decisive. ("Country be damned," roared former Virginia Governor Henry Wise to Lee. "There is no country. You are the country to these men!")

Lee paused, weighing his answer. No less than for Davis, surrender was anathema to him. Here, surely, was seduction. And in this fateful moment the aging general would affect the course of the nation's history for all time.

Throughout the years variously referred to as "guerrillaism," or "guerrilleros," or "partisans," or "Partheyganger," or "bushwhackers," guerrilla warfare is and always has been the very essence of how the weak make war against the strong. Insurrectionist, subversive, chaotic, its methods are often chosen instinctively, but throughout time, they have worked with astonishing regularity. Its application is classic and surprisingly simple: shock the enemy by concentrating strength against weakness. Countering numerical superiority, guerrillas have always employed secrecy, deception, and terror as their ultimate tools. They move quickly, attack fast, and just as quickly scatter. They strike at night—

or in the day; they hit hard in the rain, or just as hard in the sunshine; they rain terror when troops are eating or when they have just concluded an exhausting march; they assault military targets, or, just as often, hunt down random civilians. They may hit at the rear of the enemy, or at its infrastructure, or, most devastating of all, at its psyche; the only constant is that they move when least expected, and invariably in a way to maximize impact.

And as military men have often learned the hard way, guerrilla warfare does the job. By luring their adversaries into endless, futile pursuit, guerrillas erode not just the enemy's strength, but, far more importantly, the enemy's morale.

Grant's strategy of exhaustion would be turned on its head. Confronted with a guerrilla phase, the Union would not be able to demobilize its armies. Conscription would continue.

Before the coming of Christ the lightning strikes of the nomadic Scythians blunted the efforts of Darius I to subdue them; Judas Maccabeus waged successful guerrilla operations against the Syrians; the Romans in Spain required several long centuries to subdue the Lusitanians and Celtiberians. The actual word "guerrilla" came from the Spanish insurgency against France in the early 1800s, a conflict Jefferson Davis frequently referred to and which at one point was largely responsible for containing three of Napoleon's armies. Equally familiar to nineteenth-century Americans were the Thirty Years War and the French Religious Wars; the experience of Frederick the Great in Bohemia; of Wellington in Portugal; the partisan war against Revolutionary France; the Netherlands against Philip II; Switzerland against the Hapsburg Empire. And then there were the most honorable examples of all: The Swamp Fox, Francis Marion, Sumter, Pickens, Green, the Liberty Boys in Georgia... West Point

graduate and former U.S. Secretary of War Jefferson Davis knew all this.

The day after Richmond fell, Davis had called on the Confederacy to shift from a static conventional war in defense of territory and population centers to a dynamic guerrilla war of attrition, designed to wear down the North and force it to conclude that keeping the South in the Union would not be worth the interminable pain and ongoing sacrifice. "We have now entered upon a new phase of a struggle the memory of which is to endure for all ages," he declared. "... Relieved from the necessity of guarding cities and particular points, important but not vital to our defense, with an army free to move from point to point and strike in detail detachments and garrisons of the enemy, operating on the interior of our own country, where supplies are more accessible, and where the foe will be far removed from his own base and cut off from all succor in case of reverse, nothing is now needed to render our triumph certain but the exhibition of our own unquenchable resolve." He concluded thus: "Let us but will it, and we are free."

In effect, Davis was proposing that Lee disperse his army before it was finally cornered. From a military point of view, the plan had considerable merit. The Confederacy was well supplied with long mountain ranges, endless swamps, and dark forests to offer sanctuary for a host of determined partisans. Its people knew the countryside intimately and instinctively and had all the talents necessary for adroit bushwhacking, everything from the shooting and the riding, the tracking and the foraging, the versatility and the cunning, right down to the sort of dash necessary for this way of life. Moreover, given that most of them would be battle-hardened and well-trained veterans, arguably an organized Confederate guerrilla army could be among the most effective partisan groups in all of history. The Union army would then be forced to undertake the onerous task of occupying the entire Confederacy—an unwieldy occupation at best, which would entail Federal forces having to subdue and patrol and police an area as large as all of today's France, Spain, Italy, Switzerland, Germany, and Poland combined. Even in early April 1865, the Union had actually conquered only a relatively small part of the South—to be sure, crucial areas for a conventional conflict, like Nashville, New Orleans, Memphis, and, of course, the crown jewel of Richmond—but that would be largely meaningless in a bitter, protracted guerrilla war. As the Romans had found out 2,000 years earlier, cities could become useless baggage weighing down the military forces, what the ancient commanders memorably called "impedimenta."

In moving to occupy vast stretches of land defended only by small, dispersed forces, Grant's strategy of exhaustion would be turned on its head. Consider the nearly insuperable difficulties that he would face: up to that point, no more than roughly a million Union men had been in arms at any one given time. But confronted with a guerrilla phase, the Union would not be able to demobilize its armies, always problematic for a democracy. Wartime conscription would have to continue, with all its attendant political difficulties and war-weariness. Even granting the North's theoretical ability to put more than 2 million men under arms, it would be unlikely that the Federals could ever pacify, let alone manage and oversee, more than fragmented sections of the South against a willful guerrilla onslaught. Rather than having a restored United States, the country could come to resemble a Swiss cheese, with Union cities here, pockets of Confederate resistance lurking there, ambiguous areas of no-man's-land in between. Even the North would not be safe. In 1864, a ragtag group of twelve Confederates, without horses, plus ten lookouts, and financed by a mere $400 in cash from the Confederate secretary of war, had crossed the Canadian border, plundered three Vermont banks, stolen $210,000, and turned the entire state into chaos. From New York to Philadelphia, and Washington to Boston, targets would abound: banks, businesses, local army outposts, and even newspapers and statehouses. All were vulnerable. Month after grinding month, year after year, who would be under siege: the victorious Union or the hardened guerrillas?

Across most of the South, the situation would be even more daunting. In Charles Adams's famous warning, "The Confederacy would have been reduced to smoldering wilderness." As in guerrilla wars throughout history, the Union would have to station outposts in every county and every sizable town; they would be forced to put a blockhouse on every railroad bridge and at every major communications center; they would be reduced to combing every sizable valley and every significant mountain range with frequent patrols. With Lee's army and other loyal Confederates—by some historians' estimates, there were still up to 175,000 men under arms who could be called upon—dispersed into smaller, more mobile units, they could make lightning hit-and-run attacks on the invading forces from safe havens in the rugged countryside and then invisibly slip back into the population. Their molestations need not be constant, or even kill many people; they need only be incessant.

Riding past Mahone's troops, at the top of the rise Lee stopped and waited. The wind caught the flag, draping his body in Confederate red. Then a spontaneous cry from the frenzied survivors...

The military balance would be almost meaningless. In truth, more frightening to the Union than the actual casualties it might suffer would be the psychological toll as prolonged occupiers, the profound exhaustion, the constant demoralization. Where would the stamina come from? There would be no real rest, no real respite, no true amity, nor any real sense of victory. Prospects for Northern victory had seemed dim as recently as August 1864, largely because Northerners had grown weary of the war. The Northern home front had nearly crumbled first— and was saved only by the captures of Mobile and, more importantly, of Atlanta, which paved the way for a presidential reelection victory that Lincoln

himself had, just weeks earlier, judged to be an impossibility. Only the heartening prospects of sure and relatively sudden victory had sustained the Federals to this time. In a guerrilla war, all bets would be off. How much longer would the country countenance sending its men into war? How long could it tolerate the necessary mass executions, the sweeping confiscations, the collective expulsions, and all the other agonies and cruelties of a full-scale guerrilla war, which would inevitably pervert its identity as a republic? We know what the French once said of a comparable experience. As its columns sought to put down the guerrilla resistance of Abdelkader in North Africa in 1833, one urgent dispatch to King Louis-Philippe stated sadly: "We have surpassed in barbarity the barbarians we came to civilize." It is hard to imagine Americans willing to pay this price for Union.

Could the South carry it out? Grant and Sherman certainly had no doubt about the Confederacy's ability to wage protracted guerrilla war—it was their greatest fear. At one point, Grant himself ruminated, "To overcome a truly popular, national resistance in a vast territory without the employment of truly overwhelming force is probably impossible." The Union never had any systematic plans to cope with such an eventuality— all of Grant's efforts were principally designed to break up the Confederacy's main armies and to occupy the main cities. The army had failed dismally even in the more limited guerrilla war in Missouri. As General John D. Sanborn, who served under Grant's command, would later admit: "No policy worked; every effort poured fuel on the fire."

Lincoln, too, was equally concerned, and he, as much as anyone else, understood the toll guerrilla war could take on the country. On the Missouri guerrilla conflict he lamented, "Each man feels an impulse to kill his neighbors, lest he first be killed by him. Revenge and retaliation follow. And all this among honest men. But this is not all. Every foul bird comes along, and every dirty reptile rises up." Some of Lincoln's aides put it even more fearfully. Said one, guerrilla warfare is "the external visitation of evil."

Before the Civil War even began, guerrilla activity had already made its mark on the North-South conflict. On May 24, 1856, John Brown and five other abolitionists brutally murdered and mutilated five Southern settlers at Pottawatomie Creek in Kansas. Day after day for over two years, dueling bands of Free-Soil abolitionists and pro-slavery marauders burned, robbed, and killed in an effort to drive the other from "Bleeding Kansas," a grim dress rehearsal for the Civil War to follow. By the time war erupted in 1861, many on the blood-stained Kansas-Missouri border were already veterans of irregular warfare.

And once the war started, across the Confederacy, Southerners quickly took to guerrilla tactics. Sam Hildebrand roamed the woods of southern Missouri slaying scores of Unionists; Champ Ferguson tormented the Cumberland in Tennessee, knifing, mangling, and bludgeoning luckless Federals whenever he encountered them. Before he was eventually captured—and summarily hanged—Ferguson personally extinguished over a hundred lives. In the swamps of Florida, John Jackson Dickison outmaneuvered, outfought, and outfoxed the bluecoats; and anarchy reigned in Unionist Kentucky, where brutal guerrilla bands led by Ike Berry, Marcellus Clark, and scores of others sprang up across the state. At one point, Jesse McNeill and his partisans slipped into Cumberland, Maryland, and in a daring raid captured two Union generals. Whatever draconian measures the Union instituted, including confiscation of property and executions of five guerrillas for every loyalist killed, accomplished little.

Some of the Confederate's guerrillas became legendary, feared not simply in the North, but known internationally on both sides of the Atlantic. Of these, John Mosby was among the most dashing and prominent. Pint-sized, plucky, and daring, he was a bit of a Renaissance man. He read Shakespeare, Plutarch, Washington Irving, and Hazlitt's *Life of Napoleon*, and his words and writings were frequently sprinkled with passages from the classics. The twenty-nine-year-old had been expelled from the University of Virginia—he shot a fellow student—yet he later finagled a pardon from the gov-

ernor, and then, of all things, took up the law. At the outset of the war, he was actually opposed to secession and was an "indifferent soldier" at best; though after joining Jeb Stuart's cavalry, he proved himself to be a fearless courier and cavalry scout and, when he raised a company of his own under the Partisan Ranger Act of April 1862, a remarkable guerrilla leader. His fame rapidly spread with such exploits as the capture of a Northern general, Edwin H. Stoughton, in bed with a hangover—a mere ten miles from Washington, D.C., in March 1863. "Do you know who I am?" bellowed the general, upon being so indiscreetly interrupted. Mosby shot back: "Do you know Mosby, General?" Stoughton harrumphed: "Yes! Have you got the rascal?" Mosby: "No, but he has got you!" (Mosby completed the humiliation by brazenly retreating with his prisoner in full view of Federal fortifications.) Operating on horseback at night, with stealth, surprise, and swiftness, he soon earned the sobriquet of the "Grey Ghost," and the romance surrounding his exploits brought recruit after recruit to his doorstep. In turn, he was sheltered and fed by a large and sympathetic population in northern Virginia, which served as his early warning network—and his refuge. Never amounting to more than a thousand men, Mosby's partisans were confined to small platoons of several dozen. But they mauled Union outposts with such effectiveness and a whirlwind fury that the regions stretching from the Blue Ridge to the Bull Run mountains were quickly dubbed, by friends and foes alike, "Mosby's confederacy." Union supplies could not move through his territory unless well protected, and even then they were likely prey.

The destruction Mosby inflicted upon Union lines was considerable, and he was detested accordingly. Various strategies were employed—without success—to subdue him. One plan called for an elite team of sharpshooters to shadow Mosby until he was either caught or destroyed. It failed. Another promised massive arrests of local civilians in Mosby's confederacy and a wholesale destruction of their mills, barns, and crops. This also failed. While Mosby still

roamed freely, a frustrated General Sheridan, whom Mosby relentlessly foiled in the Shenandoah Valley, once thundered about the restless guerrilla: "Let [him] know there is a God in Israel!" Finally, Grant ordered that any of Mosby's men who were captured should be promptly shot. And in autumn of 1864, General George Custer obliged, capturing six men and executing them all. Three were shot, two were hanged, and a seventeen-year-old boy was dragged bleeding and dying through the streets by two men on horses until a pistol was finally emptied into his face—while his grief-stricken mother hysterically begged for his life. But the Union's hard-line tactics collapsed when Mosby began (albeit reluctantly) hanging prisoners in retaliation. Yet fearsome as he was, Mosby, like his spiritual predecessors Marion, Pickens, and Sumter, represented the civilized face of "little war." And then there was Missouri.

Missouri produced the most bloodthirsty guerrillas of the war. Topping the list was William Clarke Quantrill, a handsome, blue-eyed, twenty-four-year-old former Ohio schoolteacher. A close second was Bloody Bill Anderson, whose father was murdered by Unionists and whose sister was killed in a Kansas City Union prison disaster. Among their disciples were young men destined for later notoriety: Frank and Jesse James, and Coleman Younger.

In early 1862, Quantrill and his band of bushwhackers launched a series of strikes into Kansas that all but paralyzed the state. Then, in 1863, the revenge-minded Quantrill set his sights on a new target: Lawrence, Kansas. One would be hard-pressed to find a place more thoroughly despised by Quantrill and his comrades than Lawrence. It functioned as a Free-Soil citadel during the 1850s, then as a haven for runaway slaves, and, during the war, as a headquarters to the Redlegs, a band of hated Unionist guerrillas. Early in the morning of August 21, Quantrill and his 400 bushwhackers—including Frank James and Coleman Younger—struck. At 5 a.m., Quantrill and his men silently made their way into town. Then the killing began. With a triumphant yell, Quantrill began shouting, "Kill! Kill! Lawrence must be thoroughly cleansed… Kill! Kill!" For the next few hours, his fierce and sweaty long-haired men, unshaven and unwashed, rumbled up and down the streets of Lawrence, looting stores, shops, saloons, and houses. They systematically rounded up every man they encountered and then torched the town. By day's end, the deed was done. The city lay in ashes; 200 homes were burned to the ground. Over 150 innocent civilians, all men and young boys, had been murdered in cold blood.

The event shocked the entire country and captured the attention of the world. Thousands of Federal troopers and Kansas militiamen quickly pursued the bushwhackers, but by the next day, they were safely nestled in the woodlands of Missouri. The Federals swiftly retaliated, issuing the harshest order of the war by either side against civilians, known as General Orders Number 11. Almost as ruthless as the Lawrence raid itself, it was designed to strike at the heart of the guerrillas' power—the support given them by the civilian population. As one officer put it, the order was carried out "to the letter." Four whole counties were quickly depopulated; virtually every citizen was deported; their crops and their forage were destroyed. So were their homes, which were burned. There is no final list of how many innocent people died in the process—although some estimates suggest it surpassed the carnage in Lawrence. Nor is the list of total refugees in this mass exodus fully complete. In one town, the population dwindled from 10,000 to a mere 600. Few of these refugees returned before the war's end. Many never did. When it was all over, these Midwestern counties lay like a silent wasteland, dotted by chimneys rising above the charred debris of blackened farmhouses.

Thus escalated the vicious cycle of retaliation and revenge. For the next six weeks, Quantrill and the partisans skirmished. Yet despite a massive sweep through the woodlands of western Missouri by Federal cavalrymen, Quantrill escaped. He and his men knew the countryside personally, and friends and relatives provided them with shelter, fresh horses, and timely warning in case of pursuit. In a telling instance of the relative ease with which guerrillas operated, Quantrill himself spent much of the time in comfort, neatly residing at a house near Blue Springs with his mistress, Kate King. On October 6, his gang again struck with considerable fury, overcoming a Federal wagon train at Baxter Springs. They mauled and killed eighty-five men, including the band musicians and James O'Neal, an artist for *Frank Leslie's Illustrated Newspaper*. So great was the wave of disgust over this bloodletting that news of the guerrilla war in the West actually supplanted—temporarily at least—the clash of armies in the East. Even Confederate generals were dismayed at the wanton carnage. Noted one high-ranking military man in Richmond, "they recognize the life of a man less than you would that of a dog killing a sheep."

The Union soldiers hunted the guerrillas like animals, and in return, eventually degenerated into little more than savage beasts, driven by a viciousness unimaginable just two years earlier. By 1864, the guerrilla war had reached new peaks of savagery. Now it was no longer enough to ambush and gun down the enemy. They had to be mutilated and, just as often, scalped. When that was no longer enough, the dead were stripped and castrated. Soon, Quantrill and his men were riding about wearing scalps dangling from their bridles, as well as an assortment of other body parts—ears, noses, teeth, even fingers—vivid trophies of their latest victims.

All order broke down. Groups of revenge-minded Federals, militia and even soldiers became guerrillas themselves, stalking tormenting, torturing, and slaying Southern sympathizers. Ruthless reprisals and random terror became the norm; Missouri was dragged into a whirlpool of vengeance. New and no less bloodthirsty gangs of bushwhackers rose up, led by George Todd, John Thrailkill, and others who roved virtually unchecked, baiting and murdering Federal patrols, and bringing all affairs in Missouri to a halt. Trains were attacked. So were stage lines. Steamboats were not safe, coming under repeated sniper fire. To run the gauntlet on the Missouri, pilots started to request—and received—a thousand dollars for a single trip to Kansas. Petrified, Unionists ran, abandoning their houses and their farms, and converging on fortified towns—actually, by now they were garrisoned—which were reduced to nothing more than isolated enclaves in a sea of death. Soldiers were pinned down at their posts in a countryside dominated by guerrillas, their men as much hunted as hunters.

Missouri was something that had never been witnessed before on American soil. And the Union was utterly unable to cope with the ongoing terror. Federal policies were at once muddled, incoherent, and ineffective. A collective sociopathy reigned in Missouri, civil society was torn apart; all morals disintegrated. Both sides snapped. In a war without fronts, boundaries, and formal organization, the distinction between civilians and soldiers/partisans almost totally evaporated. Both those who sheltered the guerrillas and those who collaborated with the Unionists placed their lives in peril.

A favorite torture tactic was repetitive hanging. One father, as his family watched helplessly, was strung up three times—and only on the last try was the deed done. Another's son was walked to the noose some seven times before he met his fate. Toenails would be pulled off, one by one. Knives would be thrust into bellies—but only partially. To survive, people cheated, lied, and bore false witness against their neighbors—anything to appease the other side. Neutrality became impossible. In the words of historian Michael Fellman, life in Missouri became a "life of secret impeachments, divided loyalties, and whispered confidences."

Townsfolk couldn't trust their own neighbors, not even those they had known for years. The smallest tic in speech came to mean something ominous; the slightest arched eyebrow would be feared. Union troops fared little better. In most instances their deaths came at the hands of some unseen sniper. So all civilians were seen as enemies.

By 1864, most rural Missourians had become refugees, inside or outside the state. "We hear of some outrage every day," blithely confessed one Missourian. Wrote the *Kansas City Journal of Commerce* in 1864, even before the worst of it: "East of us, west of us, north of us, south of us, comes the same harrowing story. Pandemonium itself seems to have broken loose, and robbery, murder and rapine, and death run riot over the country." One Union general said it perhaps most poignantly: "there was something in the hearts of good and typical Christian[s]... which had exploded."

Early in the war, in an attempt to tap the growing discontent behind enemy lines, the Confederate government had legitimized guerrilla organizations with the Partisan Ranger Act of April 1862. Yet, as time went by, and even as the roaming guerrillas tied down Union troops and Union energy, a number of Confederate authorities found the guerrillas' methods distasteful. To the chivalric Southerners, war was about noble sacrifice; it was to be gentlemanly and Christian, and there was an aristocratic code of honor to be adhered to. Typically, when most rebel generals thought of guerrillas, they thought of Mosby. Missouri was another matter.

If Lee were somehow to succeed with guerilla warfare, his place in history would be assured. The temptation must have been vast.

By 1864, because of the atrocities committed by bushwhackers in the West, as well as the penchant for plunder that virtually all guerrilla bands displayed, powerful Southern voices eventually called for repeal of the Partisan Ranger Act. Finally, in early 1865, the Confederate Congress did revoke the act and the government ended its sanction of all partisan groups, with two notable exceptions: Mosby's rangers in the north, and Jesse McNeill's partisans in western Virginia. Lee himself was instrumental in the Congress's decision.

Thus on that morning of April 9, 1865, Lee had two very different faces of guerrilla war to consider: the first was the face of a Mosby. Beyond that, there was the shining example of his own

Carolina ancestors against the British Lord Cornwallis. Or, alternatively, there was the anarchic, scarlet-stained face of Missouri. In all likelihood, a guerrilla war countrywide would be a combination of the two, and, even at this late date, it could likely have an awesome impact: total conquest could be resisted, until, perhaps, attrition and exhaustion would lead the North to sue the South for peace.

The drum of history rarely beats for the men on the losing side in wars. Few are venerated in civic halls and history lessons. Lee was confronted with one last chance, one last opportunity for vindication. If he were somehow to succeed with guerrilla warfare, his place in history would be assured. The temptation must have been vast; no one should think otherwise.

So a sleep-deprived Robert E. Lee—now unable to move west, or south, or east, only north, the very last direction he wanted to go—listened to one of his most trusted advisers in the cool early morning hours of April 9. Hearing Porter Alexander out, he was doing some quick calculations in his head about the effect that generations of bushwhacking—guerrilla warfare—would have on the country. Lee, however, principled to the bitter end, was thinking not about personal glory, but along quite different lines. What is honorable? What is proper? What is right? Likely recalling Missouri, he quickly reasoned that a guerrilla war would make a wasteland of all that he loved. Brother would be set against brother, not just for four years, but for generations. Such a war would surely destroy Virginia, and just as surely destroy the country as well. Even if it worked, and perhaps especially if it worked. For Lee, that was too high a price to pay. No matter how much he believed in the Cause—his daring attempts over the last nine days were vivid testimony to that—there were limits to Southern independence. As he had once said, "it [is] better to do right, even if we suffer in so doing, than to incur the reproach of our consciences & posterity."

But Lee, more so than most other generals, also shunned making political de-

cisions. He was uncompromising about the unique American ethos of respecting the primacy of civilian leadership to make judgments about affairs of state. Yet this was surely a political decision. If he were to surrender his troops, it would be against the advice of Jefferson Davis, against the advice of his civilian authority. But on that Palm Sunday morning of April 9, he forged ahead.

Suppose, he told Porter Alexander, that "I should take your suggestion. The men would be without rations and under no control of officers... They would be compelled to rob and steal in order to live. They would become... bands of marauders, and the enemy's cavalry would... overrun many sections they may never have occasion to visit...

"We would bring on a state of affairs it would take the country years to recover from."

He continued his counsel to Alexander: "Then, General, you and I as Christian men have no right to consider only how this would affect us." We must, he stressed, "consider its effect on the country as a whole." Finally, Lee said, "And as for myself, you young fellows might go bushwhacking, but the only dignified course for me would be to go to General Grant and surrender myself and take the consequences of my acts."

Thus did Robert E. Lee, revered for his leadership in war, make his most historic contribution—to peace. By this one momentous decision, he spared the country the guerrilla war that surely would have followed, a vile and poisonous conflict that would not only have delayed any true national reconciliation for many years to come, but in all probability would have fractured the country for decades into warring military pockets. Nor is it idle to speculate that at such a late date such a mode of warfare might well have accomplished what four years of conventional war had failed to do: cleave North from South.

Just that morning, gloomily staring off into the distance, into the lifting mist, he had cried out, "How easily I could be rid of all this and be at rest! I have only to ride along the line and all will be over." But Lee weighed honor and glory against duty and will. He had already told his immediate staff with a heavy heart: "Then there is nothing left for me to do but to go and see General Grant, and I would rather die a thousand deaths." Poignantly, while tears and grief enveloped his men, he would add, "it is our duty to live."

Though Lee remained unaware, the fall of Richmond just six days before had already brought a spate of stinging calls for revenge, a grisly, thundering, roaring refrain, chanted and chanted again in an ever-rising crescendo, coming from New York, Boston, Philadelphia, Chicago, and, of course, Washington ("Burn it! BURN IT! LET HER BURN!" they cried about Richmond. On treason: "Treason is the highest crime known in the catalogue of crimes, and for him that is guilty of it... I would say death is too easy a punishment!" On Jefferson Davis: "HANG him! HANG him! Yes, I say *HANG* him twenty times!" On the Confederates who had graduated from West Point: "Those who have been fed, clothed, and taught at the public expense ought to stretch the first rope!" On those who had lifted their hands against the North: "Treason must be made odious; traitors must be punished and impoverished!... I would arrest them, I would try them, I would convict them, and I would hang them!" On pardons: "Never! Never!" And on Lee himself, a chorus cried: "*HANG LEE!* HANG LEE! HANG LEE!").

Indeed, the *Chicago Tribune* had recommended just that.

From *The American Spectator*, March 2001, pp. 69–81. © 2001 by The American Spectator, LLC. Reprinted by permission.

ABSENCE *of* MALICE

IN A NEW BOOK, HISTORIAN RONALD C. WHITE, JR., EXPLAINS WHY
LINCOLN'S SECOND INAUGURAL ADDRESS, GIVEN JUST WEEKS
BEFORE HE DIED, WAS HIS GREATEST SPEECH

"For too long," says Ronald C. White, Jr., "Lincoln's Second Inaugural Address has lived under the shadow of the Gettysburg Address. And yet Lincoln thought this was his best effort." White does too. In his new book, Lincoln's Greatest Speech: The Second Inaugural, *excerpted here, the professor of American religious history at San Francisco Theological Seminary sees the speech as key to understanding Lincoln's greatness.*

White's fascination with the 16th President was sparked at a 1993 seminar. "He was the average American, with only one year of education, a man who was really quite ugly in a certain sense—could he ever have campaigned today?—tall, awkward, gawky, clothes ill-fitting, with a tenor voice, almost a falsetto, and yet he was a huge man for his day, 6 feet 4 inches tall. Everything about him was against his being a powerful speaker. But once he began to speak, what people sensed was his integrity. He was not playing a role. And the audience of that day picked it up." More than 130 years after Lincoln's assassination, that quality still moves people powerfully. "He had the knack of asking these simple but very profound questions. In every crisis, whether it's September 11 or World War II, it is amazing how people return to Lincoln."

By March 1865 (until 1937, Presidents were generally inaugurated in March), America had been flayed by four years of a war that had lasted longer than anyone thought it would, but whose end, at last, seemed in sight. Not since Andrew Jackson, 32 years before, had any President been elected for a second term, and, says White, "there had been no expectation of it. There had been a series of one-term Presidents with not much to commend them." Nor did those gathered to hear Lincoln that rainy day—fans and detractors, newspaper reporters, Confederate deserters, black troops, plainclothes detectives fearful that Lincoln was going to be abducted—expect the 703-word speech the President delivered. What they heard was neither a recitation of achievement nor a statement of policy, but a sermon in which, White says, "Lincoln would ask his audience to think with him about the cause and meaning of the war."

In the six-minute address, Lincoln used repetition and alliteration to give his sentences a cadence White likens to poetry. Five hundred of the words are of a single syllable, "but that doesn't mean it's simple." An understated sentence such as "And the war came," says White, lifts the conflict from human event to something with a life of its own "independent of Presidents, generals and soldiers."

Now inscribed on the limestone walls of the Lincoln Memorial, the Second Inaugural Address can be understood, White believes, as a "culmination of Lincoln's own struggle over the meaning of America, the meaning of the war, and his own struggle with slavery."

And, he adds, as a blueprint for tolerance. "Lincoln hoped that this speech was laying the groundwork for a reconstruction of compassion and reconciliation."

PRESIDENT ABRAHAM LINCOLN HAD every reason to be hopeful as inauguration day, March 4, 1865, approached. The Confederacy was splintered, if not shattered. On February 1, Union General William Tecumseh Sherman led sixty thousand troops out of Savannah. Slashing through South Carolina, they wreaked havoc in the state that had been the seedbed of secession. To celebrate victories in Columbia and Charleston, South Carolina, and Wilmington, North Carolina, Lincoln ordered a nighttime illumination in Washington. Crowds celebrated these achievements in song as the harbinger of the end of the hostilities.

At the same time, Union General Ulysses S. Grant was besieging Petersburg, Virginia, twenty miles south of Richmond. Despite Confederate General Robert E. Lee's previous record for forestalling defeat, it was clear that the badly outnumbered Confederates could not hold out much longer. Everything pointed toward victory.

Apprehension intruded upon this hopeful spirit. Rumors were flying about the capital that desperate Confederates, now realizing that defeat was imminent, would attempt to abduct or assassinate the president. Secretary of War Edwin M. Stanton took extraordinary precautions. All roads leading to Washington had been heavily picketed for some days and the bridges patrolled with "extra vigilance." The 8th Illinois Cavalry was sent out from Fairfax Court House with orders to look for "suspicious characters." The problem was greatly complicated by the presence of large numbers of Confederate deserters who now roamed the capital. Stanton posted sharpshooters on the buildings that would ring the inaugural ceremonies. Plainclothes detectives roved the city keeping track of questionable persons.

After four years as a war president, Lincoln could look ahead to four years as a peace president. With no Congress in session until December to hamper him, he would have free rein to do some peacemaking on his own. Gamblers were even betting that the sixteenth president would be inaugurated for a third term in 1869. The president, who had been battered by critics in Congress and the press for much of the war, was finally beginning to receive credit for his leadership. Many were suggesting that the stakes were about to get higher. Would Lincoln, the resourceful commander-in-chief, guide a re-united nation during what was beginning to be called "Reconstruction"?

As the day for his second inauguration drew near, everyone wondered what the president would say. No one seemed to know anything about the content of Lincoln's speech. A dispatch from the Associated Press reported that the address would be "brief—not exceeding, probably, a column in length." It was recalled that he took thirty-five minutes to deliver his First Inaugural Address. The *New York Herald* reported that "the address will probably be the briefest one ever delivered." Another report said the address would take only five to eight minutes.

If reports about the length of the address were correct, how would Lincoln deal with questions that were multiplying? Would he use his rhetorical skills to take the hide off his opponents in the South and North? Was the Confederate States of America to be treated as a conquered nation? How did one demarcate between the innocent and the guilty, between citizens and soldiers? What would Lincoln say about the slaves? They had been emancipated but what about suffrage?

All of these questions involved complex constitutional issues. Lincoln had used a good portion of his First Inaugural to argue carefully and logically his understanding of the indissoluble Union in light of the Constitution. The *New York World*, a New York City newspaper that had been a thorn in his side all through the war, contended that the Second Inaugural Address "ought to be the most significant and reassuring of all his public utterances."

Just beneath the outward merry-making lay a different emotion. A weariness of spirit pervaded the nation. Government officials were fatigued from four long years of war. The agony of battle took its toll on families everywhere. Many citizens were filled with as much anger as hope. Even the anticipation of victory could not compensate for the loss of so many young men, cut down in death or disabled by horrible wounds just as they were preparing to harvest the fruits of their young lives.

And death and despair reached into nearly every home. An estimated 623,000 men died in the Civil War. One out of eleven men of service age was killed between 1861 and 1865. Comparisons with Americans killed in other wars bring the horror home. In World War I, the number killed was 117,000. In World War II, 405,000 died. In the Korean War, the death toll was 54,000. In the war in Vietnam, the number of Americans killed was 58,000. Deaths in the Civil War almost equal the number killed in all subsequent wars.

For example, New Braintree, Massachusetts, with a population of 805 shopkeepers, laborers, farmers, and their families, sent 78 young men to fight; 10 did not return. Phillipston, Massachusetts, population 764, dispatched 76 of its young citizens to fight; 9 died on battlefields. The people of Auburn, Massachusetts watched 97 soldiers go off to war; they would mourn the 15 who never returned. The people of the United States in the early 1860s felt the impact of war in their small communities. Had World War II produced the same proportion of deaths as did the Civil War, more than two and a half million men would have died.

Washington had never seen so many people as those who converged on the capital for Lincoln's second inauguration. Trains roared and smoked over the double tracks of the Baltimore and Ohio. The *Washington Daily National Intelligencer* reported, "Every train was crowded to repletion." Visitors were greeted by a band playing "The Battle Cry of Freedom." Each day the Washington newspapers listed the notables who were arriving. All knew they were coming to witness a unique event.

Hotels were overflowing. Willard's, the grand five-story hotel at Pennsylvania Avenue and Fourteenth Street, set up cots in its halls and parlors. The Metropolitan and the National were filled. "The hotels are literally shelving their guests," reported the correspondent for the *New York Times*. Lincoln-Johnson Clubs lodged more than a thousand visitors. Firehouses offered sleeping spaces.

Friends and supporters of the president, who was beleaguered during much of his first term, now declared that the recent events vindicated his leadership. In an editorial published inauguration morning, the *Illinois Daily State Journal*, a friend of Lincoln's from his earliest campaigns as a legislator, declared, "All honor to Abraham Lincoln through whose honesty, fidelity, and patriotism, those glorious results [of the war] have been achieved." The *Chicago Tribune*, also a staunch supporter, proclaimed that "Mr. Lincoln... has slowly and steadily risen in the respect, confidence, and admiration of the people."

This second inauguration, so some of his supporters argued, ought to be a time for Lincoln to crow a bit. The *Daily Morning Chronicle* agreed. "We shall not be surprised if the President does not, in the words he will utter this morning, point to the pledges he gave us in his inaugural of 1861, and claim that he has not departed from them in a single substantial instance."

In spite of the inclement weather, Friday morning, March 3, visitors crowded the streets of the capital, where spring rains had just begun to turn the grass from winter brown to green. Chestnuts and elms, planted at the turn of the century, were not quite in bloom. Cherry blossoms would not be known in the capital until early in the next century. Nothing could hide the disorder and dirt that were everywhere. The national capital, scarcely six decades old, remained an almost-city. Charles Dickens, on his first visit to the United States, in 1842, had called Washington "the City of Magnificent Intentions." He described it as "spacious avenues, that begin in nothing, and lead no-where; streets, mile-long, that only want houses, roads, and in-habitants; public buildings that need but a public to be complete."

When Lincoln had first come to the city as an Illinois congressman in December 1847, Washington had barely thirty-five thousand residents. The 1860 census counted 61,100 inhabitants. Thirteen cities ranked ahead of the capital in population. Most people would add that these cities also surpassed the capital in civility and culture. "If you want to be disgusted with the place chosen for the Capital of your country," wrote a visitor from Phil-adelphia, "visit it in the spring time, near the close of four days' rain, when the frost is beginning to come out of the ground. Whatever other objects of interest may attract your notice, the muddy streets and pavements will scarcely escape you."

The leading objects of interest were the Capitol building with its new iron dome, the Executive Mansion, the Post Office, the Patent Office, and the Treasury. European visitors dismissed the White House as an ordinary coun-try house. A great problem with the White House was its location near the Potomac Flats. This dis-mal body of water was held re-sponsible for the outbreaks of malaria that occurred in summer and autumn. The Smithsonian In-stitution stood alone as a mu-seum. A tour of all the important buildings in Washington could be completed in an afternoon.

The staggering number of war wounded and dying could not be confined to the city's hospitals. They could be found in hotels, warehouses, also schools, and lodges of fraternal orders. George-town College was turned into a hospital. Many private homes, and most churches, took in wounded. On Independence Day, 1862, some church bells could not be rung be-cause the wounded lay beneath the bells.

The Patent Office held injured Union soldiers. Visitors to the Smithsonian could hardly miss the huge Armory Square Hospital nearby, which was in fact a series of parallel sheds. Even the Capitol building had been transformed into a hospital, two thousand cots placed in corridors and even in the Rotunda.

As Friday evening wore on, a dense fog descended over the cap-ital followed by more rain, yet even the dismal weather could not dampen the spirits of the visitors. Among the arrivals were three fire companies from Philadelphia, nearly three hundred men dressed smartly in black fire hats, coats, and pants, and eye-catching red shirts. The capital became mu-sical with military bands and sere-naders. High in the fog, the lights of the now completed Capitol building created the effect of a halo over the festivities.

Within the government, there was no time yet for celebration. Lincoln met Friday night with his cabinet until a late hour, working to finish business related to the last acts of the outgoing 38th Congress. The Senate had been meeting all day and continued its session into the evening. As tem-pers flared and energy sagged, this legislative all-nighter became a strange prelude to the inaugu-ral ceremonies on the morrow.

March 4 dawned with incessant rain as more visitors poured into the city, many arriving aboard special trains the railroad compa-nies had prepared to accommo-date them. The streets oozed with soft mud, described by locals as "black plaster." The Corps of En-gineers surveyed the scene to de-termine the practicality of laying pontoons on Pennsylvania Ave-nue from the Capitol to the White House. They found the bottom too unstable to hold the anchors of the needed boats. The project was abandoned. During the early-morning hours, gale winds whipped through the city, uproot-ing trees.

The Senate and House worked on until seven o'clock in the morning. On one occasion a sud-den burst of rain suggested "an explosion inside the building," causing many "to run towards the doors." The leaders of the House and Senate convinced the members to come back to their seats.

Fog continued to hang over the city as the crowd began ar-riving at the east entrance of the Capitol, with its radiant iron dome topped by its statue, *Armed Liberty*. (Despite the war, Lincoln had insisted that the work on the dome proceed; its completion represented his hope that one day all the states and their representatives would meet again to do the nation's business.) Carriages were in great demand. The *Philadelphia Inquirer* reported that the arriv-ing throng was present "in force sufficient to have struck terror into the heart of Lee's army (had the umbrellas been mus-kets)." As visitors and residents walked toward the Capitol, they encountered military pa-trols on horseback at every ma-jor intersection.

Some in the crowd remem-bered quite a different scene four

years earlier. Trepidation and gloom had clouded March 4, 1861. Everything seemed in disarray. Sections of the dome lay jumbled near the inauguration stand, waiting for fitting. On his way from Illinois to assume the presidency two weeks before, Lincoln had to be spirited through Baltimore in disguise to avoid abduction. This episode, of which Lincoln was not proud, humiliated his supporters. Cartoonists ridiculed him, adding to the venom that was already spewing out in some of the press reports on the president-elect.

On the Saturday of the second inaugural, the rain stopped at nine-thirty. By ten-thirty, the skies were clearing. Then, at ten-forty, torrential rains came again. Open windows, crammed with sightseers, had to be slammed shut. Women tied their white handkerchiefs to their bonnets. Noah Brooks, correspondent for the *Sacramento Daily Union*, wrote that "Flocks of women streamed around the Capitol, in most wretched plight; crinoline was smashed, skirts bedaubed, and moiré antique, velvet, laces and such dry goods were streaked with mud from end to end." What should have been a brightly dressed gathering appeared instead thoroughly bedraggled by the elements of mud and wind. But as the reporter for the *New York Herald* observed, "The crowd was good-natured." They were there to participate in these grand events.

The ceremonial procedures would not differ substantially from Lincoln's first inauguration. Yet there were differences. Instead of the small clusters of soldiers in 1861, large numbers of military could be observed throughout the city. In certain sections of the capital, multiplying numbers of Confederate deserters could be seen. Twelve hundred and thirty-nine disheartened Confederate soldiers had arrived in February. All the soldiers were marked by their wounds. Ampu-

tation had become the trademark of Civil War surgery. According to federal records, three out of four operations were amputations. Too often the surgery had to be repeated. Many visitors professed shock at the sight of so many young men with amputated legs or arms.

Black soldiers had changed the composition of the army from 1861 to 1865. For the first two years of the war, the Union Army was all white. Lincoln had initiated the North's employment of African-American troops when he issued the Emancipation Proclamation on January 1, 1863. The use of black troops prompted protests both in the North and in the South, but 179,000 black soldiers and ten thousand sailors would serve in the Union forces before the end of the war. By inauguration day, black soldiers had become a common sight in Washington.

The presence of so many blacks in the inaugural crowds particularly struck the correspondent for the *Times* of London. He estimated that "at least half the multitude were colored people. It was remarked by everybody, stranger as well as natives, that there never had been such crowds of negroes in the capital." Whereas many in the crowds, because of the mud, were dressed in "old clothes," African Americans, despite the dismal weather, were noticeable also because of their dress "in festive reds, blues, and yellows, and very gaudy colors."

By midmorning, the inaugural parade, which preceded the swearing in ceremonies in Lincoln's time, was forming. Grand Marshal Ward Lamon, an old friend from Illinois, went to the White House to escort the president to the Capitol. Lamon had arranged to have thirteen brightly clothed United States marshals and thirteen citizen marshals accompany Lincoln's

carriage. Lamon did not know that Lincoln had driven off to the Capitol earlier in the morning to sign some bills, abandoning the usual protocol. As one observer noted, the parade was "the play of Hamlet with Hamlet left out."

The procession began to move at 11 a.m. from the corner of Pennsylvania Avenue and Tenth Street. At the front marched 119 metropolitan policemen. Union soldiers, many in shabby blue uniforms, followed. The three companies of volunteer firemen from Philadelphia were a hit with their smart uniforms. Chicago firemen drew their engine while they marched, as did companies from other cities. Local pride soared when the Fire Department of the City of Washington followed with its horse-drawn steam engines.

Far down the parade line was something never before witnessed at a presidential inauguration. Four companies of black soldiers, members of the 45th Regiment United States Colored Troops, marched smartly. Immediately following was a lodge of African-American Odd Fellows, a fraternal organization. The crowd cheered.

Next in line came a series of floats, patriotic but a bit dowdy. First was the Temple of Liberty, a tent made out of muslin, now soggy. The original intention had been to surround the tent with young "maidens" from each state of the Union. The rain prompted the float's organizers to replace the young girls with boys. The boys entertained the crowd by singing patriotic songs such as "Rally Round the Flag" and "The Battle Cry of Freedom." The next float—drawn by four white horses, soon spattered with mud—presented by members of the Lincoln-Johnson Club of East Washington, bore a replica of the iron warship *Monitor*.

The crowd buzzed as the third float, carrying an operational printing press, came into view. Staff members of the *Daily Morning Chronicle* busily printed a four-page inaugural newspaper that contained a program for the day, copies of which were tossed to the spectators on both sides of the avenue.

The special marshals and the President's Union Light Guard escorted Mrs. Lincoln. The crowd cheered the presidential coach along the route from the White House to the Capitol, not knowing that the president was not present.

After a festive beginning, the parade suddenly came to a halt in a snarled confusion of horses, troops, and fire engines. Following twenty minutes without movement, an impatient Mary Lincoln commanded her driver to pull out and proceed by a back way to the Capitol. The parade finally resumed, now without either the president or the president's wife.

Posters, ribbons, ferrotypes, medals, and tokens prepared for the 1864 presidential campaign were visible everywhere. One medal was inscribed "A Foe to Traitors," while another read "No Compromise with Armed Rebels." An 1864 campaign ribbon captured the now clearly understood twin goals of the war: "Union and Liberty." Another medal was inscribed "Freedom to All Men / War for the Union." The theme of human rights was captured in tokens. One side read "Lincoln," and on the other side was "Proclaim Liberty Throughout the Land." Another read "Lincoln and Liberty" on one side and, on the other, "Freedom/Justice/Truth."

The committee on arrangements was taking measures to move the inaugural ceremonies into the Senate chamber, in case the weather didn't improve. A decision to do so would be a great disappointment to the tens of thousands massing outside. At ten o'clock, the Senate galleries had opened and spectators rushed to secure seats. The press gallery of the Senate was crowded with reporters from across the nation. Undaunted by the mud on their grand skirts, women were settled above the assemblage in the ladies' gallery.

On the Senate floor, senators conversed with government officials and celebrity guests. Many eyes were riveted on the military heroes Admiral David G. Farragut and General Joseph Hooker. The diplomatic corps was resplendent in uniforms replete with gold lace and decorations. The air grew muggy. The ventilating system of the Capitol was insufficient to deal with the moisture and humidity. As more and more people crowded the Senate floor and galleries in their rain-soaked clothes, the temperature rose.

At eleven-forty-five, the official procession began to file into the chamber. The retiring vice-president, Hannibal Hamlin, and the vice-president-elect, Andrew Johnson, walked in together. The reporter for the *New York Herald* observed that Johnson, leaning on Hamlin's arm, was unsteady, but concluded that the likely reason was excitement. Lincoln was still signing bills in the president's room just off the Senate chamber.

At twelve o'clock, Hamlin, who had complained that the vice-presidency was a powerless job, began his farewell speech. Secretary of State William Seward and members of the Cabinet interrupted Hamlin's short speech as they arrived to take their seats. Next came the chief justice, Salmon P. Chase, leading in eight black-gowned elderly men, who took their places before the presiding officer's desk. Senators asked the vice-president to ask the women in the galleries to stop their "disrespectful giggling and chatter," but the request had no effect. Hamlin resumed his speech, only to be interrupted yet again when Mary Lincoln took her seat in the diplomatic gallery. Guests continued to arrive as he concluded.

Andrew Johnson was introduced and rose to give his inaugural speech. Lincoln had left the choice of a vice-president to the convention. Johnson, a war Democrat from Tennessee, had been chosen as Lincoln's running mate to symbolize the transformation of the Republican Party in 1864 into a National Union party. Lincoln had admired Johnson's courage in adhering to the Union after his state seceded. In the nineteenth century, the vice-president commanded less stature and visibility than today. Although two presidents, William Henry Harrison and Zachary Taylor, had died in office, accession to the presidency had not been a consideration in Johnson's nomination.

Lincoln arrived and took his seat in the Senate chamber as Johnson began to speak. No one in the chamber was aware of how Johnson had spent the hour before his speech. He had not been well for several weeks, and the trip from Nashville to Washington had only made things worse. The morning of the inauguration, he went to the vice-president's office in the Capitol to await the official ceremony. Feeling unwell, he asked for some whisky. He filled his glass and drank it straight. On the way to the Senate chamber he had another. And then a third.

At the new vice-president's first utterance, it became obvious to all that Andy Johnson was drunk. The traditional brief inaugural speech of the vice-president became a rambling affair. Trumpeting that he had risen to this high office from the masses, he instructed all present that they owed their positions to the people. He did not even address the Cabinet members by their titles. The assembled dignitaries and guests were shocked. Attorney General James Speed whispered to Secretary of the Navy Gideon Welles, "The man is certainly deranged." He then sat with his eyes closed. Welles in turn whispered to Stanton, "Johnson is either drunk or crazy."

The New York Herald later reported that Johnson delivered "a speech remarkable for its incoherence which brought a blush to the cheek of every senator and official of the government." Johnson, scheduled to speak for seven minutes, spoke for seventeen. Finally, Hamlin pulled at Johnson's coat tail and the tribulation ended. But not quite. After Johnson took the oath of office, he put his hand on the Bible and said in a blaring voice, "I kiss this Book in the face of my nation of the United States." He followed his words with a drunken kiss. Lincoln bent over to Senator John B. Henderson of Missouri, a marshal for the inauguration, and whispered, "Do not let Johnson speak outside."

At eleven-forty the rain had suddenly ceased, and arrangements were completed to hold the ceremonies outside. President Lincoln was escorted through a corridor to the temporary wood platform that extended from the east front of the Capitol. Noah Brooks, who was Lincoln's friend as well as correspondent for the *Sacramento Daily Union*, described the immense crowd as a "sea of heads. As far as the eye could see, the throng looked like waves breaking at its outer edges."

Soldiers were dispersed throughout the crowd. Some had come in uniform from the camps. Many more came from area hospitals. Lincoln was always the soldiers' president. He liked to mingle with enlisted men and often visited wounded soldiers. The military personnel had returned a 75 percent vote for him in his re-election the previous November. Now thousands of them were present to witness the inauguration of their president.

In the crowd, Lincoln recognized Frederick Douglass, the articulate African-American abolitionist leader, reformer, and newspaper editor. Lincoln's First Inaugural Address had dismayed Douglass. He had found Lincoln's words much too conciliatory toward the South. Douglass visited Lincoln in the White House in 1863 and again in 1864 to speak with the president about a variety of issues concerning African Americans. Douglass's attitudes about the president during the Civil War had whipsawed back and forth from disgust to respect, and from despair to hope.

Up behind the right buttress stood the actor John Wilkes Booth. Lincoln had seen Booth perform at Ford's Theatre the previous November. Booth, twenty-six years old, had been an actor since he was seventeen. Seething with hatred, Booth had been working on a plan to abduct Lincoln and take him to Richmond. Now that the South's military fortunes had taken a turn for the worse, Booth resolved that stronger measures were needed. He was in touch with the Southern Secret Service as he sought an opportunity to do something "heroic" for the South. He came to hear the Second Inaugural for his own dark motives. He must have wondered, what would this false president say?

When Lincoln was introduced, the crowd exploded. Brooks reported, "A roar of applause shook the air, and again, and again repeated." The military band played "Hail to the Chief," helping to build the enthusiasm of the gathering. The applause and cheers rolled toward those in the farthest reaches of the crowd. Finally, George T. Browne, sergeant-at-arms of the Senate, arose and bowed with black hat in hand, a signal for the crowd to become still.

Abraham Lincoln rose from his chair. He stepped from underneath the shelter of the Capitol building and out past the magnificent Corinthian columns. At fifty-six, he looked older than his years. He advanced to a small, white iron table, the single piece of furniture on the portico. We do not know how it got there. It well may be that its maker, Major Benjamin Brown French, a Lincoln admirer, simply placed it there. The table, made out of pieces from the dome's construction, symbolized for French the reuniting of the fragments of the Union. A lone tumbler of water stood on the little table.

As Lincoln rose, he put on and adjusted his steel-rimmed eyeglasses. He held in his left hand his Second Inaugural Address, printed in two columns. The handwritten draft had been set in type. The galley proof was clipped and pasted in an order to indicate pauses for emphasis and breathing.

Precisely as Lincoln began to speak, the sun broke through the clouds. Many persons, at the time and for years after, commented on this celestial phenomenon. Michael Shiner, an African-American mechanic in the naval shipyard in Washington, recorded his awe in his diary entry for March 4: "As soon as Mr. Lincoln came out the wind ceased blowing and the rain ceased raining and the Sun came out and it became clear as it could be and calm." Shiner continued: "A star made its appearance ... over the Capitol and it shined just as bright as it could be." Brooks reported the same phenomenon. "Just at that moment the sun, which had been obscured all day, burst forth in its unclouded meridian splendor, and flooded the spectacle with glory and with light."

Lincoln prepared to speak:

THE SECOND INAUGURAL

MARCH 4, 1865

FELLOW COUNTRYMEN: AT THIS SECOND APPEARING, TO take the oath of the presidential office, there is less occasion for an extended address than there was at the first. Then a statement, somewhat in detail, of a course to be pursued, seemed fitting and proper. Now, at the expiration of four years, during which public declarations have been constantly called forth on every point and phase of the great contest which still absorbs the attention, and engrosses the enerergies [sic] of the nation, little that is new could be presented. The progress of our arms, upon which all else chiefly depends, is as well known to the public as to myself; and it is, I trust, reasonably satisfactory and encouraging to all. With high hope for the future, no prediction in regard to it is ventured.

On the occasion corresponding to this four years ago, all thoughts were anxiously directed to an impending civil war. All dreaded it—all sought to avert it. While the inaugeral [sic] address was being delivered from this place, devoted altogether to *saving* the Union without war, insurgent agents were in the city seeking to *destroy* it without war—seeking to dissole [sic] the Union, and divide effects, by negotiation. Both parties deprecated war; but one of them would *make* war rather than let the nation survive; and the other would *accept* war rather than let it perish. And the war came.

One eighth of the whole population were colored slaves, not distributed generally over the Union, but localized in the Southern part of it. These slaves constituted a peculiar and powerful interest. All knew that this interest was, somehow, the cause of the war. To strengthen, perpetuate, and extend this interest was the object for which the insurgents would rend the Union, even by war; while the government claimed no right to do more than to restrict the territorial enlargement of it. Neither party expected for the war, the magnitude, or the duration, which it has already attained. Neither anticipated that the *cause* of the conflict might cease with, or even before, the conflict itself should cease. Each looked for an easier triumph, and a result less fundamental and astounding. Both read the same Bible, and pray to the same God; and each invokes His aid against the other. It may seem strange that any men should dare to ask a just God's assistance in wringing their bread from

the sweat of other men's faces; but let us judge not that we be not judged. The prayers of both could not be answered; that of neither has been answered fully. The Almighty has his own purposes. "Woe unto the world because of offences! for it must needs be that offences come; but woe to that man by whom the offence cometh!" If we shall suppose that American Slavery is one of those offences which, in the providence of God, must needs come, but which, having continued through His appointed time, He now wills to remove, and that He gives to both North and South, this terrible war, as the woe due to those by whom the offence came, shall we discern therein any departure from those divine attributes which the believers in a Living God always ascribe to Him? Fondly do we hope—fervently do we pray—that this mighty scourge of war may speedily pass away. Yet, if God wills that it continue, until all the wealth piled by the bondman's two hundred and fifty years of unrequited toil shall be sunk, and until every drop of blood drawn with the lash, shall be paid by another drawn with the sword, as was said three thousand years ago, so still it must be said "the judgments of the Lord, are true and righteous altogether[."]

With malice toward none; with charity for all; with firmness in the right, as God gives us to see the right, let us strive on to finish the work we are in; to bind up the nation's wounds; to care for him who shall have borne the battle, and for his widow, and his orphan—to do all which may achieve and cherish a just, and a lasting peace, among ourselves, and with all nations.

That night, at a reception at the White House, the President sought out abolitionist Frederick Douglass. "I saw you in the crowd today, listening to my inaugural address," Lincoln said. "How did you like it?"

Douglass demurred. "I must not detain you with my poor opinion," he said. But Lincoln pressed on.

"There is no man in the country whose opinion I value more than yours," he said. "I want to know what you think of it."

"Mr. Lincoln," Douglass replied, "that was a sacred effort."

Forty-one days later, on April 15, 1865, Lincoln was dead.

From *Smithsonian*, April 2002, pages 109–119. Reprinted with the permission of Simon & Schuster Adult Publishing Group from *Lincoln's Greatest Speech: The Second Inaugural* by Ronald C. White Jr. Copyright © 2002 by Ronald C. White, Jr.

America's Birth At Appomattox

Anne Wortham

It would of course be easy to make too much of the general air of reconciliation.… And yet by any standard this was an almost unbelievable way to end a civil war, which by all tradition is the worst kind of war there is.[1]
—Bruce Catton

On April 9, 1865, eighty-nine years after the Continental Congress declared the independence of "thirteen united States of America," the United States of America was born at the residence of farmer Wilmer McLean in the hamlet of Appomattox Courthouse, Virginia. Civil War historian James Robertson has said, "Lee signed not so much terms of surrender as he did the birth certificate of a nation—the United States—and the country was born in that moment."[2] An American nationality in the sense of a general feeling of being American above all else did not yet exist when Grant and Lee put their names to the surrender document. But there were at work nineteenth-century values, ideas, and attitudes that transcended sectional loyalties, that remained intact throughout the war, and made possible the birth of the United States as a nation.

I will look at the function of friendship, battlefield comradeship and courtesy, and shared nationality in that process; and argue that these qualities of association—as well as the high value the combatants placed on courage, duty, honor, and discipline—enabled the Federals and Confederates to achieve what Robert Penn Warren called "reconciliation by human recognition." I intend to show how reconciliation was played out in numerous meetings between Union and Confederate officers and soldiers at Appomattox between April 9, 1865, when Lee surrendered, and April 12, when the Confederates stacked their arms, folded their flags, and were paroled.

LINCOLN'S ATTITUDE

We are not enemies, but friends.… Though passion may have strained, it must not break our bonds of affection. The mystic chords of memory, stretching from every battlefield, and patriot grave, to every living heart, and hearthstone, all over this broad land, will yet swell the chorus of the Union, when again touched, as surely they will be, by the better angels of our nature. *—Abraham Lincoln*

Reconciliation was an explicit policy goal of Abraham Lincoln's, which he made clear to Generals Grant and Sherman and Adm. David Dixon Porter in a conference aboard the *River Queen* at City Point, Virginia, after his visit to the front on March 27, 1865. Lincoln knew that unless "the better angels of our nature" could be asserted by unambiguous action at war's end, there was no hope for the new birth of freedom and the national community he believed was possible. The problem for Lincoln was how to simultaneously end the war and win the peace. As Bruce Catton puts it, he argued that the Union's aim should be not so much to subdue the Confederacy as to checkmate those forces of malice and rancor that could jeopardize peace. For if the North won the war and lost the peace, there would be no way to realize his hope that "the whole country, North and South together, [would] ultimately find in reunion and freedom the values that would justify four terrible years of war."[3]

In the only existing documentation of the meeting, Admiral Porter wrote:

My opinion is that Mr. Lincoln came down to City Point with the most liberal views toward the rebels. He felt confident that we would be successful, and was willing that the enemy should capitulate on the most favorable terms.… He wanted peace on almost any terms.… His heart was tenderness throughout, and, as long as the rebels laid down their arms, he did not care how it was done.[4]

Lincoln knew that the peace and reconciliation he envisioned would not stand a chance without generous surrender terms. He expected Grant, "the remorseless killer," and Sherman, "destruction's own self," to "fight without mercy as long as there must be fighting, but when the fighting stopped they [must] try to turn old enemies into friends."

Lincoln knew his fellow citizens, and he was confident that while they were politically disunited, the raw material of reconciliation resided in their hearts.

But could reconciliation be coaxed out of defeat? There were reasons to think it possible. Lincoln knew his fellow citizens, and he was confident that while they were politically disunited, the raw material of reconciliation resided in their hearts. Indeed, friendliness and respect were present within the armies, and there was now less bitterness between them than when the war began. Yet another resource was the extraordinary resilience of the friendships between the former West Pointers leading those armies. Finally, whether he knew it or not, but must have sensed, Lincoln had a most reliable resource in the antisecessionist gray commander himself, Robert E. Lee—but not until he was defeated.

WEST POINT 1: A CHEERFUL COLLOQUY

If one would have a friend, one must be willing to wage war for him: and in order to wage war, one must be capable of being an enemy.... In one's friend, one shall find one's best enemy.

—*Frederich Nietzsche*

"The soldiers did not need to be told that it would be well to make peace mean comradeship. All they needed was to see somebody try it," writes Catton.[5] Well, on Palm Sunday, April 9, 1865, there were plenty of occasions to see the vanquished and the victorious extend the hand of friendship. On the morning of that dramatic day, white flags of truce were held aloft as messengers rode between the lines, and a cease-fire was in place until the anticipated surrender meeting between Grant and Lee. By late morning the contending armies stood on either side of the town, with their picket lines out, their guns silent, nervously contemplating the meaning of surrender and ever alert for the resumption of hostile fire. But gathered on the steps of the Appomattox Courthouse, awaiting the arrival of the two commanding generals, was a curious group of Union and Confederate generals, most of them West Point graduates, and many of them from the same graduating classes.

As historian Frank Cauble points out, because of the more significant surrender meeting that everyone was anticipating, this earlier conference of officers has been largely overlooked and seldom mentioned in Civil War histories. However, the sight of these former combatants was "a singular spectacle," wrote New York reporter L.A. Hendrick.

There were mutual introductions and shaking of hands, and soon was passed about some whiskey (General [Romeyn] Ayres furnished the whiskey and he alleges it was a first class article) and mutual healths were drank and altogether it was a strange grouping. The rebel officers were all elegantly dressed in full uniform. Gradually the area of the conference widened. From the steps the conferring party got into the street, and before it closed some were seated on the steps, and others, for lack of more comfortable accommodations, chatted cosily, seated on a contiguous fence.[6]

Gen. Joshua Chamberlain overheard two West Point classmates who had been combatants for four years renewing an old acquaintance. "Well Billy, old boy, how goes it?" the Union officer said. "Bad, bad, Charlie, bad I can tell you; but have you got any whiskey?"[7]

When we consider the pain, suffering, and death these men had inflicted upon one another and their comrades, how are we to explain their apparent lack of resentment and bitterness?

When we consider the pain, suffering, and death these men had inflicted upon one another and their comrades, how are we to explain their apparent lack of resentment and bitterness? How could one so easily drink of the cup of fraternity with someone who has been shooting at him and his comrades—and sometimes hitting the mark—for four years? Can vanquished and victor really be friends?

Well, yes—if the fellow who had been shooting at you was a friend before he was your enemy, and if he was bound to you by that precious ethos called the "spirit of West Point." Vindictiveness was not the order of the day for these men. They just wanted it over. Indeed, two months before, on February 25, Union Gen. Edward Ord met under a flag of truce with his former classmate, Confederate Gen. James Longstreet, and discussed the possibility of Lee and Grant declaring peace on the field. Now, as the officers waited for Grant and Lee, John Gibbon, a North Carolinian whose three brothers fought for the Confederacy, proposed that if Grant and Lee couldn't come to terms and stop the fighting, they should order their soldiers to fire only blank cartridges to prevent further bloodshed. By noon, when Grant still had not appeared, the West Pointers rode back to their respective lines, all hoping, as Gibbon said, "that there would be no further necessity for bloodshed."

CONDITIONAL SURRENDER

Another year would go by before President Andrew Johnson, on April 2, 1866, proclaimed "that the insurrection... is at an end and is henceforth to be so regarded." But Grant and Lee's task of reconciliation could not wait for the U.S. government's official certification of the end of the war. They knew it had to begin with the surrender terms themselves. Grant finally arrived from the field between 1:30 and 2:00 and entered the McLean house where Lee was waiting. By 3:00 the surrender documents were signed, the two commanders had shaken hands, and Lee had mounted Traveller and returned to his lines. At 4:30 Grant telegraphed Washington, informing the secretary of war that Lee had surrendered "on terms proposed by myself."

Gen. Ulysses S. Grant standing at Cold Harbor, Virginia, in June 1864 (National Archives).

They agreed that all officers and men of the Army of Northern Virginia should be paroled and disqualified from taking up arms against the government of the United States until properly exchanged; that they should turn over all arms, artillery, and public property to the Union army; but that officers should not be deprived of their sidearms, horses, and baggage. In stating that "each officer and man will be allowed to return to their homes not to be disturbed by United States authority so long as they observe their paroles and the laws in force where they may reside," Grant effectively made it impossible for Lee to be tried for treason.

Lee asked that those of the enlisted men who owned their horses be permitted to keep them. At first Grant rejected this request, but then he changed his mind. Since this was the last battle of the war, the men needed their horses to put in their spring crops, and since the United States did not want the horses, he said he would instruct the parole officers to "let every man of the Confederate army who claimed to own a horse or mule to take the animal to his home." It was ironic that for four years Grant had tried to kill these men, and now he didn't want to stand in the way of their planting their crops so they could live. But Grant now saw himself as an instrument for a lasting peace. He extended his generosity further by ordering his army to share its rations with the hungry rebels.

The surrender terms were entirely consistent with the policy of reconciliation that Lincoln had articulated back in March. According to Admiral Porter, when Lincoln learned of the surrender terms, he was "delighted" and exclaimed "a dozen times, 'Good!' 'All right!' 'Exactly the thing!' and other similar expressions." Confederate Porter Alexander was also moved by Grant's generosity at Appomattox and wrote later: "Gen. Grant's conduct toward us in the whole matter is worthy of the very highest praise & indicates a great & broad & generous mind. *For all time it will be a good thing for the whole United States, that of all the Federal generals it fell to Grant to receive the surrender of Lee*" (emphasis in the original).[8]

Union soldiers like Maj. Holman Melcher of the 20th Maine were also impressed by Grant's magnanimity and resolved to follow his example. In a letter to his brother, Melcher noted that "the good feeling between the officers and men of the two armies followed General Grant [who] set us the example by his conduct at the surrender." He went on to "confess" what no doubt many Union officers and soldiers felt—that "a feeling of indignation would rise within me when I would think of all the bloodshed and mourning these same men had caused. But it is honorable to be magnanimous to a conquered foe. And as civilized men and gentlemen, we strive to keep such feelings of hatred in subjection."[9]

Melcher's attitude confirmed Lincoln's insight that, as Catton puts it, "if the terms expressed simple human decency and friendship, it might be that a peace of reconciliation could get just enough of a lead so that the haters could never quite catch up with it." But it would require just the level of self-control that Melcher imposed on himself.

Having signed the certificate of birth, Grant and Lee still had to attend to the business of delivering a deathblow to the idea of secession while simultaneously injecting some vitality into the promise of this new beginning. They did so by word and deed. When news of the surrender reached the Union lines, the men began to fire a salute and cheer, but Grant issued orders forbidding any demonstrations. He wrote later that "the Confederates were now our prisoners, and we did not want to exult over their downfall." While Grant taught his men to resist acts of humiliation, Lee's assignment was to instill stoic dignity.

The Confederates could not believe what had transpired. Orderly Sgt. James Whitehorne of the 12th Virginia, wrote in his diary, "I was thunderstruck.... What would Jackson, Stuart, or—any of [those who had been killed fighting under Lee] say about us?... It is humiliating in the extreme. I never expected to see men cry as they did this morning. All the officers cried and most of the privates broke down and wept like children and Oh, Lord! I cried too."

The emotions of the weary and humiliated men in Lee's tattered army ranged from bitterness and anger to sadness and acceptance. But they were relieved when they learned that they would be paroled and free to go home rather than sent to Northern prisons. They were also grateful for the much-needed rations. But men need more than rations; they need meaning. And only Robert E. Lee, their beloved Marse Robert, could satisfy that most pressing of human needs by reinforcing their sense of honor, legitimating their pride, and redirecting their tired fury.

Having signed the certificate of birth, Grant and Lee still had to attend to the business of delivering a deathblow to the idea of secession while simultaneously injecting some vitality into the promise of this new beginning.

In his farewell order to the army, Lee praised their "four years of arduous service, marked by unsurpassed courage and fortitude," told them that they were brave and had "remained steadfast to the last," and urged them to peacefully return to their homes, taking with them "the satisfaction that proceeds from the consciousness of duty faithfully performed." He ended by honoring them: "With an increasing admiration of your constancy and devotion to your country, and a grateful remembrance of your kind and generous consideration for myself, I bid you all an affectionate farewell."[11]

What Lee accomplished in his address, says Bruce Catton, was to set the pattern, to give these men the right words to take with them into the future. "Pride in what they had done would grow with the years, but it would turn them into a romantic army of legend and not into a sullen battalion of death."

There were Federals, like General Chamberlain, who would not begrudge the Confederates the sentiments that Lee tried to instill in them. Although he believed they were wrong in their beliefs, "they fought as they were taught, true to such ideals as they saw, and put into their cause their best." Reflecting on the parade of Confederates stacking their arms and flags, Chamberlain, who was appointed to command the formal surrender of arms, said: "For us they were fellow-soldiers as well, suffering the fate of arms. We could not look into those brave, bronzed faces, and those battered flags we had met on so many fields where glorious manhood lent a glory to the earth that bore it, and think of personal hate and revenge."[12]

WEST POINT 2: SAM GRANT'S COMRADES

The next day, April 10, some of Grant's generals asked for permission to enter the Confederate lines to meet old friends. As he sat on the porch of the McLean house waiting for his officers to prepare his army to leave Appomattox, they began arriving with many of Grant's old comrades. Along with Phil Sheridan, John Gibbon, and Rufus Ingalls came the beloved Confederate Cadmus Wilcox, who had been best man at Grant's wedding. Confederate Henry Heth, who had been a subaltern with Grant in Mexico, was joined by his cousin George Pickett, who also knew Grant from Mexico. Pickett and Heth were friends of Gibbon, whose Union division bore the brunt of Pickett's charge at Gettysburg. Federal George Gordon and a number of others also came along.

Grant talked with them until it was time to leave. He later wrote that the officers "seemed to enjoy the meeting as much as though they had been friends separated for a long time while fighting battles under the same flag. For the time being it looked very much as if all thought of the war had escaped their minds."[13] No doubt somewhere deep in their hearts were the sentiments of the West Point hymn traditionally sung at the last chapel service before graduation:

> When shall we meet again?
> Meet ne'er to sever?
> When will Peace wreath her chain
> Round us forever?
> Our hearts will ne'er repose
> Safe from each blast that blows
> In this dark vale of woes,—
> Never—no, never.[14]

These friends were a band of brothers whom historian James McPherson describes as "more tightly bonded by hardship and danger in war than biological brothers." Now, on this spring day in April, the guns were quiet, and, as historian John Waugh points out, they "yearned to know that they would never hear their thunder or be ordered to take up arms against one another again."

By the time Longstreet arrived to join other Confederate and Union commissioners appointed to formulate the details of the surrender ceremony, Grant had apparently moved inside to a room that served as his temporary headquarters. When Longstreet walked by on the way to the room where the commissioners were meeting, Grant looked up and recognized him. He rose from his chair and, as Longstreet recalled, "with his old-time cheerful greeting gave me his hand, and after passing a few remarks offered a cigar, which was gratefully received."[15] Grant, addressing Longstreet by his nickname, said jokingly, "Pete, let us have another game of brag, to recall the days which were so pleasant to us all."[16] The two men had been best friends since West Point. They had served together for a time in the same regiment at Jefferson's Barracks, Missouri. Longstreet introduced Julia Dent, his distant cousin, to Grant and was present at their marriage vows. Three years after Appommatox, in 1868, Longstreet endorsed Grant's presidential candidacy and attended his inauguration.

Three years after Appommatox, in 1868, Longstreet endorsed Grant's presidential candidacy and attended his inauguration.

"The mere presence of conflict, envy, aggression, or any number of other contaminants does not doom or invalidate a friendship," says professor of English Ronald Sharp.[17] Much of the behavior of the West Pointers can be explained by the enormous strength of their friendships to withstand the horror of war. As Waugh points out, "It had never been in their hearts to hate the classmates they were fighting. Their lives and affections for one another had been indelibly framed and inextricably intertwined in their academy days. No adversity, war, killing, or political estrangement could undo that."[18] In his poem, "Meditation," Herman Melville, who visited the Virginia battlefront in the spring of 1864, celebrated their comradeship in the following verse:

> Mark the great Captains on both sides.
> The soldiers with the broad renown—
> They all were messmates on the Hudson's marge,
> Beneath one roof they laid them down;
> And, free from hate in many an after pass,
> Strove as in school-boy rivalry of the class.[19]

With some exaggeration, former West Pointer Morris Schaff wrote some forty years later that when "the graduates of both armies met as brothers" they symbolically "planted then and there the tree that has grown, blooming for the Confederate and blooming for the Federal, and under those whose shade we now gather in peace."[20] Our knowledge of the hatred and vengeance that Northerners and Southerners, including many West Pointers, felt toward each other and of the political conflicts attending Reconstruction might lead us to argue with the vision of West Pointers planting the tree of peace at Appomattox. But we cannot deny that, as their various diaries, letters, and memoirs document, that is what they thought they were doing.

EMBATTLED CIVILITY

A well-known paradox of the Civil War, writes Alan Nolan, was that "although fighting against each other with a devastating ferocity, the enlisted men and officers of the two sides tended to trust each other and did not see themselves in the manner of soldiers in most wars."[21] By the time Grant took command of the troubled Army of the Potomac in 1864, as Catton put it, "a fantastic sort of kinship"—"a queer combination of antagonism and understanding"—had grown up in regard to the Army of Northern Virginia. "There was no soft sentimentality about it, and the men would shoot to kill when the time for shooting came. Yet there was a familiarity and an understanding, at times something that verged almost on liking, based on solid respect." Now, on April 9, despite the fact that it was officially forbidden to prevent unpleasant contacts between members of the two armies, as soon as the surrender was announced there was quite a bit of visiting back and forth between the lines among Union and Confederate troops. Pvt. Charles Dunn of the 20th Maine reported that there was considerable trading that night.

The two picket lines were within speaking distance, and we were on speaking terms with the "Johnnies" at once. There was nothing that resembled guard duty that night.

It resembled a picnic rather than a picket line. They like ourselves were glad the war was over. We exchanged knicknacks with them, and were reminded of the days when at school we swapped jews-harps for old wooden toothed combs. The articles we exchanged that night were about the same value.[22]

Chamberlain wrote of receiving Confederate visitors all the next day. "Our camp was full of callers before we were up," he recalled. "The inundation of visitors grew so that it looked like a country fair, including the cattle-show."

J. Tracy Power notes that Confederates

were impressed by Federal soldiers who shared rations or money with them and carried on pleasant, and sometimes friendly, conversations about the end of the war. Maj. Richard Watson Jones of the 12th Virginia was visited by a Federal officer he had known before the war when they attended the same college. Sgt. James Whitehorne described the scene when the Federal entered the Confederate camp. "We saw him come up and hold out his hand—the Major did nothing for so long it was painful. Then he took the offered hand and I had a feeling the war was really over."[23]

It was in just such conduct that Bell Wiley, in his study of the common soldier, saw "undeveloped resources of strength and character that spelled hope for the country's future."[24] For his own part, Whitehorne declared, "After all, I never hated any one Yankee. I hated the spirit that was sending them to invade the south."

TWO SIDES BUT ONE IDENTITY

In his moving tribute to the men in gray, Chamberlain asserted that "whoever had misled these men, we had not. We had led them back home." While it is true that Confederates had seceded from the Union politically, they had not left the Union culturally. A significant overarching factor in the reconciliation of the former combatants was the fact that the soldiers "were not alien foes but men of similar origin." The Civil War was not a conflict between Southern Cavaliers and New England Puritans, between a nation of warriors and a nation of shopkeepers, or, as abolitionist Wendell Phillips insisted, between a civilization based on democracy and one based on an aristocracy founded on slavery. Rather, it was, in the words of Walt Whitman, "a struggle going on within one identity." Robert Penn Warren concurs in his argument that the nation that went to war "share[d] deep and significant convictions and [was] not a mere handbasket of factions huddled arbitrarily together by historical happen-so."[25]

While it is true that Confederates had seceded from the Union politically, they had not left the Union culturally.

Whether consciously acknowledged by them or not, Northerners and Southerners shared significant elements of national identity that the war could not annihilate. By national identity I do not mean nationalism, to quote Merle Curti, "in the sense of both confidence in the strength of the federal government and devotion to the nation as a whole," which in the nineteenth century was only a hope, an aspiration. Rather, I mean shared nationality in the sense that, again, quoting Curti, rank-and-file Americans "[cherish] the Union as a precious symbol of a revered past and a bright future, identifying it with abundance, opportunity and ultimate peace."[26]

The social, cultural, philosophical, and ideological differences between the combatants have been fully documented. But, as Wiley concluded, "the similarities of Billy Yank and Johnny Reb far outweighed their differences. They were both Americans, by birth or by adoption, and they both had the weaknesses and the virtues of the people of their nation and time." Alan Nolan concurs: "They shared the same revolutionary experience, the same heroes, the same Founding Fathers; and, despite the south's departure from the Bill of Rights in the effort to protect slavery, they shared, at bottom, a sense of political values."[27]

America was becoming American. Johnny Reb and Billy Yank were creating a new kind of American and a new awareness of America.

A key element of the national identity that Northerners and Southerners shared was a vision of the nation as the promised land to which God had led his people to establish a new social order that was to be, as John Winthrop said in 1630, "a city upon a hill, the eyes of all people are upon us, so that if we shall deal falsely with our God in this work we have undertaken and so cause him to withdraw his present help from us, we shall be made a story and a by-word through the world."[28]

The sense of being on show and tested before God and the world was no less true of Civil War combatants than it was for the Puritans. And just as persistent was the corollary concern of Americans that they would fall short of the vision. Because of this "fear of falling away," as historian Rupert Wilkinson calls it, Northerners and Southerners alike were faced with two basic philosophical questions: Are we worthy of our revolutionary forebears? Are we undoing, by our divisiveness, all that they worked so hard to obtain? Both sides compared America with its past and found themselves wanting. Both invoked the Revolutionary-Constitution era in seeking redemption of the Republic.

Civil War combatants were also bound by their perception of the changes swirling around them in the wider society as well as within their armies. "Always the army reflected the nation," writes Catton. And the nation itself was changing. Increased immigration, factory production, and urbanization eroded and destroyed old unities— "unities of blood, of race, of language, of shared ideals and common memories and experiences, the very

things which had always seemed essential beneath the word 'American.' In some mysterious way that nobody quite understood, the army not only mirrored the change but represented the effort to find a new synthesis."[29]

America was becoming American. Johnny Reb and Billy Yank were creating a new kind of American and a new awareness of America. As Warren points out,

> The War meant that Americans saw America. The farm boy of Ohio, the trapper in Minnesota, and the pimp of the Mackerelville section of New York City saw Richmond and Mobile. They not only saw America, they saw each other, and together shot it out with some Scot of the Valley of Virginia or ducked hardware hurled by a Louisiana Jew who might be a lieutenant of artillery, CSA.[30]

Out of the cauldron of hell into which were thrown Billy Yank, Johnny Reb, their immigrant comrades, as well as the black soldiers they all despised, came a pluralistic national community.

THE NATIONALIZATION OF LEE

In the decades following the war, as Americans became more American, so too did Robert E. Lee's image. By the turn of the century he was nationally elevated to a hero status shared by only a handful of individuals, such as Washington, Lincoln, and Jefferson. In their study of the transformation of Lee's image, Thomas Connelly and Barbara Bellows report: "A writer in *Harper's Weekly* proclaimed him 'the pride of a whole country.'... The *New York Times* praised Lee's 'grandeur of soul,' and the *Nation* called Lee 'great in gentleness and goodness.' "[31]

> The Americanization of Lee began long before he surrendered. When Brig. Gen. Samuel Crawford, in the 5th Corps of the Army of the Potomac, visited briefly with Lee the day after his surrender to Grant, he told Lee that, should he go North, he would find that he had "hosts of warm friends there." With tears in his eyes, Lee said, "I suppose all the people of the North looked upon me as a rebel traitor." Far from it. An unlikely contributor to his elevation was Julia Ward Howe, the abolitionist who wrote "Battle Hymn of the Republic":

> A gallant foeman in the fight,
> A brother when the fight was o'er,
> The hand that led the host with might
> The blessed torch of learning bore.
> No shriek of shells nor roll of drums,
> No challenge fierce, resounding far,
> When reconciling Wisdom comes
> To heal the cruel wounds of war.
> Thought may the minds of men divide,
> Love makes the heart of nations one,
> And so, the soldier grave beside,
> We honor thee, Virginia's son.[32]

The nationalization of Lee is a very American cultural practice: the elevation of worthy "native sons"—beyond the soil of their birth, beyond the privileges or lack of privileges of their class, beyond the dogma of their creed—to the position of national icon. In 1900 Virginia's son was inducted into the newly established Hall of Fame for Great Americans along with Washington, Jefferson, John Adams, and Benjamin Franklin. In 1934, Virginia presented statues of Lee and Washington to Congress to be placed in Statuary Hall in the U.S. Capitol, which houses statues of outstanding citizens from each of the states. The Lee so honored—the Lee that won over the nation and was praised by every American president—was, as Connelly and Bellows describe him, "the man of basic American values of decency, duty, and honor, the devotee of unionism trapped in 1861 by conflicting loyalties." Lee was the postwar nationalist, driven by an unswerving determination to help restore the old Union.

In truth, America had never been united, but now it was on the road toward becoming American.

But Lee is the supreme paradoxical American hero. As McPherson insightfully points out, Lee's heroism has to be seen in terms of his gigantic role in prolonging the war longer than it might have been. When Lee took command of the Army of Northern Virginia in June 1862, the Confederacy was on the verge of collapse. In the previous four months, it had lost its largest city, New Orleans; much of the Mississippi Valley; and most of Tennessee; and Maj. Gen. George McClellan's Army of the Potomac had moved to within five miles of Richmond, the Confederate capital. McPherson cites the irony of Lee's command as follows:

> Within three months Lee's offensives had taken the Confederacy off the floor at the count of nine and had driven Union forces onto the ropes. Without Lee the Confederacy might have died in 1862. But slavery would have survived; the South would have suffered only limited death and destruction. Lee's victories prolonged the war until it destroyed slavery, the plantation economy, the wealth and infrastructure of the region, and everything else the confederacy stood for. That was the profound irony of Lee's military genius.[33]

THE SIGNIFICANCE OF APPOMATTOX

In an April 12 telegram to Grant, who had departed for Washington two days earlier, General Gibbon informed him that "the surrender of General Lee's army was finally completed today," then went on to comment on the meaning of Appomattox: "I have conversed with many of the surrendered officers, and am satisfied that by announcing at once terms and a liberal, merciful policy on the part of the Government we can once more have a happy, united country."[34]

This is what Lincoln wanted. In truth, America had never been united, but now it was on the road toward becoming American. And this is how it sounded: A Confederate officer at the

head of his surrendering corps told Chamberlain, "General, this is deeply humiliating; but I console myself with the thought that the whole country will rejoice at this day." Another told him, "I went into that cause and I meant it. We had our choice of weapons and of ground, and we have lost. Now that is my flag (pointing to the flag of the Union), and I will prove myself as worthy as any of you."[35]

References

1. Bruce Catton, *The Centennial History of the Civil War: Never Call Retreat*, vol. 3 (New York: Doubleday and Co., 1965), 455–56.
2. James Robertson Jr., *Civil War Journal: Robert E. Lee: A History TV Network Presentation*, Time-Life Video (Alexandria, Va.: Time, 1994).
3. Bruce Catton, *A Stillness at Appomattox* (New York: Doubleday and Co., 1957, 340.
4. David Dixon Porter, quoted in Philip Van Doren Stern, *An End to Valor: The Last Days of the Civil War* (Boston: Houghton Mifflin Co., 1858), 103–104.
5. Catton, *Stillness at Appomattox*, 341.
6. L.A. Hendrick, "Conferences of Commanding Officers," *Freeman's Journal and Catholic Register*, 22 April 1865. Quoted in Frank Cauble, *The Surrender Proceedings: April Ninth, 1865, Appomattox Court House* (Lynchburg, Va.: H.E. Howard, 1987), 43–44.
7. Joshua Lawrence Chamberlain, *The Passing of the Armies: The Last Campaign of the Armies* (Gettysburg, Pa.: Stan Clark Military Books, 1995 reprint ed.), 244.
8. Gary Gallagher, ed., *Fighting for the Confederacy: The Personal Recollections of General Edward Porter Alexander* (Chapel Hill, N.C.: University of North Carolina Press, 1989), 540.
9. William Styple, ed., *With a Flash of His Sword: The Writings of Maj. Holman S. Melcher, 20th Maine Infantry* (Kearny, N.J.: Belle Grove Publishing Co., 1994), 219.
10. J. Tracy Power, *Lee's Miserables: Life in the Army of Northern Virginia From the Wilderness to Appomattox* (Chapel Hill, N.C.: University of North Carolina Press, 1998), 282.
11. Thomas Connelly, *Marble Man: Robert E. Lee and His Image in American Society* (Baton Rouge, La.: Louisiana State University Press, 1978), 367.
12. Chamberlain, *Passing of the Armies*, 270.
13. Ulysses S. Grant, *Memoirs and Selected Letters: Personal Memoirs of U.S. Grant: Selected Letters 1839–1865* (New York: Library of America, 1990), 744.
14. Quoted in George Pappas, *To the Point: The United States Military Academy, 1802–1902* (Westport, Conn.: Praeger, 1993), 322.
15. James Longstreet, *From Manassas to Appomattox* [1896] (New York: Konecky and Konecky, 1992), 630.
16. Jeffrey Wert, *General James Longstreet: The Confederacy's Most Controversial Soldier* (New York: Simon and Schuster, 1994), 404.
17. Ronald Sharp, *Friendship and Literature: Spirit and Form* (Durham, N.C.: Duke University Press, 1986), 120.
18. John Waugh, *The Class of 1846: From West Point to Appomattox: Stonewall Jackson, George McClellan and Their Brothers* (New York: Warner Books, 1994), 500.
19. Herman Melville, *Battle-Pieces and Aspects of the War* [1866]. Quoted in Richard Dilworth Rust, ed., *Glory and Pathos: Responses of Nineteenth-Century American Authors to the Civil War* (Boston: Holbrook Press, 1970), 177.
20. Morris Schaff, *The Spirit of Old West Point, 1858–1862* (Boston: Houghton-Mifflin, 1907), 140, 251–53
21. Alan Nolan, *Lee Considered: General Robert E. Lee and Civil War History* (Chapel Hill, N.C.: University of North Carolina Press, 1991), 158.

22. Quoted in J.J. Pullen, *The Twentieth Maine* (Philadelphia: J.B. Lippincott Co., 1957), 270.

23. Quoted in Power, *Lee's Miserables*, 283.

24. Bell Wiley, *The Life of Johnny Reb and the Life of Billy Yank* [1943, 1952], reprint, Essential Classics of the Civil War (New York: Book-of-the-Month Club/Louisiana State University Press, 1994), 361.

25. Robert Penn Warren, *The Legacy of the Civil War* (New York: Random House, 1961), 83.

26. Merle Curti, *The Growth of American Thought* (New Brunswick, N.J.: Transaction Publishers, 1991), 423–24.

27. Nolan, *Lee Considered*, 157.

28. John Winthrop, "A Modell of Christian Charity," (1630), reprinted in Daniel Boorstin, ed., *An American Primer,* vol. 1 (Chicago: Chicago University Press, 1966), 22.

29. Catton, *Stillness at Appomattox*, 216.

30. Warren, *Legacy of the Civil War*, 13.

31. Thomas Connelly and Barbara Bellows, *God and General Longstreet: The Lost Cause and the Southern Mind* (Baton Rouge: Louisiana State University Press, 1982), 83.

32. Julia Ward Howe, "Robert E. Lee," in Lois Hill, ed., *Poems and Songs of the Civil War* (New York: Gramercy Books, 1990).

33. James McPherson, *Drawn With the Sword: Reflections on the American Civil War* (New York: Oxford University Press, 1996), 158.

34. Quoted in Bruce Catton, *Grant Takes Command* [1968] (New York: Book-of-the-Month Club, 1994), 473.

35. Chamberlain, *Passing of the Armies*, 266.

Anne Wortham is associate professor of sociology at Illinois State University.

From *The World & I,* May 1999, pages 295–305, 307–309. Copyright © 1999 by The World & I Magazine. Reprinted with permission.

The New View of Reconstruction

Whatever you were taught or thought you knew about the post-Civil War era is probably wrong in the light of recent study

Eric Foner

In the past twenty years, no period of American history has been the subject of a more thoroughgoing reevaluation than Reconstruction—the violent, dramatic, and still controversial era following the Civil War. Race relations, politics, social life, and economic change during Reconstruction have all been reinterpreted in the light of changed attitudes toward the place of blacks within American society. If historians have not yet forged a fully satisfying portrait of Reconstruction as a whole, the traditional interpretation that dominated historical writing for much of this century has irrevocably been laid to rest.

Anyone who attended high school before 1960 learned that Reconstruction was a era of unrelieved sordidness in American political and social life. The martyred Lincoln, according to this view, had planned a quick and painless readmission of the Southern states as equal members of the national family. President Andrew Johnson, his successor, attempted to carry out Lincoln's policies but was foiled by the Radical Republicans (also known as Vindictives or Jacobins). Motivated by an irrational hatred of Rebels or by ties with Northern capitalists out to plunder the South, the Radicals swept aside Johnson's lenient program and fastened black supremacy upon the defeated Confederacy. An orgy of corruption followed, presided over by unscrupulous carpetbaggers (Northerners who ventured south to reap the spoils of office), traitorous scalawags (Southern whites who cooperated with the new gov-

ernments for personal gain), and the ignorant and childlike freedmen, who were incapable of properly exercising the political power that had been thrust upon them. After much needless suffering, the white community of the South banded together to overthrow these "black" governments and restore home rule (their euphemism for white supremacy). All told, Reconstruction was just about the darkest page in the American saga.

Originating in anti-Reconstruction propaganda of Southern Democrats during the 1870s, this traditional interpretation achieved scholarly legitimacy around the turn of the century through the work of William Dunning and his students at Columbia University. It reached the larger public through films like *Birth of a Nation* and *Gone With the Wind* and that best-selling work of myth-making masquerading as history, *The Tragic Era* by Claude G. Bowers. In language as exaggerated as it was colorful, Bowers told how Andrew Johnson "fought the bravest battle for constitutional liberty and for the preservation of our institutions ever waged by an Executive" but was overwhelmed by the "poisonous propaganda" of the Radicals. Southern whites, as a result, "literally were put to the torture" by "emissaries of hate" who manipulated the "simple-minded" freedmen, inflaming the negroes' "egotism" and even inspiring "lustful assaults" by blacks upon white womanhood.

In a discipline that sometimes seems to pride itself on the rapid rise and fall of his-

torical interpretations, this traditional portrait of Reconstruction enjoyed remarkable staying power. The long reign of the old interpretation is not difficult to explain. It presented a set of easily identifiable heroes and villains. It enjoyed the imprimatur of the nation's leading scholars. And it accorded with the political and social realities of the first half of this century. This image of Reconstruction helped freeze the mind of the white South in unalterable opposition to any movement for breaching the ascendancy of the Democratic party, eliminating segregation, or readmitting disfranchised blacks to the vote.

Nevertheless, the demise of the traditional interpretation was inevitable, for it ignored the testimony of the central participant in the drama of Reconstruction—the black freedman. Furthermore, it was grounded in the conviction that blacks were unfit to share in political power. As Dunning's Columbia colleague John W. Burgess put it, "A black skin means membership in a race of men which has never of itself succeeded in subjecting passion to reason, has never, therefore, created any civilization of any kind." Once objective scholarship and modern experience rendered that assumption untenable, the entire edifice was bound to fall.

The work of "revising" the history of Reconstruction began with the writings of a handful of survivors of the era, such as John R. Lynch, who had served as a black congressman from Mississippi after the Civil War. In the 1930s white scholars like Francis Simkins and Robert Woody carried the task forward. Then, in 1935, the black historian and activist W. E. B. Du Bois produced *Black Reconstruction in America,* a monumental revaluation that closed with an irrefutable indictment of a historical profession that had sacrificed scholarly objectivity on the altar of racial bias. "One fact and one alone," he wrote, "explains the attitude of most recent writers toward Reconstruction; they cannot conceive of Negroes as men." Du Bois's work, however, was ignored by most historians.

Black initiative established as many schools as did Northern religious societies and the Freedmen's Bureau. The right to vote was not simply thrust upon them by meddling outsiders, since blacks began agitating for the suffrage as soon as they were freed.

It was not until the 1960s that the full force of the revisionist wave broke over the field. Then, in rapid succession, virtually every assumption of the traditional viewpoint was systematically dismantled. A drastically different portrait emerged to take its place. President Lincoln did not have a coherent "plan" for Reconstruction, but at the time of his assassination he had been cautiously contemplating black suffrage. Andrew Johnson was a stubborn, racist politician who lacked the ability to compromise. By isolating himself from the broad currents of public opinion that had nourished Lincoln's career, Johnson created an impasse with Congress that Lincoln would certainly have avoided, thus throwing away his political power and destroying his own plans for reconstructing the South.

The Radicals in Congress were acquitted of both vindictive motives and the charge of serving as the stalking-horses of Northern capitalism. They emerged instead as idealists in the best nineteenth-century reform tradition. Radical leaders like Charles Sumner and Thaddeus Stevens had worked for the rights of blacks long before any conceivable political ad-

vantage flowed from such a commitment. Stevens refused to sign the Pennsylvania Constitution of 1838 because it disfranchised the state's black citizens; Sumner led a fight in the 1850s to integrate Boston's public schools. Their Reconstruction policies were based on principle, not petty political advantage, for the central issue dividing Johnson and these Radical Republicans was the civil rights of freedmen. Studies of congressional policy-making, such as Eric L. McKitrick's *Andrew Johnson and Reconstruction,* also revealed that Reconstruction legislation, ranging from the Civil Rights Act of 1866 to the Fourteenth and Fifteenth Amendments, enjoyed broad support from moderate and conservative Republicans. It was not simply the work of a narrow radical faction.

Even more startling was the revised portrait of Reconstruction in the South itself. Imbued with the spirit of the civil rights movement and rejecting entirely the racial assumptions that had underpinned the traditional interpretation, these historians evaluated Reconstruction from the black point of view. Works like Joel Williamson's *After Slavery* portrayed the period as a time of extraordinary political, social, and economic progress for blacks. The establishment of public school systems, the granting of equal citizenship to blacks, the effort to restore the devastated Southern economy, the attempt to construct an interracial political democracy from the ashes of slavery, all these were commendable achievements, not the elements of Bowers's "tragic era."

Unlike earlier writers, the revisionists stressed the active role of the freedmen in shaping Reconstruction. Black initiative established as many schools as did Northern religious societies and the Freedmen's Bureau. The right to vote was not simply thrust upon them by meddling outsiders, since blacks began agitating for the suffrage as soon as they were freed. In 1865 black conventions throughout the South issued eloquent, though unheeded, appeals for equal civil and political rights.

With the advent of Radical Reconstruction in 1867, the freedmen did enjoy a real measure of political power. But black supremacy never existed. In most states blacks held only a small fraction of political offices, and even in South Carolina, where they comprised a majority of the state legislature's lower house, effective power remained in white hands. As for corruption, moral standards in both gov-

ernment and private enterprise were at low ebb throughout the nation in the postwar years—the era of Boss Tweed, the Credit Mobilier scandal, and the Whiskey Ring. Southern corruption could hardly be blamed on former slaves.

Other actors in the Reconstruction drama also came in for reevaluation. Most carpetbaggers were former Union soldiers seeking economic opportunity in the postwar South, not unscrupulous adventurers. Their motives, a typically American amalgam of humanitarianism and the pursuit of profit, were no more insidious than those of Western pioneers. Scalawags, previously seen as traitors to the white race, now emerged as "Old Line" Whig Unionists who had opposed secession in the first place or as poor whites who had long resented planters' domination of Southern life and who saw in Reconstruction a chance to recast Southern society along more democratic lines. Strongholds of Southern white Republicanism like east Tennessee and western North Carolina had been the scene of resistance to Confederate rule throughout the Civil War; now, as one scalawag newspaper put it, the choice was "between salvation at the hand of the Negro or destruction at the hand of the rebels."

At the same time, the Ku Klux Klan and kindred groups, whose campaign of violence against black and white Republicans had been minimized or excused in older writings, were portrayed as they really were. Earlier scholars had conveyed the impression that the Klan intimidated blacks mainly by dressing as ghosts and playing on the freedmen's superstitions. In fact, black fears were all too real: the Klan was a terrorist organization that beat and killed its political opponents to deprive blacks of their newly won rights. The complicity of the Democratic party and the silence of prominent whites in the face of such outrages stood as an indictment of the moral code the South had inherited from the days of slavery.

By the end of the 1960s, then, the old interpretation had been completely reversed. Southern freedmen were the heroes, the "Redeemers" who overthrew Reconstruction were the villains, and if the era was "tragic," it was because change did not go far enough. Reconstruction had been a time of real progress and its failure a lost opportunity for the South and the nation. But the legacy of Reconstruction—the Fourteenth and Fifteenth Amendments—endured to inspire future efforts for civil rights. As Kenneth Stampp wrote in *The Era of Reconstruction,* a superb summary of revisionist findings published in 1965, "if it was worth four years of civil war to save the Union, it was worth a few years of radical reconstruction to give the American Negro the ultimate promise of equal civil and political rights."

Under slavery most blacks had lived in nuclear family units, although they faced the constant threat of separation from loved ones by sale. Reconstruction provided the opportunity for blacks to solidify their preexisting family ties.

As Stampp's statement suggests, the reevaluation of the first Reconstruction was inspired in large measure by the impact of the second—the modern civil rights movement. And with the waning of that movement in recent years, writing on Reconstruction has undergone still another transformation. Instead of seeing the Civil War and its aftermath as a second American Revolution (as Charles Beard had), a regression into barbarism (as Bowers argued), or a golden opportunity squandered (as the revisionists saw it), recent writers argue that Radical Reconstruction was not really very radical. Since land was not distributed to the former slaves, the remained economically dependent upon their former owners. The planter class survived both the war and Reconstruction with its property (apart from slaves) and prestige more or less intact.

Not only changing times but also the changing concerns of historians have contributed to this latest reassessment of Reconstruction. The hallmark of the past decade's historical writing has been an emphasis upon "social history"—the evocation of the past lives of ordinary Americans—and the downplaying of strictly political events. When applied to Reconstruction, this concern with the "social" suggested that black suffrage and officeholding, once seen as the most radical departures of the Reconstruction era, were relatively insignificant.

Recent historians have focused their investigations not upon the politics of Reconstruction but upon the social and

economic aspects of the transition from slavery to freedom. Herbert Gutman's influential study of the black family during and after slavery found little change in family structure or relations between men and women resulting from emancipation. Under slavery most blacks had lived in nuclear family units, although they faced the constant threat of separation from loved ones by sale. Reconstruction provided the opportunity for blacks to solidify their preexisting family ties. Conflicts over whether black women should work in the cotton fields (planters said yes, many black families said no) and over white attempts to "apprentice" black children revealed that the autonomy of family life was a major preoccupation of the freedmen. Indeed, whether manifested in their withdrawal from churches controlled by whites, in the blossoming of black fraternal, benevolent, and self-improvement organizations, or in the demise of the slave quarters and their replacement by small tenant farms occupied by individual families, the quest for independence from white authority and control over their own day-to-day lives shaped the black response to emancipation.

The Civil War raised the decisive questions of American's national existence: the relations between local and national authority, the definition of citizenship, the balance between force and consent in generating obedience to authority.

In the post–Civil War South the surest guarantee of economic autonomy, blacks believed, was land. To the freedmen the justice of a claim to land based on their years of unrequited labor appeared self-evident. As an Alabama black convention put it, "The property which they [the planters] hold was nearly all earned by the sweat of *our* brows." As Leon Litwack showed in *Been in the Storm So Long,* a Pultizer Prize–winning account of the black response to emancipation, many freedmen in 1865 and 1866 refused to sign labor contracts, expecting the federal government to give them land. In some localities, as one Alabama

overseer reported, they "set up claims to the plantation and all on it."

In the end, of course, the vast majority of Southern blacks remained propertyless and poor. But exactly why the South, and especially its black population, suffered from dire poverty and economic retardation in the decades following the Civil War is a matter of much dispute. In *One Kind of Freedom* economists Roger Ransom and Richard Sutch indicted country merchants for monopolizing credit and charging usurious interest rates, forcing black tenants into debt and locking the South into a dependence on cotton production that impoverished the entire region. But Jonathan Wiener, in his study of postwar Alabama, argued that planters used their political power to compel blacks to remain on the plantations. Planters succeeded in stabilizing the plantation system, but only by blocking the growth of alternative enterprises, like factories, that might draw off black laborers, thus locking the region into a pattern of economic backwardness.

If the thrust of recent writing has emphasized the social and economic aspects of Reconstruction, politics has not been entirely neglected. But political studies have also reflected the postrevisionist mood summarized by C. Vann Woodward when he observed "how essentially nonrevolutionary and conservative Reconstruction really was." Recent writers, unlike their revisionist predecessors, have found little to praise in federal policy toward the emancipated blacks.

A new sensitivity to the strength of prejudice and laissez-faire ideas in the nineteenth-century North has led many historians to doubt whether the Republican party ever made a genuine commitment to racial justice in the South. The granting of black suffrage was an alternative to a longterm federal responsibility for protecting the rights of the former slaves. Once enfranchised, blacks could be left to fend for themselves. With the exception of a few Radicals like Thaddeus Stevens, nearly all Northern policy-makers and educators are criticized today for assuming that, so long as the unfettered operations of the marketplace afforded blacks the opportunity to advance through diligent labor, federal efforts to assist them in acquiring land were unnecessary.

Probably the most innovative recent writing on Reconstruction politics has centered on a broad reassessment of black Republicanism, largely undertaken by a new generation of black historians. Scholars like Thomas Holt and Nell Painter insist that Reconstruction was not simply a matter of black and white. Conflicts within the black community, no less than divisions among whites, shaped Reconstruction politics. Where revisionist scholars, both black and white, had celebrated the accomplishments of black political leaders, Holt, Painter, and others charge that they failed to address the economic plight of the black masses. Painter criticized "representative colored men," as national black leaders were called, for failing to provide ordinary freedmen with effective political leadership. Holt found that black officeholders in South Carolina most emerged from the old free mulatto class of Charleston, which shared many assumptions with prominent whites. "Basically bourgeois in their origins and orientation," he wrote, they "failed to act in the interest of black peasants."

In emphasizing the persistence from slavery of divisions between free blacks and slaves, these writers reflect the increasing concern with continuity and conservatism in Reconstruction. Their work reflects a startling extension of revisionist premises. If, as has been argued for the past twenty years, blacks were active agents rather than mere victims of manipulation, then they could not be absolved of blame for the ultimate failure of Reconstruction.

Despite the excellence of recent writings and the continual expansion of our knowledge of the period, historians of Reconstruction today face a unique dilemma. An old interpretation has been overthrown, but a coherent new synthesis has yet to take its place. The revisionists of the 1960s effectively established a series of negative points: the Reconstruction governments were not as bad as had been portrayed, black supremacy was a myth, the Radicals were not cynical manipulators of the freedmen. Yet no convincing overall portrait of the quality of political and social life emerged from their writings. More recent historians have rightly pointed to elements of continuity that spanned the nineteenth-century Southern experience, especially the survival, in modified form, of the plantation system. Nevertheless, by denying the real changes that did occur, they have failed to provide a convincing portrait of an era characterized above all by drama, turmoil, and social change.

Building upon the findings of the past twenty years of scholarship, a new portrait of Reconstruction ought to begin by viewing it not as a specific time period, bounded by the years 1865 and 1877, but as an epi-sode in a prolonged historical process—American society's adjustment to the consequences of the Civil War and emancipation. The Civil War, of course, raised the decisive questions of America's national existence: the relations between local and national authority, the definition of citizenship, the balance between force and consent in generating obedience to authority. The war and Reconstruction, as Allan Nevins observed over fifty years ago, marked the "emergence of modern America." This was the era of the completion of the national railroad network, the creation of the modern steel industry, the conquest of the West and final subduing of the Indians, and the expansion of the mining frontier. Lincoln's America—the world of the small farm and artisan shop—gave way to a rapidly industrializing economy. The issues that galvanized postwar Northern politics—from the question of the greenback currency to the mode of paying holders of the national debt—arose from the economic changes unleased by the Civil War.

Above all, the war irrevocably abolished slavery. Since 1619, when "twenty negars" disembarked from a Dutch ship in Virginia, racial injustice had haunted American life, mocking its professed ideals even as tobacco and cotton, the products of slave labor, helped finance the nation's economic development. Now the implications of the black presence could no longer be ignored. The Civil War resolved the problem of slavery but, as the Philadelphia diarist Sydney George Fisher observed in June 1865, it opened an even more intractable problem: "What shall we do with the Negro?" Indeed, he went on, this was a problem *incapable* of any solution that will satisfy both North and South."

As Fisher realized, the focal point of Reconstruction was the social revolution known as emancipation. Plantation slavery was simultaneously a system of labor, a form of racial domination, and the foundation upon which arose a distinctive ruling class within the South. Its demise threw open the most fundamental questions of economy, society, and politics. A new system of labor, social, racial, and political relations had to be created to replace slavery.

The United States was not the only nation to experience emancipation in the nineteenth century. Neither plantation slavery nor abolition were unique to the United States. But Reconstruction was. In a comparative perspective Radical Reconstruction stands as a remarkable experiment, the only effort of a society experiencing abolition to bring the former slaves within the umbrella of equal citizenship. Because the Radicals did not achieve everything they wanted, historians have lately tended to play down the stunning departure represented by black suffrage and officeholding. Former slaves, most fewer than two years removed from bondage, debated the fundamental questions of the polity: what is a republican form of government? Should the state provide equal education for all? How could political equality be reconciled with a society in which property was so unequally distributed? There was something inspiring in the way such men met the challenge of Reconstruction. "I knew nothing more than to obey my master," James K. Greene, an Alabama black politician later recalled. "But the tocsin of freedom sounded and knocked at the door and we walked out like free men and we met the exigencies as they grew up, and shouldered the responsibilities."

Y̲ou never saw a people more excited on the subject of politics than are the negroes of the south," one planter observed in 1867. And there were more than a few Southern whites as well who in these years shook off the prejudices of the past to embrace the revision of a new South dedicated to the principles of equal citizenship and social justice. One ordinary South Carolinian expressed the new sense of possibility in 1868 to the Republican governor of the state: "I am sorry that I cannot write an elegant stiled letter to your excellency. But I rejoice to think that God almighty has given to the poor of S.C. a Gov. to hear to feel to protect the humble poor without distinction to race or color.... I am a native borned S.C. a poor man never owned a Negro in my life nor my father before me.... Remember the true and loyal are the poor of the whites and blacks, outside of these you can find none loyal."

Few modern scholars believe the Reconstruction governments established in the South in 1867 and 1868 fulfilled the aspirations of their humble constituents. While their achievements in such realms as education, civil rights, and the economic rebuilding of the South are now widely appreciated, historians today believe they failed to affect either the economic plight of the emancipated slave or the ongoing transformation of independent white farmers into cotton tenants. Yet their opponents did perceive the Reconstruction governments in precisely this way—as representatives of a revolution that had put the bottom rail, both racial and economic, on top. This perception helps explain the ferocity of the attacks leveled against them and the pervasiveness of violence in the post-emancipation South.

In the end neither the abolition of slavery nor Reconstruction succeeded in resolving the debate over the meaning of freedom in American life.

The spectacle of black men voting and holding office was anathema to large numbers of Southern whites. Even more disturbing, at least in the view of those who still controlled the plantation regions of the South, was the emergence of local officials, black and white, who sympathized with the plight of the black laborer. Alabama's vagrancy law was a "dead letter" in 1870, "because those who are charged with its enforcement are indebted to the vagrant vote for their offices and emoluments." Political debates over the level and incidence of taxation, the control of crops, and the resolution of contract disputes revealed that a primary issue of Reconstruction was the role of government in a plantation society. During presidential Reconstruction, and after "Redemption," with planters and their allies in control of politics, the law emerged as a means of stabilizing and promoting the plantation system. If Radical Reconstruction failed to redistribute the land of the South, the ouster of the planter class from control of politics at least ensured that the sanctions of the criminal law would not be employed to discipline the black labor force.

An understanding of this fundamental conflict over the relation between government and society helps explain the pervasive complaints concerning corruption and "extravagance" during Radical Reconstruction. Corruption there was aplenty; tax rates did rise sharply. More significant

than the rate of taxation, however, was the change in its incidence. For the first time, planters and white farmers had to pay a significant portion of their income to the government, while propertyless blacks often escaped scot-free. Several states, moreover, enacted heavy taxes on uncultivated land to discourage land speculation and force land onto the market, benefiting, it was hoped, the freedmen.

As time passed, complaints about the "extravagance" and corruption of Southern governments found a sympathetic audience among influential Northerners. The Democratic charge that universal suffrage in the South was responsible for high taxes and governmental extravagance coincided with a rising conviction among the urban middle classes of the North that city government had to be taken out of the hands of the immigrant poor and returned to the "best men"—the educated, professional, financially independent citizens unable to exert much political influence at a time of mass parties and machine politics. Increasingly the "respectable" middle classes began to retreat from the very notion of universal suffrage. The poor were not longer perceived as honest producers, the backbone of the social order; now they became the "dangerous classes," the "mob." As the historian Francis Parkman put it, too much power rested with "masses of imported ignorance and hereditary ineptitude." To Parkman the Irish of the Northern cities and the blacks of the South were equally incapable of utilizing the ballot: "Witness the municipal corruptions of New York, and the monstrosities of negro rule in South Carolina." Such attitudes helped to justify Northern inaction as, one by one, the Reconstruction regimes of the South were overthrown by political violence.

In the end, then, neither the abolition of slavery nor Reconstruction succeeded in resolving the debate over the meaning of freedom in American life. Twenty years before the American Civil War, writing about the prospect of abolition in France's colonies, Alexis de Tocqueville had written, "If the Negroes have the right to become free, the [planters] have the incontestable right not to be ruined by the

Negroes' freedom." And in the United States, as in nearly every plantation society that experienced the end of slavery, a rigid social and political dichotomy between former master and former slave, an ideology of racism, and a dependent labor force with limited economic opportunities all survived abolition. Unless one means by freedom the simple fact of not being a slave, emancipation thrust blacks into a kind of no-man's land, a partial freedom that made a mockery of the American ideal of equal citizenship.

Yet by the same token the ultimate outcome underscores the uniqueness of Reconstruction itself. Alone among the societies that abolished slavery in the nineteenth century, the United States, for a moment, offered the freedmen a measure of political control over their own destinies. However brief its sway, Reconstruction allowed scope for a remarkable political and social mobilization of the black community. It opened doors of opportunity that could never be completely closed. Reconstruction transformed the lives of Southern blacks in ways unmeasurable by statistics and unreachable by law. It raised their expectations and aspirations, redefined their status in relation to the larger society, and allowed space for the creation of institutions that enabled them to survive the repression that followed. And it established constitutional principles of civil and political equality that, while flagrantly violated after Redemption, planted the seeds of future struggle.

Certainly, in terms of the sense of possibility with which it opened, Reconstruction failed. But as Du Bois observed, it was a "splendid failure." For its animating vision—a society in which social advancement would be open to all on the basis of individual merit, not inherited caste distinctions—is as old as America itself and remains relevant to a nation still grappling with the unresolved legacy of emancipation.

Eric Foner is Professor of History at Columbia University and author of Nothing but Freedom: Emancipation and Its Legacy.

From *American Heritage*, October/November 1983, pp. 10–15. Reprinted by permission of American Heritage, Inc., a division of Forbes, Inc.

Index

Index

Test Your Knowledge Form

We encourage you to photocopy and use this page as a tool to assess how the articles in *Annual Editions* expand on the information in your textbook. By reflecting on the articles you will gain enhanced text information. You can also access this useful form on a product's book support Web site at *http://www.dushkin.com/online/*.

NAME: DATE:

TITLE AND NUMBER OF ARTICLE:

BRIEFLY STATE THE MAIN IDEA OF THIS ARTICLE:

LIST THREE IMPORTANT FACTS THAT THE AUTHOR USES TO SUPPORT THE MAIN IDEA:

WHAT INFORMATION OR IDEAS DISCUSSED IN THIS ARTICLE ARE ALSO DISCUSSED IN YOUR TEXTBOOK OR OTHER READINGS THAT YOU HAVE DONE? LIST THE TEXTBOOK CHAPTERS AND PAGE NUMBERS:

LIST ANY EXAMPLES OF BIAS OR FAULTY REASONING THAT YOU FOUND IN THE ARTICLE:

LIST ANY NEW TERMS/CONCEPTS THAT WERE DISCUSSED IN THE ARTICLE, AND WRITE A SHORT DEFINITION:

We Want Your Advice

ANNUAL EDITIONS revisions depend on two major opinion sources: one is our Advisory Board, listed in the front of this volume, which works with us in scanning the thousands of articles published in the public press each year; the other is you—the person actually using the book. Please help us and the users of the next edition by completing the prepaid article rating form on this page and returning it to us. Thank you for your help!

ANNUAL EDITIONS: American History, Volume 1

ARTICLE RATING FORM

Here is an opportunity for you to have direct input into the next revision of this volume.
We would like you to rate each of the articles listed below, using the following scale:

1. **Excellent: should definitely be retained**
2. **Above average: should probably be retained**
3. **Below average: should probably be deleted**
4. **Poor: should definitely be deleted**

Your ratings will play a vital part in the next revision.
Please mail this prepaid form to us as soon as possible.
Thanks for your help!

RATING	ARTICLE	RATING	ARTICLE
	1. Island Hopping to a New World		34. Between Honor and Glory
	2. 1491		35. Absence of Malice
	3. Slavery in the Lower South		36. America's Birth at Appomattox
	4. Pocahontas		37. The New View of Reconstruction
	5. Instruments of Seduction: A Tale of Two Women		
	6. The Pueblo Revolt		
	7. Penning a Legacy		
	8. Blessed and Bedeviled: Tales of Remarkable Providences in Puritan New England		
	9. Roots of Revolution		
	10. The American Self		
	11. Ben Franklin's 'Scientific Amusements,'		
	12. Flora MacDonald		
	13. Founding Friendship: Washington, Madison and the Creation of the American Republic		
	14. Making Sense of the Fourth of July		
	15. Hamilton Takes Command		
	16. Winter of Discontent		
	17. Founders Chic: Live From Philadelphia		
	18. Your Constitution Is Killing You		
	19. The First Democrats		
	20. The Revolution of 1803		
	21. Brains and Brawn: The Lewis and Clark Expedition		
	22. African Americans in the Early Republic		
	23. Andrew Jackson Versus the Cherokee Nation		
	24. New Horizons for the American West		
	25. The Great Famine		
	26. James K. Polk and the Expansionist Spirit		
	27. Little Women? The Female Mind At Work in Antebellum America		
	28. A Violent Crusader in the Cause of Freedom		
	29. "The Doom of Slavery": Ulysses S. Grant, War Aims, and Emancipation, 1861–1863		
	30. Richmond's Bread Riot		
	31. The Civil War's Deadliest Weapons were not Rapid-Fire Guns or Giant Cannon, but the Simple Rifle-Musket and the Humble Minié Ball		
	32. A Bold Break for Freedom		
	33. A Gallant Rush for Glory		

(Continued on next page)

BUSINESS REPLY MAIL
FIRST CLASS MAIL PERMIT NO. 551 DUBUQUE IA

POSTAGE WILL BE PAID BY ADDRESEE

McGraw-Hill/Dushkin
2460 KERPER BLVD
DUBUQUE, IA 52001-9902

NO POSTAGE
NECESSARY
IF MAILED
IN THE
UNITED STATES

ABOUT YOU

Name

Date

Are you a teacher? ❑   A student? ❑
Your school's name

Department

Address   City   State   Zip

School telephone #

YOUR COMMENTS ARE IMPORTANT TO US!

Please fill in the following information:
For which course did you use this book?

Did you use a text with this ANNUAL EDITION?   ❑ yes ❑ no
What was the title of the text?

What are your general reactions to the *Annual Editions* concept?

Have you read any pertinent articles recently that you think should be included in the next edition? Explain.

Are there any articles that you feel should be replaced in the next edition? Why?

Are there any World Wide Web sites that you feel should be included in the next edition? Please annotate.

May we contact you for editorial input?   ❑ yes ❑ no
May we quote your comments? ❑ yes ❑ no